The Power of Words

當代中國叢書

Contemporary Chinese Studies

This new series, a joint initiative of UBC Press and the UBC Institute of Asian Research, Centre for Chinese Research, seeks to make available the best scholarly work on contemporary China. Future volumes will cover a wide range of subjects related to China, Taiwan, and the overseas Chinese world.

Glen Peterson's *The Power of Words: Literacy and Revolution in South China, 1949-95* is the first book in the series.

Glen Peterson

The Power of Words:
Literacy and Revolution in
South China, 1949-95

UBCPress / Vancouver

Printed in Canada on acid-free paper ∞

ISBN 0-7748-0611-7 (hardcover)
ISBN 0-7748-0612-5 (paperback)

Canadian Cataloguing in Publication Data

Peterson, Glen, 1956-
  The power of words

  (Contemporary Chinese studies, ISSN 1206-9523)
  Includes bibliographical references and index.
   ISBN 0-7748-0611-7 (bound); ISBN 0-7748-0612-5 (pbk.)

  1. Literacy – China – Kwanztung Province – History. 2. Literacy – Government policy – China – History. I. Title. II. Series.

LC157.C5P47 1997   302.2'244'09512709045   C97-910575-7

This book has been published with the help of a grant from the Social Science Federation of Canada, using funds provided by the Social Sciences and Humanities Research Council of Canada.

UBC Press also gratefully acknowledges the ongoing support to its publishing program from the Canada Council for the Arts, the British Columbia Arts Council, and the Department of Canadian Heritage of the Government of Canada.

UBC Press
University of British Columbia
6344 Memorial Road
Vancouver, BC V6T 1Z2
(604) 822-5959
Fax: 1-800-668-0821
E-mail: orders@ubcpress.ubc.ca
http://www.ubcpress.ubc.ca

To my parents

Contents

Tables and Maps

Acknowledgments

This book originated as a doctoral dissertation at the University of British Columbia. It is a pleasure to be able finally to acknowledge the many teachers, friends, and colleagues who have given so generously of their help and encouragement over the years. I am particularly grateful to Alexander Woodside, who suggested the topic and guided my research; I have never met a more superb critic or inspiring scholar. I am also grateful to my cosupervisor, Edgar Wickberg, who first inspired my interest in the social history of Guangdong many years ago and whose deep influence on my thinking about the region is evident throughout these pages. I would also like to thank Graham Johnson for patiently teaching me about the Pearl River Delta and for facilitating my field research through his many contacts in Guangdong. Diana Lary provided much-needed support and encouragement and suggested the title for this book. I also wish to thank Ruth Hayhoe, Stig Thogersen, Charles Hayford, Elizabeth Perry, Harvey Graff, William Wray, and J. Donald Wilson for their wise counsel and encouragement over the years.

This project would never have been completed without the generous assistance and advice I received from a great many colleagues and friends in China. I am indebted to Professor Yuan Ding, whose tireless efforts on my behalf yielded many of the source materials on which this book is based. Qiao Xiaoqin and Zhou Daming kindly allowed me to join them on their regular research forays into the Pearl River Delta. Ren Gaoyu of the Guangdong Social and Economic Development Research Center provided valuable advice on the contemporary state of literacy education in Guangdong, as did Zheng Deben of the Guangzhou Social Science Research Unit. Ye Xianen helped me to see contemporary Guangdong rural education in historical perspective by sharing with me some of his vast knowledge of Guangdong's social and economic history. Zhu Yuncheng, director of the Population Research Center at Zhongshan University, patiently answered my questions and allowed me access to the centre's materials. In

Guangzhou, I also benefited from the generous assistance provided by He Zhaofa, Qiu Haixiong, Huang Shaokuan, Zhu Mohe, Zhen Ruixia, and Hong Shaowen. I would like to thank Professor Zhou Yixian of the Rural Education Research Unit of Beijing Teachers' University and, also in Beijing, Wan Dalin, Wu Yongxing, Yin Zhongmin, and Yin Zhiliang of the People's Education Press. In Hong Kong, Lee Kit Wah of the Contemporary China Collection at Baptist University guided me through the extensive files of the *Union Research Institute* collection.

The Center for Chinese Studies at the University of California at Berkeley provided an ideal environment during the initial stages of writing in 1992-3. I would like to thank Thomas Gold, Jack Potter, Frederic Wakeman, and Lu Xiaobo for reading and discussing various parts of the manuscript as it developed.

I would also like to thank Bernard Luk and the anonymous reader for UBC Press. This work has benefited greatly from their detailed criticisms and suggestions.

Turning from individuals to institutions, I wish to acknowledge the generous financial assistance of the Social Sciences and Humanities Research Council of Canada, the Commonwealth Scholarship Fund, the International Development Research Center, and the University of British Columbia.

Jean Wilson, Randy Schmidt, and Holly Keller-Brohman of UBC Press made the entire process of publishing this book a rewarding and humane experience.

This book would not have been possible without the benefit of the many happy hours of companionship shared with Michael Freeberne and Jean-Philippe Gossot. Finally, my greatest thanks go to Christine, who remained patiently supportive of this endeavour throughout.

The calligraphy for the series name was graciously provided by Mr Tse Shui-yim, Asian Library, University of British Columbia.

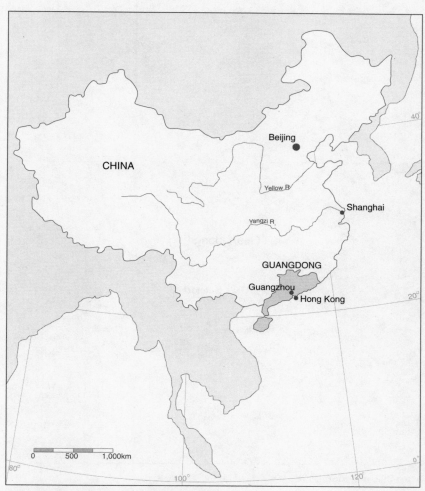

Map 1: People's Republic of China, 1950

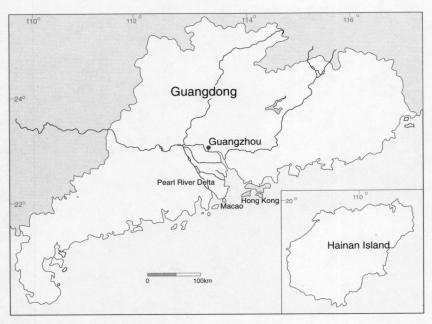

Map 2: Guangdong, 1982

The Power of Words

1

Introduction: Literacy and Society in Modern China

The pursuit of literacy for nation-building and economic development has been a central theme in the history of reform and revolution in China throughout the twentieth century. It was not until the communist revolution of 1949, however, that China embarked on a determined nationwide effort to eradicate the scourge of mass illiteracy. Indeed, the literacy programs mounted in China after 1949 constitute what is perhaps the single greatest educational effort in human history.

This is a book about the struggle for literacy in rural China from 1949 to the mid-1990s. It tries to understand how China's revolutionary leaders conceived and promoted literacy in the countryside and how villagers made use of the education and the schools they were offered. My definition of the literacy movement includes mass literacy campaigns directed at the non-school-age adult population as well as efforts to extend the school system into rural areas. This focus reflects the dual strategy employed by China's leaders (as well as those of most other countries with large illiterate rural populations) of employing mass campaigns to reach adult illiterates, while at the same time building up a rural school system to prevent illiteracy among future generations. In pursuing these questions, I focus on the history of literacy efforts in the linguistically diverse, socially complex, and politically awkward southeastern coastal province of Guangdong. I will say more about this regional focus below.

Surprisingly little has been written in Western languages on the literacy movement in the People's Republic of China. As recently as the late 1980s, when the research for this project was just beginning, there was only one Western-language monograph devoted to the subject: Klaus Belde's 1982 German-language study of adult literacy campaigns in the 1950s.[1] Although a number of scholars – including Suzanne Pepper, Jonathan Unger, and Ronald Price – considered literacy as part of their larger studies of education in the PRC, it was not until the publication in 1990 of Vilma Seeberg's Ph.D. dissertation that Western readers had access to a book-length study of the effects of national development policy on literacy levels from 1949 to the close of the Mao era.[2] Yet despite – or perhaps because of – the relative paucity of research devoted to literacy in the PRC, the subject is often dogged by controversy.

The Unstable State of Chinese Literacy Studies

Few hallmarks of the Chinese Revolution can lay claim to greater intrinsic importance yet remain as understudied and riven by competing claims and interpretations than the vexed question of the extent and significance of literacy in post-1949 China. In the words of historian Charles Hayford, the subject is marked by a 'rambunctious divergence of opinion.'[3] At one end of the spectrum are claims such as the one by Gilbert Rozman that universal literacy was 'virtually achieved' in China after 1949. Similarly, a recent UNESCO-sponsored report describes the PRC literacy movement effusively as an experiment that other Third World nations should emulate because it succeeded in making China a 'nearly literate society' in only three decades. Another scholar, comparing the developmental experiences of China and India, describes the eradication of illiteracy as one of the PRC's 'greatest achievements.' And a scholar of contemporary Chinese education describes the literacy drive as 'one of the success stories' of PRC educational policy, amid many failures.[4]

Yet Seeberg's recent study of literacy levels in the Mao era reaches an exactly opposite conclusion. Seeberg claims that despite much effort there was actually 'very little improvement' in either school-age or adult literacy from 1949 to 1979. She argues that the greatest gains in literacy were made in the initial years of the PRC, between 1949 and 1956, by full-time primary schools located in the urban areas, and that literacy expectations declined massively thereafter as 'Maoist Radicalism' held sway during most of the period up to the late 1970s. Maoist educational policies failed, according to Seeberg, because they resulted in reduced standards and lower social demand for literacy, which became excessively politicized and divorced from the traditional Confucian expectations of state service and upward mobility that continued to inform peasants' view of literacy. According to this analysis, by the close of the Mao era in the late 1970s, both school-age and adult literacy remained relatively unchanged from what they had been in 1949: 32 per cent.[5]

Seeberg's pessimistic conclusion is all the more startling because it appears to ratify the views of recent PRC scholars and observers. Much of their criticism was fuelled by the results of the 1982 national census, the first since 1964, which revealed that there were still 235 million adult illiterates in China (32 per cent of the population over twelve), and a further 40-45 million school-age children who were receiving no education.[6] The census results, combined with a relaxation of official strictures on intellectual discussion, touched off an escalating debate in the 1980s over the reasons for the alleged low 'quality' of the Chinese population. In 1988, China's esteemed dramatist, writer, and former vice-minister of culture, Xia Yan, publicly described the 'neglect of basic education' as one of the Communist Party's 'three great mistakes' (*sanda cuowu*) after 1949 (the other two were failure to control the population and failure to develop a legal system). Five years before, in 1983, Lu Dingyi, the former minister of education who had been a leader in the formulation of mass-education policy during much of the Mao era, ruefully admitted that, during the period of 'socialist construction' in the 1950s, he had failed to recognize that 'an illiterate [*meiyou wenhua*] army is a stupid army,' unable to recognize the value of a legal system or the futility of destroying forests for the sake of backyard steel furnaces. Exiled dissident and astrophysicist Fang Lizhi made what was perhaps the most serious charge of all: that far from promoting education, Mao's policies were actually designed to keep the peasantry illiterate, the better to control them. In Fang's view, China's post-1949 'emperor' relied on the same 'ignorant masses policy' (*yumin zhengce*) to govern China as had his imperial forebears.[7]

Who is right? Compared with many other large, poor, overpopulated, and nationalistic countries such as India, Pakistan, Indonesia, and Mexico, China achieved remarkable strides in eliminating illiteracy after 1949. Even bearing in mind Philip Coombs's warning that national literacy statistics are among 'the least trustworthy, and probably the most inflated, of all published educational statistics,' China's achievements appear to outrank those of most other countries at similar levels of socioeconomic development. The 1982 national census found an adult illiteracy rate (persons fifteen years of age and over) of 34.5 per cent. By contrast, the illiteracy rate in neighbouring India, a country facing a similar demographic challenge, was almost 60 per cent. In Pakistan, the rate was nearly 74 per cent. Indonesia had a slightly better rate than China at 32.7 per cent, as did Mexico at only 17 per cent. However, when rural illiteracy rates are compared, China surpasses all of these countries. As reported to UNESCO, the rural illiteracy rate among persons fifteen years and older in China in 1982 was 37.8 per cent. Mexico's rate was 39.7 per cent, and in Indonesia the rate was 37.6 per cent. In India, the rate was 67.3 per cent, while in Pakistan it was 82.6 per cent.[8] In terms of primary education, China's post-1949 achievements also rank ahead of most other 'Third World' nations. In 1979, at the beginning of the reform period, China's primary school enrolment rate was 93 per cent, which placed the country approximately 30 per cent above the average for ninety-two other developing nations. China's primary school population alone is roughly the same size as the entire population of Japan, which achieved universal primary schooling in the early years of the century. In comparative perspective, then, China's achievements in literacy and basic education since 1949 seem impressive indeed. In the words of one recent Chinese observer, in the early 1950s China's villages were still a 'vast sea of illiterates' (*wangyang dahai*). By the 1990s, this situation had been fundamentally reversed, with those still unable to read and write vastly outnumbered by a largely literate rural society.[9]

It is not my purpose, however, to measure the objective 'success' or 'failure' of China's post-1949 efforts to create a fully literate society. This book sets out to shift the focus of our attention from debates regarding the successes or failures of the PRC literacy movement. I am interested not only in the spread of literacy but also in how literacy and schools were conceived at the elite level and used at the popular level. For me, the most important question is what did it mean – socially, economically, culturally, and politically – to be considered 'literate' in Chinese rural society after 1949. In order to explore the history and multiplicity of these 'meanings,' I reconstruct the social and political history both of state efforts to impose a variety of institutions and campaigns on local areas and – to the degree possible – of local reactions to state initiatives.

Literacy is a complex and multitextured subject that does not lend itself to straightforward narrative treatment. Rather than attempting to locate a single narrative thread, I approach the subject in terms of three central aims. The first is to illuminate the various elite influences that shaped state literacy policy in the PRC. What did state leaders (at the central, provincial, and local levels) mean when they used the term 'literacy'? What conceptions of the individual and society informed their understanding of literacy's place and value? Was literacy valued primarily for political, economic, or cultural reasons? To what extent did members of the PRC political and intellectual elite disagree over the definition, meaning, and expectations of literacy? Because we are dealing with official literacy ideologies prescribed by the state for various social groups, it is crucial to understand the processes by which these ideologies were formed and articulated and how they changed over time.

The book's second aim is to reconstruct the history of local responses to state literacy programs. This is perhaps the most difficult task of the book, since the majority of the sources available to the historian of this subject are official ones that inevitably convey official expectations and understandings more than popular mentalities. Did popular conceptions and uses of literacy match those prescribed by the state? Or were popular attitudes more closely informed by local economic conditions or by traditional Confucian notions of what it meant to be 'literate'? Was literacy a tool for inscribing official orthodoxy or a new means for villagers to challenge state authority? Did peasants want to become literate?

The third aim of this book is to show how literacy is related to social structure. I argue that it is insufficient to view the history of PRC literacy education in terms of statistical growth patterns alone. Equally important are the economic, political, and social uses to which literacy is put. Conventional wisdom holds that literacy has important liberating and redistributive roles, generating social opportunities and reducing social inequalities. I argue the opposite: in postrevolutionary China, during the Maoist period, literacy ideologies contributed to the formation and reproduction of social differences.

Finally, in showing how the literacy map is also a map of class structure, this book also addresses recent theoretical controversies over literacy's role in society and history, thereby contributing to a growing body of critical scholarship that seeks to destabilize established, Enlightenment-derived narratives of literacy and societal progress. Indeed, if there is a single story line that emerges from this study, it is perhaps the tragedy of the peasants, who were largely abandoned by the revolutionary party that took power in their name. I argue that literacy education, like everything else in China, was subordinated after 1949 to the greater demands of economic development and political struggle. In Guangdong as elsewhere, this translated into frequent change and laborious progress. The mass literacy project was inseparable from the larger political project of which it was a part. That project involved creating a new class of peasants-turned-production team members, bound for life to their collectives, whose primary state-imposed obligation was to produce agricultural surpluses for China's rapidly expanding cities. The erosion and gradual breakdown of this developmental strategy since 1978 are challenging not only the official conception of literacy, which has been in place since the mid-1950s, but increasingly also the state's capacity to influence the content and uses of popular literacy.

Theoretical Perspectives

So far we have been talking about literacy as if the term itself was nonproblematic and self-explanatory. But what exactly do we mean when we speak of 'literacy'? In her seminal study of education and popular literacy in Qing China, historian Evelyn Rawski noted that 'one of the most difficult problems confronting students of premodern literacy concerns the definition of the term.'[10] Many scholars writing on Chinese literacy have stressed the traditional connection between the writing system and the state. According to Fairbank, 'the writing system began and was maintained as a pillar of the state and state-sanctioned culture ... Literacy ... was what distinguished the ruling class from the ruled.'[11] Having defined classical literacy as the standard, Fairbank then went on to argue that the nonalphabetic script represented an all but insurmountable barrier for the vast majority of ordinary Chinese peasants, who had neither money nor time for the long years of study required to memorize the characters. In one of his frequently quoted passages on the subject, Fairbank claimed that the Chinese written language 'was not a convenient device lying ready at hand for every schoolboy to pick up and use as he prepared to meet life's problems. It was itself one of life's problems. If little Lao-san could not find time for long-continued study of it, he was forever barred from social advancement. The Chinese written language, rather than an open door through which China's peasants could find truth and light, was a heavy barrier pressing against any upward advance and requiring real effort to overcome – a hindrance, not a help, to learning.'[12]

Rawski's pathbreaking 1979 study of popular literacy in the late-imperial period challenged the basic assumption underlying Fairbank's conception of literacy. Rejecting the notion that 'literacy' in Chinese meant mastery of the classical language, Rawski instead drew attention to the existence of what she termed a broad 'continuum' of reading and writing skills within Chinese society, ranging from the classically literate to those who knew only a few hundred characters, enough to 'get by' in everyday social and economic transactions. On this basis, Rawski estimated that '30 to 45 percent of the men and from 2 to 10 percent of the women in China knew how to read and write' by the late nineteenth century. Popular education was cheap and widely available, even for the poor. On average, said Rawski, late Qing China had at least one literate member per household.[13] Rawski's conclusions have been supported by subsequent research, including historian Bernard Luk's comparative analysis of Chinese fiction in the sixteenth and seventeenth centuries. By examining how these works portrayed the literacies of common characters such as clerks, secretaries, servants, soldiers, and others, Luk showed that literacy of varying degrees among commoners was widespread and gradually increased during the late-imperial period.[14]

While not questioning the notion of a 'continuum' of literacy skills, Alexander Woodside has recently sought to refocus attention on the imperial state's 'inherent desire to limit politically empowering literacy.' According to him, 'significant literacy brings with it power, which all societies ration.' Woodside suggests that late-imperial China had a 'dual system of literacy,' consisting of classical training for the elite and limited, vocationally oriented literacy for the lower strata.[15] Moreover, while popular literacy among non-elites was undoubtedly widespread, 'the dominant values, ideas, questions, and debates that prevailed in court and among officials were translated into a restricted classical language whose pronunciation was shrewdly based on the standard Mandarin dialect of the capital,' which 'only the privileged could fully grasp after years of training.'[16] Indeed, Chinese written and popular culture were suffused with notions of the cultural distinctions and achievements that marked the literati both as a social class and as individuals. In considering the continuum of literacy skills that existed in late-imperial society, we should also bear in mind real, symbolic, and perceived distinctions – political, social, and cultural – that informed popular consciousness and understanding of non-elite and classical forms of literacy.

Although differing widely in terms of their emphases and conclusions, the works described above underscore the difficulty of referring to literacy as if it were a single undifferentiated competence. This seemingly commonplace observation touches upon a major theme in recent studies of literacy, including the present one. Until recently, most studies of literacy were heavily influenced by modernization theory, which emphasized literacy's supposed transformative role in effecting a sequence of developmental changes in individuals and societies. Literacy was usually viewed in terms of a tool or technology of the intellect, possession of which granted the holder access to a wide range of modern economic, political, and cultural opportunities that would otherwise be inaccessible. According to this view, literacy was the sine qua non of modern industrial society from which sprang all of its characteristic skills, attributes, and purported cognitive dimensions (rationality, critical thinking, the capacity to think in abstract terms).[17]

Recently, however, critics have begun to question what they call the 'literacy myth.'[18] Challenging the notion that literacy is an independent variable, these critics ask how 'autonomous' the cultivation of literacy is or can be. Can literacy be studied in isolation from politics and changing social conventions? Anthropologist Brian Street calls instead for what he describes as an 'ideological' model of literacy that recognizes the significance of social context. Street maintains that 'the meaning of literacy depends on the social institutions in which it is embedded ... The particular practices of reading and writing that are taught in any context depend upon such aspects of social structure as stratification.'[19] Extending this argument further, historians, anthropologists, and sociologists who have studied reading and writing in specific ethnographic contexts have suggested that the phenomenon we call 'literacy' may be better understood in terms of specific kinds of reading and writing practices – or literacies. As Kenneth Levine puts it, 'The first step is to discard an albatross of an idea – that literacy is a single, unified competence – and to begin to think wherever possible in terms of a multiplicity or hierarchy of literacies.'[20]

Levine's argument echoes precisely the same point made by Rawski in relation to literacy in Qing China. Rawski observed that, 'with a nonalphabetic language, individuals with knowledge of a limited number of characters possessed narrowly specialized vocabularies.'[21] Indeed, the nature of the Chinese written language seems especially well suited to the concept of multiple literacies embedded in, and arising from, the social order. There are approximately 50,000 characters in the Chinese script (the famous eighteenth-century Kangxi dictionary, the most complete collection of the premodern era, listed over 48,000, while a national standard code of characters promulgated by the Chinese government in 1981 for use in international information exchange listed more than 56,000).[22] The meaning and pronunciation of each character are learned individually. Contrary to popular misconception, the majority of Chinese characters (over 80 per cent) are neither pure pictographs nor pure ideographs (only 2 to 3 per cent fall into this category); rather, most are compound symbols that contain both phonetic and semantic parts.[23] Hence, knowing the meaning and pronunciation of some characters provides clues to the meaning and pronunciation of others. Nonetheless, if we take knowledge of 56,000 characters as the definition of full literacy, few if any would qualify as literate.

How, then, were different levels and kinds of literacy generated? Modern school education was capable of furnishing knowledge of the 4,000 to 7,000 characters that statistical surveys of character frequency, first begun in the 1920s, revealed was the maximum required for unimpeded access to the full range of materials aimed at a modern reading public – newspapers, magazines, novels, and the like.[24] It would be wrong, however, to equate literacy exclusively with formal schooling. A social demand for literacy existed and was satisfied independently of the school. What one observes increasingly as one moves down the social hierarchy is a multitude of limited, highly specific literacies that were usually, though not always, occupationally based. Indeed, an excellent example of Rawski's notion of specialized occupational literacies was the 300-character primer traditionally used by fishmongers in the Pearl River Delta of Guangdong. Consisting entirely of the names of different types of fish and numerals, the primer is believed to have been used exclusively by apprentices in the local fish trade.[25] What can we say about the literacy of the Cantonese fishmonger? We might say that he or she possessed 'fish literacy.' Not the same as the literacy of the urban rice dealer, the village bean curd seller, or the itinerant fortune teller, and certainly not the same as the literacy of the imperial examination candidate or the modern university graduate; but an economically and socially deployable skill nonetheless.

For our purposes, such specialized literacies were economically and socially significant in two respects. First, they could be individually empowering. Fish literacy may have enabled the fishmonger to compete more effectively in the local fish trade through the ability to monitor fish stocks and prices. Second, such literacies were – and are – not all of a kind. They exist in a hierarchy and are part of the structure of social relations, intimately bound up with the distribution of power in society and the attendant relations of domination and subordination. Levine puts it this way:

Having argued that it is necessary to recognize a multiplicity of literacies, it would be foolish to view information as a monolithic entity ... The social and political significance of literacy is very largely derived from its role in creating and reproducing ... the social distribution of knowledge. If this were not so, if literacy did not have this role, then the inability to read would be a shortcoming on a par with tone-deafness, while an inability to write would be as socially inconsequential as a facility for whistling in tune.[26]

The varying conceptions of literacy described above underscore the fact that definitions of literacy are not objective inferences drawn from empirically calculated minimum skill requirements. We would do better to view literacy definitions as implicit or explicit ideological statements. In the words of the leading Western historian of literacy, Harvey Graff, 'virtually all approaches to literacy follow from ... historically-based assumptions: about the nature of social and economic development, of political participation and citizenship, of social order and morality, of personal advancement, and of societal progress.'[27] Viewed from this perspective, it may be more helpful to think in terms of literacy 'mentalities': ways of conceiving and representing literacy that are characteristic of a particular social or cultural group. As Alexander Woodside suggests, conceptions of literacy are 'normative prescriptions,' the understanding of which requires that 'both prescribers and those for whom they are prescribing ... be seen against their social backgrounds.' More particularly, such conceptions 'may serve as a ruling elite's image of what is possible and desirable with respect to the way they and the social classes below them will participate in economic and political life.'[28] Equipped with these observations, we can now begin to probe the changing social and political meanings of literacy in modern China.

Literacy Ideologies in Modern China

Our story begins with a telling anecdote. Early one day in 1950, medical officers in Guangzhou, Guangdong's capital, received an alarming message. Plague had broken out on the tiny island of Ban, off the Leizhou peninsula, in southern Guangdong. Local officials responded to the crisis with an urgent plea for help from experts in the provincial capital. The provincial officers in turn knew from experience that the appeal required immediate response: previous outbreaks had shown that quick action was crucial to contain the disease. Plague was hardly unheard of in this corner of southern China. Indeed, the region had seen massive outbreaks of the disease in the past, notably in the late nineteenth century when bubonic plague spread along the opium-smuggling routes from Yunnan to the port of Beihai in southern Guangxi province. Even the capital, Guangzhou, and the British colony of Hong Kong had succumbed to epidemics in years gone by.[29] In this respect, the present outbreak on a small island, away from major population centres, could almost be considered lucky – provided that the disease was contained as quickly as possible.

There were also further reasons to be hopeful. Contact between the islanders and mainlanders had increased rapidly since the arrival of the first units of the People's Liberation Army a few months previously. Now that the People's Republic was officially inaugurated, local officials on Ban were hopeful that the new government might act quickly to stop the disease in its tracks. Fortunately, too, scientific cooperation between Chinese medical specialists and their more experienced Soviet counterparts was already under way, in the name of fraternal relations between the two socialist powers and 'taking the Soviet Union as teacher' (*yi su weishi*). Indeed, by lucky coincidence a team of Soviet epidemiologists happened to be present in Guangzhou at that moment. Called upon to offer their advice and assistance, they elected to travel directly to Ban with their Chinese junior colleagues in order to investigate the situation firsthand.

Ready to oversee an emergency vaccination regime, the doctors arrived on the island only to discover that it was impossible for them to act. As they were about to begin administering the precious vaccine, the Ban islanders panicked, refusing to allow themselves to be vaccinated. The vaccinations, insisted the islanders, were really a foreign trick perpetrated by the Soviet doctors in an attempt to render the islanders infertile.[30]

The story of Ban island is significant because it encapsulates a recurrent theme in the history of twentieth-century Chinese literacy education. The fact that this story was recounted not in a medical journal but in a journal devoted to education and culture underscores the educative purpose that PRC officials ascribed to it. The plight of Ban islanders was intended to be emblematic of the potentially deadly conflict between modern civilization – represented in this case by advanced Soviet medical-scientific expertise – and China's backward peasant cultures. It also symbolized Guangdong's perceived image among northern politicians and intellectuals as a troublesome place on the fringe of the Chinese world, populated by especially unruly and superstitious peasants. On Ban island, on the periphery of a distant province, the foreign representatives of advanced scientific civilization came up against the bedrock of China's ancient peasant beliefs and mistrust of outsiders.

There were many Ban islands in the literacy journals of the 1950s. They served to keep alive the decades-old tension in the political elite's contradictory image of peasants – as an untapped source of national strength, and as the preeminent symbol of China's twentieth-century backwardness. In Zhongshan county, Sun Yatsen's birthplace, Cantonese villagers resisted cadres' efforts to encourage the use of pesticides on their fields because they

believed that 'rice without insect infestation was like heaven without drag-
ons.' Peasants in Hubei were said to have refused to combat an insect plague
out of the belief that this was heaven's revenge for their attempts to defraud
the government of taxes (*ni hong wo, wo jiu hong ni*).[31] Extirpating such fatalism and persuading peasants to 'believe in science' (*xiangxin kexue*) was one
of the Chinese literacy movement's long-standing missionary themes. In
the early 1920s, even Guangdong's first communist mass educator, Peng
Pai, scorned peasants in his native Haifeng county for what he described as
their wasteful burning of incense to propitiate the gods, their unswerving
faith in Buddha and the spirit world, and their blind obedience to the emperor and upper classes.[32] In the early 1950s, communist officials in Haifeng
boldly proclaimed that the literacy classes they were forming were intended
to empower Haifeng's peasants to finally cast off their 'ugly habit' of wor-
shipping idols. Five decades of intermittent efforts on the part of communist and non-communist elites alike had seemingly failed to extirpate the
beliefs of Haifeng's peasant culture.[33]

To China's educated leaders, instances like these proved that there was no
more onerous cultural obstacle to modernization than the tenacious peasant habit of ascribing to the gods phenomena whose real explanation
required the ability to think in secular, scientific terms. The official explanation for the fatalism of many villagers was that 'thousands of years of
feudalism have given rise to conservative, superstitious, and unhealthy habits.' Because peasants worked with their muscles and had few opportunities
to use their minds, they had developed centuries of 'closed thinking' (*sixiang
zhan bu kai*).[34] The emergence of modern technological society in China
therefore required a prerequisite cognitive transformation in peasant culture, a change that literacy would bring.

China's postrevolutionary leaders were thus heirs to a literacy crusade
several decades old. The talismanic faith in universal literacy as the touch-
stone of China's modernization began at the turn of the century as part of
the quest for national wealth and power. Inspired originally by Darwinian
fears of national extinction and the accompanying belief that the key to
Western strength lay in the 'quality' – educational and otherwise – of its
citizens, the mass literacy movement that developed after 1900 in China
expressed the complicated desire of successive generations of Chinese rulers – from late Qing reformers and warlord modernizers to Guomindang
and communist nation- and state-builders – to reform and uplift the lower
classes. Engulfed by a profound sense of national and dynastic crisis brought
on by China's humiliating defeat by Japan in 1894 and the ensuing 'scram-
ble for concessions' by imperialist powers on Chinese soil, Chinese intellectuals and Manchu court officials embarked on an earnest quest to identify
and duplicate the inner sources of Western political and military cohesion.

As part of this search, a complex new educational ideology was born that associated universal literacy with the creation of a disciplined nationhood.

Significantly, the original rationale for universal literacy was military, not economic. In this, Chinese reformers were simply following current international opinion, which had located the reason for Prussia's military victory over France in 1871 and Japan's over Russia in 1894 in the two countries' compulsory school systems.[35] Strong nations were also seen to have economically productive citizenries, which implied the need for specialized vocational training as well as politically oriented 'citizenship education' (*guomin jiaoyu*). In the words of Paul Bailey, the new educational ideology aimed to 'provide all the people with an education, one that would not only "reform" people's customs and behavior by inculcating the virtues of patriotism, concern for the public good, and hard work, but also one that would accord with the relevant economic needs of the people.'[36]

But how was universal literacy to be accomplished? The first decade of the twentieth century witnessed the emergence of what Charles Hayford describes as a 'broad, continuous, three-pronged' strategy involving (1) expansion of the formal school system, (2) creation of new forms of nonformal 'social education' to supplement the formal system, and (3) reform of the written and/or spoken language in order to make it simpler and more uniform.[37] The formal association of universal literacy with national wealth and power began in 1905 when the reformer Yuan Shikai memorialized the emperor to abolish the imperial examination system in favour of a compulsory school system.[38]

At the same time as a modern school system was promulgated in 1905 (primary education for girls was not officially sanctioned until 1907), Chinese educational reformers, inspired by Japan, were also introducing the concept of social education (*shehui jiaoyu*; in Japanese, *shakai kyoiku*), which referred to various kinds of educational activity conducted outside the formal school system. The avowed aims of social education were embedded in a modernizing discourse that contrasted the ideals of modern citizenship with the backwardness of China's unruly and localized peasant cultures. As in Japan, social education was directed primarily at the lower classes and was closely connected with increasing elite and state determination to supervise and 'reform' popular culture in the name of nation- and state-building. The main aim of social education was to educate the lower classes in, and persuade them of, the importance of social unity, patriotism, and collective interest.

The formal school system was not only seen to be of little use in this effort but was actually regarded by many reformers as a leading cause of social division. Formal schooling, with its scholastic orientation, was said to foster competitive individualism and an elitist disdain for manual labour. Social education was conceived in part as a critique of the shortcomings of formal schooling and as a means of fostering those collective values that the formal system was incapable of instilling.[39] Non-formal literacy training was only one aspect of social education, which included a virtual kaleidoscope of activities and institutions. Thus, the social education department set up under the first republican Ministry of Education in 1912 was charged with responsibility for a diverse range of activities including religion, rites, popular ceremonies and customs (*tongsu liyi*), science, museums, libraries, literature, art, music, theatre, recreational facilities, and even zoos and parks.[40]

Language reform, the third plank of the literacy movement, was a multi-faceted effort ranging from proposals to replace or supplement Chinese characters with a phonetic alphabet to efforts to simplify the characters and pleas to abolish the Chinese language altogether and replace it with Esperanto ('If you want to get rid of the average person's childish, uncivilized, obstinate way of thinking, then it is all the more essential that you first abolish the Chinese language' claimed one Esperanto supporter in the 1910s). At the level of the spoken language, initial efforts after 1900 concentrated on promoting a single standard or 'national speech' (*guoyu*). Following the May Fourth Movement of 1919, language reform centred on making this standard the basis for a common written vernacular as well. Both measures were motivated by a nationalist concern to achieve solidarity through linguistic uniformity.[41]

By the early 1920s, Chinese reformers and revolutionaries were firmly committed to the idea of universal literacy as key to China's modernization. Moreover, it did not really matter from which political camp one came. Whether it was acquired in the classrooms of Columbia University Teachers' College or in those of Moscow's University for Toilers of the Far East, all shared the same eighteenth- and nineteenth-century Western theories of the relationship of education to science and progress, wealth and power. But if the first generation of literacy crusaders viewed literacy primarily in terms of national cohesion and solidarity, the next generation was more concerned with cultural change and rural uplift. When the New Culture Movement of the 1910s and the May Fourth Movement of 1919 located the heart of China's predicament in its culture, it was the peasant problem (*nongmin wenti*) that most attracted reform-minded urban intellectuals. Beginning in the 1920s, individuals and organizations representing a diverse spectrum of ideological viewpoints began to work actively to promote literacy in China's countryside. They included James Yen's mass education movement in Hebei, Tao Xingzhi's literacy programs near Nanjing, Liang Shuming's rural-reconstruction movement in Shandong, various warlord-led efforts, and those of the Chinese Communist Party in Jiangxi.[42]

When urban intellectuals turned 'to the people' during the 1920s and 1930s, they not only discovered China's countryside for the first time but invented it for themselves and their urban audiences.[43] Mass literacy campaigners such as James Yen, Liang Shuming, and Tao Xingzhi constructed an image of China's farmers that, if not idealized, suggested that they were lacking only in modern scientific knowledge and techniques. These reformers' faith in modern science was accompanied by a corresponding tendency to downplay the significance of class structure and exploitation as causes of rural poverty. The communists, however, placed class structure and exploitation front and centre in their analysis of the peasants' plight. The Chinese Communist Party also regarded the countryside as a great but untapped reservoir of national strength. But the communist view of the peasantry was more complicated. In Marxist-Leninist terms, peasants were 'feudal,' part of an old society that had to be excoriated to make way for the new. As Myron Cohen has observed, this view led to peasants often being regarded as 'a culturally distinct and alien "other," passive, helpless, unenlightened, in the grip of ugly and fundamentally useless customs, desperately in need of education and cultural reform' brought to them by rational and informed outsiders.[44] Guangdong province, on China's southern periphery, held a special place in this view of China's peasants.

Heaven Is High and the Emperor Far Away: Guangdong in the Chinese Polity

This book is intended as a contribution to the growing field of South China studies, linked by common problems of dialect diversity, lineage activity, and the historical legacies associated with the region's unparalleled degree of foreign contact. Among the proliferation of local and regional studies in the China field in recent years, regional studies of Guangdong and South China stand out. There are a number of reasons why this has been so. In contemporary terms, South China, which includes Guangdong, Fujian, and Guangxi, is arguably China's most important region economically and politically. In addition, the level of existing knowledge as well as the historical and contemporary sources currently available to researchers are probably greater for South China than for any other part of China. By relating this study to others, we can deepen our understanding of where literacy programs fit into other programs and problems in the region. Of course, many aspects of the literacy movement covered in this book are also of national concern and relevance, so that this is not an exclusively regional study.[45] In certain key respects, however, Guangdong's experience was notable for its distinctiveness.

A recent study of educational trends in the PRC observed that China's major regions possess their own 'distinctive educational histories,' arising from the fact that 'educational trends and differentials are related to other aspects of Chinese social, political and economic history.'[46] In addition, regions of China also often possess strong subjective senses of their distinctiveness, which may range from regional stereotypes to carefully cultivated historical memories. Many years ago historian Edward Rhoads observed that, 'while every Chinese province has a sense of its own uniqueness, Kwangtung [Guangdong] has been perhaps more self-conscious than most about it.'[47] The strong sense of regional identity in South China in general and Guangdong in particular is borne out by the many studies that have sought to explicate the meaning of Lingnan culture (*Lingnan wenhua*) and its relationship to Chinese culture (*Zhongguo wenhua*).[48] Western scholars have also recently begun to pay more attention to the question of Li.[49]

Guangdong is one of China's southernmost provinces, straddling the Lingnan and Southeast Coast macroregions.[50] It occupies just 2.21 per cent of China's land area yet contains nearly 6 per cent of China's population, making it the fifth most populous province after Sichuan, Henan, Shandong, and Jiangsu. In size, Guangdong is slightly smaller than the United Kingdom. Known as a land of 'seven parts mountain, one part water' (*qishan yishui liang fendi*), almost 77 per cent of Guangdong's 85,000 square miles of territory is made up of mountains, hills, and plateaus. Since ancient times population has congregated in the valleys of the East, West, and North Rivers, the deltas of the Pearl and Han Rivers, and along Guangdong's 1,500-mile coastline. In these areas, a fertile agriculture developed, sustained by plentiful monsoon rains, a long growing season, and convenient natural waterways that facilitated commercial cropping. The dominant crop has traditionally been paddy rice, but wheat, soybeans, peanuts, fruits, vegetables, sweet potatoes, sugar cane, tea, and mulberry trees for sericulture are also important. Double-cropping is the norm, and in some areas it is even possible to harvest three crops a year.[51]

Populated originally by a branch of non-Sinitic Tai people, whom Chinese rulers called Yue ('beyond the frontier'), Guangdong was incorporated into the Chinese empire in the first century BCE. Successive waves of Han migration from the north, starting in the fifth century BCE, resulted in the gradual absorption of the Yue people or their displacement into the hilly and remote northern and western parts of Guangdong. The last major wave of Han migrants from northern China began to arrive in Guangdong during the southern Song period (1127-1280). They were labelled Hakka ('guest people') by local inhabitants, who distinguished themselves as Bendi (Punti, 'native people' in Cantonese). Thus marginalized by the dominant Cantonese majority, Hakka migrants, numbering around 4 million in 1949, tended to settle in the remote and mountainous parts of the province, especially in eastern Guangdong and the upper reaches of the East River, where their numbers remain greatest even today. Bendi also distinguished themselves from the Hoklo (Fulao) people, migrants from southern Fujian who settled in the northeast and far southern parts of Guangdong. All groups sought to distinguish themselves from the most marginalized of all Guangdong's sub-ethnic groups: the 3 million or so Tanka (Danjia) boat people, fisherfolk whose lives were spent on their boats. Finally, while the vast majority of Guangdong's people consider themselves Han (around 25 million in 1949), the remainder include a numerous non-Han minority, the largest of which are the Li (200,000, mostly on Hainan) and the Yao (100,000). By the 1990s, there were no fewer than forty-six officially recognized minority peoples in Guangdong.[52]

Extreme linguistic variation added to the complexity of Guangdong's social landscape. Excluding the minority peoples' languages, there are three major 'sublanguages' or regional dialects in Guangdong: Yue (Cantonese), Min (the dialect of southern Fujian and northeastern Guangdong, a variant of which is also spoken on Hainan island), and Hakka. Within these broad regional dialects, however, there is almost infinite variation. Geographical barriers to communication combined with ethnic and lineage feuding led to a profusion of entrenched local subdialects, which often began across the river or over the next hill. To take but one example of Guangdong's bewildering linguistic complexity, there is, in addition to the 'standard' Cantonese spoken in the vicinity of the capital of Guangzhou, the Gao-Lei version of Cantonese (named after the cities of Gaozhou and Leizhou), which is spoken along the Leizhou peninsula in the southern part of the province; as well as numerous mutually unintelligible subvarieties of Cantonese spoken in the siyi ('four counties') area southwest of Guangzhou; plus several other subdialects of Cantonese spoken in the border lands and in neighbouring Guangxi.[53]

Guangdong's linguistic diversity mirrored the complexity of its society. As Susan Naquin and Evelyn Rawski have put it, 'The society of Lingnan was thick with highly structured and complex social organizations.'[54] Frontier settlement by successive groups of migrants produced a highly stratified social landscape punctuated by powerful, fiercely competitive lineages. Especially prominent in the Pearl River Delta by the fifteenth century, lineages competed for prestige and control of territory and markets. In the realm of education, they established private schools and academies to train lineage sons for the civil service examinations.[55]

Guangdong's relationship to the central state has been traditionally complicated and frequently fraught with difficulty. Indeed, Guangdong has had a remarkable history of tension with and opposition to states in Beijing: the anti-Manchu Ming loyalists of the 1640s; the anti-Manchu triads; the Taipings and their heavenly king (a Hakka schoolteacher from Guangdong); Kang Youwei and Liang Qichao, the Cantonese reformers who wanted to change the dynastic state; and Sun Yatsen, who wanted to end it. Some of China's leading first generation communists came from Guangdong, including Peng Pai, Ye Jianying, and others. Guangdong's long tradition of greater openness to the outside world also made its relations with the central state problematic. A centre of foreign trade since the eighth century, when Guangzhou carried on a thriving trade with the Arab world,

Guangdong emerged in the modern period as China's main link to the outside world. It became a centre for the China trade after 1699 when the British established a regular trading base at Guangzhou. Guangdong had the thirteen hongs (monopoly firms licensed by the imperial dynasty to conduct foreign trade in Guangzhou) and the only port open to foreigners in the eighteenth century and the nineteenth century up to 1842, after which it was influenced by Hong Kong. The province's foreign links were sharply curtailed for three decades after 1949 but resumed with unprecedented vigour after 1978. Guangdong absorbed two-thirds of all the foreign capital invested in the Chinese economy between 1949 and 1986 and was China's leading export province by the late 1980s. The province is also the ancestral home of three-fourths of the more than 30 million overseas Chinese worldwide. Their economic, cultural, and political influence on Guangdong added to the complexity of Guangdong's relationship to the central state, especially after 1949.

Guangdong's rich heritage of powerful lineages, flourishing commerce, long-standing links with the outside world, and distinctive social and cultural practices may have contributed to a robust regional society during the late-imperial period and the early twentieth century, but to the revolutionaries who came to power in 1949, these features cast a pall of suspicion over the province and its people. The official Communist Party view of modern Chinese history describes a century-long struggle against the forces of foreign imperialism and entrenched feudalism. Guangdong's position in this narrative was ambiguous, to say the least.

We can begin to sense the revolution's ambivalence toward Guangdong by glimpsing it through the eyes of a major left-wing Cantonese cultural figure. Qin Mu, one of Guangdong's most esteemed modern writers, pointed out in 1950 that Guangdong's heritage was double-edged. On the one hand, the province had a rich revolutionary tradition, represented by the Taipings, Sun Yatsen, and the early communist movement. On the other hand, however, Guangdong society appeared to Qin to be especially feudal – more so than most provinces. Cantonese possessed a 'parochial clan outlook' (*difang zongzu guannian*), reflected in their disdain for outsiders and their love for stories of 'brilliant' Cantonese individuals. They engaged in abhorrent feudal customs such as the buying and selling of female servants, as well as modern forms of social decadence imported from the West. Many revolutions began in Guangdong only to reach fruition elsewhere.[56]

As for Guangdong's history of involvement with the West, it too was double-edged. When Shanghai was still a swamp, said Qin, Guangzhou was already a long-established international trading city. Guangdong's long exposure to the West had resulted in a greater openness to change and innovation. There was also a strong tradition of resistance to foreign imperialism in the province. But Guangdong had also bequeathed to modern Chinese history compradores and labour contractors. Not only did the heritage of Western colonialism run older and deeper in Guangdong than anywhere else in China, it also remained present in the form of continued influence from Hong Kong. There, on Guangdong's doorstep, Qin Mu pointed out, young Chinese still took English first names, believing that doing so was somehow 'glorious.' It was in this context and atmosphere that the Chinese Communist Party embarked on a concerted effort to remake Guangdong culture and society in the early 1950s. The educational revolution in Guangdong's villages was a central part of this effort.

Format and Sources
My account of the struggle for literacy in Guangdong unfolds over the course of eleven chapters. Chapter 2 examines the efforts of the new PRC state in the early 1950s to penetrate the complex local educational world of Guangdong villagers. In Chapter 3, the focus shifts to the elite level, as we consider the various ideas and influences that shaped official literacy and mass education policy after 1949. Chapter 4 looks at the role of local schoolteachers as crucial intermediaries between state and local society. Chapters 5 and 6 explore the relationship between literacy ideologies and practices, in the context of the construction, from the mid-1950s, of a collectivized rural society. Chapter 5 examines the reorientation of official literacy policy under collectivization, while Chapter 6 analyzes the aims and results of the national literacy campaigns of 1956 and 1958. Chapter 7 continues to explore the theme of state-society relations in the context of the literacy movement, this time from the perspective of the late 1950s collision between the centre's language-reform policy and the linguistic and sociocultural realities of Guangdong.

Chapter 8 focuses upon the agricultural middle school, the most important rural educational innovation to arise from the Great Leap Forward, as a means of exploring the social and political uses and limits of literacy in rural collectives. The tensions that become evident in this chapter form the backdrop for the next chapter on the Cultural Revolution. Chapter 9 analyzes the Cultural Revolution's response to the problems and tensions that had accumulated in the educational system over the preceding decade, and attempts to assess the impact of the Cultural Revolution on adult literacy and school education.

The last two chapters of the book address the question of how literacy campaigns have changed in the post-Mao era. Chapter 10 examines the contradictory effects of the post-1978 reforms on literacy and schooling in Guangdong. The final chapter locates the post-Mao era in the context of the history of Chinese literacy education since 1949, and attempts to reach some conclusions about the struggle for literacy in Guangdong and China.

My reconstruction of the literacy movement in Guangdong draws upon a variety of sources, both local and national. The local sources include hand-copied survey and conference reports, literacy primers compiled by villages and different levels of government, school histories, and local educational gazetteers. Several of the gazetteers, still in their original draft form, were generously made available to me by local educational authorities whom I visited. These sources proved especially valuable for gaining insight into the pre-1949 educational scene in different localities, since virtually all gazetteers carry sections on local education in the Qing and republican eras. I have also relied heavily on the prodigious and varied output of Guangdong's numerous provincial education journals during the 1950s and 1960s (most suspended publication in 1966 with the Cultural Revolution) and again since 1978. During the 1950s, especially, the Guangdong educational press was lively and provocative, making it a superb source for reconstructing both official debates and local scenarios. At the national level, the periodical press and recently published documentary collections and educational yearbooks provided the main source.

The largest part of the research for this book was conducted in China during 1988-9 and again for six months in 1992. On both occasions I based myself at Zhongshan University in Guangzhou. During this period I also undertook field investigations on six occasions in four counties surrounding Guangzhou: Hua, Nanhai, Panyu, and Taishan. On five of these occasions I was accompanied by two colleagues from Zhongshan's anthropology department, who were conducting their own investigation into processes of cultural change in the Pearl River Delta. Together we visited a large variety of formal and non-formal rural educational institutions, including adult literacy centres, cultural stations (*wenhua zhan*), libraries, primary and middle schools, and other facilities. During these visits I also conducted approximately twenty-five interviews with local educational officials, school principals, teachers, students, and parents. Although I will refer to these interviews and local fieldwork from time to time, they do not form a major component of this study. They did, however, serve as a valuable means for testing hypotheses, comparing and verifying information expressed in the official media, and gleaning the kinds of personal insights and opinions that are normally absent from official sources.

Finally, this study also makes extensive use of the research files of the former Union Research Institute, now held at the Baptist University of Hong Kong. These materials, consisting mostly of collated Chinese newspaper and journal clippings from across the country, remain an extremely valuable source on the 1950s in China.

2
Minban Schools and the Reaffirmation of Voluntarism in Village Education

More than any other event of the 1950s, the massive and historically un-precedented land reform that swept rural China from 1949 to 1952 signi-fied the intrusive power of the new socialist state and its capacity for radical social restructuring. Over the brief course of three years, the landlord class, which had been a permanent fixture of the rural social and political land-scape for centuries, was forcefully disempowered and its holdings redistrib-uted among the poorest sections of rural society. Western scholars have generally judged China's land reform successful in terms of avoiding severe economic dislocation or sustained popular resistance.[1] Guangdong, how-ever, was a major exception. Here land reform began later, took longer, and encountered more obstacles and resistance than in any other part of China. Complex land-tenure arrangements, the presence of large numbers of over-seas Chinese dependants whose main source of labour power was extensive overseas Chinese landholdings, and the strength of kinship-based and other forms of local resistance challenged the state's ability to impose class-based strategies of social and political change.[2]

Moreover, in terms of its effects on village education, Guangdong's land reform provoked a major unforeseen political and economic crisis. Land reform destroyed, without replacing, the institutional foundations that had provided the main fiscal and social support for rural primary and middle school education in Guangdong since the early part of the century. The exodus of students from these schools after 1949 in turn prompted an ex-plosion in the popularity of the traditional village schools, which emerged as centres of anti-communist resistance in the countryside.

This chapter examines the origins and nature of the rural school crisis that enveloped Guangdong in the early 1950s, and shows how China's so-cialist leaders attempted to grapple with the issues posed by the crisis. The rural school crisis exposed the glaring fiscal weakness of the new state and stimulated an intense search for new institutional forms and sources of fi-nancial support to replace those destroyed by the revolution. The struggle was not fully resolved until 1956, however, when collectivization created a new corporate structure within which villages once again became responsible, as they had been traditionally, for organizing and funding the basic education of their members. In retrospect, it is clear that this reaffirmation of the traditional principle of voluntarism in village education constituted one of the most significant decisions in the educational history of the PRC. In order to grasp its full significance, we first need to understand the nature of the village educational world and rural schooling in Guangdong before the Chinese Revolution.

Lineages and Modern Schooling in Guangdong

The revolution's ancien régime image of village education as dark and backward obscured the variety and complexity that characterized rural education before 1949. Guangdong possessed an especially rich educational heritage. In both the modern and premodern periods, the province's powerful lineages played a major role in providing elementary as well as advanced education to members. Since their inception in the fifteenth century, lineages in Guangdong were closely associated with what historian David Faure described as 'the spread of literacy and of the literate ideal' in Chinese society and of 'the downward percolation of that ideal in the social hierarchy.' Before the twentieth century, lineages sponsored elementary schools of various kinds as well as more advanced academies (*shuyuan*) for training lineage sons to compete in the imperial civil service examinations. Lineages that produced imperial officials were entitled to build special ancestral halls 'in the official style' and to receive other state honours signifying their official style.[3]

The attraction of the examination system for conferring prestige and political influence on lineages meant that Western-style modern schools initially held little appeal. When the first non-missionary Western-style school, the Shimin Xuetang, opened in Canton at the turn of the century, its students were jeered in the streets.[4] The social and economic attraction of modern schooling grew rapidly, however, following the abolition of the imperial examinations in 1905 and the promulgation of a modern school system. Encouraged by the Qing dynasty, which lacked the fiscal and organizational resources to create its own centrally funded national school system, and spurred by the increasing economic and political value of modern education, lineages soon emerged as the most active sponsors of modern primary schools in Guangdong.[5]

By the early twentieth century, modern schooling in prerevolutionary Guangdong rested upon a tripartite foundation of lineage endowments, commercial capital, and overseas remittances. Educational funds from the latter two were frequently invested through lineage channels. Lineage support for schools was usually in the form of endowed lineage land (*changtian*, also sometimes referred to as *taigongtian, zuchangtian,* or *zhengchangtian*). Lineage dominance in local schooling was most heavily pronounced in the Pearl River Delta region, where lineages owned up to 60 per cent of the land in some counties. But lineages were the dominant sponsors of local education in all parts of the province, due largely to their unrivalled capacity to endow land. By 1949, more than 90 per cent of primary schools in the province depended on lineage support. A mere 6 per cent were publicly owned schools, and they were confined mainly to cities and towns. More than half of the 670 middle schools in Guangdong (with a combined enrolment of 137,000) were also private.[6]

Rural schooling in prerevolutionary Guangdong was thus overwhelmingly private and lineage based. In fiscal terms, the distinction between private and public was often blurred; when the American-trained sociologist and longtime Communist Party member Chen Hansheng surveyed rural Guangdong in the 1930s, he described local elites as 'quadrilateral beings' who dominated all aspects of economic and political life. Lineage officers often served concurrently as local government officials, using the taxation powers they held under the guise of local self-government to grant private schools monopolies on selected local surtaxes. The melding of private economic interests and public office was also reflected in the existence of semiofficial bodies such as the famous Minglun Tang, the association that managed lineage school land in Dongguan county, whose heads dominated both lineage and local government.[7] With schools as with other local elite-sponsored modernization schemes that peasants paid for through taxes but seldom benefited from, there was often considerable popular resentment; the burning of modern schools by angry peasants was a recurrent phenomenon throughout late Qing and early republican China.[8]

The growth of modern schooling in Guangdong was also closely connected to lineage and local elite competition for local dominance. Lineages that formerly vied with one another to produce examination candidates and imperial officials competed after abolition of the examination system in 1905 to establish modern primary schools, while the extension of local self-government intensified lineage competition by creating opportunities for officials to favour certain schools in the allocation of taxes and subsidies.[9] Lineage competition in the establishment of schools was particularly intense in the prosperous Pearl River Delta and in the remittance-rich overseas Chinese home areas, resulting in a profusion of extremely small schools in these areas. In addition, private middle schools became an integral feature of rural political networks during the republican era, attached to competing gentry factions and local merchant associations.[10]

There were also a large number of profit-oriented private middle schools in Guangdong, established mainly by overseas Chinese. Normally located in cities and market towns, these schools were generally of poor academic quality and standards. By the 1940s, there were also a half-dozen or so middle schools in Guangdong that were affiliated with the CCP and a similar number with ties to the Guomindang. Finally, there were some sixty-six missionary-run private schools in Guangdong by 1949, some of which, like the Huaide girls' middle school in Chaoan, established in 1896, were among the oldest modern schools in the province.

According to a 1934 survey, the percentage of those who had never attended school ranged from only 9 per cent in the most developed counties of the province, where population was most heavily concentrated, to 86 per cent in the most backward counties. Primary school enrolment in Guangdong ceased to grow after the Japanese invasion of 1937 and remained at pre-1937 levels throughout the ensuing occupation and civil war. Nevertheless, by 1949 Guangdong had one of the highest primary school populations in China. There were 1.59 million children attending primary school in 1949 – a figure matched only by two other provinces, Hebei and Shandong.[11]

The Persistence of the Sishu

Guangdong's 1.59 million primary school pupils still represented less than 30 per cent of the school-age population, however. Most male children continued to attend traditional village private elementary schools, known as sishu.[12] For the better part of ten centuries, since the Song, the sishu had embodied the principle that elementary education was a voluntary concern of families and local communities. Most sishu were probably small, with fewer than a dozen pupils. Occasionally, however, they could be quite large; during the republican period, some sishu boasted more than 300 students. Sishu were known by a variety of names, depending on their size and type of sponsorship. In general, there were three main types. The most common was the 'family school' (*jiashu*), formed when one or more families hired a private tutor to provide elementary instruction to their sons. On other occasions, teachers themselves took the initiative in recruiting a small number of pupils; this practice was commonly described as teachers 'opening the door to welcome disciples.' Lineages also established their own sishu, either as charitable schools for the poor (*yixue*) or for all members (*zushu*). The different categories of sishu were not strictly separate, however. They often overlapped with one another, and the terminology itself varied from locality to locality. In Guangdong's Maoming county, for instance, there were family schools (*jiashu*), usually established by elite families; common schools (*zhongshu*), set up by local patrons for the benefit of family members; and harmonious schools (*rongxue*), located in ancestral halls and temples, where promising students were tutored by higher degree holders.[13]

The purpose of the sishu was to impart basic literacy and moral instruction to village sons. The usual practice was for all children to begin with instruction in the famous san-bai-qian trinity of classical literacy primers: the Thousand Character Classic (*Qianziwen*), the Trimetrical Classic (*Sanzijing*), and the Hundred Surnames (*Baijiaxing*). Children of elite families who were destined for scholarship would then proceed to formal study of the Four Books and the Five Classics. Children of non-elite families would receive instruction in basic practical skills such as arithmetic, bookkeeping, use of the abacus, letter writing, specialized occupational terms, and other practical knowledge contained in 'miscellaneous wordbooks' (*zazi*).

The hallmark of the sishu was its adaptability to changing rural needs and circumstances. Classes were held informally, in private homes or ancestral halls and temples. There were no age-based grades, fixed school terms, or standardized curricula or examinations. Pupils were free to enter or leave at any age, attendance was flexible and governed by the rhythms of the agricultural cycle, instruction was tailored to individuals, and costs were minimal. By the 1920s and 1930s, some sishu had begun to incorporate modern subjects, to offer specialized commercial courses, and even to teach English in areas where there was demand. In some rural sishu, portraits of Confucius, Yue Fei, Wu Xun, and Sun Yatsen hung side by side with those of Shakespeare, Darwin, and George Washington.[14]

Despite its adaptability, however, the sishu fell victim to the wholesale attack on traditional society and culture that began in earnest with the New Culture Movement in the 1910s but which originated as far back as the late 1890s. Liang Qichao wrote in 1896 that, having talked with the mean and ignorant sishu teachers in his home county of Xinhui, he knew why peasants remained mired in rural poverty all their lives.[15] Intellectuals like Liang and modern school reformers condemned the sishu as a 'backward' relic of China's feudal past, hopelessly unsuited to the educational needs of a modern nation. The sishu, according to these critics, was a product of traditional familism (*jiazu zhuyi*), which was incompatible with the modern era of military citizenship (*junguomin zhuyi*). The sishu's extinction became the avowed goal not only of intellectuals and school reformers but also of every Chinese national government this century, including the communist one.[16]

Precise estimates of the sishu's twentieth-century persistence are impossible, in part because they were often furtive, forced underground beyond the gaze of county magistrates and local educational inspectors. Nonetheless, local gazetteers, republican-period surveys, and communist records provide a wealth of evidence that suggests that sishu not only survived repeated attempts at suppression but continued to flourish throughout rural China right up to the early 1950s.

When Guangdong's early communist organizer, Peng Pai, attempted to mobilize Haifeng peasants for revolutionary action in the early 1920s, he bristled to discover that the peasants preferred to invite sixty- or seventy-year-old Teacher Eight Legs (*bagu xiansheng*) into their homes rather than send their children to a modern primary school.[17] He subsequently mounted a campaign against Haifeng's 'four olds': poverty, sickness, death, and Confucian teachers. But he also came to realize that the reason villagers feared the new schools 'the way they feared tigers' was because the new schools cost more and offered less of practical value to villagers. Eventually, Peng established his own mass-education schools, which imitated the sishu's focus on basic practical skills such as letter writing, bookkeeping, and use of the abacus while keeping out the 'feudal' learning that 'exploiting classes confer on peasants, in order to keep them as their slaves.'[18]

Around the same time as Peng Pai was coming to terms with the persistence of the sishu in Haifeng, a young Mao Zedong was busy attempting to do the same in his lectures at the Peasant Movement Training Institute in Guangzhou. In the preserved lecture notes of one of Mao's students at the institute, Mao describes to future peasant organizers why villagers 'detest the new learning':

> [They] regard the new learning as a talismanic wonder, but in truth 'A Horse Has Four Feet,' 'The Tortoise and the Hare,' and 'Come Quickly Younger Brother, We're Going to Sing a Song' are completely irrelevant ... The education that a peasant wants is for economic needs – economic liberation – but the new textbooks are full of geography, history, and other knowledge written by teachers living in the foreign concession in Shanghai. They might benefit the capitalists but contain nothing whatsoever of use to ordinary farmers ... like learning how to compile lists, law suits, field contracts, and tenancy agreements.[19]

The sishu teachers, Mao concluded, were able to 'solve many of the peasants' problems' that teachers in the new schools could not. A few years later, he related how, as a youth attending normal school in Changsha, he had detested the 'ignorance' of peasants who protested against modern schools but that, after living for half a year in the villages, 'I realized that I was wrong and the peasants were right.' They rejected the 'foreign learning' (*yangxue*) because it taught only 'city things,' which had nothing to do with the needs of the village, and flocked instead to sishu for traditional 'han learning' (*hanxue*).[20]

More than economic utility sustained the sishu's popularity, however. Equally crucial was the sishu's twentieth-century transformation into a potent symbol of village cultural resistance to the predatory incursions of modern states and foreign invaders. There were at least three occasions when the sishu had renewed appeal in the twentieth century.

The first occasion was during the early days of the republic, in response to the first state-led efforts to suppress sishu. Such efforts were frequently spearheaded by zealous county magistrates. When You Kezhen was appointed magistrate of Zijin county in Guangdong in 1912, he promptly declared his intention to abolish all sishu within his jurisdiction and to replace them with gentry-run modern primary schools. Twenty years later, Liao Hanzhao was named magistrate of Xinxing and immediately proscribed sishu on the ground that their classical curriculum was 'abstruse' and 'harmful' to pupils' minds. Neither effort was successful; six years after Liao's declaration of war on the sishu, there were still over 170 known sishu in Xinxing. In fact, local attempts to suppress the sishu frequently gave way to compromise as county authorities increasingly sought to combine recognition with control. In 1934, Huazhou county held the first countywide examination for sishu teachers. Successful candidates were awarded primary school teaching certificates. In other cases, county educational authorities granted licences to sishu that pledged to incorporate modern primary school curricula.[21]

The second occasion was during the Japanese invasion of 1937-45. The occupation served to further inscribe the sishu's status in popular culture as defender and preserver of traditional values. During the war years, sishu spontaneously changed into centres of anti-Japanese resistance in the countryside. In Zijin county, Guangdong, a new kind of sishu appeared during the war. Known as National Literature Halls (*Guowen zhuanxiu guan*), the schools taught a curriculum based on a mixture of traditional written culture and anti-Japanese patriotism. In the Shiqiao district of Panyu, where ten new sishu appeared between 1940 and 1945, a scholar and his wife founded the Strive for Wisdom School (*Qiuzhi xueshu*), which became renowned for its student theatre troupes that toured surrounding villages with plays depicting the heroism of popular defiance of Japan. In retaliation, the Japanese-sponsored puppet government in 1942 backed fifteen sishu to conduct pro-Japanese propaganda in southern Panyu. The schools were funded by the People's Food Regulation Association (*minshi shitiao hui*), a puppet association set up under the department of agriculture and forestry, which was responsible for carrying out forced rice requisitions for Japanese troops. Village sishu also became safe havens for urban students and teachers fleeing Japanese soldiers and the warplanes that regularly bombed Guangdong cities. Indeed, the closure of many urban primary schools during the occupation provided a steady stream of sishu recruits. In Taishan county alone, occupied five times from 1937 to 1945, more than 20,000 primary students were displaced.[22]

The Chinese communists expressed open support for the capacity of traditional village educational institutions to mobilize popular feelings of cultural nationalism directed against the invaders. Mao even made a personal appeal to local cadres to 'transform' sishu into a cultural weapon of anti-Japanese resistance.[23] Such culturalist sentiment was a potent force, however, which – given the proper conditions – could just as easily be turned against alleged indigenous destroyers of tradition.

The third major occasion for the sishu's renewed popularity occurred in the early 1950s. This time it was not a response to foreign invaders, but to the sudden intrusive demands of the new communist state.

The School Crisis of the Early 1950s and the Resurgence of the Sishu

The arrival of the Chinese Communist Party in Guangdong aroused as much if not more popular fear and suspicion than previous political intrusions since the fall of the dynastic state in 1912. Existing schools that were taken over by the communists were often regarded with suspicion. Volunteers for literacy classes were rumoured to be press-ganged to liberate Taiwan and exiled to Hainan if they refused; children who attended communist schools were alleged to renounce their filial obligations for loyalty to the party. It was also widely rumoured that anyone found participating in communist educational activities would be summarily beheaded by returning Nationalist forces when they reconquered the mainland. Even in Peng Pai's Haifeng, with its tradition of CCP-sponsored popular schools, it was widely alleged in the early 1950s that the party's female literacy classes were often merely a cover for male cadres who turned out the lights and secretly fondled village women.[24]

In addition to widespread suspicion regarding communist educational motives and the behaviour of communist officials, existing schools were also undermined by measures enacted to disenfranchise former elites. First the taxation powers of local elites, which had been used to subsidize private schools under the guise of local self-government, were abrogated. Then land reform fatally undermined the solvency of lineage schools, first by enforced rent reduction, which curtailed the schools' main source of income from endowed land, and then by expropriation of lineage property, which rendered lineage schools lifeless. Commercial capital fled to Hong Kong, and overseas remittances plummeted. Guangdong was in the midst of the most serious school crisis yet experienced in the province.

By 1950, the number of teachers, students, and schools was falling rapidly all across the Pearl River Delta and adjacent regions, the strongholds of lineage education in Guangdong. In the overseas Chinese county of Taishan, whose schools were especially dependent upon the flow of remittances, primary and middle school enrolments declined by 12 per cent and 49 per cent respectively within a single school term, while over the next several years the total number of schools in the county fell by 50 per cent. In southern Guangdong, a 40-50 per cent drop in middle school enrolment was recorded in most counties in 1950, while across the province the number of private middle schools fell from 360 to 260 during the first half of 1950. Altogether, the number of primary and middle school students fell approximately 80,000 by late 1950. 'Several tens of thousands' of these students may have dropped out in order to join the revolution as land reform cadres and village militia members.[25]

The collapse of school enrolments was accompanied by an explosion in the number of sishu. Contemporary sources estimated that in Guangdong sishu multiplied to between 6,000 and 10,000 in 1950-1. In Nanhai county, 100 new sishu appeared in 1950 alone, including three in Nanshan township, where previously only a modern primary school had existed. By late 1950, sishu enrolment had even surpassed that of regular schools in some areas.[26] The exploding popularity of the sishu was in some respects even more worrisome to the new government than the collapse of regular school enrolments, since the former were less easily subjected to state supervision and control. Indeed, many of the resurgent sishu adopted an openly defiant stance toward the new government.

Shen Hengsong was a leading educational official in the Pearl River Delta in charge of 'handling' the sishu 'problem.' He attributed the persistence and resurgence of sishu to both 'old' and 'new' causes. Old reasons included the sishu's tremendous adaptability to changing village educational needs. The sishu, Shen observed, had traditionally imparted basic literacy skills such as letter writing, accounting, and use of the abacus, which villagers found useful, whereas modern schools taught only academic subjects and physical education. In addition, said Shen, sishu had traditionally provided a source of livelihood for petty village intellectuals. New reasons for their continued popularity included the withdrawal of funding and the resulting collapse of so many regular schools in the province; this situation rendered the sishu the only available alternative. In addition, Shen cited a widespread misapplication of the central government's policy toward intellectuals as a reason for the sishu's resurgence. Indiscriminate firing of politically suspect schoolteachers had led many teachers to desert the regular schools and set up their own sishu in defiance of the government, taking their loyal students with them. Finally, Shen pointed out that any plan to eradicate sishu would first have to take account of the positive functions they continued to perform for the state, including providing basic literacy education to the large number of dropouts from the regular schools and absorbing the talents of unemployed intellectuals who would otherwise be a burden to the state.[27]

As in the past, how the sishu 'problem' was handled depended on the attitude of local authorities toward them, which varied considerably. In some instances, local officials attempted simply to outlaw the sishu, while many others opted for a republican-style compromise: grudging tolerance of sishu coupled with intensified efforts to 'reform' (*gaibian*) them by asserting greater control over teachers and curricula. In some localities, for example, authorities attempted to ban sishu within a radius of two *li* of regular primary schools, presumably in order to prevent students from deserting the primary schools. In other cases, local authorities decreed that sishu should begin to employ modern textbooks and add political education to their curricula; others demanded that sishu commence instruction in Mandarin. Teachers in regular schools were sometimes required to pay regular visits to sishu in order to provide instruction in modern subjects, such as physical education, fine arts, and singing, and to instruct students in proper class-room behaviour. In many cases, existing sishu were simply converted or amalgamated with regular primary schools.[28]

Amid this plethora of strategies devised for handling the sishu's resurgence, one thing quickly became clear: a policy of outright suppression was least likely to succeed. At best, suppression merely drove sishu underground, forcing them to operate on a clandestine basis beyond officials' reach. At worst, suppression of the sishu had the dreaded effect of provoking even greater popular dissatisfaction and mistrust of the new government. As Shen Hengsong put it, the 'feudal' nature of the sishu was rapidly becoming a less important problem than the rising crescendo of popular opposition toward the new government over its handling of the sishu affair.[29]

In October 1949, a special provincial-level expropriation (*jieguan*) committee was set up to supervise the takeover of privately and publicly run schools in Guangdong. Similar committees were subsequently set up in cities and counties across the province.[30] In early 1950, the committees began a program of subsidies to private middle schools with CCP sympathies or ties – including Longtian and Hepo middle schools in Xinming, Dongshan middle school in Meixian, Huaqiao middle school in Shantou – and to the pro-CCP county-run middle school in Jieyang. The committees first established control over the province's sixty-six missionary primary and middle schools (whose total enrolment approached 6,000 students) during 1951-2. The remaining 300 private middle schools were not taken over until the winter of 1953.[31]

The greatest difficulty, however, lay with rural primary education. The rural school crisis prompted an urgent debate over the organization and funding of village education. One possibility was to centralize the provision of primary schooling, creating a unified state-run system of public schooling. The other was to uphold the traditional view of village education as a voluntary responsibility of local communities.

Minban Schools and the Reaffirmation of Voluntarism in Village Education

In its earliest formulation of mass-education policy, during the period of the Jiangxi Soviet, the CCP had committed itself to a program of state-sponsored free and compulsory basic education for all. But as we have seen, Mao and other communists who worked in the countryside quickly grew disillusioned with the uniform curricula and standards imposed on the 'new' schools and were drawn instead to the flexible nature and grassroots orientation of the sishu. Decentralized village schools, modelled on the sishu, were subsequently formally embraced by the party. In 1942, the education department of the Shen-Gan-Ning Border Region government attempted to centralize the provision of schooling within the Border Region through a process of 'regularization' (*zhengguihua*), which aimed to impose unified standards and regulations on curricula, teacher qualifications, admission requirements, and examinations. The plan was short-lived. Mao attributed the desire to impose unified standards to displaced east coast urban intellectuals who dominated the Border Region education department but who knew little about the genuine educational needs of peasants – much the same way as Mao, twenty years earlier, had criticized the 'Shanghai intellectuals' who wrote the earliest modern school texts. In 1944, the party launched a campaign to promote decentralized, locally managed and funded 'people's schools' (*minban xuexiao*), which closely resembled sishu in their attempt to reflect the educational needs of local communities.[32]

The minban concept has been interpreted by Mark Selden as the product of a populist impulse within the communist movement that rejected 'domination by an administrative and technical elite operating through a centralized bureaucracy.' The party's post-1942 critique of 'officious' (*baoban*) methods and its elevation of 'people-run' (*minban*) schools were indeed based on the recognition – through hard-won experience – that successful initiative and management had to be rooted in local communities and in individual moral conscience and could not come from the top down. Yet as Selden has been careful to point out, the demand for local management was also driven by the severe fiscal crisis of 1940-1, which left the Border Region government unable to fund local-development projects as it had done in the 1937-9 period.[33]

This same combination of populist impulse and fiscal weakness of the central government argued for a continued emphasis on the development of minban schools after 1949. Initial regulations issued in 1950 stipulated that county governments should take over the former funding sources of rural primary schools, including market rents, miscellaneous local taxes, and the income generated by lineage school endowments. At least 80 per cent of the endowments was to be put toward local schools. These were temporary measures, to be employed until new structures of political authority could be established in the villages. Thereafter, former private village schools as well as newly established village primary schools and adult spare-time schools were to be designated as minban schools under the authority of township and village governments. By 1951, minban schools accounted for 33 per cent of primary enrolment across the country, up from 23 per cent the year before.[34]

Conditions in most minban schools were far from ideal. Like the former sishu upon which they were modelled, minban schools were often established in former ancestral halls and temples, without desks or chairs. The schools were usually short of teachers and funds, and a high rate of absenteeism among students and teachers alike was common. Many were short-lived: in the Chaoshan region of northern Guangdong alone, 40 per cent of the minban schools established in 1950 folded within a year.[35]

Minban schools were managed by associations comprised of local villagers; these associations were known variously as boards of school trustees (*xiaodonghui*), school trust foundations (*xuexiao jijin baoguanhui*), and later most commonly as school affairs committees (*xiaowu weiyuanhui*). They were long-standing village institutions formerly controlled by traditional local elites. Membership was now comprised of representatives from the various mass organizations established during land reform, including the peasant associations, village militia, and local Women's Federation and Youth League branches. The schools' domination by local political activists made them easily convertible into conduits for disseminating propaganda and for popularizing state policies, as we will see in Chapter 3. Yet because the new committee members often lacked the administrative skills – and sometimes even the basic literacy skills – to run the schools, they were also permitted to solicit the 'advice' and 'assistance' of sympathetic village elders and other 'enlightened personages' (*kaiming renshi*).[36]

Minban schools were distinct from the other main 'track' of the Chinese educational system. These were the state-run (*gongban*) schools located mainly in cities and market towns. They made up the skeletal public school system inherited by the communists from the former Nationalist government. State schools were blessed with superior facilities and assured state funding. In addition, they were 'regular' (*zhenggui*) schools, which meant that they conformed to uniform standards and curricula handed down from the Ministry of Education.

In November 1952, the Ministry of Education announced plans for an end to the minban and the 'regularization' (*zhengguihua*) of all primary schools in the country. Rejecting the Yanan formula of decentralized, locally funded village schools, the ministry plan envisioned the creation of a full-fledged national public school system to meet the needs of the new era. Funding for all schools was henceforth to be allocated through the state budget. This would be accomplished by means of a new agricultural surtax equivalent to 15 per cent of the state agricultural tax, which would be levied by county governments. Tuition fees were to be passed on to the state treasury.[37]

The attempt failed. Within six months, the politburo overturned the ministry's plan with a directive asserting that minban schools 'shall be allowed.'

Six months later, in November 1953, the State Council affirmed qualified support for minban schools as a suitable basis for expanding education in the countryside. The affair, which resembled more than a little the educational reforms undertaken in Yanan in 1942 and subsequently annulled by the party, represented the first direct clash between the Ministry of Education and the Communist Party over rural education policy after 1949.[38] The 1953 directive sanctioning minban schools represented, in part, a recognition of the value of local educational initiative and a desire to avoid excessive centralization. It was also partly due to the fact that, as the directive itself admitted, the postrevolutionary state, like the prerevolutionary one, lacked (*zuo budao*) the fiscal and organizational capacity to implement and enforce a unified national school system in China.[39]

The most crucial consideration underlying the reaffirmation of local educational voluntarism in 1953, however, was the need to restrict social expenditures for the sake of industrial accumulation. In 1953, China enthusiastically embraced the Stalinist model of rapid industrialization, based upon the practice of starving rural expenditures for the sake of high rates of accumulation directed into urban heavy industry. Thus, in late 1953 Zhou Enlai made the stunning announcement that, from then on, state educational spending was to be concentrated exclusively in cities and towns. The reason, said Zhou, was to build up a high-quality, state-run school system in the cities to assist industrialization. Henceforth, no additional state-run schools would be established in the countryside. Villages would be responsible for funding and managing their own schools on a voluntary basis, according to local needs and ability. State subsidies would be allocated for the purpose of defraying the cost to local communities of paying teachers' salaries, which constituted the single biggest recurrent expense in village schools.[40]

The 1953 State Council directive embraced minban schools with an apparent reluctance. While acknowledging that minban schools were 'an appropriate solution to the problem of peasant boys and girls entering school,' it also referred to the 'serious chaos' that had resulted from the 'excessive' growth of such schools in the past, without adequate safeguards for ensuring the quality of the teaching corps and school facilities. In fact central and local educational authorities attempted to curtail the growth of minban schooling after 1953 by means of a plethora of regulations and restrictions governing their operation. Funding had to be in place to cover at least two years of operation before new minban schools would be approved. Teachers were required to demonstrate a minimum 'cultural level.' As a result, minban enrolment remained low, accounting for 5 per cent of primary enrolment in 1954, 6.7 per cent in 1955, and 6 per cent in 1956.[41]

Critics later charged that continued opposition and reluctance toward minban schooling after 1953 derived from the party's worshipful infatuation with the Soviet model of education and a corresponding denigration of the party's own wartime educational heritage. Specifically, they charged that some party educators had become infected with a mania for central planning and that this mentality of 'attempting to monopolize everything' had resulted in a slighting of the party's Yanan legacy of encouraging decentralized village schools geared to local needs. It would be some years, however, before the Yanan model was revived on a large scale. In the meantime, the urban state-sponsored school system continued to grow. By 1957, the enrolment rate among urban school-age children was over 80 per cent, compared with under 50 per cent in the countryside.[42]

Rural areas suffered several disadvantages in attempting to finance their own basic education. One was related to local government finances. As Duara and others have shown, local governments in the republican period failed, for a variety of reasons, to develop the kind of rational tax structures and fiscal mechanisms necessary for the routine funding of local schools. Instead, they were forced to rely upon a plethora of ad hoc means, including miscellaneous commercial taxes and the private activities of lineages and local elites. The immediate effect of the revolution was not to solve this problem but to lay bare its weaknesses. Local governments found it even harder to sustain the existing rural school network. Following land reform, the most urgent task for local educational authorities was how to aggregate sufficient fiscal resources to replace those that had been expropriated. Once lineages were dispossessed, local governments in Guangdong had little choice but to 'mobilize' (*dongyuan*) whatever local resources were available to nourish village schools. This mobilization included 'donations' from overseas Chinese dependants and rich peasants, the 'fruits of victorious struggle' (a euphemism for wealth and property confiscated during land reform), as well as various ad hoc sources such as temple and market taxes and user fees for public toilets. Local commercial taxes, a vital source of school funds under the republic, soon dried up as the state first constricted and then abolished private commerce. To make up for lost funding sources, local authorities began to rely more heavily on student tuition fees, with the result that in village primary schools were generally higher in the early 1950s than they had been in the immediate pre-1949 period. By mid-1951, tuition in rural lower primary schools (grades 1-4) in Guangdong averaged ten catties of rice per term (with a range of four to fifty catties). In Guangdong rural senior primary schools, the amount was fifteen to twenty catties per term (with a range of five to seventy catties). Tuition fees were gradually converted to cash and stabilized at four to six yuan per year in lower primary schools, which constituted the majority of primary schools in Guangdong.[43]

Poverty and a severe shortage of educated personnel often prevented local communities from establishing minban schools that conformed to state standards. When the residents of Feie village in Guangdong's Heshang county decided to form a village school, they each contributed labour, materials, and funds to construct a small school building. Their efforts were aided by a single overseas Chinese cash donation. The school's expenses were met from the income of a small farm plot worked by the students and from students selling their urine to a local fertilizer company. The school's limited mission was to impart a knowledge of 'several hundred characters' to each of the fifty or so students. Since the village had no qualified teachers, six of the school's most literate pupils were chosen to become teachers instead. Feie's experience in setting up a village minban school was common in the 1950s.[44]

The historical constraints on local educational voluntarism caused by poverty and underdeveloped local government fiscal structures were exacerbated by the Stalinist model of industrialization adopted in 1953. This model of privileged urban development was based upon the 'enforced poverty' of rural areas, whereby rural surpluses were extracted to guarantee the profitability of urban industry and a steady supply of revenue for the central government. Little was left over for rural communities to fund educational or other social welfare activities.[45]

The problem of how to establish a firm fiscal and organizational foundation for village schooling and other social welfare activities was not effectively resolved until 1956 with the collectivization of the rural economy. The success of minban schools following collectivization is reflected in the steady increase in their share of total primary school enrolment, from just 8 per cent in 1957 to more than 25 per cent in 1958 and over 40 per cent by 1965.[46] Minban schools' expanding share of primary enrolment in this period was partly a function of the official endorsement they received from Mao and other top leaders. But it was the rural institutional structures defined by the collectives (and, after 1958, by the communes) that enabled minban schools to endure. Collectivization created a new corporate structure in the countryside – the social welfare fund of the production team – within which villages were once again able to become responsible, as they had been traditionally, for providing for the basic education of their members. Establishment of the collectives also relieved pressure on the central state to fund rural basic education by instituting what one economist has termed a 'nonmonetized program of self-taxation' for financing basic social welfare services, including schooling and medical care. Under this system of self-taxation, members of the collective financed the cost of local schooling through allocations from the collective's social welfare fund, to which all members regularly contributed a portion of their workpoints earned from collective labour, and by assigning workpoint values to the activities of teachers and school administrators.[47]

Literacy Ideologies and the Continued Reproduction of Rural-Urban Differences

The reaffirmation of local voluntarism in basic education in the form of minban schooling had critical long-term social and political implications. In the first place, it reverses a familiar theme in the literature on modern state- and nation-building: that of the national school system reaching out from the centre to override little traditions and local loyalties.[48] Instead, this reaffirmation supports the view of Vivienne Shue and others that state policies under Mao had the ironic effect of preserving and perhaps even reinforcing local identities and the traditional 'honeycomb' structure of the Chinese polity.[49] Second, bifurcation of the educational system into superior state-funded (*gongban*) schools in cities and inferior locally financed (*minban*) schools in the countryside had important social, economic, and even cultural ramifications. Two kinds of division were thereby fostered within society. One was between city and countryside; the other was within the countryside itself, between prosperous localities and regions better able to support educational development and areas less able to do so. In this way, long-standing social differences were unintentionally perpetuated and perhaps even sharpened after 1949.

The minban schools stood on one side of a crucial chasm that increasingly divided the Chinese educational system from the mid-1950s onward. The critical fault line separated the state-run primary schools confined by official fiat to cities and towns from the various collectively organized and financed forms of minban schooling. State schools often tended to have a rich pedigree. Many of the leading state-run schools in each county had long and distinguished histories stretching back to the mid-Qing period or even earlier. According to local gazetteers in Guangdong, the leading state schools in each county, which were usually located in market towns and county seats, often originated as private academies (*shuyuan*) and charitable schools (*yixue*) in the Qing period, became county and district schools during the republican era, and were designated as 'keypoint' (*zhongdian*), 'central' (*zhongxin*), and number one (*diyi*) schools in the 1950s. In Xinxing county, for example, sixteen of the county's seventeen leading state-run primary schools in the 1950s had been established before 1949. They included the Central Primary School in Tiantang town, a school originally founded in 1713 by the Xinxing county magistrate. The Xijie Primary School in Chengguan town originated as a charitable school during the sixth year of reign of the Yongzheng emperor (1728), while Shangsha-district Central Primary School began as an academy during the reign of the Daoguang emperor (1821-50).[50]

By contrast, rural minban schools were often hastily established institutions, housed in dilapidated surroundings and constantly scavenging for scarce resources. Perhaps even more important, the educational ambitions they held for students were far different and lower than those of the state schools. According to Vilma Seeberg, in rural areas where minban schools predominated, 'literacy attainment was the terminal educational goal of most schooling.' This was in direct contrast to the academic mission of the state schools. Whereas urban state-run primary schools conducted literacy education 'as part of a broader academic program,' rural minban primary schooling was 'largely confined ... to [basic] literacy.'[51]

The urban state-run primary schools and the various village-level mass-education efforts were thus intended to inculcate very different kinds of literacy, and they initiated their learners into vastly different educational worlds. The state schools placed students on the bottom rung of an educational ladder whose ultimate prize was access to the full universe of literate knowledge and culture – and to the full range of jobs and social prestige that accompanied such access. In practice, this meant university education for the most competitively adept students. The village minban schools, on the other hand, inculcated a basic, economically and socially constricted literacy. Their economic and social uses stopped at the village or production-team gate. According to Jean Robinson, rural minban schools 'offer[ed] basic character instruction, simple political instruction and propaganda, and math and science as it can be applied ... in the local community and production. They did not prepare students for further education or for vocations different from those of their parents.'[52]

The different social expectations that accompanied literacy education in urban state-run primary schools and rural minban schools may have represented a modern equivalent of the old split between elite literacy education based on primers such as the Thousand Character Classic and the Three Character Classic, which were aimed at gentry children, and the 'miscellaneous word books' (*zazi*), which taught basic, vocationally oriented occupational literacy to non-gentry children in the late traditional period. The Thousand Character Classic and Three Character Classic represented the first stage of instruction for pupils who – it was assumed – would go on to study the classics and take the examinations. The 'miscellaneous word books,' on the other hand, were aimed at 'inculcating the importance of being a farmer, of daily written business accounts, and of doing calculation by an abacus.'[53] In somewhat similar fashion, the basic literacy education imparted by rural minban schools from the mid-1950s on sought, as we will see in later chapters, to inculcate the importance of being a good production-team member, of reading and recording workpoints, and of understanding labour assignments and other written instructions. Thus, despite the widely proclaimed intention by China's leaders to use the educational system as a means of standing the old class structure on its head, the real effect from the early 1950s onward appears to have been closer to the opposite. By splitting the educational system into academically oriented state-run schools in the cities and vocationally oriented village-run schools in the country-side, China's socialist leaders effectively consecrated a dual system of lit-eracy that paralleled and reinforced the long-standing urban-rural split in Chinese society. The expansion of rural minban schooling, rather than re-ducing the differences between city and countryside, ironically served to preserve and enhance those differences.

The PRC's 1953 reaffirmation of local voluntarism as a guiding principle in the development of rural basic education thus exposed important conti-nuities in political, social, and cultural relationships, despite the supposed great divide of the revolution. As we have seen, the villages had their own well-developed educational institutions and traditions that the revolution-aries could ill afford to ignore and that they eventually sought to harness to their own objectives. The reaffirmation of local voluntarism represented the state's attempt to co-opt village educational traditions as a means to overcome fiscal constraints imposed by a Soviet-style developmental model based on the primacy of cities and of rapid urban industrialization. The results, however, were to be double-edged and fraught with controversy. On the one hand, minban schooling was destined, as we will see in subse-quent chapters, to become one of the keys to China's remarkable success in popularizing rural school education from the mid-1950s onward. On the other hand, however, the social implications of China's divided educational system, as described above, were also destined to become one of the most controversial political issues in Chinese education. In order to understand the nature of this controversy, we must first probe into the competing views and priorities state leaders held toward the rural literacy movement. That is the focus of the next chapter.

3
The Contested Priorities of Early Postrevolutionary Mass Education

When the Chinese Communist Party came to power in 1949, it possessed several decades of experience in dealing with problems of rural education. A debate quickly emerged in Chinese educational circles over whether this experience should form the basis for educational strategy in the new state. Some favoured a continued emphasis on political mobilization, while others advocated greater emphasis on developing skills and expertise. Popular education had been a central part of the communist strategy for winning rural support before 1949. But was 'guerrilla education,' as the model was disparagingly described in the 1950s by its opponents, still suitable for a country bent on rapid industrial transformation? This chapter examines the various competing views that influenced the formation of literacy and mass education policy during the first half of the mid-1950s. The central argument of this chapter is that Chinese leaders in the early 1950s were reluctant to make literacy an irreducible priority of state educational policy. During the period 1949-55, rural literacy education was repeatedly forced to take a back seat to more urgently defined priorities of mass education.

That China's leaders were, by their own admission, not that interested in literacy during the early years of communist rule may seem surprising, even contradictory, at first. After all, official pronouncements during this period frequently referred to the historical necessity of universal literacy for 'building socialism' (*shehuizhuyi jianshe*). Lenin's famous dicta that 'it is impossible to build a socialist society on a foundation of mass illiteracy' and that 'illiterates stood outside politics' were widely quoted in official China in the 1950s, as was Mao's similar injunction that 'New China cannot be established on a foundation of eighty percent illiteracy.' The Western practice of associating the Chinese Communist Party with a consuming interest in mass literacy probably originated with the pioneering interviews conducted by the American journalist Edgar Snow in the 1930s, when Snow became one of the first foreign observers to establish contact with the

Chinese communists in their isolated mountain redoubt in northwest China. Snow interviewed young 'Reds' such as Old Dog, who credited their loyalty to the party's efforts to rescue them from illiteracy. 'Did they like the Red Army?' Snow queried Old Dog, a seventeen-year-old veteran of the Long March. 'Of course,' replied Old Dog, 'the Red Army has taught me how to read.'[1]

I would argue, however, that the CCP's consuming interest in mass literacy in the pre- and immediately post-1949 periods is usually assumed rather than carefully investigated. To challenge it, as I am about to do with documentary evidence to the contrary, is to question one of the revolution's most sacred myths. The image of communist revolutionaries teaching illiterate peasants how to read in rustic classrooms, by oil lamp in the evening or in open fields under a tree during the day, was an integral part of the revolution's mystique. The revolutionaries themselves generously encouraged it, for they were aware that the literacy crusade was one of the communist movement's most sacred and powerful legitimizing symbols. As we will see, however, the party's approach to mass literacy in the early 1950s was considerably more complex and divided than has been previously assumed. In order to understand the debate over literacy education, however, we must first look at the various groups that influenced the formation of literacy and education policy in the early PRC.

The Formation of Early Literacy Policy

Education was a realm where the Communist Party felt it had particularly strong interests and responsibilities. In other less ideologically charged areas of state activity, in which the zone of political indifference was wider, the party could accommodate non-party experts and opinions with relative ease.[2] The field of education, however, was especially prone to fragmentation by competing interests and ideologies. During the early years of the PRC, there were numerous opinions on literacy policy, none of which – not even Mao's – commanded undisputed priority. It is therefore difficult to speak of 'the state's' literacy policy during this period, for how can such disparate views be reduced to the singular voice of the state? To do so would imply a homogeneity of opinion and a governing monolith that simply did not exist. We would do well to heed Elizabeth Perry's advice that, 'although we are sometimes tempted to think of the communist state as an entirely new entity, endowed with superhuman powers, it is important to keep in mind that the state was really a collection of people, whose formative experiences lay in the preliberation period.'[3] If we start from this recognition, we will be better able to reconstruct the political debates that raged over literacy and mass education policy in the early years after 1949.

Three main groups of state actors influenced the formation of literacy policy after 1949. The first consisted of professional educational circles (*jiaoyu jie*). They first appeared in China in the early twentieth century in conjunction with the growth of modern schooling. Educated for the most part either in the West or in Western-style educational institutions in China, professional educators held a liberal view of education, emphasizing its role in the realization of individual potential and insisting upon the autonomy of education and educators from politics. Professional educators entered the post-1949 state structure through their positions in central and local government educational bureaus and on the administrative and teaching staffs of schools, colleges, and research institutes. Many had also flocked to Yanan from east coast urban centres following the Japanese invasion in 1937, taking up positions in the educational bureaus of the Border Region governments. It was there that Mao first came into conflict with the professional educators, whom he referred to derisively as the 'bourgeois pedagogues.' The main institutional base of professional educational circles after 1949 was the Ministry of Education and its provincial and local bureaus.

Professional educators were locked in a constant struggle with CCP education officials – the second group – over educational policy and especially the role of politics in the educational system. Whereas professional educators tended to view education in liberal terms, as a process of individual growth, communist educators regarded education as an instrument of state power, to be used to create and sustain a particular social and political order. Many of the leading Communist Party educators, such as Lu Dingyi and Hu Qiaomu, had backgrounds in the party's propaganda apparatus. Lu headed the propaganda department within the General Office of the Communist Party Central Committee for nearly two decades from 1945 to 1965, while Hu, a long-standing expert in propaganda work and party affairs, headed the Culture and Education Committee of the State Council. In addition, many other leading Communist Party educators, including Wu Yuzhang, Xu Teli, and Chen Yi, had begun their educational careers as members of the Chinese work-study movement to France during the 1910s, where they had become involved in the first communist-led efforts to spread literacy to Chinese labourers.[4]

The third group of state actors influencing the formation of literacy policy in the PRC consisted of classically educated linguists and philologists. Although most remained non-communists, they played an important role in the PRC literacy movement through their prominent involvement in official language reform. Their primary institutional base after 1949 was in the Committee for the Reform of the Chinese Written Language, set up in the early 1950s to oversee language reform. The language reformers were responsible for devising schemes to simplify and alphabetize Chinese characters. They also ratified the party's attempts to replace regional and local dialects with Beijing-based Mandarin through philological studies of historical trends toward standard pronunciation. The language reformers' influence on the literacy movement was greatest during the 1950s and declined steadily thereafter.

The three groups of state actors were not completely isolated from one another, nor was membership in the groups mutually exclusive. Indeed, it was possible to belong to all three groups at once. Wu Yuzhang, for instance, was a prominent language reformer who was also a Communist Party member and onetime professor of Chinese at Moscow's University for Toilers of the Far East. The three groups also shared a common commitment to education and were united in efforts to defend their common turf against external encroachment or budgetary cuts.

Nevertheless, there were significant ideological differences between the groups, and these differences were interwoven with institutional conflicts. The organization and management of literacy education in the PRC was based on a Leninist state structure imported from the Soviet Union. Having adopted Soviet institutions, Chinese literacy education inherited many of the same institutional conflicts.[5] The most salient was between the Ministry of Education and the Communist Party.

The formation of literacy policy took place within several policy arenas, including, most importantly, the Central Committee and State Council on the one hand and the Ministry of Education on the other hand.[6] Supreme decision-making authority rested in the powerful propaganda department of the Central Committee, headed for many years by Lu Dingyi. Alongside it was the Culture and Education Committee of the State Council, headed by Hu Qiaomu and other leading communists, including Lu Dingyi and Chen Boda. Below these two agencies was the Ministry of Education, which held operational responsibility for literacy education. The ministry was responsible for both school education and adult literacy education. The latter was officially known as worker-peasant spare-time education (*gongnong yeyu jiaoyu*) and was grouped under a separate division of that name within the ministry. Through its Second Department of General Education, the Ministry of Education exercised nominal responsibility for all forms of primary schooling, both state and locally sponsored. In practice, however, locally run minban schools were subject to considerable decentralization with respect to funding, curricula, teacher qualifications, and other standards. Funding for minban primary schools and adult literacy education was derived nearly exclusively from local sources, with the state providing subsidies for teacher training and conferences.

As Vilma Seeberg has observed, the administration of literacy education 'continuously shifted' between the Communist Party and the Ministry of Education throughout the 1950s.[7] In 1952, the State Council established the Anti-Illiteracy Work Committee (*saochu wenmang gongzuo weiyuanhui*), modelled directly on the Soviet institution of the same name established by

Lenin in 1919. The national committee was headed exclusively by senior Communist Party educational officials, including Chu Tunan (chair), Lin Handa, and Li Chang (vice-chairs). Local branches were set up at the township level and were comprised of representatives from the party's mass organizations including the Youth League, the Women's Federation, the Educational Workers' Union, and other groups.[8]

The First Five-Year Plan in 1953, with its emphasis on formal training and skills, resulted in an enhanced role for the Ministry of Education. In late 1953 the Anti-Illiteracy Work Committee was merged with the Ministry of Education (*hebing yu jiaoyu bu*). Committee members opposed the change, not only because it removed the committee's direct link to the State Council, but also because the reorganization meant a reduced role for the committee. The ministry, staffed mainly by educators, favoured expansion of the regular school system over adult literacy work as the most effective means of spreading literacy.[9] The committee's primacy was restored in 1955, however, when anti-illiteracy associations (*saochu wenmang xiehui*) were established at all levels to carry out the national literacy campaign launched in conjunction with collectivization (see Chapter 6). When the National Association held its inaugural meeting in Beijing in March 1956, its membership was once again comprised exclusively of senior communist officials.[10]

The institutional struggle between the CCP and the Ministry of Education was overlaid in the 1950s with a debate over the continued relevance of the party's pre-1949 educational experience.[11] Some party members, led by Mao, wanted to preserve the Yanan experience of integrating education with political and social mobilization. Others, however, led by the Ministry of Education, favoured the creation of one centralized system of public schooling, state funded and regulated, with academic quality uppermost and the intrusion of political and social movements kept to a minimum. Proponents of this view condemned nostalgia for the Yanan model as a 'bad guerrilla habit' (*youji xiqi*) that advocated practices unsuited to the requirements of a rapidly industrializing society.

It would be insufficient, however, to view the conflicts over educational policy in the early 1950s solely in terms of a struggle between Communist Party 'ideologues' and Ministry of Education 'experts.' One important indication of the inadequacy of this approach was the appearance in 1949 of classical scholar Ma Xulun as the first minister of education in the new state. To describe Ma as an 'expert' in the sense in which the term is normally employed in discussions of Chinese politics – as a modern technocrat – would be seriously to misunderstand Ma's intellectual world and his place, as well as that of others like him, in modern China. Ma Xulun represented not modern technocracy but the elite tradition of classical scholarship, some of whose post-1911 leaders turned to the Communist Party for nationalist reasons during the 1930s and 1940s. Ma was perhaps the preeminent representative of this group of classically educated scholars and linguists who played leading roles in the post-1949 literacy movement.

Born in 1884, Ma Xulun was a renowned philologist and former professor of Chinese philosophy at Peking University, where he taught for nearly two decades between 1916 and 1936. Ma's earliest written works predate the 1911 Revolution, but his greatest scholarly contribution – a textual criticism of the first-century AD analytical dictionary of characters, the *Shuowen jiezi* – did not appear until 1957. Ma also published philological studies of inscriptions on Zhou dynasty stone drums, philosophical treatises on Laozi and Zhuangzi, and proposals for language reform. In addition, he had an equally long and illustrious political career, variously serving as the director of propaganda in the Beijing headquarters of the Guomindang, the vice-minister of education in the Nanking government, a cofounder of the China Association for the Promotion of Democracy, and the PRC's first minister of education from 1949 until 1952. During the May Fourth Movement, Ma led teachers on a strike in support of protesting students, but he was also one of the leading opponents of the movement in the 1920s to replace the classical language with vernacular script.[12]

What, then, was Ma's role in the new socialist state? His location in the universe of PRC officialdom implied more than simply legitimizing Mao's notion of a new democracy in which non-communists were to participate in governance, although there was certainly that aspect as well. Ma's most significant contribution lay in the perspective and ideas he brought to bear on the PRC literacy movement. Specifically, he brought to the literacy movement an elite scholar's erudite appreciation for the extraordinary historical depth and complexity of the Chinese written language. From the vantage point of more than half a century of philological scholarship, Ma was predisposed to stress the intricacies of the Chinese language and therefore to reject promises of any quick solution to the illiteracy problem. Combined with a professional dedication to simplifying the Chinese script in order to make it more accessible, he also stressed the unavoidable complexities of a person's becoming literate in Chinese. And he did so in ways that bridled impatient revolutionaries who did not share his perspective.

In nearly all of the major twentieth-century revolutions, the new states that arose rushed to embrace universal literacy as one of their most urgent goals. In Russia, Lenin proclaimed a national campaign to eradicate illiteracy within two years of the 1917 Revolution, declaring it a criminal offence for any illiterate between the ages of eight and fifty to refuse to study. Fidel Castro launched a national literacy campaign in Cuba in 1961, within two years of defeating the last Batista forces, while in Nicaragua the Sandinos launched a national literacy crusade (*Cruzada Nacional de Alfabetizacion*) within fifteen days of coming to power. And in Vietnam, Ho Chi Minh announced within a month of the 1945 August Revolution that all Vietnamese were to be able to read and write romanized Vietnamese within one year, despite the real possibility of having to fight a major war against French colonialism at the same time.[13]

In China, however, Ma Xulun began by warning delegates to the first national conference on worker-peasant education in September 1950 to resist the temptation simply to 'decree' the abolition of illiteracy in China. Raising the people's impoverished educational level, Ma told delegates, was an enormous and complicated undertaking that defied quick solutions. It could only be accomplished by 'gradually eliminating' illiteracy over an extended period.[14]

Literacy Education versus Political Mobilization
The most urgent priority, said Ma Xulun, was to raise the educational level of rural party members and activists, who included members of the Youth League, the Women's Federation, and other mass organizations whose function was to transmit central policies to local constituencies. Literacy efforts were therefore to focus initially on this group alone; only later would they gradually be expanded to other groups in society. Qian Chunrui, a leading party educational official, defended the elitist focus by pointing out that local activists and party members were 'the bridge between the masses and the state in the implementation of state policies and directives. We must therefore make greater efforts to educate them in order that their cultural and political level can be raised and their leading role and transmission function can reach its peak.'[15]

Two contending impulses stimulated mass education in the new state. One originated in a functionalist conception of literacy's role in fostering bureaucratic and economic rationalization. According to this view, expressed by Ma and others, literacy was increasingly becoming a functional requisite for local leaders, as party work shifted from military and political struggle to the complex management and administrative tasks of state-building and planned economic development. The second impulse emanated from the Communist Party's accumulated wartime experience in mass education. This tradition emphasized the uses of education for political mobilization more than education's presumed capacity to facilitate bureaucratic rule.[16] In order to understand how and why these two impulses clashed in the early 1950s, it is necessary to examine the party's wartime approach to literacy education.

During the Yanan period, the primary target of literacy education was not the populace at large but the Red Army in particular; Edgar Snow's Old Dog belonged to an educationally privileged group in Yanan society. Among the rural populace, popular education was a multimedia enterprise involving both literate and non-literate modes of communication. Moreover, it is almost certain that visual and oral media took precedence over written communications in the party's early efforts to mobilize peasant support. David Holm, the leading Western student of the Chinese Communist Party's pre-1949 efforts to communicate with illiterate audiences, writes that 'visual and oral media were far more important for mass work than media for which literacy was required.'[17] This should hardly come as a surprise, given what we know about the transformative role of modern communication technologies in creating and reaching mass audiences. Benedict Anderson has recently reminded us of the critical role played in twentieth-century revolutions by the advent of radio, which enabled elites to 'bypass' printed media and reach illiterate audiences.[18]

In the case of the Chinese Communist Party, however, rural mass-mobilization strategies involved much more than simply the adoption of modern media techniques. As Holm and others have recently shown, long before the dissemination of modern mass-communication technologies, the Chinese communists were involved in creative efforts to develop non-literate means for mobilizing popular support. Indeed, such means quickly became the very hallmark of the 'Yanan way' in popular education. Some of these means – such as pictorial magazines, cartoons, revolutionary songs, peasant dances, and public announcements – were borrowed from the Soviet Red Army.[19] Others, however, were drawn from both popular culture and a venerable repertoire of elite means for communicating with illiterate village audiences – including posters, woodblock prints, folk songs, storytelling arts (*quyi*), and popular opera. Theatre was a particularly crucial vehicle because, in the words of one scholar, 'it was the popular theatre, not books, which disseminated ... the major part of what ordinary people in the matshed audience knew about the vast complex of Chinese culture and values – both orthodox and heterodox.'[20]

Mao himself was a steadfast advocate of such non-literate means for reaching peasant audiences. Whenever he attacked the shortcomings of formal schooling (and this attack represented one of the unswerving continuities in Mao's educational thought, from the New Culture Movement to the Cultural Revolution), it was usually from the perspective of the greater mobilizational efficacy of non-book learning. 'The greatest achievements of the peasant associations,' Mao wrote in 1927, 'are always to do with popularizing political propaganda: some simple slogans, picture books, and lectures ... The results are extremely wide-ranging and rapid ... Can opening ten thousand law and political science schools succeed in popularizing politics among the peasants, men and women, young and old in such a short time as the peasant associations have been able to do [using these methods]? ... I think not.'[21]

By the 1940s, these ideas had become firmly entrenched in the CCP's approach to peasant education. According to one observer, social education (*shehui jiaoyu*) in the wartime base areas was 'stripped of much of its basic pedagogical functions and devoted instead to general political mobilization.' Rather than teaching peasants basic literacy skills, mass education was viewed as 'a means of explaining to them the importance of base area political tasks at any given time.' The motto of the communists' 1942 winter-school (*dongxue*) campaign was 'political understanding first, literacy second.'[22]

In theory, literacy among party members and activists had higher priority since they were expected to be masters of a written political canon. In fact, literacy was not a particularly significant consideration in the recruitment or training of party members and activists in the former base areas. Class background and political loyalty were far more important considerations, and they tended to be concentrated among the poorest and least educated members of village society. Illiteracy seldom posed a handicap to the pursuit of power and prestige at the village level; the popular culture sanctioned numerous non-literacy-based sources of local authority, which the party was prepared to co-opt in its effort to cultivate popular support.[23]

As a result, lower-level party functionaries in the base areas were usually illiterate. In the Shaan-Gan-Ning Border Region, literate cadres tended to be 'concentrated in the regional and district bureaucracy,' while township and subdistrict heads 'typically were illiterate peasant revolutionaries.' Even communist-appointed county magistrates were often 'illiterate or only semi-literate peasants,' who relied on better-educated cadres to handle their administrative duties. Given these trends, it is perhaps not surprising that when the Communist Party came to power in 1949, a towering 69 per cent of its members were illiterate.[24]

Ma Xulun clearly had such figures in mind when he told delegates to the first national worker-peasant education conference in 1950 that New China had inherited a large corps of peasant cadres with impeccable revolutionary credentials but 'no education.' A Ministry of Education statement around the same time was equally blunt, claiming that, while mass education in the pre-1949 base areas had been a success in terms of raising popular political consciousness and mobilizing peasants to fight the Japanese, the results in terms of raising the literacy level were 'not great.' The reason for this, according to Qian Chunrui, was that, of the three kinds of village education promoted in the wartime base areas (political education, technical education, and basic literacy training), only the first two had priority, while literacy education was deliberately neglected. Ma Xulun's solution was to recommend that within three to five years all village cadres and activists be able to recognize at least 1,000 common characters and have a preliminary ability to 'read, write and calculate.'[25]

The objective was to prevent experiences such as that of Dong Chengdui, an illiterate cadre who was nominated to attend a county conference on popularizing modern agricultural methods. Dong stayed up all night memorizing the sixteen characters that described the farming technique he was to present at the conference. But when the conference was over and Dong returned to his village, he was unable to recall any of the detailed discussions that had taken place, nor even the sixteen characters he had worked so hard to master.[26]

Dong's plight was emblematic of the problems facing the new state in its effort to consolidate control at the local level, where illiteracy was widespread (Table 1). Rapid expansion of the state's economic presence at the township level in the early 1950s created a sudden need for a sizeable literate cadre of subcounty functionaries to manage and supervise state activities such as grain harvesting, rationing, tax collection, and the like. Widespread illiteracy among the most politically reliable sections of the peasantry made these tasks difficult. Efforts to ferret out lands concealed from local tax registers were routinely frustrated by the shortage of literate cadres, while attempts to implement a surveillance system for local granaries foundered because there were not enough cadres able to 'use an abacus, make calculations correctly, and keep the accounts straight.'[27] Eliminating the 'entrepreneurial brokers' who had usurped state authority at the local level during the republican era was not just an organizational problem for the new state; it was also an educational one: recruiting cadres who were both politically reliable and literate.[28]

In the absence of such persons, authorities often had little choice but to harness the skills of intellectuals and former elites in exchange for vows of loyalty and hasty 'reeducation' classes. But this response to the situation held its own danger, namely that it was potentially delegitimizing for a state that claimed to rule in the interests of peasants and workers to draw its local functionaries mainly from the ranks of the former exploiting classes. Reports from Guangdong in 1951 spoke of illiterate village cadres who were

Table 1

Illiteracy in selected Guangdong townships, 1950

County	Township	Illiterate	Semi-literate	Per cent
Jieyang	Tanjiao	702	359	90.70
Conghua	Dongxing	399	171	63.60
Zijin	Silian	270	72	57.10
Gaoming	Jiecun	430	219	89.72
Shunde	Longjiang	941	230	65.70
Lian	Shuikou	597	260	71.42
Maoming	Wenxiu	336	489	66.70
Huazhou	Tongsheng	340	176	53.30
Wuchuan	Qidou	351	15	86.00
Total		4,632	2,002	58.70

Source: *Guangdong jiaoyu nianjian, 1949-85* (Guangzhou: Guangdong jiaoyu ting 1985), 115.

becoming increasingly resentful that intellectuals from the old society were assuming positions of power based on their superior educational qualifications. The cadres blamed the Communist Party for this situation, claiming that the party had relied upon them to win power but now relied on intellectuals to run the country.[29]

One of the first tasks for the new state was to define what 'literacy' actually meant. During 1949-50, a large number of literacy surveys were undertaken across the country. However, the effort was frustrated by 'huge discrepancies' in the criteria employed by local authorities to determine who was 'literate.'[30] In August 1950, party officials and educators met to discuss the 'common character research problem' – how many characters and which ones were to form the basis for literacy instruction. Using existing character glossaries, dictionaries, and literacy primers, including ones from different provinces, the group selected 1,589 characters – significantly more than the 1,000 characters decreed as the minimum literacy standard by the Ministry of Education in 1950. A second conference convened in December 1950; it eventually resulted in the promulgation, in June 1952, of a list of 2,000 characters. The list was designated as the basic 'reference material' for localities to compile their own literacy primers and popular reading materials. The term 'localities' referred to anything from the large regional administrations set up for a brief period after 1949 to provinces and counties.[31]

The Ministry of Education decreed in 1950 that, following three years of part-time study, illiterates (*wenmang*) and half-literates (*ban wenmang*) should be able to recognize 1,000 commonly used characters (*changyongzi*) and possess preliminary (*chubu*) reading, writing, and computation skills. Graduates would be issued certificates of official literate status (*fei wenmang zhengshu*) by the county government. The certificate qualified one to commence an additional two-year course of spare-time study, consisting of instruction in Mandarin, arithmetic, and general knowledge (*changshi*). Class length for both programs was set at 150-200 classes per year, with each class one to two hours in length.

The new official category of 'half-literate' (*ban wenmang*) is particularly intriguing. The origins of the concept are unclear. It may have originally been intended as a proxy measure of literacy based on school attendance: those who had never attended school were considered illiterate for statistics-gathering purposes, but there was still the problem of how to categorize persons who had attended a sishu for a period, as well as those who had failed to complete primary school. A more likely reason for adopting the term seems to have been the determination to borrow what was originally a Soviet concept and bend it to describe Chinese literacy. During the Soviet literacy campaign of the 1920s, separate literacy schools had been established for those considered 'half-literate.'[32] The term's precise meaning in the Chinese context, however, remained unclear. Chao Yimin, chair of the

Central-South Culture and Education Committee, identified three kinds of illiterates in 1951: those who knew no characters at all, those who knew 100 or so characters, and those who knew more than 500 characters.[33] The Ministry of Education journal reported in the same year that, 'according to standard practice' (*yiban de xiguan*), an illiterate was someone who knew between zero and 300-400 characters. Such persons, even though they could recognize bank notes and perhaps even write simple receipts, were nevertheless considered illiterate because they 'had not yet mastered the tools of writing.' A person was considered half-literate when he or she was able to recognize 500-600 characters 'more or less,' could hold a writing brush, and was therefore in a position of being 'half able and half unable to get by' in 'daily written cultural life.'[34]

Subsequent attempts to refine and clarify the meaning of 'half-literate' appear to have been equally ad hoc. In 1953, the newly formed National Anti-Illiteracy Work Committee issued a circular on literacy standards (*saomang biaozhun*) stating that a half-literate was someone who 'knew how to read' (*neng shidao*) at least 500 characters but who had still not attained the full literacy standard as measured by newly implemented literacy graduation examinations.[35]

Despite such strenuous official efforts to impose standard literacy definitions and criteria, localities frequently defied them. Some simply imposed their own definitions. Thus, for example, some Guangdong localities defined a 'literate' person as anyone who had graduated from senior primary school – a much stricter definition than the official one since, in the early 1950s, only around 10 per cent of primary schools even offered the senior-level curriculum (grades 5-6), and they were located mostly in cities. (Those with a junior primary school education were judged 'half-literate.') On the other hand, some Guangdong counties issued literacy certificates to anyone who could recognize at least 600 characters.[36]

Efforts to improve the literacy and educational level of local functionaries centred on creating a national network of special Cultural Remediation Schools (*wenhua buxi xuexiao*). The schools, which began operation in 1950, recruited their students from among township and village cadres, peasant associations, mass organizations, and the Communist Party. Their aim was to impart a condensed primary education within one to three years and to prepare selected graduates for further study in specially established 'Worker-Peasant Accelerated Middle Schools' (*gongnong sucheng zhongxue*).[37] Few such schools were established, however, relative to the magnitude of the problem they were intended to address. By late 1950, there were only eighteen Worker-Peasant Accelerated Middle Schools across the entire country. By 1955, when the experiment ended, there were just eighty-seven schools, with a combined enrolment of only 51,000 students. To put these figures in perspective, over approximately the same period the number of state cadres as a whole grew from 720,000 to over 5 million, while the number of party members increased from 4.5 million to 10.7 million.[38]

The director of the Guangdong Bureau of Education, Du Guoxiang, reiterated the official position regarding the priority of local party members and activists. More than twenty Cultural Remediation Schools and one Worker-Peasant Accelerated Middle School were set up in Guangdong during the early 1950s. The latter type, which opened for the first time in Guangzhou in February 1951, drew nearly 200 students from across the province. Four years later, however, it remained the only one of its kind in Guangdong.[39]

In Guangdong as elsewhere, the schools were beset by difficulties, starting with the educational level of the students recruited. In the first year of their operation, it was discovered that at least half of the 2,500 cadres enrolled in Worker-Peasant Accelerated Middle Schools had 'cultural levels' actually lower than those of ordinary primary school graduates. In addition, local authorities were often reluctant to allow their officials to attend the schools for fear that the latter would regard the schools simply as 'a brick to open other doors' (*qiaomen zhuan*) – that is, as a way of escaping the village for a bureaucratic job in the city. Therefore, to be on the safe side, local authorities often recommended that retired revolutionaries attend the schools, as a reward for past service, and others whom they believed they could most easily manage without.[40]

The Early 1950s Prohibition of Literacy Education

The first official directive on worker-peasant education was an ambiguous document embodying the tension between education for political mobilization and education to facilitate bureaucratic rule. While it affirmed the functional importance of literacy for bureaucratic integration, the directive also set clear limits on the allowable emphasis to be given to literacy education under certain conditions. Specifically, it stipulated that, 'in general, peasant education should emphasize literacy education first, in concert with contemporary affairs and political policy education and production and hygiene education.' However, owing to the fact that political conditions were not the same across the country, it was necessary to adjust the emphasis on literacy education in some cases. In the former base areas, where land reform was completed and the party's grip on local society had been secured, literacy education was to take precedence. In the event of 'important political movements,' however, villages in these areas were to 'strengthen the proportion of current political affairs education' and reduce the amount of time devoted to literacy instruction. In the remaining parts of the country, however, the instructions were decidedly different.

In the 'newly liberated' areas of the country, literacy education was to be prohibited until the conclusion of land reform. In 1950, this included virtually all of Guangdong. In these areas, peasant education was to focus instead on the dissemination of 'political policy and contemporary affairs education' in order to 'arouse peasants' class consciousness and raise their political understanding.'[41] Thus, the party's previous wartime distinction between political mobilization (*dongyuan* – literally, to 'shake' or 'agitate') and simple literacy acquisition (*xue wenhua* – literally, 'to learn culture') was upheld after 1949. In areas where the communists were still in the process of consolidating their power, schools were to be used as conduits for political propaganda, using the tested techniques of wartime mass education. The proven experience of the base areas was that non-literate media were a more effective means of mobilizing mass-political support than media for which literacy was needed. Peasants were not to become preoccupied with the laborious task of learning characters at a time when their mental energies were believed to be better spent cultivating the political psychology that the state regarded as crucial to the success of land reform.

The outbreak of the Korean War in June 1950 and the ensuing militarization of the Taiwan Strait tipped the balance in favour of political mobilization over literacy. The external crisis raised the twin spectre of a foreign invasion coupled with internal subversion by Nationalist remnants, especially in the south, convincing party leaders of the need to place mass education on a war footing once more. Thus, immediately following the outbreak of the Korean War, the Ministry of Education announced that the 'main educational task' of all citizens was to take part in the movement to 'Resist America and Aid Korea.' Winter schools and (in the south) seasonal spare-time schools for adults were identified as important centres for mobilization. Local officials were instructed to root out all those who insisted on clinging to the belief that 'learning culture' was more important than 'political and current affairs education.'[42]

With literacy education prohibited in Guangdong, local officials concentrated on using mass meetings and other non-print media to mobilize support for current policies. This involved instructing villagers about land reform, the new marriage law, state grain requisitions, antihoarding laws, and the prohibition of Hong Kong currency. In Fengxun county, local educational authorities organized a travelling photo exhibition that included depictions of landlord sabotage, American imperialism, Korean War battle scenes, and life in the Soviet Union. The organizers were disappointed to learn that most villagers had never even heard of Korea.[43]

Ideological education was considered especially crucial to the success of the first stage of land reform, in which outside work teams 'prepared' villagers for land redistribution. According to the Central-South branch of the party Central Committee, preparatory education was to focus on three main issues: opposing feudal enemies, feudal practices, and imperialism. The methods used included lectures (*jiangyan*) to mass audiences, seasonal and winter schools, and, for those who were literate, newspaper reading groups, wall posters, and basic primers.[44]

Following the completion of land reform in 1952, political education in Guangdong was divided into two categories. 'Current affairs political education' included the success of the campaign to Resist America and Aid Korea, achievements in the rehabilitation of the economy since 1949, and Sino-Soviet friendship, while general 'political education' included encouraging peasants to strive for 'patriotic increases' in farm output, to participate in mutual-aid teams and realize the historic importance of the worker-peasant alliance, and to consider the prospect of socialism in China. By late 1953, the focus of political education shifted to promoting the 'general line for the transition to socialism,' especially state monopolization of the grain trade and the formation of collectives. In addition, schools were to emphasize state policies concerning national defence, the liberation of Taiwan, opposition to US imperialism, and the importance of cultivating an 'international' outlook among peasants. Only passing mention was made of the importance of cultivating reading and writing skills.[45]

Since Guangdong was one of the last provinces to begin land reform in late 1950 and was the last province to complete it, in 1952, the proscription of literacy education lasted longer in Guangdong than in most provinces. It was not until 1952 that the emphasis of peasant spare-time education in Guangdong officially shifted from 'contemporary political affairs education' (*zhengzhi shishi jiaoyu*) to cultural education (*wenhua jiaoyu*), with literacy education as its 'keypoint.'[46]

The ban on literacy education had significant consequences for the educational profile of the Communist Party in Guangdong. In 1949, the communist movement in Guangdong was comprised almost exclusively of urban students and intellectuals who had joined the party during the Japanese occupation of 1938-45.[47] The preponderance of urban intellectuals can be seen clearly from party statistics. Out of a total of 129 leading Guangdong party cadres in 1950 – 88 per cent of whom had joined the party after 1938 – thirty-four were university graduates, eighty-eight had attended middle school, and only three had less than a primary school education. Likewise, when the first Guangdong People's Congress convened in 1950, 80 per cent of the political party delegates (which also included members of non-communist parties) were from non-peasant and non-worker backgrounds, while less than 6 per cent were illiterate.[48]

Over the next three to six years, however, this profile was reversed. The intellectual and student leadership was purged in the early 1950s and replaced by northern cadres, who were regarded by Beijing as having greater loyalty and more reliable class backgrounds.[49] Equally as important, however, were the party's educational and recruitment policies. The pattern of the northern base areas was repeated in Guangdong and elsewhere across the country in the early 1950s, with educated personnel recruited for county-level administrations and illiterate activists recruited to fill the lower echelons of the party-state apparatus at the township level and below. Thus, by 1953 the number of cadres in Guangdong had grown to nearly 193,000, of which 34 per cent had less than a primary school education. By 1956, a classified report estimated that as many as four out of every seven leading cadres in most Guangdong townships were illiterate.[50]

The *Sucheng* Interlude

Following the completion of land reform in 1952, a brief attempt was made to make up for the time lost as a result of the ban on literacy education in most parts of the country. Regions across China began to experiment with a new pedagogical technique for literacy instruction known as the 'accelerated literacy method' (*sucheng shizi fa*).

The creator of the accelerated literacy method was Qi Jianhua, a previously obscure cultural commissar from the PLA's Yunnan garrison. Qi claimed to have discovered the method while experimenting among illiterate army cadres and soldiers. The method purported to teach illiterates how to read and write 1,500 characters in only 150 hours, using three easy steps. First, students spent twenty to thirty hours memorizing thirty-seven phonetic symbols drawn from the old national phonetic alphabet (*zhuyin fuhao*). Second, they 'assaulted' (*tuji*) a list of 200 characters annotated with phonetic symbols, which were to be memorized at a rate of twelve to twenty-four per hour. Third, students studied simple texts to facilitate their reading and grammatical understanding. Some attention was also paid to writing at this stage, and to the range of meanings contained within individual characters. Qi claimed that the method had been tested and proven among more than 12,000 illiterate army cadres and soldiers in Yunnan, most of whom were able to achieve basic literacy in only fifteen days.[51]

The emergence of the accelerated literacy method from within the ranks of the PLA may have represented an attempt by the PLA to establish itself as the leading force in the literacy drive, similar to the role played by the Red Army in the early Soviet literacy drive. For a period of about six months, between May 1952 and January 1953, the method was feverishly embraced as a panacea. The uncritical eagerness with which it was touted during those six months portended a similar utopian optimism that infected later literacy campaigns, notably during the Great Leap Forward. The method was supposed to be used mainly among cadres and activists, but it was soon being introduced to all illiterates. In Chongqing, a group of illiterate textile workers claimed to have raised their literacy level from an average of 400 characters to more than 2,000 in only twenty-one days using the method. In Tianjin, a group of factory workers announced that they had made a similar breakthrough in just twenty-three days.[52]

Experience showed that villagers who studied in year-round evening schools needed an average of two to three years in order to master 700 to 800 characters, while even in the best evening schools, students spent roughly the same amount of time to learn 1,000 to 1,500 characters. In the seasonal spare-time schools, which met only during the slack season, progress was even slower, and study often seemed simply futile. Peasants in seasonal schools regularly complained that the characters they learned one season were forgotten the next, so that each year was like starting over again (*niannian kaixue, niannian kaitou*). So it is not difficult to see why peasants and local officials alike were quick to embrace the accelerated literacy method. In one village, peasants even refused to attend any more evening classes after they learned of the existence of the accelerated literacy method.[53]

In May 1952, the central government declared Hebei province a key experimental region for promoting the method on a national basis. The Ministry of Education obliged by publishing a teachers' guide and a two-volume literacy primer based on the method. In Guangdong, provincial education authorities prepared dialect versions of the method for the province's four main dialects. Jiangmen and Huiyang were designated as 'keypoints' for experimenting with the method. Between August and November 1952, some 23,000 teachers were trained in the accelerated literacy method and were later assigned to thirty counties and cities across the province.[54] By early 1953, national enrolment in adult literacy classes approached 20 million, of which nearly one-third were using Qi Jianhua's method.

The same month, however, critics began to openly denounce the method as 'excessively simplistic.' The following month, in February 1953, the first national conference on illiteracy eradication brought together educators, literacy activists, and officials from across the country to discuss the merits and demerits of the accelerated literacy method – marking the first time that the method was actually openly discussed and debated. The conference delegates condemned the 'blind' fashion in which the method had been promoted and implemented, and they concluded that its potential had been vastly overrated. The accelerated literacy method, they said, was actually prolonging the struggle for literacy by creating the false illusion of a quick and easy solution. The method failed to realize the 'long-term nature' (*changqi xing*) of literacy acquisition.[55]

The methods advocated by critics of the accelerated literacy method echoed the views put forward by Ma Xulun in 1950, specifically the need for a gradual, carefully managed effort that respected the complexities of the Chinese language, pupil motivation, and teacher expertise and that therefore resisted the temptation of utopian solutions. The first national conference on illiteracy eradication closed in early 1953 with a call to 'rectify' adult literacy efforts across the country and to promote the concept of a 'stable advance.' Those words in fact signalled the ascendancy of professional educators in the determination of China's literacy policy. Their views in favour of a regular state-run school system had been eclipsed since 1949, first by the influence of the Yanan mass educators who resisted giving basic reading and writing skills unchallengeable supremacy over the mobilizational uses of education, and then by Qi Jianhua's radical experiment with a miracle cure for illiteracy. A chastened official policy was announced in early 1953, calling for continued implementation of the accelerated literacy method, but on a tightly controlled basis and only under ideal conditions. In reality, the method vanished into the annals of failed literacy experiments. In most areas, adult literacy efforts stagnated. Worker-peasant education offices were closed and officials transferred to other jobs, while starting in 1953 reports began to describe a pervasive 'non-interest' in adult literacy efforts throughout the country. By the end of 1953, there were actually fewer persons enrolled in literacy classes than in 1949. It would be a full two years before the literacy movement would be rescued from stagnation in 1955 by the collectivization of agriculture.[56]

The history of rural literacy efforts during the first half of the 1950s reveals the extent to which the literacy movement was subject to elite conflicts over literacy's meaning and uses in the new state. The various state actors involved in the formation of official literacy policy – Communist Party educators, classically educated linguists and philologists, professional educators, and PLA commissars – held their own conceptions of China's rural illiteracy problem, and this diversity of views translated into frequent change and difficult progress. From Ma Xulun's cautious sobriety to the utopianism of Qi Jianhua's accelerated literacy method, from the banning of literacy instruction in areas undergoing land reform to the near-total paralysis of the literacy movement in 1953, the volatile PRC literacy movement careened from one extreme to another during the experimental years of the early 1950s.

Thus far, our discussion of the origins and development of the literacy movement has focused on state efforts to penetrate the village educational world and elite conflicts over literacy policy. Our discussion would not be complete, however, without considering the role of village schoolteachers. Standing between the state and the peasant society it wished to educate, village teachers were the indispensable intermediaries upon whom the success or failure of the literacy movement largely depended. Teachers were crucial actors in the literacy movement precisely because they intersected state and society. Yet for this very reason, their role was equivocal. Were they cultural agents of the state, serving a Leninist 'transmission belt' function of representing official values to a hostile or indifferent peasantry? Or were they more closely allied with local interests and traditional social and cultural values? In the following chapter, we will seek answers to these and other questions.

4
The Problem of the Teachers

> Our teachers of Chinese are such obstinate pedants. They are constantly mouthing expressions such as 'We read in the Book of Poetry' or 'Confucius says,' but when you come down to it, in fact, they don't understand a word. They are not aware that this is already the twentieth century; they still compel us to observe 'old rites' and follow 'old regulations.' They forcibly impregnate our minds with a lot of stinking corpse-like dead writing full of classical allusions.[1]
>
> Mao Zedong, 1923

The above passage captures well the abiding disdain and implicit distrust with which Mao and other communist leaders regarded traditional schoolteachers. His image of teachers – excessively literary, obscurantist, and hopelessly antiquated – continued to inform official thinking about the subversive danger of counterrevolutionary teachers in the PRC. What is more, Mao's comments referred specifically to teachers of Chinese – those whom Mao regarded as the most stubbornly antiquarian. As the self-appointed carriers and transmitters of China's ancient literary heritage, they could be expected to resist the Communist Party. Yet they were also crucial to the party's mass education project. How could they be made to fit? The literacy movement was, in part, a struggle between two educational worlds: the one that existed in the minds and organizational blueprints of state leaders, and the other that guided village thought and practice. To which of these two worlds did village teachers belong? In this chapter, we examine the changing nature of official attitudes toward village teachers as crucial actors in the literacy movement.

The post-1949 teaching corps was made up of two sharply differentiated groups of teachers. One consisted of teachers in state-run primary schools located mainly in urban areas. State-supported teachers (*gongban jiaoshi*) were privileged. Recruited by the state, they were generally better educated, more qualified, and better paid than teachers in village schools.

Gongban teachers were more likely to be graduates of secondary schools and teachers' colleges. Most important, they usually held the coveted urban residency status (*chengshi hukou*), which entitled them to superior rations, housing, and educational opportunities for their children. Teachers in village-run primary schools were known as people-supported teachers (*minban jiaoshi*). Whereas gongban teachers were recruited and paid by the state, minban teachers were recruited and supported by their local communities. In the early 1950s, minban teachers received subsistence-level wages, paid in kind. Following collectivization in 1956, minban teachers were attached to rural production teams, where they were paid on the basis of workpoints just as were other team members. Minban teachers rarely held urban residency status. Compared to gongban teachers, minban teachers were also far less educated and qualified. Teacher-training schools served town-based educational institutions (at the level of township, county, and district), so village primary schools normally recruited local primary graduates to serve as teachers.

Throughout the first half of the 1950s, minban teachers constituted less than 13 per cent of the primary teaching corps. The proportion of minban teachers began to rise sharply, however, with collectivization and the rapid expansion of collectively sponsored primary and middle schools in the countryside. Retrenchments in rural schooling in the early 1960s reduced the proportion of minban teachers; however, during the Cultural Revolution, the growth of minban schooling resumed with even greater vigour than before, as large numbers of primary teachers were transferred from state payrolls to local collectives. From the mid-1960s through the early 1980s, minban teachers constituted a majority of the primary teaching corps.[2]

The division of the teaching corps into superior state-supported teachers and inferior locally supported teachers thus reflected and reinforced the division between the two tracks of the Chinese educational system as a whole. Previous studies of teachers in the PRC have tended to concentrate upon urban gongban teachers. The focus of this chapter, however, is upon teachers in village-run schools.[3]

The Contradictory Image of the Village Schoolteacher

Officially and ideally, minban teachers were agents of the state, critical 'transmission belts' for communicating and popularizing the pedagogical will of the state in local society. The actual history of their plight, however, belies the image of schoolteachers as dutiful Leninist transmission belts. Perhaps no other social group was more frequently or persistently accused of resisting the revolution. Teachers were singled out as the main target of the first major campaign for thought reform carried out between 1949 and 1951. This was only the beginning. Mao later revealed that primary schoolteachers were the main target of the 1957 Anti-Rightist Campaign, comprising a third of the more than 300,000 persons labelled 'rightist' during the campaign. Political persecution of teachers reached its extreme during the Cultural Revolution, however, when an untold number of schoolteachers lost their jobs, their personal property, and in many cases their lives.[4]

The contradictory image of the village schoolteacher extended to his or her material and symbolic status as well.[5] The importance and concern with which teachers were officially viewed clashed with the popular – and largely accurate – image of village schoolmasters as tragically poor creatures, whose livelihood depended upon the charity of local communities. Moreover, the PRC inherited in teachers a rich, if somewhat ambiguous, legacy of moral leadership centred on Confucian ideas concerning the proper social and political ordering of society. There was very little celebration of the revolutionary virtues of 'blankness' by the Communist Party when it came to the role of local schoolteachers. The village schoolmaster was one of the oldest and most richly symbolic institutions in rural society. It was also, however, one of the most ambiguous. On the one hand, there was no shortage of traditional epithets exalting the moral stature of teachers. Village teachers were often affectionately referred to as 'the king of the children' (*haizi wang*). Nineteenth-century Western observers were struck by the esteemed role of teachers in village society. The American missionary Arthur Smith wrote that schoolmasters possessed 'one of the most honorable of callings' in village society. Teachers were revered partly for their access to classical knowledge contained in written texts. In addition, their leadership in local society was founded upon the literate services they provided. Daniel Kulp observed that, in Guangdong villages, classically educated teachers were 'popular among the villagers, willing to associate and converse with them in a universe of discourse familiar to them, and ready to render any kind of assistance to them.' Kulp's observation echoes the findings of Liao T'ai-chu's survey of republican-era sishu, which described how villagers depended upon teachers for a wide range of literacy-related personal and community services, including the preparation of lawsuits and wedding and funeral notices and the selection of auspicious personal names. In short, teachers belonged to what James Hayes has aptly termed the 'literate specialists' of village society.[6]

On the other hand, however, the popular image of the village schoolteacher, as conveyed in folktales and novels, was usually also that of a pathetically poor and chronically downtrodden figure.[7] Thus, while teachers may have commanded a great deal of moral respect and admiration from villagers, theirs was still an occupation that few parents directly chose for their sons. In Jerry Dennerline's apt words, village teachers were 'living proof of the separation of learning from the sources of wealth.'[8] A popular Guangdong aphorism expressed the view that 'Men who haven't hit bottom don't stoop to be schoolteachers' (*ren bujian buzuo xiansheng*), while another held that 'A family [man] with at least a couple of pecks of grain won't resort to teaching' (*jia you erdou liang, budang haiziwang*).

The split image of the worthy but chronically poverty-stricken village teacher is also expressed in Wu Jingzi's eighteenth-century satirical novel *Rulin waishi* (*The Scholars*). Among the noteworthy characters in this memorable novel dedicated to poking fun at the social manners of Qing literati was Mr. Zhou, an aging would-be scholar who at sixty years plus was still struggling to pass the lowest-level civil service examination. Old Zhou epitomized the popular image of the destitute village scholar who ekes out an existence 'plowing with the pen,' dressed in an 'old felt cap, a tattered grey silk gown, the right sleeve and seat of which were in shreds, and a pair of shabby red silk slippers.'[9] Another example drawn from popular lore was the Qing-dynasty beggar-teacher Wu Xun, who devoted his scant earnings to founding schools for the village poor and who, as a consequence, was commended by the emperor when Wu died in 1896. Of course, teaching in a village school was also the leisured pursuit of prosperous retired officials. But mostly it was the refuge of minimally literate lower degree holders and of frustrated would-be scholars like Mr. Zhou. For such thwarted scholars, teaching in a village school offered the only available, and partially face-saving, alternative to a life of manual labour.[10] The customary portrait of the village schoolmaster in Chinese popular culture was thus fraught with ambiguity: full of moral authority, but notoriously short on economic reward.

There was also a more general erosion of the traditional moral stature of teachers in Chinese culture and society after 1900. To begin with, the notion of teacher as embodiment and transmitter of classical learning was undermined by the abolition of the imperial civil service examination system in 1905. The end of this system, which for more than five centuries had moulded Chinese intellectual energies in the service of Confucian moral enquiry, also marked the beginning of a gradual but fundamental redefinition of the cultural meaning of 'teacher,' from standard-bearer of the classical written cultural tradition to transmitter of modern knowledge and skills. Moreover, within a decade of the examination system's abolition, the traditional role of teachers was overtly and vociferously challenged, as part of the more generalized intellectual attack upon Confucianism that began with the New Culture Movement of the 1910s. The end of the exam system, and the subsequent intellectual critique of Confucianism as a feudal obstacle to the emergence of a modern Chinese society, undercut the moral authority of teachers in two ways. First, the Confucian canon upon which teachers' claims to moral authority rested was reduced from the status of state orthodoxy to mere personal philosophy. Second, when New Culture intellectuals attacked Confucianism as the ugly root of Chinese feudalism and the primary cause of China's failure to modernize, they were also attacking the teachers who were the primary guardians of that heritage. By the 1920s, the disintegration of teachers' moral authority had proceeded far enough that modern-minded reformers and revolutionaries could confidently denounce Confucian teachers as one of the 'four olds,' along with poverty, sickness, and death.[11]

In the long run, however, such intellectual critiques were not as important in undermining the traditional moral status of teachers as the fact that abolition of the examination system paved the way for the enshrinement of utilitarian skills over classical knowledge as the prima facie societal rationale for learning. The twentieth-century growth of modern mass education also undermined teachers' traditional social status by lowering the scarcity value of literacy. The gradual erosion and redefinition of the teacher's role probably occurred more slowly in poorer regions, where the scarcity value of literacy continued to remain high and where occupational alternatives to teaching remained rare for literates. The educational gazetteer of Zijin county, Guangdong, describes a progressive decline in the social status of teaching compared to other literate occupations in the urban and commercialized areas of the county during the republican period. But in the poorer parts of Zijin, local schoolmasters continued to be regarded as among the most esteemed members of their communities, and they were still frequently called upon to preside at weddings and funerals, inscribe couplets for these and other auspicious occasions, and occupy the seat of honour at banquets.[12]

All of this took place within the context of the erosion and then the disintegration of traditionally clearly defined notions of literacy caused by successive modern school reforms and by the May Fourth Movement's attack on classical learning. The result was an increasing lack of consensus on what constituted 'literacy' (or the different levels thereof). And all of this occurred within the general context of 'China in disintegration,' making for even greater sociocultural uncertainty. On the whole, therefore, the social status of teachers was in a long-term state of decline for at least half a century before the Communist party-state embarked on its post-1949 attempt to transform the role of the village schoolmaster.

The Impoverished Social and Material Status of Village Teachers in the PRC

The rural teaching corps was ill prepared for the challenges that awaited it after 1949. The vast majority did not meet official qualifications; many village teachers were, in fact, barely literate themselves; nearly all lived in poverty. In early 1951, the country's two largest newspapers each inaugurated a regular series designed to draw attention to the abysmal poverty and low educational levels of most rural schoolteachers. One writer asked whether there was still any glory (*guangrong*) in being a village teacher when across the country such teachers were said to be suffering an 'inferiority complex' (*zibeigan*). Contemporary attempts to gauge popular attitudes revealed tremendous dissatisfaction with teaching as an occupation. The results of one 1952 survey of a primary teacher training college showed that fewer than 30 per cent of those enrolled aspired to teaching. Most had enrolled in teacher training either because they had failed to gain admission to more preferred educational institutions or because the tuition was relatively inexpensive compared with that for other forms of education.[13]

Despite official claims to the contrary, it appears that the material living standard of rural teachers improved but marginally during the early years of communist rule. National figures indicate that the average income of rural primary teachers, the most poorly paid of all teachers, increased by nearly 25 per cent between 1951 and 1953. However, the national figure masked enormous regional and local variations in teachers' salaries and working conditions. In mid-1951, the average salary for rural primary teachers in Guangdong was seventy to eighty catties of grain per month, well above the national average. In Zijin county, however, the figure was much higher, approximately 200 catties per month. Salaries were gradually converted to cash during the first half of the 1950s. In 1956, the central government instituted a minimum wage of twenty-three yuan per month for rural primary teachers. However, localities were often unable to guarantee teachers the official minimum, while in the poorest regions teachers continued to be paid in kind. Teachers in some parts of Yunnan received ten yuan per month on average, while teachers in Guizhou earned only four yuan per month. Press reports described teachers who had been without pay for months and therefore had been forced to subsist on food borrowed from their students.[14]

The destitute condition of most village schoolteachers thus contrasted sharply with their official role as transmission belts for inculcating the pedagogical will of the state. But there were also deeper problems associated with the state's attempt to make local teachers into purveyors of official ideology. Whereas teachers traditionally represented the community's customary values to itself, they were now expected to become the local spokespersons for a new and alien set of values, imposed from above. This meant that, to the extent the state actually succeeded in transforming teachers into transmission belts of state policy, it was often at the expense of teachers' credibility in the eyes of their local communities.

Moreover, the desire to make teachers agents of a new orthodoxy was fundamentally at odds with the state's determination to deflate, at all costs, the traditional moral authority accorded to intellectuals in Chinese society and culture. The state's conscious effort to relocate moral virtue in the 'people,' as opposed to intellectuals, undermined the cultural expectation that teachers embody moral and political orthodoxy. The moral paragons of socialist society were to be worker-heroes, such as the martyred Lei Feng. Morally heroic intellectuals like the Qing-dynasty beggar-teacher Wu Xun, however, were publicly reviled in the early 1950s at Mao's personal behest.[15]

Nor did teachers command political power. On the contrary, they were normally at the mercy of local power holders. Unlike local cadres, teachers were weak state agents, without the personalized control over the allocation of scarce resources that the former could and did use in order to mobilize support or exact compliance. Moreover, as petty intellectuals from the countryside, village teachers lacked the social status and patronage that partly shielded higher-level intellectuals from persecution.[16] While teachers lacked political power, they were also economically vulnerable. The near-total economic dependence of teachers on local communities made them particularly vulnerable to retribution from local power holders, who not only resented the economic costs of supporting local intellectuals but also sought to control the activities of schools. Indeed, an uneven struggle between teachers and poorly educated but politically powerful cadres appears to have been a regular feature of local educational life in the People's Republic of China.

Conflicts between Teachers and Village Cadres

Teachers' subordination to village political authority was ensured by the restructuring of school management committees in the early 1950s. The traditional management bodies for village schools, called 'boards of school trustees' (*xiaodonghui*), were taken over. Membership on the boards, formerly vested in lineage elders and prominent members of the local elite, was now reserved for party members and representatives of the newly established mass organizations, including the peasant association and local branches of the Youth League and the Women's Federation. Their mandate was to exercise both administrative and political leadership over the schools.

Tensions between teachers and their new political overseers came to a head in 1957 when, as part of the Hundred Flowers Movement, teachers were officially encouraged to vent their grievances and to offer frank assessments of the party's failure to 'link up' with the schools. Teachers complained of the tendency of local cadres to 'look down' upon them with an air of political superiority. Cadres were accused of routinely refusing to take teachers' opinions into account when deciding on educational matters. Party cadres, with no teaching experience and very little formal education, were placed in charge of compiling political texts for use in the schools. One teacher complained in 1957 that, when cadres talked with students about education, their attitude was patronizing and insincere; they talked excessively about the importance of having 'correct political viewpoints' but not at all about 'life problems, educational work, [and] study problems.' As a result, said this teacher, students found it difficult 'to feel close to' the Communist Party.

Another critic attributed the superior and disdainful attitude of cadres toward village schoolteachers to the new village political elite attempting to ape the ancient mandarin habit of arrogance toward petty village intellectuals. The mentality of local cadres, said this critic, was 'vivid with the remnant thought of the ruling classes of the old society.' Their behaviour toward teachers was castigated as a 'manifestation of the sectarianism that discriminates against [low] intellectuals.'[17]

Unlike the mandarins of the past, however, party cadres were normally poorly educated, often illiterate, peasant activists. Thus, their deliberate mistreatment of teachers may have reflected not so much an effort to imitate mandarin traditions as a determination to assert the primacy of revolutionary class background over educational attainment (or even basic literacy) in the distribution of rank and power in New China. Of course, the reverse was sometimes also true: poorly educated cadres deferred to better-educated intellectuals, and often for very traditional reasons. Mao himself was well aware of this tendency, apparently regarding it as serious enough to warrant his comment in 1958 that 'We have been afraid of professors ever since we came into the towns. We did not despise them, we were terrified of them.'[18]

Political pressure and interference were not the only problems teachers faced in their dealings with local cadres. Of crucial significance was the fact that local cadres controlled the social welfare funds that paid teachers' salaries in kind and provided for their upkeep. Local cadres were therefore in a position to pressure or punish teachers by withholding or threatening to withhold the essentials of life. Such tactics were not uncommon. Moreover, the costs to local communities of supporting teachers were often prohibitive, especially in poorer villages. Teachers' salaries accounted for the single greatest recurrent cost – up to 90 per cent – of running schools. State subsidies covered only a small proportion; local authorities were to generate the rest. Not surprisingly, there was often resistance and resentment. In one Guangdong collective, cadres remarked of the local teacher that she was 'trying to grab a few workpoints in whatever way she could' at the expense of other members of the collective. By 1956, ill treatment of teachers by village cadres had become so widespread that the central government issued directives requiring local party committees and judicial organs to discipline cadres who violated the 'human rights' of teachers. Such violations included beating teachers and withholding food from them.[19]

The Real and Potential Subversiveness of Village Schoolteachers

As noted, teachers were usually poverty stricken and lacked formal political authority. They did, however, possess considerable cultural resources for mobilizing popular thought and action. The new state's most urgent concern with respect to teachers after 1949 was their political loyalty, especially their capacity to mobilize popular resistance. There were several reasons why teachers were inherently suspect in the eyes of the new state. First, those who had taught in the old society tended to come from the ranks of the 'exploiting classes' (*boxue jieji*). The shortage of trained teachers forced the new government to continue to rely on the services of this group. In 1951, Chao Yimin, chair of the Central-South Culture and Education Committee, observed that the majority of 'unemployed intellectuals' recruited to teach basic literacy in communist-run winter schools that year were from landlord and rich peasant families.[20]

Land reform broke the economic power of the old elite. Chinese press accounts of this period, however, abound with cases of former elites attempting to reestablish local dominance via village schools. Although officially excluded from serving as school board trustees, members of the former elite were often the only persons with sufficient literacy and managerial skills to teach in and administer village schools. Thus, when villagers in Longlou, Hainan, decided to establish a village school in 1950, they found that only five out of seventy-nine persons in the village had any previous education and that the five were all from landlord and rich peasant families. A former landlord, Wang Nengchen, became the school's teacher. Shortly afterward, Wang was accused of using his position to disguise his class background. He was subsequently arrested and replaced by several minimally literate activists from neighbouring villages. The 'hundred-character teachers' (*baizi xiansheng*), as they were popularly known, made Wang Nengchen's 'crimes' the focus of study.[21]

State suspicion of teachers was also grounded in an acute historical consciousness of the personal bonds between teachers and their students. Such bonds had historically served as a basis for collective action, with rebellious teachers often at the front of popular movements against the state. Guangdong, with its surfeit of frustrated examination candidates and lower degree holders, abounded with subversive schoolteachers. Hong Xiuquan, leader of the Taiping movement that shook the imperial state to its core in the mid-nineteenth century, began his revolutionary career as a village schoolteacher in Hua county, just outside Guangzhou. Similarly, Sun Yatsen began his revolutionary career as a sixteen-year-old iconoclast who, in 1883, embraced Christianity and was subsequently expelled from his home village for smashing and mutilating temple idols, as Lyon Sharman puts it, 'to drive superstition forcibly out of men's minds [and] make an entrance for new ideas.'[22] From the apocalyptic vision of the Taipings to the republican vision of Sun Yatsen, Guangdong nurtured some of China's most radical antiestablishment visions.

The tradition of political activism by local schoolteachers was not only emblazoned on the historical memories of rulers; it was firmly embedded in the popular culture as well. Alexander Woodside points out that 'Confucian societies recognized the existence of an important tradition of the poor, idealistic backwoods scholar-teacher who dreams of making, and sometimes does make, a dramatic intervention in politics.'[23] The tradition explains why Chinese governments never failed to take seriously the ideological rumblings of lowly village schoolteachers. The Guomindang government demanded that primary schoolteachers take loyalty oaths. The Chinese socialist state emerging in the early 1950s likewise could not afford to take the loyalty of schoolteachers for granted when its own moral authority – not to mention its political and administrative structures and policing power – was still only weakly constituted.

Problems of Professionalism versus Party Control

The party-state's wariness toward teachers was not based exclusively upon their tradition of political activism, however. The perceived threat posed by educational circles (*jiaoyu jie*) in the new state also had distinctly modern foundations. The development of modern education since the turn of the century led to a significant professionalization of teaching in certain parts of the country, especially in the big eastern coastal cities and provincial capitals and their surrounding hinterlands. With the growth of modern schooling after 1900, teachers in these areas established their own professional associations. Often they became involved in efforts to separate education from politics – no easy task under the predatory politics of warlordism. In 1920, the National Association for Educational Autonomy was founded in Beijing. Together with the National Education Association, it was partly responsible for a wave of teacher strikes that swept across Guangzhou, Wuhan, Tianjin, Beijing, and other major cities during the 1920s, in protest against warlord-government interference in education.[24]

After 1949, teacher opposition to the new state continued to find expression in the form of an ideology of professionalism. Non-party educators persisted, much to the chagrin of party officials, in cultivating a professional ethic that directly contradicted the state's hegemonic claims over the educational domain. From the perspective of communist educators, apolitical schools were neither possible nor desirable. But this did not prevent teachers from denouncing party interference in the running of schools or attempts to introduce politics into what they regarded as 'purely educational' concerns.[25] Local education bureaus often sympathized with teachers' complaints. Concerned with maintaining the academic standards of schools, they actively supported the principle that the primary obligation of teachers was teaching, not politics. In the overseas Chinese county of Taishan, county educational authorities in 1953 issued regulations that strictly limited the amount of school time that teachers and students could spend participating in political and social movements. Teachers were to devote no more than twelve hours per month to political movements. Primary school pupils were allowed to spend no more than one and a half hours per week on political movements, junior middle school students no more than three hours per week, and senior middle school students no more than two hours per week. The regulations came in response to a State Council directive of late 1953 that attempted to correct what it called the 'excessive' participation in recent years of teachers and students in 'social movements' and other 'non-teaching activities.' The directive stipulated that 'the main responsibility of teachers is to teach' and of 'students to study,' and it called for all primary school activities to be placed under the 'unified leadership' of local education departments; 'other units' had no control over school activities and were to refrain from further interference.[26]

Teachers also raised professional concerns when they argued that the rapid expansion of mass education would necessarily lead to a decline in educational quality and standards. Some even invoked imported Western theories of hereditary intelligence to attack the government's mass education policy, arguing that it was fruitless to waste scarce resources on literacy education among the poor, who allegedly lacked the innately superior learning abilities of the upper classes.[27] There was, of course, a vast difference between teachers whose opposition to state educational policy was articulated on the basis of their familiarity with Western theories of hereditary intelligence and teachers who were barely literate themselves but who were nonetheless respected guardians of an older moral tradition. However, the variety of opposition only serves to illustrate the diverse nature of the difficulties faced by Chinese leaders in their quest to make rural schoolteachers the instruments of a new national ideological uniformity and cohesiveness.

For their part, Communist Party educators fought back against teachers' claims to professional autonomy with stinging denunciations of their alleged aloofness from society and their arrogance toward common people. Teachers were said to have adopted the condescending view that ideological education was a matter for mere 'factory leaders,' not intellectuals, whose mission was to impart culture (*wenhua*), not ideology (*sixiang*). Teachers adopted a nonchalant attitude toward the problem of economic development and were loathe to 'descend to the factory floor.' When they did, they were unable to communicate with ordinary workers and needed a dictionary just to look up routine production terms. They considered ancient poetry and literature 'tasteful' but deemed communist literature not even worth discussing in the classroom.[28]

Few things rankled Communist Party educators more, however, than the tendency of teachers to stress their professional interests while ignoring or decrying political concerns. Teachers who raised the banner of professional detachment from politics were regarded as naïve dupes who unwittingly served the interests of the exploiting classes. The notion of 'education for education's sake' was little more than a fanciful self-deception; all educational activity was perforce rooted in ideology and class relations. As Qian Chunrui described the communist view in 1950, 'People who say "I don't serve anyone, I don't participate in politics, I'm for education for its own sake" are deceiving themselves ... Regardless of what your subjective hopes [are], objectively you would always be unable to avoid becoming an instrument of the reactionaries ... Say as much as you like that you are for "education for its own sake," objectively you would then docilely administer the reactionary's educational policy.'[29]

The origins of the 'bourgeois' theory of education for education's sake were attributed to the adoption of a foreign – specifically American – model of education in China in 1922, a theory that now had to be forcefully expunged. Again, in Qian Chunrui's words, 'at first glance it seems to be very lofty for you to say ... "I won't participate in politics, I won't serve anyone, I won't be used by anyone," while all the time behind your back there is a small group of people who secretly applaud you and say "bravo." This small group is now sitting in Taiwan and Washington; they believe your loftiness can perform the function of splitting up the Chinese people's strength and weakening the Chinese people's dictatorship.'[30]

Thus, teachers who continued to advocate education's independence from politics in the new state were to be regarded not only as naïve but also as a potential fifth column of foreign and reactionary forces attempting to undermine the Chinese Revolution. The outbreak of the Korean War in 1950 dramatically heightened concern over teachers' loyalty to the new state. As the twin spectre of invasion and counterrevolution loomed in the minds of the new leaders and as the country was mobilized against all manner of real and imagined foes, teachers became the most heavily targeted group. In the first political campaign directed expressly at schoolteachers, primary and middle teachers became the objects of a fierce effort to expunge what the Cantonese communist educator Zhou Ping described as a mentality of 'My job is to teach. I care only about teaching the various subjects, and that the students do well on the examinations. Your social reforms are not a part of my responsibility.' 'Reeducation' classes to resolve teachers' 'attitude problem,' 'standpoint problem,' and 'whom to serve' problem began as part of the Resist America and Aid Korea movement and subsequently became a regular feature during future campaigns against teachers.[31]

Guangdong, more than most parts of China, was heavily associated with foreign models and philosophies of education introduced into China since the turn of the century. Communist educators in Guangdong attempted to equate foreign influence in Chinese education with an elitist disdain for the culture of the Chinese masses. In 1950, Zhou Ping delivered a long speech at Lingnan University (later Zhongshan University) comparing the 'old' and the 'new' education in China. He began by decrying the Western educational model that had been 'mechanically copied' in China since the 1920s. In his view, the dominance of the American model since 1922 had led teachers and students to worship everything in American civilization as superior and to consider everything in Chinese civilization inferior by comparison. The teachers and intellectuals responsible for promoting the American model had caused the Chinese people to 'forget their roots' (*liule ben*). Teachers in missionary schools in Guangdong flaunted their scientific knowledge to attract students, then used religion to deceive them.

To provide evidence of the damaging effects of this teacher-directed foreign worship, Zhou Ping told of classes that taught appreciation for the literature and art of Europe and America, which Chinese students found difficult to comprehend and often repugnant to their own cultural values, while ignoring Chinese cultural achievements. Teachers graduated students who knew foreign languages and literature but who could not write essays in Chinese or even speak Chinese well.

For Zhou Ping, therefore, 'sinicizing' (*Zhongguo hua*) Chinese education meant making it more populist in content. And this approach corresponded exactly with the Communist Party's efforts to promote mass culture and arts (*dazhong wenyi*). To provide examples of what he termed 'national' (*minzu*) education, Zhou cited the village schools, winter schools, popular libraries, folk songs, and other forms of mass education developed by the Communist Party in Yanan during the 1940s. The 'old' education was alien and elitist, while the 'new' education was national, indigenous, and populist in orientation.[32]

Deprofessionalization of teaching was a crucial plank in the state's strategy for both attacking the elitism of the old educational system and undercutting the independent authority of teachers. The effort to deprofessionalize teachers centred on their ideological and organizational redefinition as 'educational workers.' That required destruction of the autonomous organizations that had fostered teachers' sense of collective professional identity and independence from state authority during the previous half-century. In Guangdong, the locus of teachers' autonomous self-help efforts was the local teachers' alliances (*jiaolianhui*). Beginning in 1951, the alliances were replaced by an official educational workers' union (*jiaogonghui*), modelled on the Soviet Teachers' Union. Branches of the union were subsequently established in every county. Local branches were represented at the national level by the All China Union of Educational Workers, formed in 1950. The educational workers' unions were to formally represent the interests of Guangdong's 70,000 primary and middle schoolteachers. However, as in the case of the Soviet *Rabpros* upon which they were modelled, the unions comprised all personnel attached to the schools, including clerical workers, custodial staff, and other non-teaching employees. The unions therefore did little to advance the specific interests of teachers.[33]

The reason for deeming teachers members of the 'working class' was not only to reduce the differences in status that distinguished intellectuals from manual workers. The label was also intended to delegitimize teachers' professional demands. From now on, the special demands of teachers could be dismissed as elitism and breaches of 'class solidarity.' The designation of teachers as part of the 'working class' was designed to minimize their social bargaining power. Western scholars have used interest group theories to elucidate the ways in which teachers in urban state schools exerted bargaining power under socialism.[34] It is crucial, however, to distinguish relatively well-educated and well-paid urban state schoolteachers from poorly educated and lowly paid village schoolteachers. The latter possessed scant bargaining power, which is why rural primary teachers were often the worst victims of teacher persecution in the PRC.

Nonetheless, it appears that rural teachers on the whole continued to view their social role and responsibilities in pedagogical rather than transmission belt terms. In this respect, teachers' self-conception was probably determined more by their position in the social division of labour than by the policies of the state.[35] One measure of the mutual distrust that continued to exist between teachers and the new state and its local functionaries was party membership. In 1957, only 4 per cent (5,687) of Guangdong's primary schoolteachers were members of the Communist Party.[36] In Xinxing county, there were no party members among schoolteachers in 1949. Not until 1958 were Communist Party members mentioned among Xinxing's teaching corps, according to the Xinxing county educational gazetteer. In that year, 17 per cent of primary and middle schoolteachers were party members. In Huazhou county, fewer than 10 per cent of more than 300 middle schoolteachers were party members by 1956, while a mere 6 per cent of the county's 1,800 primary schoolteachers joined the party. By the mid-1950s, however, generational divisions had begun to emerge among teachers in Guangdong. The split was between 'old hands' (*laopaizi*) who had been teachers before the revolution and a 'new force' (*xin liliang*) of teachers educated after 1949 who were more thoroughly imbued with the revolution's values.[37] The division suggests that the majority of the prerevolutionary teaching corps may have remained outside the Communist Party after 1949. Party recruits were probably drawn mainly from the younger generation educated after the revolution.

The preceding discussion has shown that the literacy movement experienced frustration precisely at the point where state met local society, in the person of the village schoolteacher. Ideally, village teachers would have been highly trained and dedicated agents of the socialist state, embodying and representing the state's values before a rural audience. But the communist state inherited a complex legacy in teachers. On the one hand, village school-masters were often poorly educated and poverty stricken, which made them less than ideally suited to serve as icons of the new socialist order. At another level, professionally minded educators decried what they regarded as unwarranted political interference by the party and declining educational standards. Moreover, both groups had a cultural role as mobilizers of village resistance against intrusive state authority. Ironically, the Communist Party depended most heavily for the transmission of educational policy at the local level upon persons whom it trusted the least. The explosive relationship between schoolteachers and the state was undoubtedly one of the critical weaknesses affecting the literacy movement after 1949. By the mid-1950s, however, what seemed to matter most to China's expectant literacy planners was not the unreconstructed political loyalty of schoolmasters or the overwhelming shortage of formally qualified teachers but the sheer collapse of the literacy movement in general since late 1953. As we will see in the following chapter, with China's lunge toward rapid farm collectivization in mid-1955, the question of reviving the literacy movement suddenly acquired unprecedented urgency. Teachers, students, villagers, local authorities, and the central state alike were summoned to action.

5
Collectivization and the Increased Importance of Literacy

To this point, I have argued that China's leaders initially did not consider universal literacy an irreducible priority in the new state. Early postrevolutionary mass education policy carried on the wartime tradition of using schools as conduits for political propaganda. This meant that popular educational activities – those that were outside the formal school system – continued to be predominantly oral in nature. Compelling pedagogical and practical reasons explained the predominance of non-literate modes of popular political instruction. Mobile theatre troupes, lantern slide exhibitions, mass lectures, and other techniques were proven methods for reaching illiterate audiences. Moreover, non-print-based methods eliminated the need for trained teachers, textbooks, paper, ink, and writing utensils, all of which were in short supply. Literacy was considered an urgent priority only for rural cadres, in order to facilitate bureaucratic communication and comprehension of written political texts.

The collectivization of Chinese rural society in the mid-1950s challenged the wartime educational model and forced China's leaders to revise their view of the importance and timetable for achieving mass literacy. The collectivization of Chinese agriculture is well documented.[1] The literacy campaigns that accompanied collectivization, however, are largely neglected in existing Western scholarship on the rural transformations of the 1950s. This is rather surprising given that the architects of collectivization attached enormous importance to the task of raising rural literacy levels. Mass literacy was seen as crucial for both the immediate consolidation of collectives and their long-term success as agents of economic development and cultural change.

The purpose of this chapter is to examine how China's leaders viewed the increased importance of literacy in the context of agricultural collectivization. Their conception of the relationship between literacy and collectivization was grounded in assumptions regarding literacy's role in promoting scientific agriculture, efficient farm management, and planned economic development. In the 1950s, collectivization was still what it has been for most of this century: one of Marxism-Leninism's most sacrosanct shibboleths. Mass literacy was its inseparable companion. As we will see, the urgency with which China's leaders came to regard literacy in the countryside was a result of their reading of recent Soviet history and of the worried comparisons they drew between literacy levels in the two countries on the eve of collectivization.

Literacy Targets under the First Five-Year Plan

Chinese economic journals of the early and mid-1950s were filled with detailed prescriptions for creating a fully 'organized' (*zuzhi*) and 'planned' (*jihua*) economy. The gospel of planned economic development first received concrete expression in 1953, with the promulgation of the First Five-Year Plan for China's 'transition to socialism.' By replacing private property with public ownership, economic activity would henceforth be organized on a more rational basis. Rather than the haphazard nature of economic growth under capitalism, a centrally planned economy would be designed to benefit the national economy and society as a whole.[2] The presumed capacity of the socialist bureaucratic state to achieve historically unprecedented levels of rationality in the social organization of production created a new expectation of Chinese education. Furthermore, this expectation differed significantly from the older aims of political mobilization that had characterized mass education policy during the guerrilla period and on into the early 1950s. As we saw in Chapter 2, economists and others increasingly regarded the decentralized and politically oriented Yanan model as a leftover 'guerrilla habit' (*youji xiqi*) that was unsuited to the present needs of a rapidly industrializing society. Education's new credo centred on its role in planned economic development.

Chinese planners were not the first to view education in these terms. 'Human capital' theory – the concept that educated labour is itself a form of capital investment – originated in the Soviet Union in the 1930s. It was developed by the Russian educational theorist and leading member of Gosplan (Central Planning Agency), Stanislav Strumilin, during the Soviet industrialization drive of the 1930s.[3] Given that China's industrialization drive of the early 1950s was heavily patterned on the earlier Soviet one, it is not surprising that the human capital concept also emerged as a prominent component of Chinese economic planning. The First Five-Year Plan (1953-7) introduced the practice of educational 'production quotas,' set by the central planning commission and passed on to provincial and local authorities as part of the overall objectives of the plan.

The First Five-Year Plan called for a carefully calibrated annual increase in the number of literates and other kinds of educated 'talent' (*rencai*). An estimated 20-23 million new literates were required to meet the needs of economic development from 1953 to 1957. The aggregate figure was subdivided into 3-4 million new literates per year and then broken down into more specific regional and provincial targets.[4] In addition, the national and provincial plans also set targets for the number of primary, secondary, and postsecondary graduates from the urban state school system, as well as for various kinds of specialized technical personnel (*jishu renyuan*). Guangdong's target under the First Five-Year Plan called for eliminating illiteracy among 6,370,000 persons. Only 20 per cent of these new literates (1,274,000), however, were expected to achieve an educational level equivalent to primary school completion by 1957.[5]

The literacy targets announced in 1953 assumed, however, that collectivization was not imminent in China. The First Five-Year Plan was predicated upon the official policy that collectivization was to be a carefully controlled process, unfolding gradually over the course of three or more five-year plans. Since the main objective was rapid industrialization of urban areas, the literacy targets set forth in the First Five-Year Plan represented primarily the state's projections of urban literacy requirements. In fact, even the rural literacy quotas announced in the plan were explicitly aimed at fulfilling urban literacy requirements. China's urban population grew by nearly 60 per cent between 1949 and 1957, from 58 million to 92 million, representing an enormous surge in rural-urban migration. Anticipating this increase, educational planners cited it as a main justification for expanding literacy education in rural areas.[6]

Chinese Literacy Levels in the Mid-1950s and the Debate over Collectivization

China's policy of gradual collectivization was implicitly intended to avoid the spectre of large-scale peasant resistance and state violence that accompanied collectivization in the Soviet Union.[7] In addition, however, those in charge of plotting the transition to socialism in the countryside were also well aware of the implications of collectivized farming for rural mass education. In any society, reading and writing serve different functions and therefore take on different emphases in literacy movements.[8] In the context of rural China in the mid-1950s, reading for political propaganda was not urgent since there were other well-developed means available for spreading the CCP message. But writing for economic growth and development was urgent. Hence, certain choices had to be made concerning the contents of literacy to be taught. As early as September 1949, communist writers identified the various literacy skills peasants would need to function in a collectivized rural economy. These included the ability to write production plans and reports, draw up collective work schedules, and calculate and record workpoints.[9] The scarcity of such skills was considered manageable so long as China adhered to a policy of gradual collectivization.

By the mid-1950s, however, a vigorous debate was beginning to unfold between party leaders over the pace of collectivization. On one side were those, led by the economist Chen Yun and others, who comprised the majority of the central leadership, who favoured the existing gradual pace. On the other side was Mao, who advanced both economic and political arguments for increasing the speed of collectivization. In July 1955, Mao resolved the debate in characteristically unilateral action by going over the heads of the Central Committee leadership to present his case for rapid collectivization before an assembled group of provincial and regional party bosses gathered in Beijing. That Mao's policy reversal was greeted with opposition by the rest of the central leadership was suggested by the manner of the official response to his action.[10]

Western coverage of the mid-1950s collectivization debate has concentrated on the issue of mechanization: whether collectivization was viable before the mechanization of agriculture or whether, as Mao and others argued, collectivization would actually speed up the process of mechanization by creating economies of scale.[11] The question of literacy levels also entered the debate. Mao's decision to press for rapid collectivization brought the question of the relationship between literacy and rural economic development to the foreground of official considerations. Interestingly, however, Mao himself appears to have been little bothered by rural illiteracy. On the contrary, if relative silence is to be taken as any indication, he appears to have evinced considerable unspoken confidence in the peasantry's ability to rapidly master the literacy skills demanded by collectivization. In his July 1955 speech, for example, Mao did not even mention the rural illiteracy problem. Nor did he refer to it in his first (unpublished) preface to the Central Committee's magisterial three-volume compendium on the progress of collectivization, *Zhongguo nongcun de shehui zhuyi gaochao* (The High Tide of Collectivization in Chinese Villages), which was designed specifically for use by cadres involved in implementing collectivization.[12] For officials responsible for the literacy movement, however, Mao's sudden policy reversal on collectivization nullified all of the carefully laid plans for a gradual increase in rural literacy.

When party leaders and planners discussed the literacy requirements of collectivization, nothing weighed heavier in their calculations than the experience of the Soviet Union. Chinese officials writing in the mid-1950s were convinced that the Soviet Union had embarked upon collectivization in 1929 with a literacy rate far superior to China's in the mid-1950s. Owing to a variety of factors, from the nature of the Chinese written language to the Soviet state's ongoing efforts since 1919 to eradicate illiteracy, the Soviet Union was considered to have been far more educationally prepared than China to launch a successful collectivization drive. Chinese officials pointed out that the Soviet literacy rate on the eve of collectivization in 1929 was around 80 per cent. But in China, the situation in 1955 was ominously reversed: 80 per cent were still illiterate. Moreover, China's illiteracy rate on the eve of collectivization was still basically unchanged from what it had been six years earlier, suggesting that there had been little, if any, real progress since 1949.[13]

It hardly mattered that China's appraisal of the Soviet literacy rate in 1929 (based on Soviet claims made to Chinese leaders in the early 1950s) was seriously exaggerated.[14] What counted was perception. To buttress their argument that China was educationally ill prepared for collectivization, Chinese educational writers also pointed out that universal primary education had been implemented in the Soviet Union as early as 1925 and was fully realized by the early 1930s, whereas in China barely half of primary school-age children were enrolled in school in 1956. In response, the PRC drew up its first compulsory education plan that year.[15] Finally, the nature of written Chinese also had to be taken into consideration in deciding whether China was ready for collectivization. In his major 1955 speech on the literacy movement, Hu Yaobang, then head of the Youth League, declared that, owing to the non-alphabetic nature of Chinese and the difficulty of memorizing characters, it was unlikely that China would be able to emulate the Soviet Union's experience in illiteracy eradication.[16]

The growing sense of alarm generated by comparisons of Chinese and Soviet educational experience was further heightened by China's failure by 1955 to have met even the minimal literacy targets set down in the First Five-Year Plan. As noted previously, the plan had called for an increase of 23 million new literates over five years. By 1954, there were 24 million persons enrolled in literacy classes nationwide, of which only 2 million, however, were expected to meet the state's minimum literacy requirement by the end of the year. Altogether, by 1955, perhaps as few as 4 million, and certainly no more than 9-10 million, persons had acquired literacy since 1949. Most of them, moreover, had received instruction before the literacy movement collapsed in early 1953.[17]

The situation was equally grim with respect to the literacy level of local cadres. This was particularly alarming to educational planners since cadre education had earlier been declared an urgent national priority. In Guangdong, according to a 1956 classified report prepared by the provincial education bureau, as many as four out of every seven leading cadres were illiterate in most Guangdong townships. According to another source, when collectivization was launched in Guangdong, most village cadres were so poorly educated that although they 'had mouths they were unable to speak[, and] their writing brushes never moved.'[18]

One delegate to a Youth League forum convened to debate the reasons for the lack of progress in illiteracy eradication pointed out that, at the Ministry of Education's current projection of just over 3 million new literates in 1955, it would take more than sixty years to eliminate illiteracy among the more than 180 million illiterate persons between the ages of fourteen and fifty – to say nothing of the millions added to the illiteracy roster each year until the universalization of primary education![19] Echoing the sense of urgency, the head of the Guangdong branch of the Youth League pointed out in 1956 that rapid collectivization had created a desperate need for certain kinds of new literate 'talent' in the countryside: team leaders, accountants, technicians, veterinarians, health care workers, and agricultural workers. He estimated that a minimum of 500,000 such personnel would need to receive 'backbone' leadership training for the province's collectives. Some of these leaders, it was noted, would be drawn from the 300,000 primary and junior middle school students graduated in Guangdong since 1953; still others could be recruited from among literate demobilized PLA veterans, who were offered financial support to settle in collectives.[20] Yet even when these sources were taken into account, there was still a desperate shortage of literate talent needed to guarantee the viability of the collectives.

Guangdong, like other provinces, was finally feeling the effect of the sluggish pace of adult literacy education since 1949. Two million persons had participated in seasonally based winter schools and literacy classes in Guangdong between 1950 and 1953, out of a total adult illiterate population of approximately 12 million. Of these participants, however, fewer than 10 per cent – barely 180,000 – achieved the state's minimum literacy standard of 1,000-1,500 characters. Guangdong's illiteracy rate, like the national one, was officially unchanged in 1955 from what it had been six years earlier, around 75-80 per cent. Faced with the daunting prospect of rapid collectivization, Liang Weilin, head of the Guangdong Bureau of Education and a leading member of the Guangdong Anti-Illiteracy Association, openly lamented that '50,000, even 100,000,' new literates per year in Guangdong would not be sufficient to keep pace with the newly envisioned speed of economic development. At the current pace, Liang said, it would be 'decades, even a century,' before illiteracy was banished in Guangdong.[21]

Illiteracy and Problems of Collective Management

Liang was aware that many mutual-aid teams and cooperatives in Guangdong were foundering because of the lack of literate skills. In 1955, the vice-minister of education and vice-chair of the National Anti-Illiteracy Association, Dong Chuncai, identified what he considered to be the three most important uses of literacy under the collective system. First, literacy was necessary to strengthen collective management. The evaluation of work, the recording of workpoints, the formulation of production plans, and the registration of personal property with the collective, said Dong, all required the ability to read, write, and calculate. Second, literacy was necessary to promote technological advances in the countryside, because advanced scientific knowledge was contained in and transmitted by the written word. The use of chemical fertilizers, soil-improvement techniques, pest control, the design and operation of modern agricultural implements – all required the ability to read and write. Third, Dong pointed to literacy's increasingly important political function. Teaching local cadres and peasants how to read books, reports, and documents made it simpler and more effective for the party to communicate its messages to villagers, said Dong. Furthermore, written communication was more easily directed at individual audiences than was oral communication. Written communication would thus better enable peasants to grasp 'their individual responsibilities under the new social system.'[22]

Often, efforts to form collectives were frustrated by the lack of basic literacy skills. Villagers were quick to develop imaginative, if ultimately ineffective, ways around the illiteracy problem. When the farmers of Fengtang township in Luoding county formed mutual-aid teams, they found that five of the eight households in one of the teams lacked a single literate family member. In order to keep track of each household's labour contribution, the team members decided to distribute a piece of paper to each of the eight households. Using an incense stick, families were told to burn one hole in their piece of paper for each day worked. Before long, however, one family's sheet of paper accidentally caught on fire. The team disbanded because the families could not agree on an alternative method of keeping track of labour contributions. In another case, peasants in Charong township formed a cooperative only to realize that none among them was literate enough to maintain the accounts. They decided that, instead of keeping books, each member would leave a section of bamboo with the cooperative leader. At the end of each day's work, team members would go to the home of the leader and deposit one yellow bean in his or her section of bamboo for each full day worked. A single grain of rice was deposited for each half-day of work. In another newly formed cooperative, youths who knew more than 100 characters were appointed as accountants; however, their knowledge proved so limited that they were forced to rely upon abstract symbols such as lines and circles to represent various agricultural activities. After a time, no one could remember what the symbols were originally meant to signify.[23]

Illiterate cooperative leaders were often accused by team members of inflicting unnecessary waste and chaos. In Guangning county, Guangdong, Qiu Lianfang was elected leader when his village formed a cooperative in 1955. Unable to read or write, Qiu wrought chaos on the cooperative when he attempted to rely upon his memory alone rather than solicit help from others. Members turned against him after Qiu repeatedly confounded the distribution of workpoints and work assignments, dispatching large teams to labour on tiny plots and vice versa.[24] In another example, Chen Fengying was assistant team leader in the Pule cooperative in Lechang county, Guangdong. Because he was illiterate, he was constantly forced to rely upon others to compile his reports and to explain written communications from senior levels of government. Chen lost face, and his standing as a leader fell.[25]

Organizational and management problems caused by the shortage of literate personnel were major causes of the widespread dissolution of cooperatives that took place across the country in 1955. Estimates range from 20,000 to as many as 200,000 mutual-aid teams and cooperatives dissolved between February and July 1955.[26] Xiang Nan, a leading figure in the national branch of the Youth League, described the situation thus:

> The development of the co-operativization of agriculture is changing the outlook of all rural work, and one of these changes is the demand of the peasants for the study of the written language which becomes more and more urgent. For the running of the co-operatives calls for the drawing up of plans, the keeping of books, and if the people are illiterate, these tasks cannot be well done. This is why [the peasants] say, 'Co-operatives are really good, but without knowledge of characters, we cannot run [them] properly.'[27]

Lin Handa and the Official Ideology of Peasant Literacy

Lin Handa was one of the most articulate exponents of the official conception of peasant literacy centred on collective farming. A former schoolteacher who had once spent three years in Colorado studying for a doctorate in education before 1949, Lin emerged in the mid-1950s as one of the leading figures in the PRC literacy movement. In 1950, he had been appointed the first head of the Ministry of Education's social education division, and from that point onward he played a central role in virtually all of the major bodies responsible for determining literacy and mass education policy in the 1950s. In 1952, Lin was appointed vice-chair of the newly established Anti-Illiteracy Work Committee. He later served as vice-minister of education from 1954 to 1957 and simultaneously became a leading member of the newly established Committee for Reform of the Chinese Written Language, an organization that was to play a crucial role in formulating literacy during the national literacy campaigns of the late 1950s. When the National Anti-Illiteracy Association was established in 1956 to oversee the literacy campaign, Lin was named secretary-general.[28]

In late 1955, barely four months after Mao's dramatic acceleration of rural collectivization, Lin Handa oversaw a major reassessment of the nature and purpose of rural literacy education.[29] His sharply worded, incisive analysis of the failure of previous PRC anti-illiteracy efforts stands as one of the crucial – and hitherto largely overlooked – statements in the history of the PRC literacy movement. Not only was Lin responsible for launching a blistering attack on previous conceptions and methods of literacy cultivation, perhaps more importantly he was also responsible for articulating the ideology upon which 'peasant education' (*nongmin jiaoyu*) was to be based for the next two decades in China.

Lin's critique of existing literacy education centred on the notion, which he regarded as a deeply ingrained feature of traditional Chinese educational philosophy, that the purpose of acquiring literacy was to become initiated into the world of academic learning. In Lin's words, it was misguided to think that 'the purpose of eliminating illiteracy is simply to be able to recognize characters, and that the purpose of being able to recognize characters is to enable one to *study*' (emphasis added). Lin considered the tenacity of this concept the root cause of all the ills that, in his view, had continued to infect village-level education since 1949. Continued emphasis upon the importance of academic learning was responsible for the regrettable practice of village schools striving to imitate – without much hope of success – the curriculum and standards of the regular state-run schools in the cities. The belief that basic literacy instruction was simply preliminary training for advancement up the school ladder not only encouraged unrealistic social expectations on the part of peasants; it also fostered a false notion that the most important ingredients of a successful literacy campaign were such things as school space and equipment, funds, teacher qualifications, and the number of specialized cadres to oversee the campaign.

Lin drew several critical inferences from what he considered the chief sociological effects of an excessively academic approach to popular literacy instruction. He argued that the 'best' students in village literacy classes – those who attended regularly and scored highest on examinations – were not the cadres, activists, and peasant workers whom the state regarded as the main targets of the literacy movement. Rather, Lin argued, the best students tended to be 'young girls and old village women.' The reason was that village literacy education had become divorced from the real economic and political needs of the main village labour force. Cadres, activists, and team members were simply too busy and hence unwilling to engage in the arduous effort of memorizing how to read and write characters that had no recognizable practical purpose. Similarly, Lin argued, the reason why urban workers had come to value literacy more than peasants did was because the former had followed the experience of the Soviet Union in striving for ways to use literacy to improve technology and production. For workers, therefore, the link between literacy and economic development had become clear. But in the countryside, the reason why 'men were not as good as women' and 'activists were not as good as the masses' was that literacy instruction was not sufficiently integrated with economic construction. The way to overcome the problem, Lin argued, was to alter the nature and purpose of rural literacy education: henceforth, village literacy instruction ought to be closely integrated with the local bureaucratic-economic requirements of collectivization.

The purpose of literacy education in rural production teams was not to groom peasants for further academic study, said Lin, but to prepare them to become productive team members. Rural literacy education ought therefore to focus on the inculcation of local economic skills. Knowledge pertaining to broader economic and political spheres would gradually be added to later stages of the curriculum. To this end, Lin advocated the adoption of a three-tiered model of literacy education. The first tier would emphasize local production knowledge, the second would stress vocabulary drawn from a slightly larger catchment area, and the third would emphasize national concerns. The model was subsequently enshrined in the 1956 anti-illiteracy decree and formed the basis for rural literacy efforts for the next four decades.

Although Lin did not emphasize the point, the three-tiered model originated with Mao. It appears to have been developed by state literacy planners on the basis of Mao's personal endorsement of the efforts of a Shandong collective to set up special 'workpoint-recording classes' (*jigong xuexi ban*) for team members. 'This experience ought to be widely popularized,' proclaimed Mao in an editorial comment he attached to the official report describing the workpoint-recording classes set up in Gaojialiugou village following collectivization. 'Such classes should be emulated and established everywhere!' Mao then went on to suggest that rural literacy education be expanded to include two additional levels of instruction. According to Mao,

After the peasants form co-ops, they demand to be taught to read and write ... The first step, to meet the need in recording workpoints, is to learn the names of people and places in their own villages, the names of tools, and the labels for different sorts of farm work and other necessary vocabulary – this requires a knowledge of about two or three hundred characters.

The second step is to learn more advanced characters and vocabulary. Two kinds of textbooks must be compiled. The first type of textbook ought to be compiled by the local intellectuals with the help of the comrades who are guiding the work of collectivization. Each locale should compile its own textbook; we cannot use one unified text. This type of textbook need not be checked by the authorities. The second type of textbook also ought to be compiled by the local intellectuals with the help of the comrades who are guiding the work of collectivization and should be based on the affairs of a relatively small area (for example, a county or a special district) as well as affairs and vocabulary pertaining to a province (municipality and autonomous region) and to the nation as a whole. These, too, should only contain a few hundred characters. This type of textbook need not be uniform from one place to another, either, but it should be examined promptly by educational organizations at the county, the special district, or the provincial (municipal and autonomous region) level. After having taken these two steps, a third step ought to be taken; the educational organizations of each province (municipality and autonomous region) should compile a third type of textbook containing general material. The cultural and educational organizations at the Center ought to give this matter appropriate guidance.[30]

Vivienne Shue and others have described how the institutional reorganizations of Chinese agriculture in the 1950s added up to an encystment of rural communities, a paradoxical turning inward in economic and social terms even as the village's links with the state became unprecedentedly more direct.[31] The ideology of peasant literacy embodied in the three-tiered system of literacy primers contributed to this process of encystment, through its attempt to foster localized economic competence and community solidarity, together with limited incorporation into the world beyond the production team on terms and in ways determined by the state. The anti-illiteracy decree of 1956, which marked the formal beginning of the national literacy campaign, formalized these objectives by prescribing a knowledge of 1,500 characters to be acquired in stages according to the three-tiered format described above. The basic-level literacy primer was to be compiled by 'local intellectuals' (*dangdi de zhishi fenzi*) with 'guidance and help' from cadres responsible for collectivization. This primer was to be comprised of 'around two to three hundred characters' chosen on the basis of their association with the local economy: place names, names of locally used farm tools and farm activities, crop names, weights and measures, basic arithmetic, and items of daily vocabulary. The second-level primer, also comprised of several hundred characters, was to be drawn from a wider political-geographic realm, equivalent to the local county or special district. It would consist of vocabulary for 'commonly seen things' (*changjian shiwu*) and 'commonly used words and phrases' (*changyong yuci*), as well as some provincial and national-level vocabulary (*ben sheng he quanguo xing de changjian shiwu he changyong yuci*). The second-level primer was also to be compiled by local intellectuals, with the assistance of cadres in charge of collectivization. This primer, however, had first to be 'checked' (*shencha*) and approved for use by provincial or district government educational organs. Finally, the third-tier primer was to consist of several hundred characters emphasizing provincial- and national-level vocabulary. It was to be compiled by the educational bureaus of provinces, autonomous districts, and centrally administered municipalities. Upon completion of all three primers, peasants were expected to be able to recognize 1,500 characters, as well as to read and understand 'simple' (*qianjin tongsu*) newspapers and magazines, keep simple accounts, write simple notes, and perform simple calculations on an abacus. It was estimated that peasants would require an average of three to four months of part-time study in order to complete the two basic-level primers, followed by a further seven months of study to complete the provincial-national primer.[32]

Lin Handa's frank assessment of the failures of the literacy movement up to 1955 and of the need to integrate rural literacy education more closely with the bureaucratic and economic requirements of collectivization could not have come at a more opportune moment. The dissolution of so many cooperatives due to management and accounting difficulties, the growing sense of disappointment and alarm over the slow progress of literacy efforts since 1949, and, perhaps above all, the haunting comparisons with literacy rates in the Soviet Union had fuelled a growing sense of despair among those involved in the literacy movement. In 1956, China's leaders sought to abolish this widespread pessimism and to reverse the uneven progress of the past half-decade by launching an unprecedentedly ambitious national literacy campaign, designed to catapult China into the status of a universally literate society. Subordinated still to the greater demands of economic development, literacy education – now seen to be in the service of collectivization – was on the verge of becoming an urgent national priority for the first time since 1949.

6
The National Literacy Campaigns of 1956 and 1958

The 'anti-illiteracy decree' jointly issued by the Central Committee and the State Council on 29 March 1956 launched an epic campaign that was intended to rid China of illiteracy within five to seven years. The decree divided the adult population into several target groups to which varying objectives and criteria were to be applied. Illiteracy among cadres was to be completely eliminated within two to three years; among 95 per cent of urban factory and enterprise workers within three years; and among 70 per cent of peasants within five to seven years.[1] Persons aged fourteen to fifty were to comprise the main focus of anti-illiteracy work, but participation by persons over fifty 'ought to be welcomed' (*yinggai huanying*). In addition to a timetable for eradicating illiteracy among various social groups, the 1956 decree also prescribed different literacy standards for villagers and urban residents. Urban workers were required to master 2,000 characters 'more or less.' The requirement for peasants was lower, only 1,500 characters. Peasant literacy education was furthermore to be based closely upon the principles of 'integrating the practical' (*lianxi shiji*) and of 'learning for the purpose of applying' (*xue yi zhi yong*), and it should proceed 'from [that which is] close to [that which is] far' (*you jin ji yuan*) – meaning that the emphasis should be placed first and foremost upon local knowledge, expanding gradually outward on the basis of the three-tiered model of literacy instruction described in the previous chapter.

A major concern of literacy campaign organizers centred on how to prevent persons from 'relapsing' (*fumang* or *huisheng*) into illiteracy once the literacy campaign ended. The issue was addressed in a 1955 State Council directive calling for the establishment of spare-time senior primary school classes for peasants who had completed the three-tiered model of basic literacy instruction. Such schools were to be set up in areas where 'the cultural level is relatively high and the supply of teachers adequate' and where peasants' demand for further education was 'relatively strong.' A subsequent decree stipulated that, in order to graduate from the spare-time primary schools, peasants would be required to demonstrate, through examinations, knowledge of 2,700 characters 'more or less,' plus mastery of primary school-level arithmetic. In reality, however, it appears that most peasants only received the initial phase of literacy instruction.[2]

This chapter examines the national literacy campaign from its much-heralded inception in March 1956 to its dispirited demise four years later in 1960. The years from 1956 to 1960 constitute the single greatest effort to eradicate illiteracy in modern Chinese history. Indeed, it is probably fair to say that never in the history of the world has there been a national literacy campaign of comparable scale and intensity of human effort. As many as 80 million persons may have received some form of literacy education during this brief four-year period. The magnitude of the endeavour is evident from a comparison of literacy enrolment figures immediately before and after the launch of the campaign. Official PRC sources estimate that during 1955, on the eve of the campaign, a total of 3.68 million adults had acquired basic literacy. In 1956 and 1957, the number increased sharply to 7.43 million and 7.20 million, respectively. An even more spectacular increase was registered during the Great Leap Forward, when some 40 million were described as having acquired literacy in 1958, followed by a further 26 million in 1959. On the basis of such claims, the illiteracy rate was nearly halved, from 80 per cent in late 1955 to 43 per cent in 1959.[3]

Guangdong's official statistics tell a similar story. Out of approximately 13 million adult illiterates in the province in 1954, only 987,000 were enrolled in literacy classes. In 1955, the number fell even further, to only 843,000. But by 1956, the number had risen to 2.7 million. In 1958 any where from 2.6 million to 5.5 million persons acquired basic literacy, depending on which official source is used. The official Guangdong educational yearbook, published by the provincial education bureau in 1986, claims a figure of 4,860,000 new literates in 1958. On this basis, the illiteracy rate among 12-40 year olds in Guangdong was reduced from 80 per cent in 1954 to 40 per cent or less by the end of 1959.[4]

The problem with such claims, of course, is that the most spectacular increases in literacy are registered for the period in which, most scholars agree, official PRC statistics are most notoriously inflated and unreliable (Table 2). The entire state statistical system was in disarray from 1958 to 1960, at the height of the Great Leap Forward. Given widespread scepticism of and rejection by most observers of other Great Leap 'production' statistics, should we view statistical claims made by literacy campaign organizers during this period as any more reliable? In the following pages, we will see how the ambitious expectations and utopian claims made by literacy campaign organizers were undermined in the late 1950s by the reality of a nation in severe economic collapse. Yet despite the hugely tragic consequences of China's failed leap toward communism – including horrific famine – the

Table 2

Number of adults acquiring basic literacy, 1949-81

Year	Number of persons (millions)
1949-53	7.01
1954-65	95.71
1972-6	12.66
1977-81	26.07
Total	141.45

Source: *Zhongguo jiaoyu nianjian* (Beijing: Zhongguo da baike quanshu chubanshe 1984), 578.

patently exaggerated claims of the literacy campaign should not detract from the monumental nature of the effort itself, which deserves serious scrutiny, if only to reveal its unintended complicity in the ill-named human catastrophe known as the Great Leap Forward.

Influence of the Soviet Union

The 1956 national literacy campaign embodied numerous influences, including a Leninist organizational structure, Stalinist 'storming' methods, and YMCA-inspired James Yanist techniques of grassroots mobilization. Soviet influences, in particular, were numerous and critical. It is often assumed that the Soviet influence on postrevolutionary Chinese education was most pronounced and consequential in the field of higher education and considerably less significant in areas such as elementary schooling and adult literacy, areas in which the party possessed its own considerable and much-valued body of experience accumulated in the revolutionary base areas.[5] It is time to revise this view. As we saw in Chapters 1 and 2, the party's pre-1949 experience in adult and primary education was widely criticized in the early 1950s as unsuited to the needs of an industrializing socialist power. It is clear that PRC leaders intended from the beginning to pattern their country's anti-illiteracy efforts closely upon the prior experiences and institutions of the Soviet Union.

As early as 1950, for example, the first official statement of PRC educational aims, announced by vice-minister of education Qian Chunrui, made only slight mention of peasant education in the 'old liberated areas.' Most of Qian's comments with respect to literacy education related to the experience of the Soviet Union, which he urged China to follow. Qian described in detail Lenin's famous 1919 anti-illiteracy decree, which imputed 'criminal responsibility' to anyone who avoided or obstructed the decree. Qian also reported on the role of the Soviet national anti-illiteracy committee, which held overall responsibility for the literacy campaign, and described the formation of the Soviet Union's great 'cultural army' of more than 10,000 anti-illiteracy 'soldiers.' And he lauded the Soviet Union's apparent success, using these methods, in eradicating illiteracy among its nearly 200 million people within the space of only two decades by 1939.[6] We have also seen that Chinese literacy planners in the early 1950s adopted Soviet-style literacy organizations and directly borrowed certain Soviet concepts such as the 'half-literate' category. We have seen, too, that on the eve of collectivization, anxious Chinese educational officials debated Chinese and Soviet literacy rates. It was during the literacy campaign of 1956-7, however, that Soviet influence on Chinese literacy efforts reached an apogee.

The organizational structure, financing, implementation methods, even the official imagery of the 1956 literacy campaign – all were closely modelled on the previous Soviet literacy campaign. Responsibility was vested in the National Anti-Illiteracy Association, modelled after the All-Russian Extraordinary Commission for the Eradication of Illiteracy set up by Lenin in 1919. Like its Soviet counterpart, the Chinese association was composed of leading Communist Party officials. Lin Handa, who had served as vice-chair of the Central Anti-Illiteracy Work Committee, the forerunner of the association, was made secretary-general. Other members included veteran linguistic revolutionary Wu Yuzhang; Liao Luyan, a leading specialist in agricultural policy; chief party propagandists Hu Qiaomu and Lu Dingyi; and Hu Yaobang, Qian Chunrui, Lin Feng, and Chen Yi (chair).[7]

Following Soviet practice, branches of the association were subsequently established at all levels of the administrative hierarchy down to the township. In Guangdong, a provincial branch was established in 1956, comprised of thirty-nine leading provincial Communist Party officials, headed by Gu Dacun. In order to buttress party control over the movement in Guangdong, the provincial party committee established a supervisory body, the anti-illiteracy 'leadership group' (*lingdao xiaozu*), also headed by Gu Dacun. By the end of 1956, anti-illiteracy commissions had been established in over 80 per cent of Guangdong counties. By 1957, there were some 6,500 commission branches in place at all levels in Guangdong, with a combined membership of 484,200.[8]

As in the Soviet literacy campaign, the role of local educational bureaus was limited to administrative aspects, including the provision of literacy primers and school space. Primary responsibility for mass mobilization rested with the local anti-illiteracy commissions and, in particular, the commissions' Youth League components. The central role played by the Youth League was also modelled directly on Soviet experience. In 1955, Hu Yaobang, as head of the league, described it as the 'natural helping hand' (*tianran zhushou*) of the literacy movement in the villages, echoing Stalin's identical reference to the Komsomol (Young Communist League) as the 'helping hand' of the Soviet literacy drive.[9]

In both countries, moreover, the Youth League was charged with imparting an atmosphere of militant struggle to the campaign. According to Sheila Fitzpatrick, Soviet literacy campaigns had been associated since the Civil War period with coercion. In the early 1920s, the Soviet anti-illiteracy campaign was even headed by a special unit known as the illiteracy *Cheka* (Secret Police). When the Komsomol assumed responsibility in 1928, it proceeded to organize the literacy effort 'as if it really were a military campaign.' Komsomol volunteers were referred to as 'cultural warriors' and 'liquidators of illiteracy' who carried out 'cultural-political reconnaissance' (*razvedka*) of villages and set up illiteracy 'liquidation points' (*likpunty*) across the countryside – a term that acquired particularly menacing overtones following Stalin's 1929 announcement of the policy of 'liquidating' the *kulak* class. (Among the rumours circulating about those sent to the *likpunty* was that girls weighing sixty-three kilograms or more were kidnapped and sent to China as slaves!) As Sheila Fitzpatrick observes, Soviet illiteracy 'liquidators' seemed 'constantly on the brink of treating the village as occupied territory, and its illiterate population as the enemy.'[10] China's literacy campaign organizers directly copied the militaristic strategy and vocabulary of the Soviet campaign. Just as the Komsomol spoke of raising a 'cultural army' to attack illiteracy (and illiterates), members of the Chinese Youth League were officially known as the 'advance troops' (*xianjun*) of the literacy campaign, conducting propaganda work and arranging the procurement of benches, desks, and lamp oil for students. Literacy instructors themselves were described as 'anti-illiteracy assault troops' (*saomang dui*). Anti-illiteracy 'command posts' (*zhihui bu*) were set up, reminiscent of the Soviet *likpunty*.[11]

The organizers of the 1956 literacy campaign did not look exclusively to Soviet experience, however. They also looked to the efforts of neighbouring Asian countries. Faced with troubling comparisons of Soviet and Chinese literacy rates on the eve of collectivization, and doubtful of China's capacity to replicate Soviet experience, Chinese literacy planners in the mid-1950s turned to Ho Chi Minh's Vietnam. Ho's Vietminh had carried out a successful literacy campaign in the 1940s, which Chinese literacy campaigners set out to study. Educational delegations were dispatched to Hanoi to investigate the Vietnamese experience, while Chinese educational journals began to run numerous articles on Vietnamese mass literacy efforts. At the first national conference of anti-illiteracy activists held in Beijing in 1956, representatives of the Hanoi Municipal Education Bureau were even on hand to award silver medals to Chinese literacy activists.[12] Why the turn to Vietnam? True, northern Vietnam was a fraternal socialist state. But Vietnam was also, perhaps more importantly, a neighbouring Asian society with a large peasant population and a shared Confucian educational heritage. Moreover, Vietnam was also an example of the successful adoption of a roman script for a tonal language – a feat that was very much on the minds of Chinese literacy strategists in the mid-1950s (see Chapter 7). The turn toward Vietnam may even have been symptomatic of Mao's growing disillusion with the Soviet Union and an increased Chinese interest in Southeast Asia.

Mass Mobilization

The party's pre-1949 educational experience was evident in the literacy campaign's determined attempt to mobilize every conceivable human and material resource – over the objections of professional educators who deplored the rejection of uniform standards for teachers, texts, and schools. The Communist Party organizers of the 1956 literacy campaign rejected the principle of educational 'standardization' (*zhengguihua*) that had dominated mass education policy since 1953; instead, they sought to revive the base area principle of decentralized initiative and management. Uniform standards were regarded as a hindrance to mass action. The absence of formal school buildings would be overcome simply by utilizing whatever space was available, including former lineage halls and temples. The shortage of trained teachers would be overcome by summoning to duty everyone who possessed some degree of literacy, from schoolteachers to school children. The guiding principle was to be one of 'relying on people to teach people' (*yimin jiaomin*). On this basis, Lin Handa estimated, China was capable of mobilizing an 'anti-illiteracy army' of several million. It would include the 7 to 8 million peasants who had experienced some form of literacy education since 1949, all 'available' primary and middle school graduates (by 'available,' Lin specified graduates living in the countryside), and the more than 1 million primary schoolteachers already living in the villages.[13] In 1956, Guangdong authorities announced the mobilization of a 'great anti-illiteracy army' (*saomang dajun*) of 2 million, comprised of some 400,000 Youth League members, 500,000 primary and middle school graduates, 110,000 primary schoolteachers, 600,000 senior primary school students, 300,000 middle school students, and 20,000 middle schoolteachers.[14]

Literacy classes were to adopt a multiplicity of organizational forms (*duoyang de zuzhi xingshi*) suited to local needs. The three most common types included graded classroom instruction (*banji jiaoxue*), small group instruction (*xiaozu jiaoxue*), and individual instruction (*gebie jiaoxue*). The first referred to literacy instruction in minban schools and classes, the management and financing of which were now to be taken over by the newly established rural collectives. Instruction was to be on a year-round basis rather than on the seasonal basis of former 'winter schools.' The second type of instruction took place in informal small groups, such as the outdoor 'foot-of-the-field group classes' (*ditou xiaozu*) of South China and the 'bedside reading groups' (*kangtou xiaozu*) of North China. The third type involved informal teaching on a one-to-one basis. Sometimes known as 'taking characters to the doorstep' (*songzi shangmen*), this technique was often employed by school children who instructed their parents at home. It also referred to personal instruction for women who were tied to their homes because of domestic chores or because their husbands forbade them to attend classes outside the home.[15]

Provinces, cities, counties, districts, and townships were required to submit detailed plans and timetables for the eradication of illiteracy within their jurisdictions to the National Anti-Illiteracy Association by mid-1957. A classified document prepared by the Guangdong education bureau in 1956 detailed Guangdong's plan to organize 45 per cent of the province's 12 million illiterates between the ages of fourteen and fifty into literacy classes by the first half of 1956 and the remainder by the end of 1956. The bureau projected that illiteracy would be eliminated in Guangdong by 1961 – well in advance of the seven-year objective set forth in the 1956 anti-illiteracy decree. Before central authorities had a chance to respond to the plan, however, the provincial Youth League branch publicly pledged that Guangdong would complete the task even sooner, by 1959.[16] In terms of literacy education, the Great Leap Forward habit of bumping up quotas and shortening target dates had already begun.

Problems in the Supply and Distribution of Literacy Primers

The success of the literacy campaign depended not only upon mass mobilization, however, but also on the capacity of individual localities to compile, publish, and distribute enough of their own basic-level township literacy primers. From the outset, the literacy campaign experienced severe logistical obstacles, among the most serious of which were difficulties in the production and supply of local literacy primers. Production efforts were bedevilled by chronic shortages of even the basic raw material, paper. At local levels, paper manufacture in the mid-1950s was still largely a household-based seasonal handicraft industry. Neither local household production nor limited modern factory output was able to adequately cope with the sudden surge in demand caused by the literacy campaign. The assertion of central control over the modern publishing industry during the 1950s only created additional bottlenecks in production and distribution.[17]

Literacy campaign organizers at the centre also assumed smooth cooperation between publishing houses and the rural collectives and township governments. However, this was rarely the case. For one thing, the publishing industry as a whole was biased toward the production of reading materials for an urban educated public. In this respect, the shortage of popular reading materials did not emerge suddenly with the literacy campaign in 1956; indeed, there had been a severe shortage of such material since 1949. Out of a total of 950 million books printed nationwide in 1954, only about a third could be classified as suitable for poorly educated persons with limited reading ability, despite the fact that such persons constituted the vast majority of the reading public.[18]

A second problem related to conflicts between publishing houses and the local authorities responsible for compiling the literacy primers. Locally produced primers were supposed to be printed and distributed by local branches of Xinhua, the state publishing agency, which maintained a nationwide distribution network. All other locally distributed popular reading materials were normally edited and published by the state publishing house for educational materials, the People's Education Press in Beijing. These materials were then printed by local People's Press publishing houses in the provinces and distributed by local Xinhua bookstores. During the literacy campaign, however, local authorities frequently accused local Xinhua branches of failing to meet agreed-upon production and distribution schedules. Local Xinhua managers, for their part, accused local education departments of chronic overordering, which resulted in a pileup of unused literacy primers in some localities. They also complained that the reason they were unable to meet supply schedules was that inexperienced local literacy authorities were constantly requesting last-minute changes and additions to literacy primers as they went to press.[19]

Bureaucratic delays and wranglings like these nearly brought the literacy campaign to a standstill shortly after its inception. The situation had become so severe by spring 1956 that the Ministry of Education was forced to take extraordinary measures to save the campaign. Because of the extreme shortages of local literacy primers, the ministry decided to allow three literacy primers from the northern province of Hebei to serve as national models. It agreed to allow the adoption of these primers by villages in all parts of China until problems in the composition, production, and distribution of local literacy primers were sorted out. Copies of the Hebei primers were subsequently circulated to all provinces for local distribution in the summer of 1956. The decision to promote northern literacy primers for use throughout the country represented a flagrant violation of one of the central principles of the literacy campaign: to foster local knowledge by promoting decentralized and non-standardized curricula. Even this move, however, was not enough to overcome the shortage of locally available primers. Thus, in 1956 it was further stipulated that, in areas where adult literacy primers were still unavailable, regular primary school texts could be temporarily substituted.[20] This, too, represented a violation of the campaign's stated principle of emphasizing practical knowledge and skills, since the regular school curriculum was academically oriented. In addition, the decision also meant that adult learners would be exposed to texts based on children's learning psychology, which professional educators dismissed as inappropriate and ineffective for adult learners.

Participation and Resistance

Did peasants want to become literate? Popular motives for participating in the literacy campaign varied greatly, as did the motives of those who resisted it. And among those who did participate, their motives were often not the same as those envisioned by the campaign's organizers. Campaign organizers correctly anticipated the widespread stimulatory effect of collectivization on popular demand for certain basic literacy skills associated with collective living. The leap from private family farming to bureaucratic collectivism entailed participation, on a day-to-day basis, in a new kind of literate world revolving around workpoints (*gongfen*), task lists, team ledgers, receipts, accounts, promissory notes, personal records, permission slips, and other written practices associated with the collective economy. We can call these various written practices 'workpoint literacy.' As enshrined in the 1956 anti-illiteracy decree, workpoint literacy remained the core of peasant literacy education throughout the collective era. But whereas the official view of these skills emphasized their contribution to 'building socialism' in the countryside, villagers-turned-production team members often viewed them as 'survival skills' for coping in the new rural order.[21]

The list of literacy survival skills was not limited to workpoint-related matters alone. It also entailed mastery of a new political vocabulary. Michael Schoenhals has recently demonstrated the extent to which formalized language formed an integral aspect of political power in the People's Republic of China. Through an administered system of formalized language, the state strove to construct a formal discourse for describing social reality, one that would be far more effective in regulating public expression than outright censorship.[22] The literacy campaign was one of the state's most important vehicles for inculcating the language of revolution among non-schoolgoers. Villages were no longer villages but 'production teams' and 'production brigades,' ruled by 'team leaders' and 'party secretaries' rather than village and lineage elders. The food that team members produced was no longer sold in market fairs but to 'supply and marketing co-ops.' Farmers were no longer farmers but 'peasants' whose social identity was, in theory, no longer rooted in village and kinship relations but in their membership in a 'revolutionary class' engaged in an epochal struggle of historical transformation. The use of such new linguistic labels was a crucial aspect of the revolution in the villages. Acquisition of the formalized state vocabulary was an act of political survival as well as of political ambition. In China, as elsewhere, the state language was not 'hegemonic' but was rather a linguistically based political skill to be mastered, manipulated, and wielded for advantage in certain circumstances. One is reminded here of the village cadre in Gu Hua's perceptive novel *A Small Town Called Hibiscus* for whom phrases such as 'Marxism-Leninism' and 'class struggle' kept 'pouring from her lips ... for hours at a stretch ... as if she had been to a college to learn revolutionary terminology.' Gu's subtle commentary captures the curious combination of alert respect and contained mockery that characterized popular attitudes toward the state language.[23]

Despite all this, revolutionary idealism was undoubtedly also a powerful motivating force on the part of many who participated in the struggle for literacy. Clifford Geertz has argued for the importance of the symbolic dimensions of state power: the state is not merely an instrument of governance but a normative order, which seeks to embody, in ceremony and practice, the common moral beliefs of the polity. The literacy campaign was, in effect, a kind of state ceremony and participation in it a form of politicomoral activity focused on the state. Seen from this perspective, literacy campaigns in the People's Republic embraced not only utilitarian aims but moral and political ones as well. Literacy campaigns not only imparted knowledge and skills to illiterates but also served to link state and society, leaders and led, in a new form of state ritual. Christel Lane has defined state ritual in Soviet society as the 'behavioural dimension of ideology,' encompassing phenomena such as mass political rituals (public commemorations of the Russian Revolution or its heroes, for instance), rituals of initiation (into social and political collectivities such as the army, the Young Pioneers, or the working class), and rites of passage (such as 'socialist' wedding and funerary rites). The literacy campaign in China, with its mass character, daily public reaffirmation of devotion to learning, symbolic displays of initiation (into the world of reading and writing), and passage (*tuomang* – literally, 'casting off illiteracy') performed a similarly crucial symbolic function in the cultural construction of Chinese socialism, serving as both a symbol of the state's devotion to educational salvation of the masses and a symbolic means for the masses, through participation in its rituals, to affirm support and solidarity with the state.[24]

The motives for participating in this new state ritual were not always voluntary or consensual, however. It is important to realize that the anti-illiteracy decree created a new stigmatized social category of 'culturally blind' (*wenmang*) persons. Whereas illiteracy was traditionally an anonymous feature of village society, those who were unable to read or write now suddenly found themselves members of an officially labelled outcast group to be pitied, cajoled, and compelled into learning. The literacy campaign thus spawned enormous social as well as political pressures for villagers to 'cast off their blindness' (*tuomang*).[25] The stigmatization of illiterates lent a distinctly inquisitorial tone to the literacy campaign, a tone reminiscent of the earlier Soviet literacy campaigns described above. Krupskaya's dramatic description of the tensions that accompanied a typical literacy campaign meeting in the Soviet Union could just as easily apply to China: 'In the front rows sit the liquidators [of illiteracy], the organizers of the campaign and the *aktiv* ... At the back and on the side, crowded shoulder to shoulder, stand the masses who are to be taught – tense, motionless, listening ... They are waiting, tensely waiting: What does it mean? Is it serious, or is it just talk?'[26]

Finally, we should not imagine that there was universal support for the literacy campaign. Evidence suggests that passive and active forms of resistance were both widespread and frequent, and not only among villagers: local officials were often equally adept in evading and resisting the literacy campaign. Collectivization was a higher and more immediate political priority for the state than literacy education; this meant that local officials were far more likely to be castigated for failing to meet production quotas than for failing to meet literacy targets. Moreover, production efforts yielded immediate, tangible results, whereas the outcome of literacy work was less certain and took longer to achieve, and its economic value was difficult, if not impossible, to quantify. In the eyes of literacy campaign organizers, this situation made for several 'deviationist' tendencies on the part of local officials. One was a tendency to view the literacy campaign as simply a quota exercise: meeting – or pretending to meet – the official targets handed down from above became the exclusive preoccupation of those in charge, with little regard for the educational effort itself or its results. Others took the view that literacy work was simply ineffective (*ke you, ke wu*) in terms of its stated goal of promoting local economic development. Finally, some local officials described adult literacy efforts as positively wasteful. During the height of collectivization, team and brigade leaders frequently opposed the literacy movement and refused to set up literacy classes on the ground that they interfered with production and were a worthless diversion of scarce economic resources. In the Nanpu district of Guangdong's Yangyun county, the local party secretary even went so far as to ban literacy education in 1956 because, he said, the production of food and other agricultural necessities came from peasants working in the fields, not from their learning how to read and write. Others refused to release villagers from their labour obligations in the collective so that they could attend literacy classes. Some collective leaders took the position that it was the function of the collectives to raise agricultural production and the responsibility of the schools to educate, and that the two were unrelated, and potentially at odds. Spreading literacy would not raise the food supply; on the contrary, literacy classes deprived the collective of precious labour power.[27]

Resistance on the part of team members themselves was also widespread during the campaign. Memorizing characters was a long, time-consuming process, full of drudgery. Especially in the heat of the collectivization campaign, when local cadres were pressuring peasants for production increases, the thought of spending evenings or lunch breaks in the fields learning characters must often have been greeted with dismay, if not open resistance. Many team members were said to be of the opinion that 'taking part in the cooperative movement is like riding a train, but participating in a literacy class is like riding in an ox cart.' Others voiced scepticism that the literacy campaign could really produce quick results: 'A hen fed in the morning can't lay eggs by afternoon.' A Guangdong official described villagers' concern that attending literacy classes would interfere with their labour obligations to the collective as one of the three great fears (*san da pa*) that infected the 1956 literacy campaign (the other two were not enough teachers and insufficient primers).[28]

The official view was that collectivization would stimulate popular demand for literacy. In reality, however, this was not always so. During the height of the collectivization campaign, many parents in Guangdong and elsewhere actually withdrew their children from schools so that they could join newly formed production teams. By the spring of 1956, the problem had become severe enough that the vice-secretary of the Guangdong party committee felt compelled to issue a warning that collectivization was leading to mass dropouts in some areas.[29]

The Great Leap Forward Literacy Campaign
The literacy campaign stalled briefly in 1957, during a respite between the end of collectivization and the beginning of the commune movement. In early 1958, however, it was revived on an even grander scale than before.[30]

The first indication that the literacy campaign was about to heat up again came in early 1958 when Chen Yi, head of the National Anti-Illiteracy Association, predicted an imminent 'atomic explosion' in culture in conjunction with the communization movement.[31] In Guangdong, there immediately followed a rapid escalation of literacy targets. A conference on educational work convened in April 1958 to discuss preparations for reviving the literacy campaign. Qu Mengsheng, one of the highest ranking educational officials in Guangdong, declared at the conference that illiteracy should be completely eliminated in Guangdong within four years. This was not a particularly extravagant goal; it reflected the original target date put forward in 1956. Later that month, however, the Guangdong education bureau published an official 'correction' to Qu's figure.[32] The correction stated that what Qu had 'meant to say' was that literacy work in Guangdong would be completed 'within three years,' one year earlier than Qu had estimated.

This was only the beginning. In the same issue of the journal that contained the 'correction' was another report, which stated that the Guangdong party committee was determined to see illiteracy completely eliminated within one year! In response, the provincial education bureau, representing the more cautious opinion of professional educators, issued a sober statement declaring that Guangdong needed a minimum of seven more years to successfully eradicate illiteracy within its borders. The following month, however, the propaganda chief of the Guangdong party committee astounded delegates to a May 1958 meeting of 'advanced anti-illiteracy units' by announcing that Guangdong was to become a 'fully literate' province before 1 October 1958 – barely five months away. A literate Guangdong, he said, would be the province's gift to the nation for national day.[33]

The adventurism of the 1958-60 literacy campaign was also evident in changing definitions of the time required to acquire literacy. When the literacy campaign was first mounted in 1956, the Central Committee stipulated that peasants would require at least sixteen months of spare-time study to achieve the minimum literacy standard of 1,500 characters. Starting in early 1958, however, literacy campaign organizers embraced the Great Leap Forward motto that 'one year is like one day' (*yinian ru yiri*). In the spirit of 'socialist competition' (*shehui zhuyi jingsai*) that characterized all official endeavours during the Great Leap, localities began to compete with one another to produce the most miraculous literacy claims. A factory in Jiangmen claimed to have eliminated illiteracy among its workforce in a mere nine days. An illiterate overseas woman who had returned to China was said to have learned 2,800 characters in just five days. A commune in Shantou claimed to have achieved a 99.9 per cent literacy rate in thirty-eight days. Prosperous Shunde county in the Pearl River Delta claimed a literacy rate of 100 per cent, while nearby Huiyang county declared itself illiteracy free in July 1958, after only sixty days of heroic effort.

As part of an officially encouraged effort to revive the 'Yanan spirit' of hard work and thrifty self-reliance, former base areas were elevated during the Great Leap. In Guangdong, such areas emerged during this period as leading models for anti-illiteracy work in the province. Puning county in northeastern Guangdong, one of the oldest CCP base areas in Guangdong, became the most esteemed of all. Puning became the first 'literate' county in Guangdong in June 1958. Only weeks earlier, Baoya village in Puning had received the distinction of becoming the first officially 'cultured' village in Guangdong. Puning joined Jieyang county, another former base area located close to Puning in the Shantou district, Ningan county in Heilongjiang, and Dengfang county in Henan as national models for the Great Leap Forward literacy campaign.[34]

Puning was said to have set a target of fifty days for eliminating illiteracy among its 69,700 illiterates. In keeping with the Great Leap Forward habit of not only meeting but also surpassing quotas, Puning claimed to have accomplished the task in only forty-five days! Its 'assault' on illiteracy involved the creation of what might be described as a 'total learning environment.' Literacy 'checkpoints' were set up at strategic locations on village paths to intercept and test illiterates. Characters were posted on trees, in doorways, inside homes – anywhere illiterates were to be found. Shops were required to place character cards alongside their goods; peasants unable to read the cards were not allowed to purchase the goods.

Mutual-responsibility systems were set up to ensure that literacy quotas were respected and fulfilled. In one case, there was a celebrated tale of a fifty-year-old woman who had taught herself to write using pig grease for ink because ink was unavailable in her village. These well-publicized official examples of literacy work in Puning and other former base areas conveyed the Great Leap message that no material obstacle was too great to overcome when confronted by steel will.

An Illiteracy-Free Province?

On 27 September 1958, Guangdong declared itself an official illiteracy-free province. Only one other province had claimed this status; Heilongjiang had become the first a few months before. Guangdong leaders claimed that fully 88 per cent of twelve to forty year olds in the province had met the state's minimum literacy standard of being able to read and write 1,500-3,000 characters, plus write 300-500-character essays and read simple books and magazines. This, they said, included 86 per cent of all peasants in the province, 98 per cent of cadres, and 92 per cent of all urban workers. Having 'basically eliminated illiteracy,' the official task now was to overtake Liaoning and Jiangsu within three years as the most educationally advanced province in China.[35]

Retrenchment

The Great Leap Forward literacy campaign continued throughout China until the latter part of 1960. Guangdong authorities were aware at least a year before, however, that the province's literacy achievements had been grossly exaggerated. Previously, official figures had claimed that 5.5 million persons acquired literacy during the first nine months of 1958. In 1959, authorities admitted, however, that at least 30 per cent had subsequently 'relapsed' (*fumang* or *huisheng*) into illiteracy – up to 60 per cent in some counties.[36] In one commune in Puning, at least 50 per cent of the new literates in 1958 had relapsed into illiteracy. In Shunde, which months before had claimed 100 per cent literacy, 40 per cent of peasants in the Mingzhu commune had relapsed by 1959.[37] The very use of the term 'relapse' was misleading in this context. Were peasants who participated in thirty- to sixty-day crash courses ever meaningfully 'literate?'

The demise of the Great Leap Forward literacy campaign followed a series of top-level party meetings held between July and August 1960. These meetings marked the renunciation of Great Leap policies as a whole and the mounting of new economic plans designed to rescue the country from famine and economic collapse.[38] The end of the literacy campaign was formally marked by a Central Committee decree ordering the bureaucratic responsibility for village literacy education to be taken out of the hands of local anti-illiteracy associations and placed in the village work departments (*nongcun gongzuo bu*) of the agriculture bureaus of county governments.[39]

By the end of 1960, the focus of anti-illiteracy work in Guangdong had shifted from educating illiterates to discovering how many illiterates truly remained in the province. As with nearly every other form of mass activity during the Great Leap Forward, exaggerated claims, false reports, and administrative chaos led to a complete breakdown of the statistical base in education.[40] Restoring it required the comprehensive collection of local data, followed by administrative measures to verify the numerical claims submitted by local authorities. Thus, the Guangdong education bureau stipulated in 1960 that, in order for a rural production team to declare itself officially literate, it would first have to undergo a series of on-site inspections by team and commune officials. The team would then be required to submit to further verification by three additional administrative levels: production brigade, commune, and county.[41] The verification procedure adopted by county governments involved the familiar method of dispatching work teams (*gongzuo tuan*) to conduct on-site investigations. However, inspection teams normally inspected only a third or at most two-thirds of the production brigades in a commune. This meant that as few as one-sixth of the brigades within any given county were actually visited by the inspection teams.

Moreover, the inspections themselves did not entail testing individual performance. Rather, the main part of the verification process consisted of the presentation of written and verbal progress reports by brigade officials to the inspection team, coupled with the team's own on-site observations. Literacy statistics were thus based on self-reporting by brigade officials, rather than on the aggregation of individual test scores. Indeed, it appears that actual testing for individual literacy played little if any role in the inspection process. Finally, as Vilma Seeberg has observed, the very concept of 'inspection' was problematic. As Seeberg points out, inspection was primarily a political tool for enforcing party discipline, not a procedure for measuring individuals' literacy competence. If current policy called for all-out effort and quick results, then inspection teams looked for evidence of such. Likewise, if current policy called for moderation and retrenchment, then the main task of inspection teams was to enforce local compliance and to discipline those who deviated. Politics, in this sense, remained in command.[42]

Nonetheless, the results of the investigations were often enlightening. For instance, as a result of one such investigation in Guangdong's Chaoan county, it was discovered that the number of illiterates in late 1960 was actually one and a half times higher than the number reported two years earlier. Local officials, it was revealed, had falsely reported the number of illiterates at the outset of the Great Leap in order to magnify the extent of their subsequent 'achievement.'[43] Such revelations provided ample fuel for intellectual critics, who, in the aftermath of the Great Leap demise, launched their most blistering attacks to date on the literacy campaign.

Critics of the Literacy Campaign

The normally muted voices of intellectual critics of the literacy campaign rose to the fore on two occasions during the late 1950s and early 1960s: in 1957, during the period of intellectual liberalization known as the Hundred Flowers Movement, and again in the aftermath of the Great Leap debacle. On both occasions Guangzhou and Shanghai emerged as bastions of intellectual opposition to the Communist Party's mass-campaign approach to literacy education.

In 1957, a leading Shanghai educational journal published an article that took direct aim at the principle of 'people teaching people' (*yimin jiaomin*), which underpinned the entire literacy campaign. The authors challenged the Communist Party's ability to achieve the educational salvation of the peasantry on the basis of a mass campaign, pointing out that adult learning psychology was extremely complex, demanding special pedagogical training and skills. How, then, could the party justify using unqualified and barely educated 'mass teachers' (*qunzhong jiaoshi*) to accomplish this task? The party was really demeaning Chinese peasants by taking the position that anyone could teach them. The authors also accused the Communist Party of applying a double standard in its policy toward adult peasants. After all, the party expected children to be taught by graduates of normal school, so why apply a different standard to adult learners? If adult education was to succeed, adult learners needed specially designed learning materials and specially trained teachers who understood the different and complex psychology of adult learners.[44]

Guangdong educators mounted a different but equally devastating critique of the party's campaign-style approach to mass education. Their first publicly punishing judgment appeared in the provincial education bureau's journal in January 1960. This critique, together with two subsequent treatises published in 1962, showed just how opposed some Guangdong educators were to CCP literacy policies. All three works began from the position that there could be no such thing as a 'leap forward' in education. To suggest otherwise was to defy an 'objective law' of education, namely that the accumulation of knowledge progresses incrementally, 'from little to much, from shallow to profound, from simple to complex, from a low level to a high level, progressively upward.'

Schools, these critics complained, 'cannot be equated with production units' (*xuexiao buneng gen shengchan danwei dengtongqilai*). They cited Marx's observation that, while it took relatively little time to grow wheat or raise cattle, it took much longer for other kinds of 'production,' especially 'spiritual production' (*jingshen shengchan*). And whereas it might require mere hours to produce a pair of shoes on a factory assembly line, it took nine years to 'produce' a junior middle school graduate, twelve years to 'produce' a senior middle school graduate, and sixteen to seventeen years to 'produce' a university graduate. Why? Because unlike the factory production of shoes, the accumulation of knowledge requires time for each new bit of learning to be absorbed and consolidated. Since education could not be compared to modern factory production, it was folly to use a 'production campaign' (*shengchan yundong*) approach to increasing the number of literates. Extending the analogy even further, critics pointed out that, 'if there is wastage in the production of steel, the waste can still be recycled' (a veiled reference to the infamous failed backyard furnace campaign of 1958). Sadly, however, this was not the case for 'wastage in the training of human talent.' Because the educative process was by nature long and costly, all attempts to defy this nature by making 'sudden and quick assaults' (*tuji*) on illiteracy were bound to fail.

Finally, one writer went so far as to invoke the legacy of Confucius to call for an end to mass literacy campaigns. Citing the sage's admonishment of 'sustenance and then instruction' (*fu erhou jiao*), the author wanted literacy campaigns put on hold until economic livelihoods were restored. This critic was writing at the height of the great famine of 1959-61, in which as many as 30 million or more Chinese peasants may have perished. [45]

Thus, despite the immense human and bureaucratic effort, the legacy bequeathed by the mass literacy campaigns of 1956 and 1958-60 is far from certain. Western scholars such as Evelyn Rawski have pointed to the 'limited efficacy' of literacy campaigns in China to produce significant and sustainable improvements in literacy rates over time.[46] Judging from the criticisms presented above and the subsequent redirection of official literacy efforts in the 1960s away from adult literacy campaigns and toward the universalization of primary school education, a similar de facto conclusion appears to have been reached in Chinese educational circles by the early 1960s. What is perhaps most striking, however, is that official China has yet to undertake a definitive reassessment of the Great Leap Forward literacy campaign. On the one hand, the authors of the official Guangdong educational yearbook, published in 1986, acknowledge that the number of peasants who took part in the 1958-9 literacy campaign and who subsequently 'relapsed' into illiteracy was around 40 per cent, 'more or less,' and up to 60 per cent in some units.[47] Yet, on the other hand, the original inflated literacy statistics that were announced at the height of the campaign continue to be reprinted uncritically in virtually all official documents that describe the progress of literacy in China since 1949. In recent years, however, a number of PRC scholars have taken advantage of the loosening of strictures on intellectual expression to offer a more candid reappraisal of the past. Among them, the educational historian Chen Bixiang is perhaps the most unflinching in his criticism of the mass literacy campaigns of the late 1950s. The number of persons who became genuinely and permanently literate during the Great Leap Forward, Chen concludes, was actually 'very few.' The campaign method failed, in his view, because it was predicated not upon the genuine and carefully researched educational needs of illiterate villagers but upon a utopian desire to 'sweep away' illiteracy in one fell swoop. Consequently, Chen argued, not much was really learned by villagers who participated in the campaign. And the little that was learned was quickly forgotten as popular enthusiasm evaporated once the true scale and difficulty of the undertaking became clear. From this perspective, he implied, the state's ill-conceived effort to 'sweep away' illiteracy amounted to a cruel, if well-intentioned, hoax perpetrated upon a captive population.[48]

If collectivization imposed unprecedented demands for literacy among Chinese peasants, the mass literacy campaigns generated in response also revealed the state's hubristic belief in its educative power. If turning China into a literate society within seven years was a utopian prospect, so too was the literacy campaign's other major expectation: that Chinese peasants could be easily persuaded to abandon their local speech in favour of official Mandarin and to write using roman letters. As we will see in the next chapter, the literacy campaign was not only about teaching peasants how to read and write; it was also about the state's attempt to impose an artificial written and spoken language on China's peasants. Our investigation of the literacy campaign's organizational structures and implementation has revealed that there was frequently a lack of fit between official aims and popular thought and between central policies and local interests. This proved to be an even greater problem when it came to the controversial question of language reform.

7
Beijing's Language Reform and Guangdong's Opposition

Thus far we have considered the literacy campaign from several different perspectives: the economic pressures for it, brought on by collectivization; the massive organizational and mobilizational efforts involved; and popular participation and resistance. Alongside these perspectives, however, lies another story that we have yet to consider. The literacy campaign was not only about cultivating local economic competencies and regime support; it also embodied the state's unprecedented attempt to impose a single written and spoken language on China's diverse peasant cultures. More than any other feature of the literacy campaign, this pursuit of national unity through imposed linguistic uniformity aroused tremendous and passionate resistance at the local level. And nowhere was the resistance greater than in Guangdong.

Language reform embraced three key objectives: replacement of dialect speech with Beijing-based Mandarin, replacement of the existing characters with simplified ones to facilitate literacy acquisition, and adoption of phonetic writing as an aid to character recognition and correct Mandarin pronunciation. These sweeping changes to the linguistic environment were announced in a series of decrees promulgated by the State Council and the Central Committee over a five-year period from 1955 to 1960. Mandarin-based phonetic writing was to be promoted across the country and at all levels of society to facilitate the replacement of local dialects with Mandarin and, it was argued, to speed literacy acquisition. Schools and literacy classes nationwide were to adopt an official list of 515 simplified Chinese characters (eventually increased to more than 2,000). And all primary and middle schools (with the temporary exception of those in minority areas) were to begin disseminating Beijing-based vernacular, which was to become the 'common speech' (*putonghua*) of the Han ethnic people. In order to expedite the use of phonetic writing, even the traditional vertical style of writing was to be abandoned in favour of horizontal writing.[1]

This chapter focuses upon the conflict that erupted between Beijing and Guangdong over the question of language reform. The central state's attempt to unify China's disparate peasant cultures by imposing a single north-ern-derived and standardized written and spoken language engendered fierce resistance in multilingual Guangdong. Moreover, opposition to this ill-fated effort was expressed not only by Guangdong villagers, incensed at what they regarded as costly elite experiments imposed from afar, but by senior provincial party officials as well, who openly defied Beijing's orders. In the end, a combination of popular resistance and elite opposition defeated Beijing's attempt to replace Guangdong's cacophonous linguistic anarchy with an artificial standard imposed from above.

In order to fully understand why language reform met with such staunch resistance in Guangdong, we must begin with a brief overview of the complex and controversial history of language reform in twentieth-century China. Beijing's concern with Cantonese linguistic parochialism can be traced back at least as far as the eighteenth century. Qing emperors decreed the establishment of Correct Pronunciation Academies (*zhengyin shuyuan*) for examination candidates from Guangdong and Fujian, in an effort to improve the Mandarin spoken by southern officials.[2] However, the official state desire to foster uniformity of popular speech – as opposed to the speech of scholar-bureaucrats – dates only from the appearance of modern nation-alism at the turn of the century. In 1903, the newly formed Ministry of Education observed that while the 'spoken language of every country is nationally unified,' in China 'people [still] speak their own dialects,' with the unfortunate result that 'even people from the same province cannot understand each other.' The ministry's school regulations proclaimed that Mandarin or 'official speech' (*guanhua*), a term that had been in use from the Yuan period in reference to the Beijing-based lingua franca of official-dom, should henceforth become 'the spoken language of the whole Em-pire,' to be used by all of its citizens. Guanhua was to be taught in the new, modern school system, from higher primary to normal school.[3] At this stage, however, guanhua was promoted solely for its value as a common spoken language, while classical Chinese remained the written standard. It was not until the May Fourth Movement abolished the old national written lan-guage of classical Chinese and replaced it with the northern dialect as an imposed standard that the republican government officially adopted the concept of 'national language' (*guoyu*) in the sense of a common spoken and written vernacular.[4]

The leaders of the Chinese Republic established in 1912 were committed to unifying China linguistically and sought to promote Mandarin as the republic's lingua franca. Ironically, however, just as modern nationalists were beginning to regard the profusion of local and regional dialects as an obsta-cle to national unity, the disintegration of the imperial state resulted in an erosion of Mandarin's traditional roles as lingua franca of the ruling class and marker of elite status. The end of the examination system and the political decentralization that accompanied the 1911 Revolution may actually have reduced the normative value and social demand for Mandarin outside its spoken area. The rise of the provinces after 1911 was not limited to greater political assertiveness. In Guangdong, it was also expressed in a flourishing movement for Cantonese literature centred in Guangzhou and Hong Kong. Even the traditional 'stage Mandarin' (*xitai guanhua*) of Cantonese opera disappeared after 1911.[5] In China, as elsewhere, the pressure to build a modern national state ironically led to sharpened senses of local and regional difference, as well as to fiercely contested definitions of national identity. Thus, when the republic's Ministry of Education convened its first Conference on the Unification of Pronunciation in 1913 and announced that Mandarin was to become the 'national language' (*guoyu*) of the Chinese Republic, southern delegates to the conference promptly revolted and walked out, protesting vehemently the ministry's decision to 'Force the South to Follow the North.'[6]

Dialect speech was also strengthened in early-twentieth-century Guangdong as a result of efforts to develop romanization schemes that would aid literacy acquisition for local dialect speakers. The interest in making written Chinese more 'Western' by writing it with roman letters appeared first in Guangdong. Nineteenth-century Christian missionaries in Guangdong and Hong Kong devised the first alphabetic schemes for Chinese. These schemes were based not on Mandarin, however, but on the plethora of local dialects and subdialects spoken by the peasants among whom the missionaries lived, worked, and attempted to convert. Between 1890 and 1904, missionaries in China produced over 130,000 romanized Bibles (or portions thereof), of which a mere 2 per cent were based on Mandarin and the rest on local dialects. The Cantonese Christian missionary Wang Bingyue was among the first Chinese to devise a romanization scheme for Chinese. A pastor of the London Missionary Society, Wang published his *Pinyin zibu* (Guide to the Alphabetic Writing of Chinese) in 1897. The method employed a combination of stenographic symbols and roman alphabet letters to represent Cantonese sounds and tones.[7]

The May Fourth Movement marked the beginning of the elevation of Mandarin – or, to be more precise, the Beijing version of it – as modern China's 'national language' (*guoyu*). Subsequent Nationalist efforts at linguistic unification during the republic centred on promoting Mandarin (interestingly, Beijing speech was still taken as the standard, even though the Nationalists made their capital in Nanjing) and the annotated use of phonetic symbols to facilitate standard pronunciation. In 1918, the republican government officially adopted a phonetic alphabet for Mandarin, *Zhuyin zimu*, based on Japanese *kana* symbols. It was officially superseded in 1928 by the National Language Romanization Scheme (*Guoyu romazi* or *gwoyeu romatzyh*). Dialect-based phonetic writing and literature were strictly prohibited by the Guomindang government after 1928; those who continued to advocate it were charged with leading a movement of 'cultural traitors.' The Chinese communists, however, took a somewhat different approach to the question of dialect speech and literature during this period.

The CCP's Support for Dialect Romanization before 1949
When it came to language policy, the CCP in the 1930s adhered to Stalin's concept of federal nationalism, which entailed promoting a unified 'common speech' while at the same time championing dialect standards of reading and writing as legitimate, non-treasonous expressions of local culture. Indeed, it is no exaggeration to say that the CCP's language policy and official romanization scheme originated in the Soviet Union. The persons most responsible for their early development included Qu Qiubai, the CCP leader who fled to Moscow in 1927 to escape Chiang Kaishek's purge of communists, and Wu Yuzhang, the veteran linguistic revolutionary who followed Qu to the Soviet Union. Although he was completely lacking in formal linguistic training at the time, Qu was recruited by Soviet linguists to aid in the development of a romanization scheme for use among the 100,000 members of the largely illiterate Dungan Chinese minority in eastern Siberia. In 1929 Qu published the *Zhongguo ladinghua zimu* (Chinese romanized alphabet), which was based on the Shandong version of Mandarin spoken by the Dungan Chinese. Following Qu's return to China in 1931, Wu Yuzhang continued the effort, publishing the first handbook on the scheme in 1931. Wu eventually also returned to China and became one of the leading figures in the PRC literacy movement, holding leading positions in the National Anti-Illiteracy Commission and the Committee for Reform of the Chinese Language.[8]

Qu Qiubai coined the term 'common language' (*dazhongyu, putonghua*), which the CCP later officially adopted, along with a version of Qu's phonetic alphabet, to describe the general northern dialect spoken by 70 per cent of Chinese, a dialect that Qu believed would eventually spread throughout China. His advocacy of a new written and spoken language of the masses grew out of his Marxist critique of the elitist social base of the New Culture Movement. Qu called for the replacement of Western-influenced *baihua* with a written language based on the street vernacular of the urban working class. However, he rejected rural vernaculars as a basis for the new written language because he viewed them as primitive and obscure.[9]

Qu accepted Marx's prediction that dialects would disappear eventually as a matter of objective necessity, the unification of language proceeding inevitably from the unification of the economy and of the state under socialism. But Qu also held fast to his view that the 'dialects cannot be forcibly unified,' a position that he took up in earnest when he became commissioner of education in the Jiangxi Soviet upon his return to China in 1931. The Communist Party formally adopted Qu's Mandarin-based romanization scheme, now called the New Script Alphabet (*Sin wenz*) in 1937. But Sin Wenz was also simultaneously adapted to create separate romanization schemes for the eight major regional dialects of the country, and it was even modified to take account of subdialect variations between villages in the Yanan area. The various schemes were incorporated into an officially endorsed, dialect-based 'people's literature,' which also received the backing of leading populist writers such as Lu Xun and Mao Dun, who supported dialect romanization because they believed that it helped to bring writing closer to the daily speech of ordinary people ('From the lips of living people take words and phrases that are full of life and transfer them to paper,' Lu Xun had written). Unlike the Nationalists, the CCP in the 1930s and 1940s was firmly committed to the support of dialect-based romanization schemes and literature.

At Yanan, the CCP also formally committed itself to the goal of abolishing Chinese characters entirely and replacing them with a phonetic alphabet. The official position was that abolishing characters was essential for achieving universal literacy. As Mao told Edgar Snow in 1936, 'Chinese characters are so difficult to learn that even the best system of rudimentary characters, or simplified teaching, does not equip the people with a really efficient and rich vocabulary. Sooner or later, we believe, we will have to abandon characters altogether if we are to create a new social culture in which the masses fully participate.'[10] This passage is particularly significant because Mao appeared to be questioning whether the 1,000-character archetype for basic literacy instruction used in China for centuries and adopted by the Mass Education Movement and the Chinese Communist Party alike could really serve as an effective basis for achieving universal literacy in China. By the latter 1930s, Mao and other senior communist educators such as Xu Teli concluded, at least temporarily, that universal literacy could only be achieved by eliminating Chinese characters altogether and replacing them with phonetic writing.[11]

The CCP's Changed Policy after 1949

Two important changes occurred in the CCP's language reform policy after 1949. First, the party reversed its previous policy of supporting dialect-based romanization schemes and dialect literature and mounted a policy of strict opposition to what were now described as unacceptable manifestations of linguistic and cultural 'localism.'[12] The revolutionary task of cultivating local constituencies gave way after 1949 to a nation-building imperative that identified national solidarity with linguistic uniformity. Thus, phonetic writing continued to be promoted after 1949, but its exclusive purpose was now to facilitate standard Mandarin pronunciation and character recognition during literacy training. Second, the idea that phonetic writing should replace characters altogether, a popular idea in communist linguistic circles during the 1930s, was now effectively abandoned and replaced by an urgent effort to simplify the existing characters.[13] These policy changes crystallized in 1955-6 with the promulgation of the above-mentioned measures designed to promote the nationwide use of Mandarin speech, Mandarin-based romanization, and character simplification.[14] The first two measures are most important for our purposes, for they had the greatest impact upon the literacy campaign in Guangdong. Before we proceed, however, let us briefly consider the decision to promote character simplification.

In 1956, the State Council promulgated the first list of simplified characters, consisting of 515 simplified characters plus fifty-four simplified particles. In 1964, the number of simplified characters was increased to over 2,000. The effort to popularize simplified characters met with little, if any, overt popular resistance. Rapid dissemination of simplified characters through the school system and the official print media appears to have facilitated their universal acceptance and use within a short period. However, recent research by Chinese and Western linguists and learning psychologists has called into question whether simplified characters actually facilitated literacy acquisition. While simplified characters have been shown to be easier to write than the old characters because they contain fewer strokes, there is no scientific evidence to indicate that simplified characters are easier to recall than the old characters.[15] Indeed, the recent conclusion of Chinese researchers, following empirical testing, is that 'in recognition [of characters] ... there is no marked difference between simple and complicated characters.'[16] In fact, there is reason to believe that simplification in some cases may actually retard character recognition by eliminating cultural cues that formerly may have aided recognition and by reducing the distinctiveness of individual characters.

Language reform was motivated more by political considerations, however, than by the empirical observations of linguists and learning psychologists. Indeed, herein lurks the tension at the heart of language reform in China: language reform was a technical undertaking entrusted to skilled professionals, but the rationale and objectives were always deeply political.[17] Nationalism and cultural attachment to the traditional writing system informed the decision not to replace Chinese characters with an imported foreign alphabet and to embark instead on a concerted effort to simplify the existing characters.

Nationalist imperatives also underlied the party's policies for promoting the nationwide use of Mandarin and Mandarin-based phonetic writing. Particularly striking was Mao's 1952 intervention over the question of what kind of phonetic writing system the People's Republic of China should adopt.

Mao delivered a set of personal instructions to Ma Xulun, minister of education and chair of the newly established Committee for Research into the Reform of the Chinese Written Language, on the issue, the effect of which was abruptly to reverse the party's previous long-standing support for Sin Wenz. Mao did so simply by declaring that 'The writing system must be reformed, it should take the phonetic direction common to languages of the world; it should be *national* in form, the alphabet and system *should be elaborated on the basis of the existing Chinese characters*' (emphasis added).[18] His rejection of the roman-based Sin Wenz alphabet and his demand that language reformers create a new alphabet based on 'the existing Chinese characters' were not rooted in a careful linguistic assessment of the relative advantages and disadvantages of different kinds of phonetic writing; Mao was not a linguist. Rather, his instructions to Ma Xulun may have been motivated by the fact that Mao was then embroiled in his first great post-1949 confrontation with Western imperialism in Korea. Nationalism was a priority, and that meant purging roman-based Sin Wenz and replacing it with a more authentically Chinese alphabet.

Mao's instructions threw the Language Reform Committee into a frenzied search to come up with a new alphabet to match his prescription. As Wu Yuzhang told the Language Reform Committee following Mao's remarks, 'We must do away with the idea that it is necessary to use the Latin or Cyrillic alphabet.' As a result, between 1950 and 1958, no fewer than 1,700 different phonetic schemes were proposed, an outpouring that Charles Hayford remarks was 'rivalled in the West only by the search for a perpetual motion machine.'[19] In the end, however, none was deemed acceptable, and the committee reverted to its original search for an acceptable system of phonetic writing based on roman letters. The end result was the *Hanyu pinyin* scheme adopted in 1958, which was based upon a combination of elements drawn from Sin Wenz and the other major romanization schemes developed earlier in the century.[20]

Beijing's effort to promote the use of Mandarin in Guangdong, particularly among officials, began with the arrival of the first PLA troops. In 1950, Mandarin was declared a compulsory subject at the senior level in the village spare-time schools that had been hastily set up to identify and train local activists for land reform. Peasants in one such school, the Yellow Bamboo Drop spare-time school in Huiyang county, spent a total of 540 class hours learning to speak Mandarin compared to only 180 class hours learning how to write characters. Mandarin was also the principal subject taught in the cultural remediation schools (*wenhua buxi xuexiao*) set up to train Guangdong cadres in the early 1950s. The schools taught Mandarin as well as mathematics, natural science, geography, history, politics, physical education, and music. However, in the first year, Mandarin occupied sixteen of twenty-eight classes during the first term and twelve of twenty-eight classes in the second term. In the second year, Mandarin still occupied ten of the twenty-eight classes in each term; the next subject in importance was mathematics, which took up only seven of the twenty-eight classes in both years. In addition to these measures, village peasant associations were instructed to convene Mandarin classes and to hold Mandarin-speaking competitions.[21]

From the beginning, the central state's promotion of Mandarin in Guangdong was linked to its effort to weaken the forces of Cantonese 'localism' and to nurture the loyalty of local officialdom, which Beijing regarded as riven with parochial ties. Many Cantonese cultural figures who welcomed the communist revolution agreed with this view. The esteemed Cantonese writer and cultural critic Qin Mu, for instance, attributed the strength of localist sentiment in Guangdong in 1950 to the profusion of local dialects. The 'local clan outlook' (*difang zongzu guannian*) characteristic of most Cantonese, said Qin, was rooted in the fact that there were no fewer than four major dialects in Guangdong, each of which in turn split into a bewildering variety of subdialects. A Mandarin-speaking educational official transferred to Guangdong in 1950 echoed Qin's criticism when he complained that linguistic parochialism was one of the chief causes of what he called the 'feudal personal relations' (*fengjian guanxi*) characteristic of many Guangdong cadres. The state's work was being frustrated, he said, because Guangdong cadres clung to their local dialects and insisted that outsiders learn them if they wished to have any local dealings.

Although measures to promote Mandarin in Guangdong were in place since the earliest days of the PRC, as mentioned above a coherent national policy for the universalization of Mandarin did not appear until the mid-1950s. Following a national conference on language standardization in 1955, sweeping measures were instituted for use of Mandarin in the language and literature classes in schools at all levels across the country. Zhang Xiruo, one of the project's architects, explained its significance this way, in terms that echo somewhat those used in the 1903 school regulations:

> The People's Republic of China is a nation which is highly unified. The government, economy, culture and national defense have all realized an historically unprecedented unity ... [But with respect to linguistic divisions,] there are still some rather serious distinctions which pose an obstacle to the exchange of ideas between people from two different regions. In order to meet the needs of all the nation's people, strengthen their unification, advance their culture to meet the needs of socialist construction, and insure the success of the First Five Year Plan and future plans for building the economy, we should energetically promote the teaching of the standard vernacular and broaden its dissemination; this is a serious political

responsibility ... We call on everyone to learn this form of pronunciation, to train their own tongues and ears, and gradually achieve the ability to hear, read, and speak it.[22]

The main pedagogical device for training peoples' 'tongues and ears' in Mandarin pronunciation was to be the new romanized system of phonetic writing known as *Hanyu pinyin*. The pinyin scheme was published in 1956 and formally adopted in 1958.[23] Mandarin and pinyin were to be promoted simultaneously throughout the school system, but there was still the question of how to reach the millions who were outside the school system. From the mid-1950s, the national literacy campaign became the most important vehicle for promoting Mandarin among non-schoolgoers. The implications of this decision for literacy training in Guangdong and other non-Mandarin-speaking parts of the country were crucial, for literacy was now to be defined as the written form of Mandarin.

Guangdong's Resistance

Guangdong authorities reacted cautiously at first to the central state's plans for nationwide promotion of Mandarin and *Hanyu pinyin*. In 1956, the provincial education bureau announced plans for rapidly popularizing the use of Mandarin. With the exception of minority areas, Mandarin instruction was to be introduced in the language classes of all primary and middle schools and teacher training institutes in the province. Within six months, all county and city governments were to begin providing Mandarin instruction for their teachers, and committees for the promotion of Mandarin were to be set up at every administrative level from the province to the county. But the education bureau also made it clear that it foresaw major problems and resistance to popularizing Mandarin owing to the 'complexity' of the dialect situation in Guangdong. In addition to embracing four mutually unintelligible major dialects – Cantonese, Chaozhou, Hakka, and Hainan – some parts of the province were also marked by an extraordinary profusion of subdialects. Particularly in the Cantonese- and Chaozhou-speaking areas of the province, dialect differences often seemed to appear literally over the hill or across the river.[24]

The use of Mandarin in Guangdong schools frequently met with a lukewarm response from teachers and students. In 1956, Mandarin teachers in the Chaozhou region reported that their students believed the use of Mandarin in classrooms was lowering teaching standards and unnecessarily increasing the burden on students. In addition, students who could not speak Mandarin well were subjected to laughter and ridicule by their classmates. Many students were also deliberately ignoring their Mandarin lessons, gambling that doing so would ultimately result in their gaining an edge over students who devoted greater study time to Mandarin.[25] The emphasis on Mandarin was also sometimes undermining classroom discipline, as teachers frequently found themselves the brunt of student laughter and derision as they struggled in vain to speak Mandarin after hours of self-study at the prodding of local authorities. The methods employed to persuade teachers and students of the value of learning Mandarin were mainly hortatory. For instance, teachers in a Muslim primary school in Guangzhou told their students that because Chairman Mao spoke Mandarin they would need to learn Mandarin if they wanted to understand his speeches (ironic, since Mao's heavily accented Hunan version of Mandarin was notoriously difficult to comprehend). And teachers in another school informed their students that Mandarin was necessary if they wished to understand the heroic tales of PLA veterans who visited the school.[26]

The most critical confrontation, however, was over whether to use Mandarin-based pinyin as the basis for adult literacy training in Guangdong. Official policy statements on this issue were contradictory throughout the latter 1950s. In his 1955 speech on the literacy movement, Lin Handa suggested that pinyin should be used in areas 'where dialect conditions permit,' implying that the use of pinyin and Mandarin in the literacy campaign ought to be confined to Mandarin-speaking parts of the country. A Ministry of Education directive similarly stated that pinyin might 'help' adult literacy acquisition and reading 'in cities and in villages in the northern speech region,' while a 1959 Central Committee and State Council directive called on 'all Mandarin speaking regions of the country' to experiment with pinyin-annotated characters as the basis of literacy instruction.[27] At the same time, however, other leading officials in the literacy movement advocated Mandarin-based pinyin as the basis for literacy instruction in all regions of the country. Thus, in 1956, Hu Yaobang called for township-level literacy primers across the country to adopt pinyin. Furthermore, Hu made the rather astounding claim (without any supporting evidence) that the use of Mandarin-based pinyin would actually speed literacy acquisition, even in non-Mandarin-speaking regions of the country.[28]

It was not until 1959, however, at the height of the Great Leap Forward, that the movement for phonetic reading reached a feverish pitch all across China, following its endorsement by the highest levels of party and government. Against a backdrop of mounting economic chaos and a foundering literacy campaign in which tens of thousands of newly literate villagers were 'relapsing' into illiteracy across the country (up to 60 per cent in some Guangdong counties), the authorities of Shanxi province convened a national conference in December 1959 to discuss the reputedly remarkable achievements of the people of Wanrong county, Shanxi, in using pinyin to eliminate illiteracy and promote Mandarin. All of the fifteen attending provinces, with the exception of Fujian, were Mandarin speaking. Guangdong did not attend.

Wanrong officials claimed that youth needed only fifteen to twenty hours to master the basics of pinyin transcription, followed by a further 120 to 130 hours to attain a basic reading and writing knowledge of some 1,500 simple characters. Subsequent spare-time reading courses for new literates with knowledge of pinyin could be shortened from three years to only one year.[29] Moreover, claimed Wanrong officials, pinyin was like 'a tree that yielded two kinds of fruit': it not only facilitated literacy but also helped villagers to achieve proper Mandarin pronunciation.

In April 1960, the Central Committee endorsed Wanrong's experience, claiming that Wanrong had successfully solved the 'two great problems of the literacy movement': preventing the widespread phenomenon of peasants relapsing (*fumang* or *huisheng*) into illiteracy as soon as they ceased to attend literacy classes, and providing a learning method that enabled those with basic literacy to consolidate and improve their reading skills without the continued presence of teachers. Wanrong's experience was hailed as a 'shortcut' (*jiejing*) to literacy, to be emulated across the country.[30] The use of Mandarin-based pinyin in the literacy movement served different purposes, however, depending on the region. Within the broadly defined Mandarin-speaking areas that accounted for 70 per cent of China's population, pinyin was promoted mainly for the purposes of indicating standard Beijing pronunciation and facilitating reading skills. But in Guangdong and other non-Mandarin-speaking areas, the promotion of pinyin was expressly linked to the centre's aim of replacing local dialects with a unified national standard.[31]

The use of Mandarin-based pinyin in Guangdong did not, however, make it either easier or quicker for dialect speakers to become literate. On the contrary, it made it more difficult. In the Mandarin-speaking regions of the north and southwest, phonetic writing was at least based on a form of speech broadly familiar in pronunciation and grammatical patterns. But for dialect speakers in Guangdong as elsewhere, the use of Mandarin-based pinyin in literacy instruction imposed a double burden. First, there was the burden, shared by all students of pinyin, of having to become familiar with a thoroughly alien form of script that was completely without historical and cultural roots in the society into which it was suddenly and forcibly implanted. Guangdong villagers referred to the strange and squiggly looking symbols of pinyin as 'chicken-guts letters' (*jichang zi*) and 'foreign writing' (*yangwen*).[32] Then there was the additional burden of learning to pronounce these symbols in a form of speech that was also essentially 'foreign,' based on utterly different sounds and grammatical constructions. That Chinese leaders actually promoted this method as a 'shortcut' to literacy stands as one of the most brazen miscalculations in the history of PRC literacy education. So, too, does the statement by H.S. Bhola, writing for UNESCO, that the use of Mandarin in literacy education in China 'received widespread acceptance throughout the country and among groups of all ages.'[33] In fact, Guangdong villagers and political leaders alike openly resisted these efforts to impose an artificial linguistic environment.

Official resistance centred on an effort to revive the party's pre-1944 policy of promoting dialect-based phonetic schemes as the basis for literacy education in the province. Such schemes were, as previously noted, strictly forbidden after 1949; according to DeFrancis, even the possibility of separate alphabetic treatment for regional dialects became a 'virtually tabooed subject' after 1949.[34] Yet such schemes did appear in Guangdong during the late 1950s. A leading member of the PRC Language Reform Committee has recently said that such schemes were drawn up by a renegade 'group of linguists in Guangdong' but were 'actually not used at all.'[35] In fact, not only were the schemes implemented in Guangdong, they were also personally endorsed by the most senior Communist Party officials in the province, who advocated their use in open defiance of Beijing.

In June 1960, six months after the Wanrong conference, the Guangdong provincial party secretary, Qu Mengjue, quietly announced that Guangdong 'might' undertake 'some experiments' with dialect-based phonetic alphabets in Hakka-, Chaozhou-, and Hainan-speaking areas in order to see whether such alphabets could form a basis for literacy education given the 'complicated linguistic features' of Guangdong. Two months later, as the national campaign to emulate Wanrong got under way, another leading member of the Guangdong party committee, Che Mu, published a strenuous rebuttal of the Wanrong model entitled 'Why We Should Use Dialect Phonetic Alphabets for Literacy.' Che pointed out that Mandarin-based pinyin contained many letters representing sounds that did not even exist in Guangdong dialects, such as *zh*, *ch*, *sh*, *r*, *e*, and *u*, among others. How, then, could Guangdong villagers be expected to learn these letters easily when the sounds they represented were as unfamiliar as the symbols themselves? Guangdong had therefore decided to fashion its own pinyin schemes based on the four major dialects.[36] Without specifically referring to it, Che Mu resurrected the debate that had taken place at Yanan two decades earlier over the legitimacy of dialect-based writing as a 'transitional' form before the eventual universalization of *putonghua*.

Just as the Yanan CCP had accepted the use of dialect-based romanization schemes as necessary 'transitional' forms, Che Mu also argued for the temporary necessity of a 'two-step' (*liangbu zou*) method for cultivating literacy in Guangdong. Persons would first achieve the state's minimum literacy requirement of 1,500 characters in their own dialect, with the aid of a phonetic alphabet. They would then proceed to the second step, which involved gradually learning *Hanyu pinyin* and Mandarin in spare-time evening schools. Che was careful to defend this approach as not only necessary but also appropriate under Guangdong's complex linguistic circumstances, and he was adamant that Guangdong's unilateral language policy in no way conflicted with the central government's long-term aim of replacing dialect speech with Mandarin.

More than a little symbolism appears to have been intended in the place that Guangdong leaders chose to showcase their defiant effort. The small Cantonese village of Sanyuanli outside Guangzhou was known to all Chinese for its heroic resistance to British invaders at the time of the Opium War, and the village was virtually synonymous with patriotism in China. In its new role as a literacy model, Sanyuanli was held up by the Guangdong government as the province's proof of the power of its new 'magic weapon' (*fabao*) in the fight against illiteracy, dialect-based phonetic writing. In late 1960, the provincial education bureau proceeded to publish dialect pinyin schemes for the province's four main regional dialects.[37]

It quickly became apparent, however, that the various dialect pinyin schemes were overwhelmed by difficulties of phonetic representation, as well as by the sheer degree of subdialect diversity in the areas for which they were intended. Part of the difficulty stemmed from an attempt to limit the schemes to letters used in official *Hanyu pinyin*. This meant that dialect sounds not present in Mandarin, of which there were an abundance, had to be represented by the awkward and frequently inadequate method of combining letters used in *Hanyu pinyin* and by additional diacritical markings. Thus, the Cantonese scheme incorporated diacritical markings on the letters e and o in order to represent sounds absent from Mandarin. As an added complication, the sounds represented by z, c, and s were indistinguishable in the Cantonese dialect from j, q, and x respectively. This in turn imposed the additional burden on writers of having to decide which letter to represent on the basis of the letter that followed.

Such complexities represented only part of the problem, however. More serious was the fact that the four basic regional dialect schemes concealed a bewildering diversity of subdialects with varying degrees of resemblance to one another in terms of pronunciation and grammatical structure. Thus, for example, the Hakka pinyin scheme was based on the main variant of Hakka spoken in Meixian county and had to be repeatedly modified for use in other Hakka-speaking parts of the province. Similarly, the Chaozhou scheme was based upon Shantou speech and had to be modified for use in subdialect areas such as Chaoan, Denghai, Puning, and other Chaozhou-speaking counties. The Hainan scheme was based upon the version spoken in Wenchang county and had to be altered for use in other areas of the island. The degree of subdialect variation was even greater among Cantonese speakers, who represented the largest single group of dialect speakers in the province. The made-in-Guangdong dialect schemes were thus every bit as artificial as the one made in Beijing.

By late 1960, the literacy campaign in Guangdong and all across China was collapsing under the weight of its own errors and the catastrophic economic failure of the Great Leap Forward. The Central Committee, which shunted Mao and his supporters onto the sidelines of political authority in mid-1960, embarked on a series of measures to restore order as the spectre of famine loomed.[38] In the field of literacy education, the committee took the unprecedented step of removing responsibility for literacy education from linguistic experimenters and placing it in the hands of local agricultural bureaus, whose main concern was to increase the food supply. Shortly afterward, in November 1960, Chen Ziyun, vice-director of the Guangdong Bureau of Education, announced that Guangdong was waiving the dialect pinyin literacy requirement for those who already knew at least 700 characters, as well as for anyone who 'found it difficult' to master roman letters.[39]

At the same time, Mandarin requirements were raised for members of the village elite – brigade cadres, militia leaders, Youth League members, and others – as part of the effort to restore central control.[40] Knowledge of Mandarin was reaffirmed as a badge of elite status, as it was traditionally among those who ruled the village in the name of the state. After 1961, the phonetic-reading movement faded for the most part, continuing to form the basis for adult literacy instruction only in individual localities with the backing of local authorities. The villagers of Wanrong revived their phonetic-reading movement following the Cultural Revolution, but the 'Wanrong model' never again achieved national status. In the meantime, the state's quest to spread Mandarin among peasants and elites in rural Guangdong continued. My own research in Guangdong villages during the late 1980s revealed that many older village and township cadres in the areas I visited spoke Mandarin poorly or not at all. Inevitably, this was a source of embarrassment. But it was also, more importantly, a source of status gradations among rural officials. Ability to speak Mandarin was and is a form of political capital, to be deployed on certain occasions but not others. In instances when one wishes to speak with the authority of the state or the party, Mandarin is a badge of one's qualification to do so. If, on the other hand, one wishes to defend local interests against the state or to show that one has local interests at heart, then local dialects are the preferred means of communication. One cannot but be reminded of the peasants in Eugen Weber's classic study of rural France, who used patois to discuss local politics but switched (if they were able) to French when discussing national issues.[41]

Thus far, we have been examining the literacy campaigns of the late 1950s as a process of state-societal interaction, examining various aspects of the fit – or lack of it – between state aims and popular thought. In the following chapter, we will take up the theme of state-societal interaction from another perspective, focusing on popular uses and expectations of literacy in the collective era. As we will see, these popular expectations were shaped both by long-standing beliefs inscribed in popular culture and re-inforced by local economic circumstances, as well as by the historically un-precedented power of the socialist state to control distribution of the social and economic rewards that literacy conferred.

8
Literacy Expansion and Social Contraction: The Agricultural Middle School Experiment, 1958-65

Did the spread of literacy bring economic, political, and cultural empowerment to Chinese peasants? Or did it merely make possible the opposite: the historically unprecedented entrapment of production team members within bureaucratic webs of communication and control? China's leaders expected it would do both. For them, the creation of a literate rural citizenry was inseparable from the goal of a strong state capable of mobilizing the masses for political and economic tasks. In this chapter I examine how the expansion of literacy paradoxically occurred within the context of a simultaneous contraction of rural social and economic boundaries under collectivization. I will use the concept of literacy expansion and socioeconomic contraction to explain the ways in which literacy in China's collectivized rural society was economically and socially restricted within the closed confines of rural production teams. I focus on the role of the agricultural middle school (*nongye zhongxue*). The agricultural middle school was the most important educational innovation to arise from the Great Leap Forward.[1] It was a prominent fixture of Chinese rural education from 1958 to the early 1960s and again from 1964 to 1966, when it came under severe attack as part of the Cultural Revolution's attempt to discredit the 'double-track educational system' (*liangzhong jiaoyu zhidu*).

From the inception of the agricultural middle school, state leaders sought to invest it with substantial symbolic and economic-political significance. The school would implement the Marxist pedagogical ideal of combining work and study and of uniting education with productive labour (*jiaoyu yu laodong shengchan xiang jiehe*). In doing so, the school would serve the revolution by creating a new kind of socialist worker who was both 'red' and 'expert' (*youhong youzhuan*). The ideological importance attached to the agricultural middle school was combined with a strong economic argument in favour of its existence. By emphasizing self-reliance through the productive labours of students and their teachers, the agricultural middle school would form the basis for a rapid expansion of rural middle school education at minimal cost to the state. And since graduates would be trained to serve their local communities, the agricultural middle schools would not add to the already serious oversupply of educated job-seekers in the cities. To put in another way, the agricultural middle school would serve as an outlet for the literate aspirations of peasant children who were largely excluded from participating in the urban state school system – where the opportunities for real social advancement were to be found. The agricultural middle schools offered children of peasant families the chance for a limited form of social mobility, within the confines of the collective. Lastly, the agricultural middle schools were envisioned as future centres of scientific experimentation and technical innovation in rural areas. This vision was fraught with latent tension, however, for it implied the prospect of a new literate elite emerging in the countryside whose source of power and prestige – scientific and technical knowledge – was independent of the Communist Party. It was one thing to impart basic literacy focused on the ability to read and record collective labour assignments. It was potentially quite another matter to nurture and entrust a cadre of rural scientists and technicians to creatively transform the countryside. As Kenneth Levine observes, the inculcation of mass 'functional' literacies that emphasize elementary reading skills and are adequate to address only a restricted range of printed materials (such as instructions, forms, form letters, and the like) can often serve merely to 'reproduce or further institutionalize existing social arrangements.' Higher-level writing competencies, however, are capable of 'initiating change [because] ... writing conveys and records innovation, dissent, and criticism; above all, it can give access to political mechanisms and the political process.'[2] The CCP thus regarded the training of school graduates who were 'both expert and red' as not only ideologically important but politically imperative. The agricultural middle school experiment revealed not only the Communist Party's aspirations but also its anxieties over the potentially empowering effects of literacy.

In order to grasp the full social and political significance of the agricultural middle school experiment, we must begin by examining the social and economic context in which the expansion of literacy and rural education took place during the collective era. The expectation of a quick transition to universal 'workpoint' literacy was shattered with the failure of the Great Leap Forward by 1960. The rural people's communes that emerged during the Great Leap, however, remained intact as the basis of rural social organization.[3] As such, the collective system shaped the social construction and popular expectations of literacy among rural residents for more than two decades, down to the time of its dissolution in the early 1980s.

Contraction of the Village under Collectivization
The changes in land tenure that began with land reform in 1949 and

culminated with the formation of rural people's communes in 1958 brought about a revolution in rural Chinese social organization that went well beyond the immediate economic issues of land ownership and redistribution. They also revolutionized the relationship between villagers and the state. Historically, the state-society relationship in Guangdong was mediated by supra-village networks of economic, religious, and political affiliation dominated by local elites. For villagers who participated in these networks, they were sources of involvement and identification with wider economic, social, and even cultural environments whose boundaries extended well beyond the village. For the state, such networks constituted the social tissues through which it was forced to negotiate or 'broker' its authority in local society. Elimination of these intermediate networks and the elites that controlled them in the 1950s represented a crucial historical change in state-society relations, paving the way for the construction of a new rural political economy based on farm collectivization.[4]

Two features of the new political economy stood out. First, the state now confronted villagers directly, in their collectives. Second, the social and economic horizons of peasants in production teams were circumscribed to a degree that was unprecedented in Chinese history since the breakdown of feudal manors in the Tang period. The 'liberated' Chinese peasant was much less free, socially and economically, than his or her forebears under the free-wheeling societies of late-imperial and republican China. The late-imperial state was able to regulate social mobility to an extent through manipulation of examination quotas and, indeed, by the social appeal of the examination system itself. But in a society with a thriving free market in land and extraordinary population pressures, the imperial state was largely powerless when it came to controlling the geographic mobility of its peasant subjects – witness the spectacular internal and external peasant migrations of the late-imperial period, to the exasperation of Qing emperors. By contrast, the post-1949 state, through a series of extraordinary administrative measures, succeeded in turning the collective system into a powerful instrument for controlling not only peasants' geographic mobility but their social mobility as well.

The two were closely linked. As early as 1953, communist writers were beginning to express consternation over the political consequences of the uncontrolled movement of peasants into cities. Some even cited the Qing-dynasty scholar-official Guo Tinglin's admonition that, 'when the masses dwell in the villages, order prevails; when the masses flock to the cities, disorder prevails.'[5] In response to these concerns, the first major move toward instituting a system of state controls over population movement occurred in 1953 with the state's monopolization of the grain trade and introduction, shortly afterward, of a rationing system. As Jean Oi explains, the key to the state's power over the peasantry lay in 'China's decision to add the element of rationing to the basic Soviet procurement model and create a monopoly for the purchase and sale of grain (*tonggou tongxiao*). This effectively controlled the distribution of grain and had broad political and economic implications for China. Rationing devalued money as an effective currency of exchange and tied peasants to the countryside and collectives for subsistence. Markets were closed and peasants were confined to closed corporate villages.'[6]

The process by which this transformation took place occurred over several years. In 1954, a household registration system (*hukou dengji*) was erected, far more stringent than the earlier *baojia* system and other pre-twentieth-century methods of population registration used in China. The PRC *hukou* system classified all households as either urban (*jumin hukou* or *feinongye hukou*) or rural (*nongmin hukou* or *nongye hukou*). Initially, the designations were used only to determine state grain entitlements and not to control population movement. Persons with an urban hukou were entitled access to heavily subsidized state grain reserves, while those with a rural hukou were required to obtain their grain stocks from their collectives. Throughout the remainder of the 1950s, peasants continued to move freely to cities, causing the urban population to grow by some 60 per cent between 1949 and 1957. Many were permitted to settle permanently in cities and exchange their rural hukou for the coveted urban status. Starting in 1959, however, hukou status became the basis for a new law of internal migration, which assigned legal residency status on a permanent, inheritable basis. Furthermore, in a society that otherwise continued to be organized on a patrilineal basis, hukou status was inherited maternally. This feature was designed to minimize future increases in the number of urban hukou-holders, since the limited opportunities for acquiring an urban hukou, such as by joining the army or becoming a state official, were more likely to occur among males than females. By assigning hukou status through the maternal parent, the opportunity for upwardly mobile fathers to bequeath urban hukou status to their offspring was eliminated. As a result of these measures, rural-urban migration was virtually eliminated in China by the early 1960s and remained so for the next two decades.[7]

From the state's point of view, the elimination of residential mobility through hukou controls was partly a means of avoiding the politically and socially destabilizing costs of untrammelled rural-urban migration, including a shortage of food and housing stocks, inadequate and overburdened transport, and rising levels of crime and unemployment. Equally important, however, was the fact that hukou controls had become 'intimately bound up with state development policies.'[8] The Stalinist economic model sought to avoid the higher costs of supporting more people at the privileged urban standard of living. Hukou controls were the state's primary mechanism for allocating – and denying – access to a wide range of state-supplied goods and services: schooling, food, housing, employment, consumer products, and other benefits. Following the great famine of 1959-61, moreover, China's leaders came to regard a peasantry bound legally and permanently to the land as the most effective means of guaranteeing the country's precarious food supply.

From the perspective of Guangdong villagers, however, the system imposed historically unprecedented limits on their social and economic activity. As explained by Sulamith Potter and Jack Potter, on the basis of anthropological research conducted in Guangdong's Dongguan county, villagers were now 'structurally immobilized in their teams ... separated from urban residents by legal restrictions creating a caste-like barrier against both geographical and social mobility that was virtually impenetrable.'[9] Moreover, by 'fixing peasants on the land, and having the team control their labour, the Marxist state created a set of serf-like conditions more classically "feudal" than the pre-Liberation society, in which peasants controlled their own labour, and could leave their villages ... [Under collectivization,] villagers were inextricably suspended in the collective social and economic webs spun by the state.' The result was a form of virtual 'bureaucratic serfdom' in which 'the Maoist peasant was fixed as firmly in his [production] team as the serfs of feudal Europe were fixed on the manor.' Likewise, Helen Siu writes that peasants in Xinhui county, Guangdong, discovered in the 1950s that 'the world outside their administratively created collectives had shrunk to a minimum. The team, brigade, and commune gradually became their sole source of economic livelihood, social identity, and political status ... Villages might have retained their physical boundaries, but the social meaning of their existence was being changed from within by the Maoist paradigm.'[10]

The changes just described also had a significant impact on popular motives for acquiring literacy. In pre-1949 Guangdong villages, there were numerous motives for becoming literate. One was a Confucian reverence for learning itself. In addition, there were also practical motives for literacy. One was the examination system, followed after 1905 by modern schooling for urban occupations.[11] A second was the thriving rural commercial economy, which required and encouraged literacy of various kinds and degrees, starting with the simple need to know enough to avoid being cheated in the marketplace. A third was to join the ranks of those whom James Hayes has described as the 'literate specialists' of Cantonese village society: the coterie of geomancers, fortune tellers, herbal doctors, and assorted other literate masters whose specialized knowledge of written texts was an essential aspect of village social and religious life and the transmission of culture.[12]

After 1949, these traditional stimuli to literacy were either eliminated or driven underground. Literate specialists were denounced and forced to renounce their former 'feudal' occupations. Collectivization abolished the commercial motive for literacy, as private commerce all but disappeared save for the limited and closely regulated exchange of a few household 'sideline' products (*fuye*). The *hukou* system made urban state schools – which were always remote from villagers – effectively out of the reach of most production team children. Under the collective system, there were only three possible means for peasants to break through the castelike barrier that separated them from urban residents. One was to join the Communist Party, a second was to join the army, and a third was to gain entry to the state school system. Of the three, entrance to state schools appears to have been the most rare.[13] Literacy and education *were* means of advancement under the collective system – but only within the closed corporate confines of the production team or brigade.

Literacy as a Means of Restricted Social Mobility within Collectives

Collectivization created two new strata of rural managers. One was the political leadership, composed of team and brigade leaders and party secretaries. The other consisted of the various administrators, technicians, and clerks who staffed the collective's administrative and technical bureaucracy. The former group wielded political power, but literacy for them was less important for garnering popular support and legitimacy than other personal qualities, such as charisma, the ability to maintain 'good feelings' (*ganqing*) with others and to dispense patronage, dedication to community welfare or expert knowledge of farming. As we saw in Chapter 3, this stratum of political leaders was drawn mainly from the ranks of illiterate poor peasant activists who were recruited into the party-state structure during land reform. With collectivization, many of these 'land reform cadres' (*tugai ganbu*) became team and brigade leaders. They remained in these positions until the 1970s, when they were succeeded by a new generation of better-educated middle school graduates.[14]

In contrast, the second stratum of rural managers was defined by their literate abilities. Bureaucratization of village and township economies enlarged local occupational hierarchies and called into existence a new stratum of literate functionaries who staffed the collective's administrative and technical organs. In this way, collectivization replaced the old village literate order of classically educated scholars, merchants, and assorted ritual specialists with a new literate cadre of team accountants, bookkeepers, workpoint recorders, cashiers, storehouse keepers, finance deputies, and various other 'technical personnel' (*jishu renyuan*) responsible for the collective's economic functions.

In the basic-level production team (*shengchan dui*) – equivalent to the former village – the most critical literate functionaries were the accountants and record keepers. Among the eight or so key functionaries who normally administered team affairs, at least five were predominantly concerned with accounting and record keeping. They included the deputy for finance and economy, cashier, storehouse keeper, accountant, and workpoint recorder. Most important were the accountant and workpoint recorder. The latter was responsible not only for keeping records of the team members' labour contributions but also for going personally to the fields on a daily basis to certify that the labour tasks assigned to individual team members were completed according to agreed-upon standards. The workpoint recorder then entered the appropriate workpoints for each team member in his record book for the accountant's use. The accountant's job was perhaps the most onerous and difficult of all. It was the accountant who assumed overall responsibility for managing the team's income and redistributing members' proceeds. The latter was especially onerous due to the complexity of the accounting procedures employed. Since teams endeavoured to distribute workpoints as equitably as possible, and since team members were equally set on receiving their fair share, extremely elaborate accounting procedures were used to ensure maximum fairness for all concerned, procedures that far surpassed those necessary in any small- to medium-sized privately owned enterprise.[15]

Beyond the basic-level production team, the next level of commune administration was the production brigade (*shengchan dadui*), a mainly administrative unit where the commune's social welfare functions were based. The production brigade supported a sizeable literate bureaucracy of secondary and tertiary graduates responsible for running middle schools, hospitals, clinics, agricultural research, and the like. The next and highest level of commune administration was the commune headquarters, a purely administrative unit. The commune level was the site at which state bureaucracy and commune administration intersected and where the two 'castes' of urban and rural residents met. Thus, some commune-level officials were state cadres (*guojia ganbu*) who possessed the coveted urban residency status and its attendant privileges, including access to urban state schools, while others were collective cadres (*jiti ganbu*), tied permanently to the collective.

It was here, in terms of staffing the closed occupational structure of team, brigade, and commune, that literacy under the collective system assumed its greatest importance. In the cellularized rural society of production teams and brigades to which peasants were forcibly confined, literacy offered one of the only prospects for restricted social mobility within the collective. It has been argued that socialist systems, by eliminating the private economic sector, tend to foster an especially close motivational link between education and state service.[16] In China, of course, the link between education and state service was a central feature of the Confucian tradition. Ironically, collectivization may actually have imparted new significance to the traditional notion that one studied in order to become an official (*dushu zuoguan*).

What is especially significant is that the Chinese socialist state seems not only to have recognized this irony but also to have promoted the notion as a way of stimulating popular demand for literacy in the collectives. With collectivization, said one writer, peasants would no longer regard the pursuit of literacy as a 'dead angle' (*sijiao*) leading nowhere. Instead, noted another, collectivization had stimulated young people's enthusiasm for 'studying to become one of the three new kinds of rural personnel' (*xuexi dang sanyuan*) – accountants, technicians, and tractor operators. Local Youth League branches subsequently set up 'Three Kinds of Personnel Night Schools' (*sanyuan yexiao*) to train such persons across the country.[17] It was in this context that the agricultural middle schools were conceived in 1958 as a magnet for attracting the literate aspirations of rural youth.

Agricultural Middle School Experiment
The agricultural middle schools were intended to serve as the key educational institutions for staffing the administrative and technical bureaucracies of communes. In early 1958, Liu Shaoqi called for the formalization of a 'double-track education system' (*liangzhong jiaoyu zhidu*) to satisfy the country's need for 'two kinds of labour': a small corps of highly trained experts to lead the modernization effort, and a large pool of citizens with basic education oriented to local needs. The former would be educated in the urban, state-run school system, while the latter would attend rural minban schools financed and operated by collectives. While the state schools were to retain an academic focus, the minban schools were to emphasize 'local production knowledge.' And while the state schools were to operate on a full-time basis, rural minban schools were to be run on a basis of 'half-work, half-study' (*bangong bandu*). As one Guangdong writer put it in 1960, rural work-study schools imparted basic literacy and production knowledge, but it was the responsibility of the urban state schools to 'lead our country's march towards a world class advanced scientific level.'[18]

The double-track model announced by Liu in 1958 upheld the 1953 decision to restrict state educational funding to urban academic schools while leaving rural areas to finance their own schooling. But it also added to that earlier decision in two important ways. First, it contributed the additional feature of combined work-study, thereby resuscitating a concept whose roots in Chinese educational reform stretched back to the early part of the century.[19] Different sections of the party supported the work-study concept for different reasons. Maoists emphasized its promise of dissolving the distinction between mental and manual labour and sought to extend the concept to the state schools as well. Others emphasized more the economic advantages of work-study, particularly the savings in investment to the state. Second, the double-track model sought to elevate the concept of 'two kinds of education' to a long-term strategy for national development. What is especially crucial for our purposes is that the evaluation of the double-track model as a long-term developmental strategy coincided with the elimination of physical and social mobility through *hukou* controls and the creation of two separate 'castes' of rural and urban residents. Educational ideology was thus an integral component in the structural immobilization of rural residents from the late 1950s. The enshrinement of this social schism as a hallowed principle of state educational policy in 1958 was like a political charge waiting to be detonated. It would take about eight years – until the Cultural Revolution – for it to explode.

Liu Shaoqi identified four major 'contradictions' constraining the growth of Chinese mass education that necessitated the creation of a double-track system.[20] The first contradiction, which was potentially destabilizing, was rising demand of rural primary school graduates for further education. 'Our country shouldn't fear having too many intellectuals, or too many schools,' Liu is reputed to have said in response to critics who complained that basic schooling had increased too rapidly since 1949 relative to the economy's capacity to absorb graduates; 'what we ought to fear are too few schools.' Growth in middle school education had failed to keep pace with the much more rapid expansion of primary schooling in the 1950s, leading to what educational planners frequently described as the 'tense problem' of primary graduates unable to advance to further study. As Education Minister Lu Dingyi lamented, 'Every year, the number of senior primary school graduates is more and more, but the regular middle schools are unable to absorb them all.'[21] Between 1952 and 1957, the number of primary school graduates across the country more than tripled to just under 5 million, but only 44 per cent of them advanced to junior middle school in 1957.[22] In Guangdong, growth in middle school education was especially sluggish during this period; in 1956, there were just 153,000 junior middle school students in the province – around the same as in 1946 and only slightly more than the 140,000 students enrolled in 1949.[23]

The problem was that large-scale government-funded expansion of rural middle school education to satisfy this need would have constituted an intolerable burden on state finances given the steadfast commitment of all sections of the party leadership, Maoists included, to a Stalinist fiscal regime of privileged urban development.[24] Thus, in order to 'reduce the state's burden' (*jianqing guojia de fudan*), Liu called for a sharp increase in collective-sponsored minban middle school education operated on a work-study (*qingong jianxue*) basis.

The second contradiction involved the problem of school graduates who were inadequately equipped – psychologically or in terms of skills – for life in the village. Since the majority of primary and middle school graduates did not advance to further study, a purely academic education was unsuitable for them. Work-study would better prepare the majority of school graduates to return to their villages with needed skills and commitment.

The third contradiction Liu cited was the problem of universalizing rural education. Once again, the crux of the problem was fiscal. The work-study formula promised universalization of rural school education without diverting state funds from the privileged urban sector. Lu Dingyi pointed out that it cost the state more than 180 yuan per year to educate a student in a state middle school, compared with only ten yuan per year to educate the same student in a locally sponsored agricultural middle school. As Lu explained, without the double-track system, 'Our country would find it very difficult to institute universal primary and secondary education and would have no hope at all of instituting universal higher education, because the state has no way of carrying the huge burden of expenditure involved without heavy damage to production.'[25]

The fourth contradiction involved the need for greater 'ideological and moral education' as part of the process for preparing school graduates to return to the agricultural sector. Work-study would instil proletarian consciousness and capacity for engaging equally in both mental and manual labour, without preference or distinction.

The agricultural middle school was to be the centrepiece of the work-study movement in rural education. The schools, which were established by communes, recruited primary school graduates between the ages of thirteen and sixteen for a three-year program of politics, mathematics, language and literature, as well as courses in animal husbandry, soil fertilization, crop planting, crop care, and other technical subjects. The schools maintained their own experimental plots, provided by the commune, where students were to earn income to support the school while striking scientific and technical advances to benefit the commune. As much as possible, curricula in the schools were to be integrated with local farming practices.[26]

In addition to the work-study rationale provided by Liu Shaoqi, agricultural middle schools were clearly intended to serve several other purposes as well. Guangdong authorities openly expressed their hope that the agricultural middle schools would alleviate popular dissatisfaction with the structural inequity of the double-track system by providing graduates with opportunities for limited upward mobility. This aspect of the agricultural middle school calls into question oft-repeated claims that the schools aimed to abolish distinctions between mental and manual labour. On the contrary, it seems, the schools' promoters sometimes endeavoured to preserve that distinction as a way of raising the schools' prestige in local society. Local and central state authorities alike chose to measure the schools' success in terms of the number of graduates who left the fields for bureaucratic postings. Thus, Hetang agricultural middle school in Xinhui county, one of the province's leading models, was the subject of a joint survey by the Ministry of Education and the Guangdong education bureau that portrayed Hetang's success primarily in terms of the social mobility achievements of its graduates. The survey emphasized that, out of 350 students graduated from the school, a fifth went on to higher education, while more than half of the remaining 280 were employed by the commune in various non-labour management positions as accountants, workpoint recorders, and statistical personnel, and seventeen had become team leaders.[27] In another instance, local authorities compiled a list of the social mobility achievements of the more than 500 graduates of a school in Xinhui, of whom 155 had gone on to higher education and ninety-seven had been assigned to work as accountants, clerks, and record keepers in supply and marketing co-ops, as managers of pumping stations, and in other positions. Although 300 of the graduates had been sent back to their production teams, the report noted that forty-nine were assigned jobs as accountants, two became assistant team leaders, and one was put in charge of militia. Such claims were not limited to Xinhui. Gulang agricultural middle school in Xingtan commune, Shunde, was said to have produced nearly all of the commune's 'backbone' cadres; of a total of ninety-seven graduates, seventy-eight were working as accountants, veterinarians, grain officials, and officers in the local supply and marketing co-ops.[28]

While agricultural middle schools provided an outlet for the social mobility aspirations of children of peasant families who were cut off from the regular school ladder, some proponents also envisioned the schools as future leading centres for scientific experimentation and innovation in agriculture. They emphasized the 'scientific' mission of the schools and saw them as an opportunity for advanced science and technology to penetrate the countryside. Lu Dingyi and Yang Xiufeng, both of whom served as education minister, were leading exponents of this view. Yang pointed out that in twenty years the Guomindang government had managed to produce a paltry 13,183 agricultural and forestry school graduates, most of whom never set foot in a Chinese village. But the current graduates of agricultural schools would do better, said Yang. They were to settle down in the countryside, taking up work in district-level agricultural extension stations and on collectives and state farms, using their scientific and theoretical knowledge (*kexue lilun zhishi*) to solve the concrete problems of local (*dangdi*) economic development.[29]

It was this future 'scientific' role of the agricultural middle school, rather than the Maoist vision of transforming consciousness through labour, that Guangdong leaders usually chose to highlight. As early as 1956, Lin Liming, vice-secretary of the Guangdong party committee, spoke of what he described as the 'new industrial revolution' currently sweeping the world and of China's urgent need to participate in it by cultivating a corps of scientists who would carry this revolution – symbolized for him by transistors, computers, and nuclear energy – into the countryside. The agricultural middle schools were to be the primary agents of this transformation, developing enhanced seed varieties, innovative farm implements, better fertilizers, more reliable weather prediction, and other scientific improvements. They were to become local 'strongholds' (*judian*) of scientific and technical expertise in the countryside.[30]

The desire to make the agricultural middle schools into self-reliant centres of scientific and technical innovation was offset, however, by a fear that, in becoming thus, the schools might eventually evolve into independent bastions guarded by a new literate elite of scientists and technocrats, who were both outside and beyond the reach of the Communist Party. The schools, it was feared, might be in a position to convert their monopoly of technical and scientific knowledge into power over economic and political life. Apprehensions over the schools not being securely under party control were apparently well founded, even if the grandiose scientific expectations of the schools were not. Statistics gathered in the late 1950s and early 1960s revealed that the Communist Party's grip on the schools was far from complete. An investigation of 875 agricultural middle schools in Guangdong in September 1959, for example, emphasized that only about half of full-time principals were party members, while a mere 3.2 per cent of the schools' full-time teachers had joined the party.[31] Even in Xinhui's Hetang model agricultural middle school, the first party cell was not established until 1962.[32]

Official anxieties that the Communist Party could end up being held hostage by the very rural intelligentsia whom it was striving to cultivate led to two constant policies toward the agricultural middle schools. One was a strict insistence that the schools be firmly under the control of the Communist Party. The party cell was to become a school's 'nucleus' (*hexin*). Wherever possible, principals were to be chosen from among party secretaries in the commune administration. The second was to insist that the schools harbour no sentiment of exclusiveness from their surrounding communities but strive to become perfectly integrated with them. The danger of this not happening seemed real enough. As explained by Qu Mengjue, secretary of the Guangdong party committee, many experts who wielded specialized technical knowledge were prone to holding the defiant view that 'I have my technical expertise and my specialization, and I am not afraid if you [the Communist Party] don't like it. Technology is like an iron rice bowl. Redness is for others who don't have it.'[33]

Popular Attitudes toward the Agricultural Middle Schools

That this anxiety over a new technocratic elite arising through education came to rest so intensely upon the agricultural middle schools was testimony to the extravagant expectations Chinese leaders heaped upon the schools as engines of modernization. In the end, however, both the hopes and the fears were sorely misplaced. Both were founded upon the schools' ideal conception as centres of scientific experimentation and innovation in agriculture. In reality, their role in rural modernization was a great deal less exalted.

For one thing, there was a substantial gap between official expectations of the schools and popular thought toward them. How did rural production team members perceive the schools and the education they offered? Recent work by comparative education specialists has shown that villagers frequently are opposed to government efforts to impose curricula 'relevant' to local needs. Parents often prefer their children to be educated in the regular school system, for social-mobility reasons and the intrinsic benefits of a general education.[34] In socialist China, too, state efforts to make rural education serve local production needs frequently collided with popular expectations of literacy and schooling. Moreover, in China this popular resistance appears to have been rooted not only in basic sociological realities arising from the continued poverty of the countryside, which sustained the view that schooling was a means to 'jump over the village gate' (*tiaochu nongmen*), but also in historically based cultural assumptions about what constituted 'schools.' Alexander Woodside has pointed out that schools are historically among the most heavily ritualized of Chinese social institutions.[35] For this reason, Woodside argues, there was historically in China a strong 'symbolic dissociation' between schools and more mundane forms of vocational instruction. The ritualized association of schools with the examination system and academic learning precluded use of the term 'school' to describe educational institutions dedicated to more plebeian forms of vocational training. A similar mentality appears to have underwritten popular opposition and/or indifference to the agricultural middle schools and the various other 'irregular' forms of minban schooling organized by rural collectives. Indeed, the dissociation between the academically oriented state schools and the vocational aims of the agricultural middle schools was actually reflected in official ideology itself: whereas state schools were subject to heavily ritualized standards with respect to everything from textbooks and examinations to school size and student-teacher ratios, the operative principle of the agricultural middle schools was to build them 'out of nothing' (*baishou qijia*). As a consequence, the latter were, for the most part, 'tiny, scattered, hastily improvised schools' that averaged only three teachers each.[36] In practical terms, the official exhortation to build schools 'out of nothing' meant that such schools were often quickly set up, without proper equipment or facilities, in abandoned temples, ancestral halls, or, as often happened, in tool sheds, warehouses, and the like.

The glaring difference between these schools and the closely regulated state schools was hardly lost on peasants. Significantly, one of the most common complaints of villagers was that the agricultural middle schools were 'not like real schools' (*buru xuexiao*). The Baita agricultural middle school in Jieyang county, Guangdong, for instance, was set up in an abandoned goose shed because that was all that commune authorities were willing to turn over to the school. Villagers referred to it disparagingly as the 'goose hut middle school' (*eliao zhongxue*). And in Puning county, leaders from seven production teams in the Meitang commune refused outright to turn over land for use by agricultural middle schools on the grounds that 'These educated youth might know a few characters and understand a bit of theory, but they know nothing about farming. We'll be dead without agriculture; how can we risk the team's land by turning it over to these novices to experiment with?' In such instances, the schools were valued neither as centres of academic learning nor as centres of vocational training.[37]

Some schools did manage to win the support of their local communities. Students in one agricultural middle school in Puning used their knowledge of chemistry to help local farmers determine the correct application of an imported ammonia-based fertilizer whose instructions were in a foreign language. In another instance, the Zhongfeng agricultural middle school in Lianyang county developed a new device for transplanting rice as well as a seed drill, vine cutter, and water dispensing mechanism for chicken coops, demonstrating that the schools sometimes did contribute to local agricultural development.

More often, however, the schools were disparaged and scorned by local society for their disappointing results. A 1961 survey of the graduates of Longtian agricultural middle school in Guangdong's Xingning county revealed that many graduates lacked genuine technical skills and even had a poor understanding of the basic principles and practices of farming. Many were unable to perform simple calculations using an abacus or keep accounts. Teachers and students in the school were less interested in scientific experimentation and innovation than they were in growing established sideline crops that could be freely sold to maximize the school's income. Indeed, the problem of schools concentrating on the market opportunities afforded by sideline products was one upon which state leaders frequently commented.[38]

The poor showing of most agricultural middle schools was also reflected in their completion rates. A total of 23,000 agricultural middle school students were recruited in Xingning county, Guangdong, between 1958 and 1965, but only 2,200 – fewer than one-tenth – actually graduated. During 1958-9, many of the schools simply folded in the face of mass dropouts, forcing Xingning county officials to convene a conference to discuss the schools' future. The conference revealed that two charges were most frequently levelled at the schools: they were inferior to regular state-run schools, and they did not teach useful knowledge. The agricultural middle schools in Xingning survived, but mainly as a result of pressure from above. In 1961, however, in the midst of the post-Great Leap Forward famine, county authorities announced plans to close down the schools, on the ground that they were competing for urgently needed agricultural labour. In the end, they spared the schools but forced all students aged sixteen and over to withdraw to their production teams. In 1963 the debate over the schools' future flared yet again, this time over whether they ought to drop their technical and vocational orientation, adopt an academic focus, and seek to emulate the state schools. This kind of constantly recurring debate over whether or not the schools served any worthwhile purpose was replicated throughout the province and country.[39]

The cherished notion that schools could be fashioned from scratch by dint of local effort – with just a shed, a few benches, some rudimentary writing utensils, and the enormous dedication of teachers and students – was a product of the CCP's wartime experience, which Mao and others in the party had sought to reinvigorate in the late 1950s and 1960s as the 'Yanan Spirit' in education. But what of the villagers themselves? No doubt some continued to abide by this faith. But for most, the inferior quality of the agricultural middle schools, the fact that they were intended for those denied access to state schools, and the strikingly different career paths of their graduates clearly indicated that the agricultural middle schools were second-rate alternatives and not 'real schools' at all.

That the agricultural middle schools were the product of changing elite educational strategies rather than a genuine reflection of popular values is also illustrated by the erratic fluctuations in their numbers. The first such school was founded in Tianjin in May 1958, and by 1960 the schools came to account for 27 per cent of junior middle school enrolment nationwide. Over the next three years, however, the number fell from 30,000 with 2.9 million students to only 3,700 with a mere 240,000 students. In 1964, the number of agricultural middle schools surged again, from 3,600 in 1963 to 13,000 in 1964, and to over 54,000 in 1965, while total enrolment rose from 240,000 in 1963 to 3.16 million in 1965. By early 1966, the schools accounted for more than one-quarter of all middle school enrolment in China.[40]

Guangdong's agricultural middle schools also rose and fell according to policy shifts in Beijing. In 1958, there were around 1,000 agricultural middle schools in Guangdong, with an enrolment of approximately 80,000, but by 1962, the number had fallen to only 150 schools and 11,000-15,000 students. Enrolment then soared to 84,000 in 1964, and reached 200,000 in 1965. Enrolment peaked at 240,000 in early 1966, when agricultural middle schools accounted for 40 per cent of all middle school enrolment in the province. Yet by 1972, only seven of the schools remained, with a mere 700 students.[41]

When the agricultural middle schools were criticized in early 1966 as part of the Cultural Revolution's unfolding attack on education, it was not because they had become the bastions of a powerful new technocratic elite. It was because they were accused of consigning the children of rural production team families to inferior work-study education, while the children of urban residents and the political elite attended the 'real' state-funded schools. The tensions that had been building in the Chinese educational system since the early 1950s over the social distribution of schooling were about to burst forth with a vengeance.

9
The Cultural Revolution

The Cultural Revolution erupted in the spring of 1966. Significantly, the opening shots in Guangdong were fired in the province's leading educational journal. The target was the lyrics of a revolutionary song published by *Guangdong Education*, the official journal of the provincial education bureau. In a self-criticism that appeared in the journal's May 1966 issue, the editors admitted to having glossed over several 'gross errors' in the song's lyrics when they made their original decision to publish it. The mistakes reflected not just a bad choice of words, they confessed, but also a seriously flawed understanding of politics, for the song was now recognized as a veiled criticism of Mao's disastrous policies during the Great Leap Forward.[1] Critics of the journal were unsatisfied, however. In the following issue, two members of the political education department of Huanan Teachers' College in Guangzhou led a scathing attack on the journal. Entitled 'Who Does Guangdong Education Serve?' the article roundly criticized *Guangdong jiaoyu* for its 'sloppy work' in publishing the conspiratorial song. In addition, the article went on to attack the journal's editors for refusing to comment on the future Cultural Revolution's leader Yao Wenyuan's sharp rebuke of historian and playwright Wu Han's recent play, 'Hai Rui Dismissed from Office.' Wu's metaphorical play relied on historical allusions to denounce Mao's 1959 purge of Defence Minister Peng Dehuai after Peng criticized Mao's Great Leap policies for heaping economic hardship on the peasantry. This neglect, the critics said, proved that the journal had become 'seriously divorced from politics' and had failed to carry out Chairman Mao's directives on education.[2] Days later, the journal ceased publication. The Cultural Revolution had begun.

In order to understand the Cultural Revolution's impact on literacy and rural education, we need to go back to the early 1960s and the lessons that Chinese leaders drew from the failure of the Great Leap Forward. The most important change in literacy strategy following the Great Leap Forward was a shift in emphasis from adult literacy campaigns to improvement and expansion of the school system. The shift signalled a growing recognition that adult literacy campaigns were at best a rearguard action in the struggle against illiteracy and that the only effective long-term solution to the problem lay in the achievement of universal schooling. Adult literacy efforts virtually ceased for two full years following the Great Leap. The retrenchment was partly a response to the severe economic crisis of the early 1960s. Yet it also signified a recognition of the literacy campaign's failure – as demonstrated by the 40 per cent or so of campaign participants who quickly 'relapsed' into illiteracy – to effect substantial and sustainable improvements in the literacy rate. The number of adults who acquired basic literacy subsequently dropped from an all-time high of 40 million in 1958 to a mere 167,000 in 1962. Adult literacy efforts were not revived on a significant scale until 1964, when they were reintroduced, albeit on a much smaller scale, as part of Mao's attempt to resuscitate rural class struggle.[3]

While the emphasis on adult literacy subsided in the early 1960s, Chinese educational leaders began to pay greater attention to the problem of developing rural school education. Although all could agree on the need to develop rural school education, they disagreed sharply over the means. Professional educators tended, as we saw in previous chapters, to favour a centralized, state-run school system, with uniform standards and curricula, while others favoured a decentralized system modelled on the party's post-1942 Yanan educational reforms. What had emerged, in practice, since the mid-1950s was a hybrid system of urban state-run schools and decentralized, rural minban schools run by collectives. This formula, known as 'walking on two legs' (*liangtiaotui zoulu*), was hailed in the 1950s as a necessary and creative solution to the problem of expanding rural education in a large country with a big peasant population and relatively few fiscal resources.[4]

Minban schooling under the auspices of production teams and brigades expanded dramatically during the late 1950s. As a result, primary school enrolment jumped from 64 million to 84 million from 1957 to 1958. As we saw in Chapter 8, middle school enrolment also expanded dramatically in the form of commune-run agricultural middle schools. Critics maintained, however, that the massive increase in minban enrolment during the late 1950s had been accompanied by an equally massive deterioration of educational standards and quality. With Mao relegated to a lesser position of authority for his role in the Great Leap disaster, the post-Leap leadership centred on Liu Shaoqi and Deng Xiaoping sought a restoration of academic quality and standards. At the same time, the severe economic crisis of the early 1960s necessitated severe retrenchments in all sectors of the educational system.

Thus, in the early 1960s, state schools were purged of the productive labour requirements imposed in the late 1950s, and greater emphasis was placed upon academic studies and examination results. 'Keypoint schools' (*zhongdian xuexiao*), established systematically since 1959 (but with origins dating back to the Yanan educational reforms of 1942), whereby the best resources and students were concentrated in a network of elite schools stretching from kindergarten to university, were reaffirmed and strengthened. In December 1962, Zhou Enlai proclaimed the centrality of gongban (state) schools in the PRC educational system. He advised that, while minban schools would continue to be established in the future, it was 'incorrect to take them as the policy' (*zuowei fangxiang budui le*). Minban schools located in the cities were either closed or incorporated into the state sector. Rural minban schools that did not meet state standards were closed.[5]

The result was a massive decline in minban enrolment in the early 1960s. Total primary school enrolment fell by at least 20 million nationwide between 1959 and 1962, from 91 million to 69 million. In Guangdong, primary school enrolment fell from a reported 86 per cent of school-age children in 1960 to only 69 per cent in 1963. Altogether, between 1960 and 1961, a total of 170,000 primary pupils in Guangdong were taken out of school and sent back to their production teams in order 'to reduce the number of persons dependent on commodity grain.' In Jiangping commune, on Manwei Island, the percentage of school-age children attending primary school was actually lower in 1963 than it had been a decade earlier in 1954. Cutbacks were equally severe in the middle school sector. As noted in the previous chapter, the number of agricultural middle school students in Guangdong fell from 150,000 in 1958 to a mere 15,300 in 1963. State-run middle schools were hit equally hard. In 1960-1, enrolment in state-sponsored middle schools in Guangdong fell by 122,000, from 297,000 to 175,000.[6]

In 1963, the Chinese press began to publish a large number of rural educational surveys purporting to demonstrate that, in addition to a declining rate of primary school attendance overall, the problem of non-attendance and dropouts was greatest among the poorest sector of rural society. Particular attention was drawn in these reports to the educational plight of the children of peasant families who had been classified during the land reform as 'poor and lower middle peasants' (*pinxia zhongnong*). A 1964 survey of school attendance in the Dongan commune in Guangdong's Gaozhou county, for example, claimed that 49 per cent of school-age children were not attending primary school, of which fully 84 per cent were children of poor and lower middle peasants. Reports like these, replicated across the country, formed the basis for a large-scale campaign to revitalize and expand the importance of minban schooling and work-study.[7]

Half-Farming, Half-Study Primary Schools
In early 1964, Liu Shaoqi reiterated the need for a 'dual track education

system' (*liangzhong jiaoyu zhidu*). One track would consist of the urban, academically oriented, state-sponsored school system, operating on a full-time basis, whose primary purpose was to train expert talent for China's economic modernization. Alongside it would be a locally financed, vocationally oriented, work-study track for expanding mass education in the rural areas. The two-track formula would thus solve the dual tasks of the educational system to 'elevate' (*tigao*) a group of highly trained experts and to 'popularize' (*puji*) the availability of basic education, especially in the countryside.

Liu's model further envisaged a broadening of the work-study formula to cover not only middle school education, in the form of a revival of the agricultural middle school, but primary schooling as well, in the form of a new rural educational institution to be known as 'half-farming, half-study primary schools' (*bangeng bandu xiaoxue*).[8] The number of such schools rose rapidly following Liu's announcement. Nationally, more than 40 per cent of primary school enrolment in 1965 was in minban schools, of which approximately 20 per cent was in half-farming, half-study schools. By 1965, the primary school enrolment rate reached 85 per cent. The percentage was similar in Guangdong, where, by September 1965, a total of 1.3 million students were enrolled in half-farming, half-study primary schools. This represented 17 per cent of the total primary school population in Guangdong. In the Zhenjiang special prefecture, 45 per cent of primary school students attended minban schools in 1965, of which 29 per cent were enrolled in half-farming, half-study primary schools. Provincewide, the primary school enrolment rate reached 91 per cent by 1965, up from only 63 per cent in 1963 and higher even than the 86 per cent rate claimed in 1959. By 1966, most production teams in Guangdong supported at least one half-farming, half-study primary school.[9] The advent of half-farming, half-study primary schools thus appears to have contributed to a dramatic increase in the availability of rural primary schooling after the severe retrenchments of the early 1960s.

Popular reaction to the schools is difficult to measure, but it is clear that many people regarded them as yet another 'temporary wind' (*zhenfeng*). The schools were set up on an ad hoc basis, with students working and studying according to formulas decided upon by local authorities. The work aspect often consisted of performing team tasks, such as tending cattle, undertaking child care, and cleaning, in exchange for workpoints. The academic curriculum was limited to basic literacy. In one school, located in a mountainous area of Xinyi county, the students' families all held sideline contracts to produce bamboo hats for the brigade. Hence, students learned only contract vocabulary.[10] Teachers in the schools were generally poorly qualified and, in hard economic times, often strongly resented. They were described as 'illiterates teaching other illiterates' and as parasites in search of 'rice handouts.' In addition, the schools were sometimes established by local authorities simply as a means of legitimizing the use of child labour. The manager of the Niaoshi state farm in Raoping county, Guangdong, decided to set up a half-farming, half-study primary school rather than expend adult labour on tending the farm's eighty head of cattle. Twenty-three students were selected to attend the school against the wishes of their parents. They tended the farm's cattle and received character lessons during lunch hour.[11]

The half-farming, half-study schools were also criticized by professional educators. Qiu Tian, a member of the teaching research office in the education department of Jiaoling county, described the practical component of the schools' curricula as a sham. He cited the teaching manuals of some schools that instructed children on how to become familiar with the shape of a hoe, its purposes, and how to operate it. This, said Qiu, was pure 'formalism': any child growing up in a rural commune knew such things from daily practice and did not need classroom instruction in them. The party's effort to bring the worlds of education and farming closer together had simply revealed how little party educators themselves actually knew about rural life.[12]

Socialist Education Movement

At the Tenth Plenum of the Eighth Central Committee in 1962, Mao and his supporters sought to reaffirm the doctrine of class struggle as a guiding force in China's revolution. They were particularly opposed to the liberal economic policies adopted in the early 1960s by Liu Shaoqi and Deng Xiaoping. In order to restore agricultural production, the Liu-Deng leadership sanctioned the revival of private plots and periodic markets and allowed production teams to contract production quotas as well as team land to individual families. Fearing that the changes would lead to a restoration of capitalism in the countryside, and anxious to wrest back power, Mao launched a campaign designed to make the countryside the focus of an ideological struggle over the proper values of a socialist society. The Socialist Education Movement began officially in 1962, but its major effect was not felt until several years later.[13]

The Socialist Education Movement relied upon two forces to return politics to peasant education: the People's Liberation Army under the leadership of Lin Biao, and rusticated urban educated youth. The army's involvement in rural education and propaganda work had a long history, as we have seen, dating back to the Red Army's creation in 1927.[14] The role of rusticated youth, however, was new and closely related not only to ideological objectives (the training of a new generation of 'revolutionary successors') but also to practical considerations associated with the contraction of enrolment in higher education in the early 1960s. The tightening of entrance requirements for middle and tertiary education resulted in a significant increase in the number of primary and middle school graduates in the labour market. Since the cities could not absorb all of these graduates, and since the countryside had a chronic shortage of educated personnel, state authorities opted to 'send down' an increasing number of urban graduates to the countryside for work. As early as 1962, Guangdong authorities had proposed that the 100,000 or so urban school graduates nationwide who returned to their rural production teams every year be used to revive the flagging literacy movement.[15] In June 1963, the Central Committee called upon provinces to submit fifteen-year plans for the large-scale transfer of educated urban youth to the countryside. In 1964 alone, some 300,000 educated youth were relocated to rural areas, a number that far surpassed the 100,000 students similarly relocated during 1962-3. It was precisely these sent-down students who were to play a leading role in the Socialist Education Movement as so-called 'Mao Zedong Thought Counsellors.'[16]

The Socialist Education Movement unfolded in two stages. The first, known as the Four Cleanups campaign, was ostensibly aimed at eliminating corruption and the abuse of collective property. The second stage involved organizing production team members into ad hoc literacy classes and recital groups to study the works of Chairman Mao and other revolutionary models. It was in this latter stage of the movement that the educative function rose to the fore. Guangdong set a target of 1 million adults to be enrolled in rural spare-time educational activities in 1964, three-quarters of whom were to be between the ages of fourteen and thirty. Local authorities were also instructed to prepare for the Socialist Education Movement by stepping up literacy work among rural youth. By the following year, nearly 1.5 million adults were enrolled in rural literacy and spare-time education classes, compared with almost none a few years earlier.[17]

Spare-time evening schools, set up by rural production teams, became the chief 'battlegrounds' (zhendi) of the movement. In some counties, the schools were known as 'night schools for communism' (gongchanzhuyi yexiao). The Promote the Proletariat and Exterminate the Capitalists Spare-Time School (xingwu miezi yeyu xuexiao) was established in 1964 in Sihui county by Lu Yubiao, a rusticated youth. Lu set up the school in order to incite struggle against another village youth, Luo Tianrui, whom Lu accused of attempting to seduce the other youths in the village with 'pornographic' books from the old society. Hechun commune, Lianjiang county, was selected as a keypoint area for implementing the movement. Spare-time schools were set up to 'organize the class troops' for struggle and purification, which involved compiling students' family histories (jiapu) in order to identify positive and negative role models. A great deal of emphasis was placed on comparing the prerevolutionary past with the present and, in the case of Guangdong, the 'stinking harbour' of Hong Kong with life in socialist Guangzhou. Students were urged to recognize the world of difference between Kowloon and Shenzhen, even though just a narrow river separated the two.[18]

Guangdong's leading educational journal identified the Socialist Education Movement as a struggle between the 'small morals' (*xiaode*) around which peasant communities traditionally revolved – respect for one's social superiors, deference to authority, family honour, and the maintenance of 'good feelings' between persons – and the 'big morals' (*dade*) that the Central Committee and its educated youth messengers were attempting to instil in peasants.[19] The big morals were concerned not with the maintenance of village harmony but with a grand philosophy of history. They were those that, in Richard Madsen's words, pitted individual farmers 'on various sides of vast struggles that would change the shape of Chinese and indeed world history.' The big morals instructed villagers to think of themselves not as members of a family, village, or lineage but as members of social classes (*jieji*). Classes, in turn, were like 'great modern armies ... knit together like a huge machine' engaged in a 'titanic military struggle.' Enshrining the 'big morals' of class struggle in villagers' consciousness was not always easy, however, for villagers often conceived of class status in ways other than those intended for them. For villagers, as Madsen points out, having a good class label 'was like having an extra supply of money in the old society ... One could use it to extend one's influence within the community, to provide security and honor for one's family, and perhaps to help one's whole community to prosper and thus ensure that one's heritage would be gloriously remembered for generations to come.'[20] The 'small morals' of the village frequently subverted the big morals of the party.

The big morals of the Socialist Education Movement were often represented by Mao's works. One of the most widely used texts during the movement consisted of three essays written by Mao. The essays, known as the 'three constantly read works,' were 'Serve the People,' 'In Memory of Norman Bethune,' and 'The Foolish Old Man Who Moved the Mountain.' Often they were chanted for maximum effect. Chinese novelist Gu Hua provides a vivid description of one such session:

> 'Now, comrades, all hold up your little red books and stand facing the red sun!' Wang boomed, ... then gave a demonstration. Standing to attention, chest out and head thrown back, he gazed into the distance, his left arm at his side, his right elbow bent to clasp the little red book to his heart. He then stood sideways looking at the glorious image and recited: 'First we salute our most respected and beloved great leader, great teacher, great commander-in-chief, great helmsman, the red sun in our hearts – long life

to him! May he live forever!' ... Wang had raised his little red book level with his head to wave it rhythmically during this incantation ... Carried away by his own splendid performance, his throat hoarse, his eyes filled with hot tears, he felt boundless strength and pride.[21]

The relationship of orality to writing in the Socialist Education Movement lay in the almost sacred power ascribed to revolutionary texts, which made their recitation a form of ritual in itself. Texts were treated as *'Writuals*, requiring listeners to become readers. Doing so put education at the center of the redeeming project.'[22] It also granted the educated youth, who were appointed official Mao Zedong Thought Counsellors (*Mao Zedong sixiang fudao yuan*) because of their superior knowledge of the canonical writings, a privileged role in the movement. As explained by Richard Madsen, the Maoist paradigm for moral discourse 'can lead to coherent moral discussion only if all members of a group are intimately familiar with the details of the authoritative teaching ... Such a system ... works best among people who are literate and have the time to study the authoritative writings thoroughly. The way is then open for such people to claim that they form a moral aristocracy within communities of illiterates.' If Mao Zedong Thought Counsellors claimed moral prestige by virtue of their access to Mao's writings, the texts themselves were becoming imbued with even greater powers. Under the Socialist Education Movement, Mao's thought was treated not only as an increasingly important guide to correct political action but also 'a sacred Word, awesome and magically powerful.'[23] Guangdong schoolteacher Li Wenhui, for example, claimed to have achieved extraordinary results when growing vegetables as a result of reading Mao's essay 'In Memory of Norman Bethune.' On the other hand, however, not everyone appears to have been as convinced of the miraculous powers of Mao's thought. At least one Guangdong peasant claimed that reading Mao's works to solve practical problems was even 'more useless than taking a correspondence course.'[24]

Cultural Revolution Attack on Education

The Socialist Education Movement gave way to the Cultural Revolution in the spring of 1966. Tensions had been gathering for several years in the country's schools, among students, and among the leadership as Maoists struggled with the post-Great Leap leadership of Liu and Deng over basic issues of educational policy. At the middle and tertiary levels of the regular school system, the issue centred on the role of class background versus academic criteria in the competition for school places.[25] An even deeper issue was the bifurcation of the school system as a whole into full-time gongban schools and work-study minban schools, a division that had been a simmering source of tension within the educational system for more than a decade. These tensions might have persisted indefinitely, however, were it not for Mao's attempt beginning in the spring of 1966 to oust his party opponents from power.[26]

The Cultural Revolution's critique of the educational system centred on three key issues surrounding the role of education in a socialist society: who goes to school, what is taught there, and what schools are for.[27] The first criticism maintained that children of 'poor and lower middle peasant' families had been effectively barred from the greater part of the educational ladder as a result of certain institutional features, including the emphasis on examinations, marks, and age limits, as well as tuition and boarding fees and other expenses that the poor could not afford. The second criticism centred on the length of studies, the weight and bookish nature of curricula, and teachers' emphasis on cramming and rote memorization. Too much 'useless' knowledge was being taught. And the third criticism accused the entire educational system of being consumed by Soviet revisionism and bourgeois tendencies. As a result of the pernicious influence of bourgeois educators and revisionists such as Liu Shaoqi, education had become divorced from its real purpose, which was to promote class struggle.

The greatest criticism, however, was reserved for the 'double-track education system' (*liangzhong jiaoyu zhidu*), the blame for which was now heaped entirely on Liu Shaoqi. Liu was accused of promoting, in concert with 'bourgeois educators,' a 'capitalist-style' educational system whereby privileged urban residents and children of cadres attended elite state-run schools while the sons and daughters of peasants and workers were consigned to inferior work-study schools. Mao and his supporters now began to argue that a 'two-line struggle' between Maoists and revisionists headed by Liu Shaoqi had existed ever since the founding of the PRC.[28]

As Suzanne Pepper has shown, however, the Cultural Revolution's indictment of Liu Shaoqi reflected current intraparty struggles rather than long-standing historical differences over educational policy. Liu's 1964 'double-track educational system' was in reality simply a reformulation of Mao's earlier 'walking on two legs' formula, which had been hailed by Mao as a creative solution to the problem of expanding rural education at little cost to the state. The differences between Mao and Liu emerged primarily in the early 1960s, when Mao grew opposed to the heavy emphasis Liu accorded to full-time state schools. Mao was also determined not only to revive the minban sector but also to reintroduce productive labour and ideological requirements in the state schools as well in order to prevent them from becoming bastions of elitism. Liu supported the former objective but was opposed to the latter. He therefore sought, unsuccessfully, to 'promote his own "two kinds of education systems" as a means of circumventing Mao's line,' the strategy being 'to divert Mao's demands for labour and practical training into the work-study stream while leaving the full-day schools unchanged.'[29] As part of Mao's campaign to unseat Liu, however, the Cultural Revolution's polemic sought not only to exaggerate the differences between the two but to push them back in time to the very founding of the PRC. Liu thus became the Maoist symbol of everything that was now judged to have gone wrong in education policy since 1949.

Between 1966 and 1969, the entire administrative structure for education was dismantled and its officials either reassigned or purged. Many of the leading figures who had been involved in the literacy movement – including Lu Dingyi, Qian Chunrui, Dong Chuncai, Lin Feng, Hu Qiaomu, and Ma Xulun – were criticized or condemned as 'counterrevolutionary revisionists.' The Ministry of Education itself was dissolved and not reconstituted until 1975. It was replaced by a Science and Education Group under the nominal control of the Cultural Revolution Group, Mao's 'steering group' for implementing the Cultural Revolution. The Science and Education Group was formally in charge of carrying out Mao's plans for decentralization and deregulation of the educational system. But with the centre in chaos, local officials had to glean whatever policy directions they could through newspaper reports, editorials, and anything else that filtered down to local levels, usually in the form of 'draft' or 'experimental' decisions that reflected the continuing uncertainty at the top. Until the Ministry of Education was reestablished in 1975, schools and adult education activities were administered by local committees comprised of non-educational personnel supervised by student-led Red Guard units, the party, and the army.

Collapse of Literacy Education
The dismantling of the central administrative structure for education brought adult literacy efforts to a grinding halt in 1966. 'During the ten years of chaos anti-illiteracy work was stopped,' is the stock phrase one encounters in official texts on this period. This was not entirely true, for adult literacy education was revived in a limited way beginning in 1972. Yet the verdict reached at the Second National Work Conference on Peasant Education in November 1979 was broadly true: peasant education during the Cultural Revolution 'was seriously ruined, the administrative structure rescinded, full-time cadres dismissed, and work came to a standstill for a long period of time, causing a huge regression.'[30] In Guangdong, the administrative structure for literacy and spare-time education was disbanded and its personnel transferred to other areas. Those adult education activities that continued to exist after 1966 were mounted on a local basis. In Xinxing county, only one commune sponsored literacy classes from 1966 to 1971: the Shuitai commune operated six Red Evening Schools in which 270 youth studied Mao's works. In Panyu, the peasant educational bureaucracy was disbanded in 1966, to be reestablished only in 1977.

Cultural Revolution attitudes toward literacy education varied from initial critiques of the failure of the 'old' educational system to redress the problem of widespread peasant illiteracy to later claims by the Gang of Four that illiteracy no longer existed in China. But the Cultural Revolution's critique of education had relatively little to say about illiteracy per se. It was far more concerned with the alleged defects in the orientation of the entire educational system, especially its overly academic focus. What is important, however, is that Mao's accusation that postrevolutionary Chinese education was excessively bookish did effectively proscribe educative efforts such as basic literacy training, whose purpose was the purely intellectual task of learning to read and write. This could lead to striking conclusions: in 1966 education officials in Guangdong's Xinfeng county declared that 'there was no harm in being illiterate' (*wenmang wuhai*). They also praised Mao's assertions that 'study was useless' (*dushu wuyong*) and that, 'The more knowledge one has, the more reactionary one becomes' (*zhishi yueduo yue fandong*).[31]

Methods of literacy instruction that 'put intellectual development first' (*zhiyu diyi*) were condemned for avoiding politics. This included the traditional method of memorizing individual unrelated characters, which had been heavily criticized by Lin Handa and others during the 1956 literacy campaign but which had been revived since the late 1950s in elite schools such as Beijing's Heishan Beiguan and Jingshan primary schools. Heishan Beiguan developed a modified version of the traditional pedagogy, known as the 'concentrated character recognition method' (*jizhong shizi fa*), that combined the traditional practice of memorizing individual characters with mnemonic methods based on modern psycholinguistics. Students first learned pinyin and then memorized characters grouped together on a phonetic basis. Although it was reputedly highly effective, the method was criticized during the Cultural Revolution for its failure to integrate literacy instruction with political study. Cultural Revolution methods of literacy instruction were to be based on the principle of 'linking together a single red line' (*yi tiao hongxian chuanqilai*). This meant that characters could not be taught individually or in phonetic groups but only in politically meaningful sequences. Thus, for example, the character *bai*, meaning 'white,' could only be taught as part of a sequence of characters, such as Bai Qiuen, Norman Bethune, the Canadian doctor mythologized by Mao for his revolutionary spirit.[32]

As part of the Gang of Four's attempt to revive Cultural Revolution policies in the fields of education and culture, literacy and spare-time educational activities were revived in some areas starting in 1972. Between 1972 and 1974, adult education efforts centred on the creation of 'political evening schools' (*zhengzhi yexiao*). Based on the model experiences of a Tianjin commune brigade, the schools devoted themselves mainly to the study of

Cultural Revolution documents, including the campaign against Confucius and Lin Biao, and to being village forums for denouncing 'the capitalist viewpoint.' In Xinxing county, an organizational structure for adult literacy education was reestablished at the county level in March 1973 after a seven-year hiatus. In 1973, some 6,000 Xinxing peasants were recruited to study in 129 political evening schools set up across the county. The schools' main subjects were 'taking class struggle as the key link' and 'continuing the revolution under the dictatorship of the proletariat.'[33]

In 1975, the Guangdong provincial education bureau convened a conference to discuss the 'three nothings' (*sanwu*) of literacy education in Guangdong: no organizational structure, no personnel, and no activity. The conference agreed on the need to boost literacy enrolments, which subsequently reached 232,000 by the end of 1975.[34] The curricula remained, however, a curious mixture of Cultural Revolution political slogans and simple instructions for daily living. One primer, designed for Yunfu County Red Evening Schools in 1972, included an exhortation by Mao to raise hogs and domestic animals placed alongside illustrated glossaries of the animals, as well as other Mao quotations (such as 'The fundamental way out for agriculture lies in mechanization') alongside illustrated glossaries of tractors, pumps, and vegetable oil presses. A 1973 Shandong literacy primer for use by rural commune members also included Mao quotations, as well as a biography of Chen Yonggui (leader of the Dazhai commune promoted by Maoists in the 1970s as a national model of self-reliance) and Mao's essay 'In Memory of Norman Bethune.' In addition, however, this two-volume primer contained lessons on family planning, household sanitation, kinship terms, letter writing, and dictionary use; a lesson on China's first satellite; and basic geography and history.[35]

The conflation within the same literacy primer of Maoist political slogans and lessons on traditional kinship terms signalled that the Cultural Revolution forces were weakening and that former officials were beginning to regain their influence over education. The Cultural Revolution was formally declared a disaster for rural literacy education at the Second National Work Conference on Peasant Education in November 1979. In Guangdong, it was subsequently estimated that from 1966 to the close of the Cultural Revolution in late 1975, approximately 5 million persons had 'relapsed' into illiteracy. Official sources also later estimated that adult illiteracy in Guangdong rose from 25 per cent to 32 per cent between 1966 and 1976.[36]

Cultural Revolution Model of School Education
The Cultural Revolution also witnessed a wholesale attack on all levels of the school system from primary schools to universities and colleges. Primary and middle school education was widely suspended in the spring of 1966 and did not resume until 1967-9, when students and teachers were

called back to 'resume classes and make revolution' (*fuke nao geming*). Some universities, however, remained closed for a decade.

The effort to restructure formal schooling began in 1969. The objective was to eliminate all of the invidious distinctions that had come to pervade the educational system under the pernicious influence of 'revisionists' such as Liu Shaoqi – distinctions between gongban and minban schools, between full-time schooling and work-study, between vocational and regular education, and between key versus ordinary schools. The changes were set forth in a 'Draft Programme for Primary and Middle School Education in the Chinese Countryside,' issued in May 1969. Under its terms, rural (that is, town-based) state-run primary schools were transferred to production brigade management. They were to be run by management committees composed of poor and lower middle peasants – the 'most reliable allies of the working class.'[37] In practice, this meant that the school committees were set up according to a 'three-in-one' formula of representatives from the army, party, and mass organizations. Middle schools were to be run by communes or brigades, depending on local conditions. The minban-gongban distinction was thus abolished by decentralizing financial and management responsibility for state schools to the level of the localities.[38]

The double-track concept of two separate school streams consisting of work-study and vocational education for some and academic education for others was also rejected. Instead, all schools were to implement the principle of 'open-door schooling' (*kaimen banxue*), whereby academic study was mixed with heavy doses of labour, practical learning, and politics. A 1970 newspaper editorial described open-door schooling as 'going out' (*zou chuqu*) into society: students were to be sent out on a regular basis to work and study in factories and with rural production teams; urban schools were to set up rural branches (*fenxiao*); and workers and peasants were to be invited to schools to serve as teachers. The avowed purpose of open-door schooling was to dissolve the distinction between schools and society and to carry the class struggle into the classroom.[39]

The length of primary schooling was also reduced from six years to five and, in some cases, four years. The 'old' academic curriculum was replaced with Cultural Revolution tracts. In Xinxing county, Cultural Revolution newspaper editorials became the main foundation of the primary school curriculum. In Huazhou county, the primary school curriculum of the early 1970s consisted of locally compiled Worker-Peasant-Soldier Textbooks (*gongnongbing keben*), in accordance with Mao's directive that educational priority be given to these groups. The previous 'marks-in-command' approach, with its emphasis on examinations and pass/fail criteria, was abolished in favour of a system of recommendation in which class background and 'redness' counted most.[40]

It is difficult to gauge the effect of the Cultural Revolution reforms on school education, because they were never systematically implemented. The patchwork system that emerged after 1968 'was never officially standardized on a nationwide basis ... On many points, its tentative nature continued until the autumn of 1976. The result was a provisional system that varied from place to place, from school to school, and even from department to department within schools.'[41] Nevertheless, it is possible to draw some general observations. First, the distinctions between different types of schools were never completely obliterated. The expansion of commune-based schooling in the early 1970s produced enormous variations in the quality and content of education, depending on the wealth of the locality, the priorities of local leaders, and the degree of state assistance. State subsidies, which went largely to pay teachers' salaries, the single biggest recurrent cost in local educational financing, continued under the Cultural Revolution 'model' and in some cases even exceeded the local contribution. This occurred both in some extremely poor areas, where the state contribution was often the only one, as well as in the most prosperous regions, such as Guangdong. Thus, by the mid-1970s, the majority of primary schools in some parts of Guangdong were predominantly state financed.

A second observation is that the placing of all schools under commune jurisdiction made possible the near-perfect control of students' and teachers' residential and social mobility. Between 1970 and 1976, communes in Guangdong received annual quotas from state authorities for the number of students they could nominate for higher education, but the quotas were usually allotted to urban 'sent-down' youth rather than to local school graduates. The main principle, widely adopted, was that 'those who reach senior middle school shall not leave the commune, those who reach junior middle school shall not leave the brigade' (*shang gaozhong buchu gongshe, shang chuzhong buchu dadui*).[42]

Among the worst affected by the transfer of schools to commune authority were teachers in the former state schools. They lost not only their former salaries but often their coveted urban residency status as well, which in turn meant reduced food rations, no more access to state-subsidized grain stocks, restrictions on mobility, and the elimination of a host of other privileges, from housing to the type of school one's children were entitled to attend. All teachers were now paid in workpoints, a portion of which usually came from teaching and another portion from field labour. In Guangdong between December 1968 and May 1969, virtually the entire primary teaching corps in the state sector was reassigned to communes to 'make workpoints' (*jigongfen*).[43]

The Cultural Revolution represented the darkest hour for schoolteachers. Identified as the 'stinking ninth category' (*choulaojiu*) behind eight other 'reactionary' social groups, teachers bore much of the blame for the 'old' education. Altogether, some 29,000 primary and middle schoolteachers in Guangdong were persecuted and dismissed from their jobs between 1966 and 1976. To take but one example, 250 primary and middle schoolteachers were 'criticized' in Guangdong's Xinfeng county during the Cultural Revolution, of whom some 190 were said to have been severely 'persecuted.' Eight were killed.[44]

Finally, the Cultural Revolution also witnessed a widespread expansion of rural school education nationwide, at both the primary school and, to a lesser extent, the middle school levels. Nationally, the rate of primary school enrolment rose from 85 per cent in 1965 to more than 95 per cent in 1976, with most of the increase taking place in the countryside. In Guangdong, the enrolment rate rose from an estimated 91 per cent to 96 per cent over the same period. At the same time, many primary schools, after reducing the length of schooling from six years to five, began to add one or two years of junior middle school education for their graduates. The first to adopt this practice in Guangdong was Heyuan county, a former base area, in 1968. This practice subsequently spread to most other areas as well. By 1977, nearly 20,000 schools – 67 per cent of all primary schools in the province – had added junior middle school classes, thereby substantially enlarging the pool of rural middle school graduates.[45]

The only region where rural school education appears to have suffered greatly in Guangdong during this period was in the overseas Chinese home areas. Here extensive retrenchment occurred due to the forced closure of many if not all overseas Chinese-funded schools. Such schools were not part of the double-track educational system. They were classified neither as minban schools nor as state schools. Rather, they were a special category of privately funded schools that had been widely set up in the overseas Chinese home areas (especially in the delta counties and the adjacent four counties of Taishan, Xinhui, Kaiping, and Enping, as well as in the Chaozhou region of northeastern Guangdong) since the 1950s when the central state formulated a special policy toward dependants of Chinese overseas.[46] Reviled during the Cultural Revolution for their 'foreign connections' (*haiwai guanxi*), the schools remained closed until they were revived, on a much larger scale, beginning in 1977.[47]

The results of the Cultural Revolution 'model' were thus deeply mixed. A significant expansion of rural educational opportunities took place, but at the cost of a curriculum heavily laden with crude ideological indoctrination. The abolition of the double-track system, moreover, did not so much eliminate educational disparities as entrench them, by making educational development even more contingent than before upon the capacity and willingness of localities, both of which varied. In terms of adult literacy efforts, however, the impact of the Cultural Revolution seems to have been largely negative: six years of paralysis, followed by four years of stultifying political indoctrination.

In August 1977, one year after Mao's death, the Chinese Communist Party, at its Eleventh National Congress, officially proclaimed the end of the Cultural Revolution. There was initially little observable difference, however, in post-Cultural Revolution literacy education. In 1975, opponents of the Gang of Four had accused the gang of using education as a tool in their struggle for power. Yet this is also precisely how the early post-Mao leadership seems to have viewed education in the late 1970s. With the political struggle against Maoists still in high gear, literacy primers now concentrated on vilifying the Gang of Four and blaming them for the disasters of the past decade. Hua Guofeng, Mao's apparent anointed successor who held power from the time of the gang's arrest until 1978, was fond of reiterating Mao's dictum (borrowed from Lenin) that it is 'impossible to build socialism in a country congested with illiterates,' but the thrust of literacy education spoke of political retribution more than socialism. Peasant literacy education continued to be used by the victors in elite political struggles to marshal public support and channel blame.

Change, however, was just around the corner. After August 1977, officials set about undoing the educational system built up over the previous decade. Between 1977 and 1978, the Cultural Revolution reforms in education were systematically dismantled and pre-Cultural Revolution arrangements gradually restored. On the surface, it looked like a return to the past. In reality, however, China was on the threshold of a major change that would soon take the country in directions that no one could have foreseen in 1978. Led by Deng Xiaoping, thrice-purged Communist Party veteran, former close associate of Liu Shaoqi, and now the country's paramount leader, an economic revolution was about to unfold, and it would transform Chinese education and society over the coming decade and beyond.

10
Literacy and Economic Development in the Post-Mao Era

Mao's death in September 1976 signalled the end of an era in China. Within two years of the chairman's passing, his anointed successor, Hua Guofeng, was eclipsed by Mao's long-time rival, Deng Xiaoping. A ranking member of the original Long March generation of Chinese communists and a shrewd politician in his own right with a proven record of opposing Mao, especially on matters of economic policy, Deng had been the chief target, along with Liu Shaoqi, of Mao's Cultural Revolution crusade to rid the party of alleged 'capitalist-roaders.' Now, with Mao gone and Hua Guofeng's titular authority all but removed, Deng wasted little time in launching China on a path of bold and far-reaching economic reform.[1]

The decision to embark upon a wide-ranging program of economic reforms, beginning in the agricultural sector, was made in December 1978 at the Third Plenum of the party's Eleventh Central Committee. Interestingly, from their outset, the post-Mao reforms in agriculture were closely identified with the unfinished tasks of rural education. One month before the Third Plenum convened, the State Council renewed the original 1956 anti-illiteracy decree and called for the eradication of illiteracy throughout China by 1982 'or perhaps a little longer' in some areas. The decree laid out a three-pronged strategy for achieving this objective. Described as *yidu, ersao, santigao* ('first block, second wipe out, third raise'), the plan placed the greatest emphasis upon 'blocking' (*du*) the appearance of 'new illiterates' (*xin wenmang*) through the rapid implementation of five years of universal primary education (although the primary school enrolment rate in 1978 was 94 per cent, the figure concealed major regional and local variations). The plan also affirmed the continued importance of relying upon spare-time education and mass literacy campaigns to eliminate (*sao*) illiteracy among the non-school-age population (calling for the elimination of illiteracy among 85 per cent of twelve to forty-five year olds within four years). Finally, the strategy also emphasized the importance of raising (*tigao*) adult literacy standards by providing opportunities for continued study. Adults with minimal literacy skills were now expected to raise themselves to a primary school educational level within two or three years.[2]

The relationship of the literacy movement to the post-Mao rural reforms involved more, however, than simply reinvigorating (*huifu*) existing literacy programs and strategies that had lain dormant during the long hiatus of the Cultural Revolution. The reforms also demanded a rethinking of the basic theoretical premises underlying the literacy movement since collectivization in the mid-1950s. The dismantling of the collective system and the restoration of family farming, the rapid growth of commercial agriculture, the takeoff of township-based industry and de facto urbanization – all made for unprecedented transformation of the rural socioeconomic environment. Peasants and state educational planners alike found themselves suddenly forced to reconsider the socioeconomic significance of literacy.

This chapter begins with the official effort to reformulate literacy's role in an era of reform (*gaige*) and openness (*kaifang*). It then goes on to examine the actual impacts of decollectivization on rural education, revealing the complex and often unexpected, sometimes contradictory, ways in which the post-Mao reforms affected the provision of and demand for rural literacy and school education. The final section of this chapter examines the ways in which literacy and rural education have both contributed and responded to the dramatic economic metamorphosis of Guangdong in the 1980s and 1990s.

Redefining Literacy's Role in the Post-Collective Economy

For nearly three decades until 1979, rural literacy campaigns had been predicated upon a state vision in which collective agriculture was seen as the sine qua non of successful economic development and the realization of a true socialist society. The single most radical theoretical rupture undertaken by Mao's successors was the admission that collectivization – one of the greatest shibboleths of twentieth-century Marxist-Leninist revolutions – was not, after all, an essential requirement of socialist economics.[3] There is, of course, a great deal of debate among scholars as to whether the centre initiated decollectivization or simply acceded to it in the face of popular pressure from below.[4] Whichever the case, Mao's successors were quick to legitimize the return to family farming and to construct a new set of theoretical principles intended to guide rural development in the post-collective era.

The single overriding objective of rural reform was to 'enliven' (*gaohuo*) the rural economy by restoring material incentives and granting greater play to market forces. In order to achieve these objectives, a production responsibility system (*shengchan zeren zhi*) was sanctioned in 1979. The system was based on previous experiments sanctioned by Liu and Deng in the early 1960s, in the wake of the Great Leap famine, under which production teams were allowed to contract production quotas (*baochan*) to smaller groups of producers, including, in some instances, individual households. The aim was to link reward to output by encouraging production above quota for the market. Except in some localities, where collectively organized production created much-needed economies of scale (in which cases decollectivization was strongly resisted), the reappearance of the responsibility system in 1979 was greeted with widespread and enthusiastic grassroots support. By early 1983, the dominant form of the responsibility system across the country involved contracting full responsibility to the level of the individual household (*baogan daohu*), often on a long-term or semipermanent basis. This meant, in effect, the demise of collectivized farming in China.[5] Formal dissolution of the commune system began in the fall of 1983. Guangdong, whose rural residents had greeted the responsibility system with particular enthusiasm, became the first province officially to complete decollectivization in the spring of 1984. Decollectivization involved not only a significant decentralization of economic decision-making power but a massive administrative reorganization as well. Guangdong's 386,924 production teams were formally disbanded and reconstituted into nearly 97,000 natural village (*cun*) councils; 26,583 production brigades were recombined to form nearly 20,000 administrative villages (*xiang*) and 350 towns (*zhen*); and the province's 1,982 communes became 1,836 districts (*qu*).[6]

The emerging theoretical premise for rural development in the reform era centred on the notion that China was reembarking upon the delayed transition to a 'commodity economy.' Senior rural policymaker Du Runsheng explained the main features of this transition and how it had been distorted by previous policies. Development of a commodity economy (*shangpin jingji*) was said to be a universal feature of historical development, one that was 'indispensable to the development of productive forces' and therefore could not be 'bypassed.' In China, production of commodities for the market was said to have originated in ancient times during the period of slavery and Zhou-era feudalism and to have reached a level of 'universal development' with the rise of capitalism in the late-imperial period. China's commodity economy continued to develop into the twentieth century until 1957, when, according to Du, its development was suddenly arrested.

Du conceded that the country's low level of mechanical development, combined with rapidly increasing population pressure and a shrinking land base, was partly to blame for this arrest. Far more significant in Du's view, however, were state policies with respect to collectivization and urban industrialization. Three features of the post-1957 political economy were particularly said to account for the 'retardation' of commodity production. First, the inability of food supplies to keep pace with the needs of rapid urban industrialization had led the country's rulers to adopt the policy of 'taking grain as the key link.' The universal emphasis upon grain production, even in areas such as Guangdong, whose natural economic advantages lay in other forms of agricultural and non-agricultural activity, was said to have reduced both the number and scope of commodities in circulation. Second, the workpoint method of remuneration employed under the collective system further hindered the development of commodity production, since team members now cared only about the number of workpoints they earned, not about the saleability of what they produced. Third, said Du, the severe mobility restrictions imposed upon peasants in order to guarantee collective production hindered their ability to engage in market-related economic activities outside the collective sector. In each of these instances, the culprit was deemed to have been the socialist state and its efforts to eliminate the market and replace it with state planning and collective production.[7]

The reformers' effort to furnish a theoretical justification for enhancing the role of the market thus entailed a critique of the collective system that centred on the negative effects that resulted from denying economic decision-making power to peasant households. The critique had direct implications for literacy and other forms of rural education. Reformers argued that the loosening of state controls over agricultural production and the accompanying restoration of household decision-making power would perforce have a profound impact upon the value that peasant households attached to literacy in the post-collective era. Under the collective system, with its emphasis upon food-grain production, local self-sufficiency, and the near absence of commercially based exchange, peasants were required to master a set of relatively uniform and interchangeable basic literacy skills – what I earlier termed 'workpoint literacy' – in order to carry out their responsibilities as team members. And since both geographical and social mobility were tightly constricted under the collective system, there were few opportunities and outlets for literate expression available beyond the boundaries of the collective. But with decollectivization, literacy had become a potential ingredient in mobility strategies and a significant factor in determining the economic choices available to peasants and their families. And with peasants increasingly able to travel and even relocate, the scope for additional forms of literate expression, economic and otherwise, was substantially greater than before. Operating in the future as 'comparatively independent commodity producer[s],' peasant households would be more 'free to choose what they want to produce *in light of their own special skills and abilities'* (emphasis added).[8]

Reformers envisioned that the educational 'knock-on' effects of decollectivization and commodity production would propel further changes in the economy, which would in turn have an effect on educational demands. The economically motivated demands of independent peasant 'commodity producers' for specialized skills would compel the advancement and spread of technical agricultural education. Increasing specialization on the part of skilled farmers would herald a genuine diversification of agriculture, and the rise of a genuinely diversified and commercialized agricultural economy would in turn give birth to a society of peasant entrepreneurs in need of specialized business and managerial skills. As increasing numbers of peasants left the land to become workers, technicians, and managers in the rapidly developing village and township commercial and industrial enterprises, literacy and other forms of specialized training would become increasingly important. Literacy's prescribed role in the post-Mao agricultural reforms was thus to equip China's peasants for their new roles as specialized entrepreneurs, business managers, and technical experts.

Yet despite the new emphasis upon commodity specialization and decentralized decision-making power, the reformers' view of the future ironically continued to echo many of the themes and expectations contained in similarly euphoric discussions of the early 1950s on the anticipated benefits of central planning. It is true, of course, that Deng Xiaoping won the support of intellectuals early on with what appeared to be a clear renunciation of the Maoist position on education and science. In March-April 1978, Deng created a stir among delegates to the National Conference on Science and the National Education Work Conference with his candid admission that since 1949 the state's science and educational policies had been based on the 'mistaken belief' that the two belonged to the realm of 'superstructure' when they were really 'productive forces' in their own right, capable of propelling economic advances. Intellectuals and educators welcomed Deng's remarks, for they seemed to signal not only greater official recognition of and respect for the value of education and educators but also the possibility of greater state investment in education in the future.[9] Yet Deng's assertion that science and education were productive forces in their own right was hardly radical; the notion had long been incorporated into PRC educational policy as the 'human capital' premise that had undergirded educational planning throughout the prereform era. There were further echoes of the past as well. This was nowhere more so than with respect to the prophetic role ascribed to science by both Maoists and reformers alike. The theory of China's transition to a commodity economy was firmly embedded in the same – to use Alexander Woodside's term – 'Saint-Simonian' prophecy that informed the earlier gospel of central planners. In both instances, educational visions of the future were embedded in the anticipation of an emergent industrial civilization, in which advanced scientific, technical, and managerial skills were the key to growth and prosperity.[10] Woodside cites as an example one of the most optimistic prophets of this transition, who wrote in 1985 that China was poised on the verge of a major world historical breakthrough. 'A new agricultural great power is about to appear in the world,' wrote this prophet, referring to the advent of what he termed 'intellectual agriculture' (*sikao nongye*) in China.[11] Thus, the China

Association of Science and Technology began awarding titles of 'technician' and 'assistant technician' to farmers for the first time in the 1980s, while local authorities issued 'science and technology certificates' to model rural households (*keji shifan hu zhengshu*).[12]

The technocratic and managerial ethos of rural education also found expression in official views of the impact of foreign investment on education. In 1986, Li Peng, minister in charge of the newly formed State Education Commission, chided delegates to a national adult education conference with the question 'Why are Chinese products uncompetitive on world markets?' Not because Chinese raw materials were inferior to those of other countries, Li responded, but because the human resources that produced them were inferior to world-class standards. He was confident, however, that the problem would soon be solved by the role of 'market forces,' as the increase in joint ventures with foreign firms would create demand for foreign language ability, technical and managerial training, and other skills required for competing effectively in a global economy. Others attempted to draw lessons for China's education from the history of industrialization in the West. Some pointed to the rise of management science in the West in the late nineteenth century as a crucial factor in the rapid industrialization of the United States and Europe, while others cited the arguments of Western historians, such as Corelli Barnett, that Britain had been condemned to industrial decline by a shortage of sufficiently trained workers.[13]

But if the reformers' expectant vision of an emergent industrial civilization based on advanced scientific, technical, and managerial skills resembled more than a little that of their central-planning forebears of the 1950s, the means they chose to achieve it – foreign direct investment, free markets, and private farming – were radically different. The deradicalization of China's economic development strategy received the immediate and overwhelming approval of international monetary and financial institutions such as the World Bank and the International Monetary Fund, which have since laboured hard – and not always with success – to bring China's economic and fiscal institutions and practices into conformity with the established norms of the capitalist world economy. Moreover, as Juergen Henze and others have shown, the 'search for higher efficiency' extended to education as well, as international bodies such as the World Bank and other UN institutions encouraged and aided the restructuring of Chinese educational institutions and practices to bring them into greater conformity with Western-based international norms.[14] One result of this process was a parallel deradicalization of the official terminology and vocabulary of rural education. The formerly used term 'worker-peasant education' (*gongnong jiaoyu*), for example, used since 1949 to describe mass educational activities outside the formal school system, was increasingly replaced in the 1980s by more politically neutral and internationally accepted terms such as 'adult education' (*chengren jiaoyu*) and 'continuing education' (*jishu jiaoyu*). In 1985, the Guangdong education bureau altered the official title of its spare-time education division from Worker-Peasant Education Division to Adult Education Division. Whereas the former implied education to enable workers and peasants to carry out their state-prescribed tasks as members of a particular class, the latter clearly implied a conception of education based on the developmental needs of individuals at various life stages.

Impact of Decollectivization on Rural Literacy and Schooling

In attempting to understand the impact of decollectivization on rural literacy practices, it is important to distinguish between immediate and longer-term effects. It is also necessary to take account of regional and even local variations, since decollectivization gave rise to literacy practices far more closely associated with the economic ecology of diverse localities than was ever the case under the collective system. Thus, while the immediate effects of decollectivization on literacy were broadly similar on a national scale, shaped primarily by the sudden dismantling of the fiscal and institutional foundations that had underpinned rural basic education for more than two decades, important regional and local differences in literacy trends began to emerge by the late 1980s. These differences reflected above all the unequal distribution of economic resources and opportunities and the hardening of regionally based economic inequalities under reform. Thus, while the initial effects of decollectivization in Guangdong may not have been much different than those in most other parts of the country, this was no longer the case once the reforms were firmly established and allowed to achieve their maximum effect. As we will see, by the latter part of the 1980s, literacy and rural education trends in Guangdong more closely reflected the province's ability to capitalize – with active central government support – upon its unique locational and historical advantages. The following section first examines the immediate effects of decollectivization nationwide, then goes on to discuss the longer-term impact of the post-Mao reforms on literacy and basic rural education in Guangdong.

In the short term, decollectivization was accompanied by shrinking enrolments and rising dropout rates in both adult literacy classes and rural school education. Despite an overall improvement in the national illiteracy rate during the 1980s, from 23 per cent in 1982 to 16 per cent in 1990, the number of persons attending literacy classes actually fell steadily throughout the decade. Between 1980 and 1985, for example, enrolment in adult literacy classes fell by more than 57 per cent, from 12.2 million to 5.2 million. Similarly, the number of adults completing literacy classes dropped from 3.52 million in 1985 to 2.39 million in 1986 and to only 1.44 million in 1988. The decline in literacy class enrolments during the 1980s stands in sharp contrast to the situation in the late 1970s, when

the central government concentrated on reviving literacy programs abandoned during the Cultural Revolution. Thus, during the four years from
1977 to 1981, more than 26 million persons nationwide acquired basic literacy. Yet over the following seven years, from 1982 to 1989, only around
19 million persons met this goal.[15]

The situation was worse in the countryside and among women, with rural women faring the worst. According to the national sample population
survey conducted in 1987, rural residents comprised 92 per cent of the country's 220 million illiterates. The illiteracy rate among the rural population
was 44 per cent, nearly double the national rate of 23 per cent. Nationally,
nearly 80 per cent of illiterates were women. To be sure, there were important demographic differences between women of various age cohorts, differences that reflected the influence of pre-1949 conditions and the steady
progress after 1949. Thus, for example, over 95 per cent of women sixty
years and over were illiterate. But even among women aged thirty to thirty-
four – that is, women who were born after 1949 and reached school age in
the late 1950s – the illiteracy rate was still over 40 per cent.[16]

Decollectivization and the rise of the responsibility system also produced
a similar decline in rural primary school enrolments. Suzanne Pepper has
documented this decline across the provinces. Despite the fact that the primary school enrolment rate surpassed 97 per cent in the late 1980s, the
number of students actually enrolled fell from a high of 150 million in
1975-6 to 136 million in 1983 and to 128 million by 1987. These are national figures; in poorer provinces such as Anhui and Yunnan, the decline
was much steeper.[17]

The number of primary school dropouts also increased during the 1980s.
These dropouts averaged over 4 million per year during the 1980s, equivalent to 3 per cent of the total primary school population. While some of
these dropouts possessed basic literacy, officials estimated that in the late
1980s there were approximately 2 million 'new illiterates' (*xin wenmang*)
appearing each year due to a combination of dropouts and the absence of
universal primary and middle schooling. Altogether between 1980 and 1987,
some 30 million primary and middle school students dropped out.

As with adult illiteracy, the situation was worst for female students. Nearly
83 per cent of children not attending primary school in 1988 were female,
as were 70-80 per cent of all school dropouts. Perhaps not surprisingly, an
estimated 85 per cent of all child labourers (*tonggong*) aged sixteen and under were also female. This was despite the fact that the 1986 compulsory
education law (see below) forbade child labour under the age of sixteen.
One report on the subject noted that nearly half of young girls did not
complete primary school.[18]

The long-standing rural-urban gap in literacy and educational levels
that preceded 1949 and was, ironically, perpetuated by Maoist policies of

self-reliance also continued in the reform period. Thus, whereas 81 per cent of seven year olds in the cities were enrolled in primary school in 1983, the figure was only 58 per cent among rural residents. Without exception, cities offered six years of primary schooling, but as of 1990 fully half of all primary schools in the countryside offered five years or fewer of primary education. If the countryside as a whole remained disadvantaged relative to urban areas, the situation was worst in the poorest parts of rural China. In the late 1980s, the central government sanctioned a truncated three-year version of primary schooling for poor areas. Known as 'minischools' (*jiaoxue dian*) or 'simplified primary schools' (*jianyi xiaoxue*), they offered only basic literacy and arithmetic. Although difficult to quantify, such truncated primary schools may have accounted for as many as 20 per cent of all rural primary schools during the late 1980s.[19]

What factors account for the decline in rural school enrolment and adult literacy classes in the 1980s? Was it the result of a slackening of official efforts or the weakened ability of local governments to enforce literacy and school attendance? Were peasants – despite the optimistic projections of reformers – actually less interested in literacy and school education under the reforms?

The decline in school enrolment was partly attributable to the one-child policy of birth control introduced in 1979, which had the effect of eventually reducing the absolute size of the school-age population. As Suzanne Pepper has pointed out, however, given subsequent official admissions in the late 1980s concerning the laxity of family-planning measures in rural areas, this factor should not be overemphasized. The economic reforms themselves appear to have had a much more direct effect on rural literacy and school education. The effects of reform on rural education can be divided into two main categories: first, the effect upon the institutional structure of rural education and, second, the effect upon the value that peasants placed on literacy and school education.

As we saw in previous chapters, China's rural collectives supported a system of minban ('people-run') schooling, based on a non-monetized system of taxation in which workpoints substituted for a regular fiscal base. Under this system, collectives used their authority to determine the value and distribution of workpoints to sustain a wide range of social welfare services, including health and education. The system worked reasonably well so long as agricultural production continued to be carried out on a collective basis and the collective retained its authority to distribute collectively owned resources. As soon as changes were made in the organization of agricultural production, however, in the words of one prominent economist, 'the entire complex of rural services collapsed in most parts of the country.'[20] It is not difficult to see why. As the responsibility system granted households increasing authority to make their own production and exchange decisions, collectives began to lose control over local income and, with it, the ability to fund rural services.

Decollectivization thus created a vacuum of responsibility for local social welfare functions in the countryside, including education. This situation in turn gave rise to a protracted debate and considerable confusion over which levels of the shifting post-collective rural administrative structure ought to be responsible for such functions. The confusion – but not the debate – was partly resolved in 1985, when the central government issued its formal decision on reforming the educational system. The decision is discussed in the following section.

The increase in household decision-making power under the responsibility system also affected the ways in which rural families viewed the prospects of literacy and schooling in the reform era. Literacy was now, in theory, a potential ingredient in family-based mobility strategies. In cases where households pursued economic strategies involving regular commercial activity or the acquisition of technical skills, there was increased demand for the various specialized literacy skills associated with these undertakings. Local governments attempted to meet such demand by vastly increasing the number and range of short-term specialized training classes for adults (also described below). Equally important, however, was the fact that the responsibility system often had the opposite effect on popular demand for literacy. The system also encouraged families to rely upon the intensification of field labour to increase household income. In such cases, household income rose by devoting less, not more, time to educational pursuits. Believing that 'study is useless' (*dushu meiyou yong*), many parents in the reform era withdrew their children from school for the opportunity to earn quick money. Likewise, rural industrialization and the sudden lure of factory labour drew many children out of school.[21] Indeed, by the mid-1980s, the problem of school dropouts, non-attendance, and declining enrolments in adult literacy classes had grown serious enough that the central government felt compelled to introduce a series of radical measures designed to reverse the trend.

Official Efforts to Strengthen Literacy and Rural Education in the Reform Era

Official efforts to strengthen literacy and rural basic schooling in the reform era involved changes to the organization, management, and funding of rural education. In the early 1980s, the central government responded to the problem of declining enrolments in adult literacy programs by calling upon local authorities to adopt their own version of the responsibility system. The concept of 'production contracts' as used in the agricultural sector was to be applied to literacy work as well. Under the 'anti-illiteracy responsibility system' (*saomang zeren zhi*), contracts to undertake literacy work were to be drawn up at all levels; counties were to contract with communes, communes were to establish contracts with production brigades, and brigades were to contract with teams (following decollectivization in 1983, these collective units were replaced by their corresponding units of local government). At the basic level, teachers and learners also entered into contracts, which stipulated precise teaching and learning objectives and set a scale of bonuses and punishments. Under one such contract, local literacy teachers were required to post a three-yuan bond for each student. If they reached their literacy target within the time and according to the criteria stipulated in the contract, the bond was returned and a three-yuan bonus paid to the teacher. If the target was not met, however, the three-yuan deposit was forfeited and a three-yuan fine levied on the teacher.[22]

In 1983, the state attempted to address the problem of mounting confusion and disagreement over administrative responsibility for local education following decollectivization by announcing a major restructuring of the educational system. The 1985 Decision on Reforming the Education System stipulated a division of responsibilities based on the principle (cumbersome in translation but succinct in the original) of 'multiple-levels-run schools with separate levels of management' (*duoji banxue fenji guanli*). Primary schooling was to be the responsibility of village (*cun*) governments, junior middle school education the responsibility of township (*xiang*) and town (*zhen*) governments, and senior middle school education the responsibility of county (*xian*) and city (*shi*) governments. Higher education was to be the responsibility of the state (*guojia*), provinces, and centrally administered cities. The Decision on Reforming the Education System was followed in 1986 by a new Compulsory Education Law, designed to halt the problem of declining school enrolments and rising dropout rates engendered by the rural reforms. The law called for the phased institution of nine years of compulsory schooling across the country, to be achieved by 1990 in the economically advanced coastal areas and cities and by 2000 in the least developed parts of the country. In addition, the law also provided for a large-scale expansion of the secondary vocational track. In future, middle school education was to be divided equally between regular academic schools and vocational-technical schools. In the latter, at least 30 per cent of the curriculum was to be devoted to 'agricultural [vocational] technology' (*nongye [zhiye] jishu*) and 70 per cent to basic 'cultural knowledge' (*wenhua zhishi*). The technical-vocational component would be geared toward skills such as chicken and pig breeding, clothing manufacture, house construction, and specialized crop production.[23]

The most controversial issue facing the central government's effort to strengthen literacy and rural basic education in the reform era involved funding. In 1979, at the outset of reform, national expenditures on primary education were derived from three main sources: 56.8 per cent from the state budget, 27.2 per cent from local budgets, and 15.9 per cent from tuition fees.[24] The same year, however, the central government proclaimed its intention to shift a greater proportion of the already substantial fiscal burden for primary education onto localities. Ironically, the educational burden placed on localities had also emerged as a major element in the unfolding critique of the commune system. Early 1980s critics argued that the commune system had enabled the state to 'cunningly shift to teams and brigades many burdens and expenses that should rightfully have been borne by the state ... Using revolutionary-sounding slogans about popular management and control, [the state made] peasant collectives liable for public service expenditures' such as schools, clinics, public transport, and civil administration.[25] But as Suzanne Pepper informs us, a major article published in an official educational journal in 1980 revealed that the central government's emerging policy on funding basic rural education in the reform period actually called for 'restoring' (*huifu*) the 'two kinds of educational system' (*liangzhong jiaoyu zhidu*), which had been destroyed during the Cultural Revolution. Arguing that the policy of 'walking on two legs' – the division of the educational system into state-funded and locally funded schools – was still necessary if China was to achieve universal schooling as rapidly as possible, the authors of the article summarily declared that 'our state presently cannot afford to spend more money on education.'[26] Later the same year, the State Council and the Central Committee issued their Joint Decision concerning Some Problems in Popularizing Primary Schooling. It reiterated this view, emphasizing that, in a large country such as China with a huge population and a still undeveloped economy, it was simply 'impossible' to depend completely on state financing for basic education. The reaffirmation of educational voluntarism was subsequently enshrined in Article 19 of the 1982 constitution, which stipulated that, in addition to state funding for education, 'the state encourages collectives, state enterprises, and other social forces [*shehui liliang*]' to establish schools.[27]

Indeed, it is hard to see how the fiscal logic of the reform process could have permitted the central government to do other than increase its reliance on 'social forces' for funding basic education. The central state's fiscal base was seriously eroded by the decentralizing reforms of the 1980s. This prompted a major effort to overhaul the country's tax structure in the early 1990s as a means of enhancing state fiscal powers. The immediate effect, however, was to make it even more difficult for the state to assume an increased share of the responsibility for funding basic rural education than was the case in the Mao era, when local self-reliance was promoted for ideological as well as fiscal reasons.

The reform period thus saw an increasing reliance upon non-budgetary sources of educational financing, known as 'multiple funding channels' (*duoqudao jizi*). One such channel consisted of ad hoc levies by local governments and educational authorities. Under the terms of the 1986 compulsory education law, primary schooling was to be 'free,' which meant the absence of tuition. However, local governments were authorized to collect a surtax in support of local educational undertakings, as well as to levy special 'miscellaneous educational fees' (*xue zafei*). The fees, which quickly became a focus of popular resentment, were levied upon students, teachers, and parents in order to pay for specific costs such as desks, lamps, heating fuel, and school improvements. In one widely publicized case, a peasant woman was driven to suicide after local cadres confiscated her television and bicycle for failing to pay a 320-yuan 'family planning and education fee' levied by local officials. Other non-budgetary channels of funding included 'donations' (sometimes voluntary, often coerced) from successful local entrepreneurs, specialized households (*zhuanye hu*), collectives, enterprises, and from overseas Chinese and compatriots from Hong Kong and Macao, as well as income from school-owned enterprises. To counter stories such as that of the peasant woman driven to suicide by the predatory acts of local officials, authorities went to great lengths to extol local cadres who were willing to sacrifice their own resources to support education. One such case involved a Guangdong cadre who, in a sudden change of heart, decided to donate the 600-yuan he had been saving for a lavish wedding celebration to the local education fund.

Despite official efforts to carve out multiple funding channels, critics of central government policy continued to argue throughout the 1980s and 1990s that the state's low level of support for basic education was a leading cause of the perceived low 'quality' (*suzhi*) of the Chinese population. The criticism was fuelled in large part by international comparisons of state educational funding, made possible for the first time in the 1980s by China's incorporation into the educational databases of international agencies such as the World Bank and UNESCO. Such comparisons revealed, for example, that China's level of state educational spending fell significantly below the median of eighty-two other developing countries (3.1 per cent of GNP compared with a median 3.9 per cent). During the 1980s, China devoted 6.6 per cent of central budgetary expenses to education, compared with an average of 15.1 per cent in other less developed countries and 15.6 per cent in the industrialized nations. Through its own official commentary, the World Bank appeared to confirm the pessimism of China's domestic critics, observing, for example, that 'Chinese [state] spending on primary and secondary education is inadequate given the high percentage of unqualified teachers, often poor physical facilities and lack of teaching materials.' The same report went on to conclude that China had 'shifted much of the cost of education to local authorities and ... families' and that 'the family contribution to education ... particularly in primary and secondary schools' was significantly greater than in most socialist countries (in 1985, China allocated 3.4 per cent of GNP to education, compared with 8.7 per cent in the Soviet Union). As one Chinese commentator wrote in 1992, 'For many years our country has failed to recognize the full importance of education ... especially basic education ... Whether from the perspective of proportion of GNP or as a proportion of state financial expenditures, China is among the lowest countries in the world.'[28]

The fiscal burden on localities was made more difficult during the reform period by a simultaneous strengthening of centrally imposed standards with respect to schools, teachers, and curricula. As Jean Robinson has observed, the 1980s and 1990s witnessed an 'unprecedented increase in state control' over primary education, involving the imposition of unified national standards for curricula, textbooks, teacher qualifications, and the physical infrastructure and equipment of schools.[29] The pattern of the Deng era thus became one of decentralized financing coupled with increasing centralization of standards and curricula. The ultimate effect of this pattern was to lay bare the disparity in the ability of different regions and locales to create and maintain healthy, well-funded, basic educational systems in accordance with state standards. In the 1980s and 1990s, educational disparities in China became ever more closely intertwined with imbalances in economic development.

Literacy and Rural Schooling in Post-Mao Guangdong

Guangdong leaders began to restore pre-Cultural Revolution adult literacy programs as early as 1977. They focused initially upon promoting the achievements of two model counties: Dingan, a poor county on Hainan island (in 1985, Hainan became a separate province), and Conghua, a relatively prosperous county near Guangzhou. In September 1978, four months before the State Council renewed the 1956 anti-illiteracy decree, the Guangdong Revolutionary Committee issued its Opinion Concerning Opening Up Literacy and Spare-Time Education Work, which called on localities to cooperate with mass organizations to reinvigorate anti-illiteracy work. Within one year of this proclamation, nearly twenty-five counties and cities in Guangdong had declared themselves officially 'illiteracy free,' led by Conghua and Dingan.[30]

It was not until 1979, however, that rural education in Guangdong truly entered the reform era. In early 1979, the central government decided to grant Guangdong and neighbouring Fujian a 'special policy' that gave the two provinces greater autonomy to decide policy in areas such as agriculture, commerce, industry, wages and prices, transport, education, foreign trade, and fiscal affairs. The decision reflected an admission that the rigid model of bureaucratic socialism adopted since the mid-1950s had failed Guangdong in many respects. In the frank words of one of the province's leading economic geographers, the centre's determination for three decades to impose a single model of rural development upon all regions was 'divorced from Guangdong's reality' (*tuoli le Guangdong de shiji*). Policies such as stressing heavy industry over agriculture (*anzhong qingnong*) made little sense in Guangdong, while the policy of 'taking grain as the key link' (*yiliang weigang*) distorted Guangdong agriculture, which was better suited to the production of commercial crops. Moreover, the Maoist policy of self-reliance had prevented Guangdong from tapping the potential of its various 'special features' (*tedian*), which ranged from historical to locational. They included, most importantly, Guangdong's unrivalled commercial heritage in China, its long tradition of foreign trade and greater openness to the outside world, its proximity to capitalist Hong Kong, and its close economic and cultural connections with Chinese overseas.[31] As Ezra Vogel notes in his magisterial survey of Guangdong under reform, the slogan adopted by the province's reform leaders in 1979 aptly captured their intentions: 'To the outside, more open; to the inside, looser; to those below, more leeway' (*duiwai, gengjia kaifang; duinei, gengjia fangkuang; duixia, gengjia fangquan*).[32]

In Guangdong, as elsewhere, decollectivization ended the enforced poverty of the agricultural sector, freeing up rural households to engage in a variety of agricultural and non-agricultural pursuits. As explained by anthropologist Graham Johnson, the rural economy that emerged in Guangdong by the late 1980s had at least four key components: (1) the peasant household economy, including families engaged in pursuits ranging from cash crops to livestock breeding, aquaculture, fruit growing, transport, and wholesale and retail business; (2) the 'new economy of associated peasant producers' (*xin jingji lianheti*), comprised of peasants engaged in cooperative business ventures with others in order to achieve economies of scale, such as in the case of fish, poultry, and pig farming; (3) the economy of collectively owned township (*xiang*) and town (*zhen*) enterprises, engaged in activities ranging from food processing to export industries; and (4) a residual collective economy, in which village councils or other organs of local government managed public resources such as irrigation facilities, forests, and social welfare (including education).[33] These changes implied a significant diversification of agriculture and a proliferation of related occupational categories.

Many of these new agricultural activities, business ventures, and urban occupations required specialized technical skills of one sort or another. The increase in demand for business-related literate skills such as accounting and management was greatest among the 'specialized households' (*zhuanye hu*) and 'keypoint households' (*zhongdian hu*) that appeared after 1979. They were defined as rural households whose economic activity was concentrated in one or a few specialized undertakings; in official terms, specialized households were those that concentrated at least 60 per cent of household production and labour in a single sector. By this definition, there were an estimated 270,000 such households in Guangdong in the early 1980s and around 22.5 million nationally (14 per cent of the rural population). In Guangdong, the greatest concentration of specialized households was in the Pearl River Delta, where agricultural diversification, commercialization, and industrialization were most developed. Indeed, Johnson suggests that by the mid-1980s it was becoming increasingly difficult to identify specialized households as such in the delta, because most rural families were engaged in 'distinctive household strategies' involving several economic sectors. Such households were like minicorporations. In one admittedly exceptional case, a specialized household in prosperous Shunde county counted some twenty-seven members, with its business empire spanning everything from aquaculture to brick kilns.[34] The proliferation of commodity markets that aided and accompanied these changes added to an increasingly literate rural business environment in the 1980s. Peasant entrepreneurialism depended more and more upon steady access to market information, much of it written, in order to make informed business decisions. This burgeoning need for information in areas such as prices and price trends, transportation costs, and market opportunities led to the establishment of the first rural business newspapers in the mid-1980s.

The changes described above received an added boost in 1985 when the central government's reform policy began to focus on measures to diversify the rural economy. State procurement quotas were abolished in 1985 for all but the most essential agricultural commodities as an incentive for peasants to shift production into high-value agricultural commodities such as vegetables, sugar, fish, livestock, tree farming, and vegetable oils. The policy also sought to promote multisectoral development by reviving the Great Leap Forward strategy of rural industrialization, with the Pearl River Delta emerging as national leader. Local governments there, often in conjunction with Hong Kong and Macao investors, established a wide range of collectively owned enterprises producing food, textiles, shoes, electronics, toys, and other products for both international and domestic markets. Industrial activities in the Pearl River Delta, which were valued at less than 4 billion yuan in 1978, generated more than 20 billion yuan in 1986.[35] This process of rural industrialization, which accelerated even more rapidly after 1990, led to important sectoral shifts in the rural labour force as increasing numbers of peasants 'left the land but not the countryside' (*litu bulixiang*) to take up temporary urban residences and occupations. In Foshan, at the hub of the delta, some 90 per cent of the rural population was engaged in agriculture in 1978 and only 10 per cent in industry. Yet by 1984, the number of rural residents engaged in agriculture fell to only 40 per cent, while 60 per cent were engaged in industry and commerce.[36]

Local adult education departments attempted to meet the burgeoning demand for specialist knowledge and skills by offering short-term technical training classes (*jishu peixun ban*). By 1984, there were more than 2 million peasants enrolled in such short-term classes, compared with only 550,000 enrolled in spare-time primary and middle schools. In the late 1980s, I visited adult education projects in the Pearl River Delta counties of Nanhai and Panyu, where there was a frantic effort by local adult education bureaucracies to keep up with demand for such short-term training courses in everything from aquaculture to accounting, from tree-fruit cultivation to small-appliance repair. Indeed, the demand for such skills was so great that by the late 1980s specialized households were even contracting privately with provincial colleges and universities to pay the expenses for their members to take specialized training courses. Other specialized households, with the encouragement of local governments, set up their own private schools and training centres.[37]

By 1984, the number of people enrolled in short-term training courses exceeded the number of those pursuing spare-time primary and middle school degrees. Demand for such courses continued to escalate rapidly through the 1980s and 1990s, while enrolments in literacy classes and spare-time primary and middle schools dwindled. Between 1990 and 1992, for example, enrolment in various kinds of basic-level vocational training rose from 22,000 to more than 161,000, while over the same period enrolment in spare-time regular schooling fell from more than 1 million to fewer than 670,000.[38] The pattern suggests how economic reform may have altered the popular demand for literacy skills in Guangdong. Under the collective system, spare-time school degrees were valued because they offered the greatest chance of mobility, while specialized technical training remained a relatively minor component of adult education. Now that the acquisition of such specialized technical skills was linked to the pursuit of private wealth and personal mobility, the demand for such skills soared. School degrees remained highly valued among those seeking government jobs (indeed, educational writers complained of the increasing problem of credentialism (*wenping zhuyi*) in adult education in the 1980s), but among the growing legions of peasant entrepreneurs, specialized technical skills – not school degrees – were the means to social and economic advancement.[39]

In 1980, Guangdong leaders set a target date of 1985 for eradicating illiteracy among twelve to forty year olds. Within two years, more than half of the province's rural counties had officially met the target. Significantly, most of these counties were located in the greater Guangzhou-Pearl River Delta region, where the pace and degree of economic reform were most advanced. According to the 1982 national census, Guangdong registered a total of 9.7 million illiterates aged twelve years and older. However, only 4.7 per cent (1.25 million) were within the state's targeted age cohort of twelve to forty year olds, compared with 25 per cent nationally.[40] By 1985, the official illiteracy rate among this age group had been reduced to 2.5 per cent (620,000). Official accounts claimed that illiteracy was now 'basically eliminated' in 95 per cent of all counties in the province, with a further six awaiting 'verification.' It is important, however, to bear in mind the criteria under which localities were judged to have 'basically eliminated illiteracy.' In Panyu county, for example, the adult education committee, following central guidelines, employed a 60 per cent pass mark in testing for adult literacy. The test was based on a 1,200-character literacy textbook published by the Guangdong education bureau in the early 1980s. On this basis, Panyu had achieved more than 90 per cent literacy by 1982.[41] Once a locality submitted its claim to have 'basically eliminated illiteracy' according to official criteria, the claim was subjected to official verification by a senior administrative level. As in the past, the verification procedure was based on administrative reporting by a sampling of units rather than on actual testing. Once these reports were approved, the claim became official. Obviously, the lack of testing and the reliance upon self-evaluation and administrative reporting raise legitimate questions concerning the criteria for localities declaring themselves officially 'illiteracy free.' Nevertheless, on this basis Guangdong declared itself, for the second time since 1949 (the first was in 1959, at the height of the Great Leap Forward), an officially 'literate' (*wu wenmang*) province in 1985.[42]

Guangdong continued to be held up throughout the 1980s and 1990s as a national model for adult literacy and spare-time education in the reform era. By 1989, the number of illiterates aged twelve to forty had been further reduced to only 520,000. Thirteen counties and over 150 townships were yet to achieve official illiteracy-free status, most of them in poor mountainous areas. Nationally, the illiteracy rate among persons twelve years and older was still 16 per cent, compared with only 11 per cent in Guangdong. The province was ahead of all provinces except Liaoning and neighbouring Guangxi. Moreover, as provincial officials were fond of pointing out, Guangdong's adult education scene was now more robust than at any previous time since 1949, thanks to the popular demand generated by the economic reforms.[43]

Turning from adult literacy to school education, it must be pointed out that the post-Mao economic reforms initially affected adult and school education in quite different ways in Guangdong. Whereas the reforms appear to have had a mainly salutary effect on popular demand for adult education, especially in the realm of short-term technical training, the situation of rural primary education was more complicated. The challenge facing local governments by the 1980s was how to retain the significant gains in school enrolment made during the 1960s and 1970s, in the face of fiscal constraints imposed by decollectivization and the lure of new economic opportunities for school-age children created by economic reform.

On one hand, the overall trend was definitely one of strengthening and improvement in the provision of basic schooling. By the latter part of the 1980s, rapid commercialization and industrialization of the Pearl River Delta had made local governments flush with revenue and profit. A strong commitment was made in most counties to use this expanded revenue to strengthen and improve local educational systems. Thus, by 1988 large parts of the delta had successfully implemented nine years of compulsory schooling as laid down by the 1986 compulsory education law, while three out of four counties identified as national models for popularizing the nine-year system were located in the delta (Shunde, Xinhui, Dongguan). Dongguan in particular attracted national attention in 1988 when it announced that it was raising recurrent spending on primary and middle school education by 92 per cent over the previous year.[44] The situation in the province as a whole was likewise impressive. By 1985, fully 98 per cent of school-age children were attending primary school in Guangdong, while the completion rate stood at 95.3 per cent, making Guangdong one of the top three provinces in China in terms of success in 'popularizing' (*puji*) primary school education.

The delta region and adjacent areas were also well placed to take advantage of the central government's policy of establishing 'multiple funding channels' (*duoqudao jizi*) for basic education by virtue of the large overseas Chinese population. The 1980s saw a resurgence of overseas remittances and investment in overseas Chinese home counties, a significant proportion of which was directed into the improvement of local educational systems. As early as 1983, it was estimated that since 1979 some 1,500 schools and universities had been built with overseas Chinese assistance in Guangdong and Fujian.[45] The authors of a recent book on educational reform in the Pearl River Delta describe 'mobilizing' educational contributions by local overseas Chinese and compatriots from Hong Kong/Macao/Taiwan as constituting one of the 'most important' means of raising educational funds in the delta. In Taishan, one of the main overseas Chinese counties, local authorities raised more than 81 million yuan for education from overseas Chinese sources between 1986 and 1990 – slightly more than the total government contribution over the same period. Some 60 per cent of primary and middle schools in Taishan received overseas funding between 1978 and 1986, including 107 new schools established by overseas Chinese. They included schools endowed by overseas surname associations (*xingshi ban*) and by prominent overseas Chinese individuals. In addition, many of the overseas-Chinese-funded schools that had been set up in the 1950s (in Taishan alone, twenty-three overseas-funded schools were established during the 1950s) and then closed during the Cultural Revolution were reopened in the 1980s.[46] Sociologist Yuen-fong Woon has described overseas Chinese contributions to schooling in Guangdong's Kaiping county.

They included both money and materials such as building supplies, classroom furniture, electric fans, tape recorders, movie projectors, videocassette recorders, lab equipment, computers, and foreign language texts. Altogether, between 1979 and 1987, overseas Chinese funding supported forty different elementary and junior middle schools in one of Kaiping's main towns, almost as many as the sixty schools funded by collectives and the local government.[47]

On the other hand, however, Guangdong was hardly immune from the pressures that decollectivization and rural reform exerted nationwide on local school funding and attendance. With decollectivization initially weakening the ability of localities to fund basic education, in the early 1980s Guangdong local governments increasingly resorted to the principle of 'whoever studies pays the costs' (*shei dushu shei chuqian*). The increased cost of educating children, coupled with the sudden opportunity to increase household income by sending sons and daughters to work in fields and factories, caused a significant number of parents to withdraw their children from school. By 1985, there were 800,000 fewer primary school students in Guangdong than there had been in 1980 – a drop of 1.1 per cent. It was not until 1990, following passage of the compulsory education law and stricter enforcement of funding and attendance, that primary school enrolment in Guangdong returned to its 1980 level.[48]

Yet even these measures were not enough to halt the problem entirely. Between 1985 and 1989, there were a total of 1.12 million primary school dropouts in Guangdong. Moreover, the problem of dropouts and nonattendance was not restricted to poorer regions but was also characteristic of the most rapidly developing parts of the province. As recently as 1991, for example, in Maoming city, situated in less affluent southern Guangdong, more than 22 per cent of six to eleven year olds were not enrolled in primary school.[49] But even in Dongguan, the most rapidly industrializing county in the province, located adjacent to Shenzhen, there were more than 1,500 school dropouts in 1986, and some 70 per cent of them were female. The problem of school dropouts and non-attendance was worst among girls – the mainstay of the workforce in Guangdong's fast-growing textile, plastics, and electronics export industries. Indeed, the situation became so serious that internally circulated county educational bulletins in the late 1980s warned of senior primary school classes in some counties becoming so devoid of female students that they were popularly referred to as *nanshengban* ('male student classes').[50] The problem of female school attendance was eventually partially resolved in the 1990s through a combination of stricter enforcement of school attendance and, more importantly, the growth of a huge migrant labour force composed of young, unmarried females from the interior provinces seeking work in Guangdong's export factories.[51]

Finally, teachers were also adversely affected by the reforms, especially during the first decade of reform. Salaries of both minban and state-paid teachers failed to keep pace with the rapidly increasing costs of living in Guangdong, forcing many to seek alternative jobs or supplementary income. By the late 1980s, high inflation had severely eroded teachers' salaries, with some reports claiming that teachers' real purchasing power was actually lower than it had been in 1949-50. Instances of local minban teachers going without pay for extended periods were widespread in Guangdong throughout the 1980s as local governments debated their educational responsibilities and struggled to create or maintain a fiscal base. Lured by higher wages and better living conditions in other occupations, Guangdong teachers quit in increasing numbers during the reform period. In the Pearl River Delta, where the lure of more lucrative occupations was greatest, the number of employed teachers fell from 12,500 in 1985 to 11,100 in 1987.[52]

Studies of the growth of literacy in Europe suggest that the experience of the Pearl River Delta under reform was not unlike that of other societies that have experienced rapid industrialization. In studying the Industrial Revolution's impact upon education in Europe, for instance, Carlo Cipolla concluded that, with the rise of child labour, formal education may actually have declined among the poor during the early stage of industrialization, as the appearance of factory labour increased the 'opportunity costs' to parents of keeping children in school. Similarly, in their meticulous study of the growth of literacy and schooling in France, French historians Furet and Ozouf found that in the nineteenth century literacy was 'dragging its feet' in localities that experienced sudden, wide-scale industrialization.[53] These comparisons reinforce the view, stated at the outset of this chapter, that the relationship of the post-Mao reforms to rural education was neither as clear-cut nor as unidirectional as the reformers had hoped and theorized, and that the great economic changes of the reform era – decollectivization and the return to family farming, growth of commerce and industry, and the open-door policy – affected rural literacy in complex and often unexpected ways.

11
The Struggle for Literacy in Guangdong

Revolutions seek to transform society, but the results often reflect the uneven distribution of political, economic, and cultural resources in the old society as much as the intentions and efforts of the revolutionaries. In the late 1980s, Fudan University demographer Dai Xingyi suggested that China could be divided into three model zones in terms of literacy success: Zone A, where illiteracy is minimal, which includes Guangdong, Beijing-Shanghai-Tianjin, and Liaoning, Jilin, Heilongjiang, Hunan; Zone B, the middle or relatively average zone of lesser literacy but considerable cultural richness (Jiangsu, Henan, Shandong, Sichuan, Zhejiang, Shaanxi, Guangxi, Shanxi, Hubei, Anhui, et cetera); and Zone C, the western border provinces, where literacy education has floundered (Gansu, Qinghai, Tibet, et cetera).[1] Guangdong's location at the top of Dai Xingyi's national literacy map underscores its success at the national level (Table 3). At the same time, however, Dai's national literacy profile masks significant literacy and educational differentials within Guangdong. What are some of the factors that account for these internal variations? Are literacy differentials primarily related to levels of economic development? To proximity of towns and cities? Or to some other measure of development? How have the distinctive economic, political, and social features of Guangdong contributed to the successes and failures of literacy education within it?

The sources available to historians of literacy in China do not permit the kind of exhaustive, systematic analysis of regional variations in literacy patterns over time that distinguishes works such as Furet and Ozouf's masterly study of the growth of literacy in modern France.[2] Nonetheless, the broad outlines of Guangdong's internal variations in level of educational development were suggested in a 1986 report published by the Guangdong education bureau. The report divided the province into three zones of literacy and educational development – a simpler provincial version of Dai Xingyi's national literacy map (Map 3).

Table 3

Illiterates aged fifteen years and older by province, autonomous districts, and directly administered cities, 1990

	Number of persons		Per cent	
	Male	Female	Male	Female
Total	47,071,222	107,011,373	15.74	37.11
Beijing	123,955	281,796	11.77	25.99
Tianjin	90,464	246,645	9.48	25.23
Hebei	2,581,747	5,855,125	15.00	34.24
Shanxi	905,130	1,770,635	12.40	25.16
Neimengu	937,754	1,676,792	18.81	37.44
Liaoning	678,374	1,450,867	9.23	20.67
Jilin	645,967	1,148,775	12.30	23.36
Heilongjiang	842,709	1,609,079	12.62	25.92
Shanghai	207,659	603,394	11.96	32.67
Jiangsu	2,730,729	7,369,652	13.81	37.29
Zhejiang	1,703,063	3,933,489	15.42	37.52
Anhui	3,973,290	8,488,980	23.86	53.49
Fujian	970,002	3,101,786	12.14	40.19
Jiangxi	1,470,480	4,069,949	14.32	41.77
Shandong	3,420,519	8,059,150	15.54	36.32
Henan	4,021,464	8,789,077	15.86	35.01
Hubei	2,119,754	5,005,409	15.40	38.37
Hunan	1,883,120	4,763,148	10.36	28.09
Guangdong	956,224	3,846,493	7.17	29.15
Guangxi	1,028,628	3,155,007	8.47	28.02
Hainan	196,653	596,363	11.83	37.47
Sichuan	4,831,180	10,468,545	14.49	33.17
Guizhou	2,126,529	4,924,835	23.95	58.89
Yunnan	2,968,739	5,831,337	27.80	56.56
Tibet	370,676	553,661	61.80	88.51
Shaanxi	1,855,873	3,527,908	20.38	40.40
Gansu	2,020,367	3,699,355	32.11	61.79
Qinghai	400,985	718,837	35.66	68.35
Ningxia	323,886	600,514	29.56	56.44
Xinjiang	685,302	864,770	20.78	28.30

Source: *Zhongguo 1990 nian renkou pucha ziliao*, vol. 2 (Beijing: Zhongguo tongji chubanshe 1990), 276-7.

The agriculturally prosperous, rapidly industrializing, and heavily urban-ized and commercialized Pearl River Delta and other urban and suburban areas of the province constituted the zone of greatest literacy and educa-tional development. Illiteracy in this zone was basically eliminated and universal primary schooling firmly established by 1986. The middle

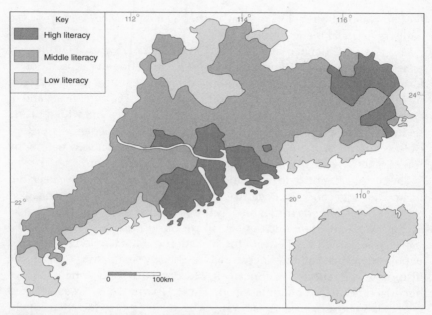

Map 3: Literacy zones in Guangdong, 1986
Source: 'Jiji fazhan nongmin jiaoyu,' *Guangdong jiaoyu* 10 (1986):15-16.

educational zone encompassed the remaining parts of the province, with the exception of mountain, coastal, and minority-populated areas. The middle zone was characterized by an 'average' (*yiban*) level of cultural development as determined by the 1982 national census. Approximately half of Guangdong's population belonged to the middle zone. The third zone, representing the lowest level of educational development in the province, was comprised of official minority districts, the remote mountainous parts of the interior, and the poor coastal regions. Anti-illiteracy work and universalization of primary education comprised the most urgent task in the third zone. County by county, literacy figures from the 1982 census generally conform to this pattern (Appendix).[3]

The 1982 census, the first since the end of the Mao era, revealed that literacy education in postrevolutionary Guangdong fared best in those parts of the province where it was traditionally highest, and remained low in areas where literacy had traditionally been lacking. More specifically, the census figures revealed that literacy was highest in two areas in particular: the Pearl River Delta, writ large to include the greater Foshan-Guangzhou commercial region, and in Meixian county in northeastern Guangdong. The greater Foshan-Guangzhou region alone accounts for nearly 60 per cent of the total Guangdong population. Thus, together with Meixian, the greater

Foshan-Guangzhou region is what pushed Guangdong to the top of Dai Xingyi's national literacy profile.

The fact that Meixian and the Pearl River Delta are both high literacy zones in Guangdong is significant because it confounds any expectation of a simple correlation between economic development and literacy attainment. The delta has been the economic, political and cultural heartland of Guangdong for at least six centuries, since the Ming period, which makes its literacy success seem perhaps less surprising. But Meixian has historically been one of the poorest parts of Guangdong, populated mainly by Hakka 'guest people.' Why has literacy fared best in Meixian?

The historical motive for education in Meixian appears to have been bureaucratic, not economic. Poverty is what historically drove Meixian villagers to seek livelihoods through education, as reflected in a popular Hakka saying: 'Without economic outlets, all we can do is study' (*Meiyou chulu suoyi dushu*). Traditional esteem for education in Meixian, long celebrated in popular culture and now increasingly studied by Guangdong educational historians, was reflected historically in Meixian's disproportionate share of imperial officials and examination graduates.[4] In the 1980s, it was reflected in Meixian's unsurpassed literacy rates. The literacy rate in Meizhou City in 1982 was 91 per cent – the highest in Guangdong. It was well above the literacy rate in the Cantonese heartland cities of Guangzhou, the provincial capital, at 85.8 per cent and Foshan, the province's main commercial centre, at 86 per cent.[5]

If poverty stimulated literacy in Meixian, then the rural-urban commercial heritage and the related legacy of lineage-sponsored schooling were critical historical influences on literacy and educational development in the Pearl River Delta. Historian David Faure has shown how the growth of the lineage in the Pearl River Delta was linked to the spread of literacy and of the 'literate ideal' in the region since the fifteenth century.[6] The legacy of lineage schooling may have benefited post-1949 educational development in the delta in two ways. First, the tradition of lineage sponsorship of education for economic and political reasons bequeathed a rich legacy of well-established schools, many with histories stretching back several centuries. As previously noted, many of the 'keypoint' and 'central' schools set up in the 1950s originated as academies and charitable schools during the Qing period. County educational histories also show that lineages led the way in establishing modern primary schools following the abolition of the imperial examination system in 1905. Moreover, lineage domination of local education also made for an especially rich proliferation of village sishu ('private schools') in the delta. Subsequently established minban schools, run by single-surname production brigades and teams, were thus perpetuating a long-established local tradition of community sponsorship of schools. Overseas remittances channelled through lineage ties, though reduced after 1949, also continued to fortify schools in the overseas Chinese home areas. Lineage schooling thus provided the foundation for a solidly established school system to emerge in the delta after 1949. Finally, the delta's rich heritage of lineage-based schooling may have helped in another way as well, by fostering a school culture that may not have existed to the same extent in regions that lacked this tradition.

Schools themselves cannot, however, account for all of the delta's pre-1949 educational success. As Furet and Ozouf point out with respect to the spread of literacy in rural France, 'the school is not the substance or the heart of the literacy process, but merely its form.' What is more significant, in the final analysis, are the 'social pressures' in favour of literacy.[7] Confucian values attached to learning, whether for self-cultivation or state service, certainly constituted one such stimulus. Commercialization was another. Historically, in agrarian societies the role of commerce was often critical in the spread of literacy. In France, for example, the growth of literacy 'by and large conformed to the laws of uneven economic development: literate France was ... open-field France, with high farm productivity and well-to-do villages and peasant communities. The spread of literacy was born of the market economy, which contributed to the division of labour and to the growth of written communications.'[8] Likewise, developmental economists have found a correlation between education and agricultural productivity, 'particularly in modernizing agricultural conditions such as marketing mechanisms.'[9]

The Pearl River Delta was historically one of the most heavily commercialized regions of China. The commercial activity that formerly gave rise to localized occupational and mercantile literacy in the delta was all but eliminated under the cellular economy of the collective era. Collectivization in the mid-1950s severed the dense commercial networks that formerly linked the delta economically to local and regional market towns, cities, and even beyond, via Hong Kong, to the world market. The literate practices that sustained those networks, however, may have continued to play a role. While local commerce shrivelled under state socialism, we might reasonably expect commercial activity to have continued to stimulate literacy at higher levels of the marketing hierarchy, such as in the case of regional hubs that retained their traditional role as centres for surplus transfer and redistribution. Literacy figures from the 1982 census lend some support to this hypothesis. The highest literacy rates in the Pearl River Delta were in Foshan (86 per cent) and Jiangmen (87 per cent), the traditional commercial hubs for the central and southwestern parts of the delta, respectively.[10]

The trend supports Skinner's argument that post-1949 institutional reorganizations worked best when built on 'natural' socioeconomic units rooted in marketing networks.[11] Skinner pointed out that the collective units into which Chinese rural society was parcelled after 1949 rested on a historical foundation of marketing arrangements with deep roots in the economic geography of the countryside and in the social and economic life of the peasantry. While the traditional link between marketing and literacy was severed or transposed into workpoint literacy at the level of the pro- duction team, it may have survived intact at the level of regional marketing centres. Of course, there are numerous other variables, difficult to isolate, that may also help to explain why literacy rates tend to be highest in re- gional centres. State schools, with their superior budgets and opportunities for social advancement, tended to concentrate in such locations. Local edu- cational budgets in general were also bigger in major centres. And urban parents may have, in general, possessed a greater sense of the opportunities that education brings. Proving the effect of any one of these factors, how- ever, is extremely difficult.

If the post-1949 successes of literacy education in Guangdong were strongly regionally and historically based, so too were the failures. Skinner has re- cently provided a sophisticated analysis of spatial variation within the Lingnan macroregion with respect to literacy and nine other socioeconomic indicators.[12] His conclusion is that spatial inequality in Lingnan (of which Guangdong constitutes the major part) 'is stark, at least as stark as that in any other Chinese macroregion.' These spatial inequalities closely parallel the region's internal core-periphery structure. Thus, levels of development in the most rural areas of Lingnan's far periphery are comparable with those of the poorest nations in Asia, while development in Lingnan's urbanized inner core, centred on the Pearl River Delta, is now nearly on a par with that of South Korea and Taiwan. Illiteracy increases sharply as one moves out into the hinterland of lower-level towns and cities in the periphery. Lingnan's relative advantage – which also explains why Guangdong was pushed to the top of Dai Xingyi's national literacy profile – lies in the fact that, compared with North China (where population density is only weakly correlated with agricultural productivity), population in Lingnan is dispro- portionately concentrated in the most productive parts of the province. Population density in the delta often exceeds 600 persons per square kilo- metre, whereas densities of 50-200 persons per square kilometre are not uncommon in the hilly regions of the north, east, and west of the province. As noted, the delta and greater Foshan-Guangzhou area accounted for nearly 60 per cent of Guangdong's population.

But in the mountainous districts and counties that accounted for nearly 42 per cent of Guangdong's population, educational progress was much slower. Whereas by 1990 educational officials in the Pearl River Delta were openly discussing the need for a distinctive 'Lingnan coastal educational' strategy that could absorb the latest foreign achievements and experiences, mountain regions remained preoccupied with more basic concerns.[13] Al- though primary schooling was 'basically' universalized in the mountain counties by 1985, the numbers of non-attendees, dropouts, and overage students were all significantly higher in the mountain counties than in the delta. As recently as 1990, the primary school completion rate in one district in Liannan county was only 27 per cent. And whereas provincewide about 30 per cent of total educational expenditure was invested in improvement and development, in the mountain areas the figure was less than 10 per cent, with more than 90 per cent devoted to maintaining existing programs.[14]

Literacy fared least well in the minority-populated areas of the province, making Guangdong a microcosm of all China in this respect. In the Yao counties of Liannan and Ruyuan in northeast Guangdong, for instance, illiteracy rates in 1982 were 30 per cent and 35 per cent, respectively, while in parts of Hainan the figure rose to 48 per cent (Hainan became a separate province in 1988). According to reports in the mid-1980s, the illiteracy rate in some minority areas of Guangdong was still a staggering 90 per cent.[15]

Finally, there is also the question of gender differentials in literacy and educational attainment in Guangdong. According to Chinese demographer Peng Xizhe, gender differentials in education are especially marked in Guangdong. In particular, says Peng, there is a strong household preference for males in the allocation of primary schooling in Guangdong.[16] Whereas in many provinces gender differences in school attendance appear minor, Peng points out that in Guangdong over 88 per cent of school-age males were enrolled in primary school during the 1980s, compared to only 64.4 per cent of females. Other provinces with high gender gaps in school attendance, such as Anhui and some western provinces, were less developed and therefore slower to implement national policies. But Guangdong was economically an advanced province, so why did it lag behind? In Peng's view, Guangdong's relative 'backwardness' in this and other gender-related issues (Guangdong was also the first province to sanction a second child if the first was a girl) was primarily due to the tenacity of what Peng called its 'little traditions' and 'special institutional settings.' Specifically, he attributed Guangdong's 'very staunch resistance' to national policies of gender equality to the persistence of 'feudal' ideologies of 'clan superiority' that ranked males over females. Such ideologies persisted because of the continued influence of overseas Chinese and the province's 'special political history,' by which Peng presumably meant Guangdong's long tradition of tension with and resistance to the central state in Beijing.

A similar argument has been advanced by educational demographer Jacques Lamontagne, whose work also suggests that Guangdong's gender-based literacy differential is anomalous in China. What he terms the 'female-male inequality ratio' – the ratio of female to male illiterates – is higher in Guangdong than in any other Chinese province: 4:11 compared with a national low of 1:36 (in Tibet).[17] It is important to realize, however, that such ratios may sometimes mislead. When actual female illiteracy figures are compared for different provinces – as opposed to female-male ratios – Guangdong emerges as one of the country's leading provinces in progress toward eliminating female illiteracy. In terms of the percentage of total population, for example, female illiteracy in Guangdong is actually among the lowest in China: 37 per cent in Guangdong as compared with 45 per cent nationally, 57 per cent in neighbouring Fujian, 52 per cent in Shandong, 51 per cent in Henan, 50 per cent in Jiangsu, and 64 per cent in Anhui. Moreover, female illiteracy in Guangdong, as elsewhere in China, is most heavily concentrated among the elderly and declines steadily among younger age cohorts. According to a 1987 population sample, among females sixty years of age, over 82 per cent were illiterate. But illiteracy among forty-year-old females was only 26 per cent, among twenty year olds 7.4 per cent, and among twelve year olds only 6 per cent.[18]

Guangdong's post-1949 progress in eliminating male-female differences in illiteracy also compares favourably with the experience of other Asian countries at similar levels of economic development and with similar patrilineal family traditions. In 1982, a total of 7.67 per cent of Guangdong males and 31.45 per cent of females were illiterate (population aged twelve and over). These figures compared with India's illiteracy rate of 45.2 per cent of males and 74.3 per cent of females; to Pakistan's illiteracy rate of 64 per cent among males and 84.8 per cent among females; and to Indonesia's illiteracy rate of 22.5 per cent among males and 42.3 per cent among females.[19] Guangdong's male illiteracy figure of 7.67 per cent was not only lower than those of the countries cited above but also significantly lower than those of all other Chinese provinces. Thus, the most salient point about gender differences in literacy attainment in Guangdong seems to be not that female literacy has lagged behind but that male literacy is so far ahead, both nationally and internationally.

Turning from Guangdong to China as a whole, we may pose some larger issues raised by this study. To what extent do the 'failures' of the PRC literacy movement reflect the nature of the Chinese Communist Party, the People's Republic of China, or Mao Zedong personally? To what extent do they represent authentic dilemmas inherent in the situation of modern China? What role are we to assign, for example, to factors such as the chronic fiscal weakness of the twentieth-century Chinese state? Or the organizational complexities of governing a large and poor country such as China? Or the overwhelming demographic challenge of extending basic education to more than 800 million rural dwellers? Most would probably agree that, compared to most other large and poor countries at a similar level of development, the PRC has responded remarkably well to the demographic challenges facing mass education over the past five decades.

But at what cost? Did the PRC model of mass education, with its empha-sis on local voluntarism for the countryside, while maintaining a privileged state-funded school system in the cities, not end up perpetuating rural-urban differences and regionally based educational inequalities? More than twenty years ago, historian Donald Munro asked, 'If local areas not only have self-management but also provide a substantial amount of their own financing, does this [not] mean that poor areas will provide educational facilities infe-rior to those of prosperous areas and, thus, that the problem of equity will not be solved at all?'[20] Twenty years of educational development appear to have proved Munro correct. Regional and local educational inequalities persisted, perhaps even widened, under Mao.

Could China have pursued a different course? The reaffirmation of local educational voluntarism represented, in part, a deliberate choice necessi-tated by what economist Barry Naughton has termed China's 'stunted fiscal structure,' which was based on the Stalinist formula of rich industry-poor agriculture and the 'enforced poverty' of rural areas.[21] The Stalinist model of channelling state investment into urban industrialization – a pattern that Mao never broke with – precluded large state outlays for education and social welfare services in China's vast countryside. The reaffirmation of lo-cal voluntarism was also partly a result of the general fiscal poverty of the Chinese state in the twentieth century, a situation that post-1949 leaders exacerbated with Stalinist policies. Yet local educational voluntarism was embraced partly for positive reasons as well. Mao, like important Confucian thinkers before him, believed that successful initiative and management had to be rooted in local communities.

The dilemma of how to create a national educational system that re-sponds to and is not divorced from the genuine educational needs of local communities has confronted every agrarian society in the twentieth cen-tury.[22] In China, the inadequacy of the formal school system for meeting rural needs has been a common concern of educational reformers through-out this century, ever since the first plans for a national school system were laid in 1904. During the 1930s, a famous League of Nations report on Chinese education heavily criticized the republican school system for its urban bias and basic irrelevance to the educational needs of the vast ma-jority of China's rural citizens. One of the authors of the report, R.H. Tawney, described Chinese higher educational institutions as seemingly 'suspended in the air' – completely divorced from the needs of the rural majority.[23] Not only did educational reformers with divergent ideological views share such concerns but they also tended to concur in the solutions they put forward: an emphasis on locally relevant curricula and local financing, often drawing – as Mao himself had done since the mid-1920s – on the old-style village schools as models. The efforts of republican-era non-communist mass educators such as James Yen, Tao Xingzhi, and Liang

Shuming were firmly based upon the premise that what was taught ought to be of use in people's daily life.[24]

In fact, all of the major debates that tore through Chinese education after 1949 had their origins in the early twentieth century. As Paul Bailey has shown, when Mao belittled formal schooling and academic instruction, condemned examinations, and stressed practical learning and manual labour, he was echoing the criticisms of late-Qing and early-republican reformers who had blasted the new schools for fostering elitism and disdain for manual labour. The post-1949 problem of balancing the conflicting demands of 'elevation' (*tigao*) and 'popularization' (*puji*) also mirrored the early-twentieth-century struggle between advocates of 'education for talent' (*rencai jiaoyu*) and advocates of 'general education' (*putong jiaoyu*). And when Mao battled Liu Shaoqi and Deng Xiaoping over the relative emphasis to be given to building up a well-endowed and centralized formal school system versus decentralized spare-time schools, the protagonists were reliving earlier struggles by proponents of non-formal social education who had seen the formal system as unresponsive to the educational needs of workers and peasants.[25]

The socialist state after 1949 promoted local literacy among rural citizens partly, it is true, from the genuine and highly responsible desire to make education in the villages relevant and responsive to local needs. Another hope was pedagogical: the idea that the written language was more easily grasped if learning was integrated with daily life. But yet another was political. The mass literacy efforts in China's countryside after 1949 cannot be understood apart from the state's larger political project of creating a class of statutory peasants, tied permanently to their collectives. The ideological premise underlying the literacy drive was crucially involved – along with ration cards, residential status (*hukou*), and other mobility restrictions – in the 'pinning down' of the Chinese peasantry to the land, where the production of China's precarious food supply occurred.

Yet in the final analysis, there was perhaps also an equally significant positive aspect – not easily denied – of the legacy of local voluntarism and workpoint literacy. The strategy of minban schooling and adult literacy education was successful in creating a 'broad base of simple skills' among the rural population, which in turn 'laid the foundation for a spurt of agricultural and other economic growth in the countryside after 1981.' Without the fundamental investments in human capital made during the 1950s and 1960s, it is doubtful whether the agricultural reforms enacted after 1978 would have produced the same dramatic effect in China's countryside.[26] Anthropologist Brian Street has argued that the traditional literacy taught in Iranian village Islamic schools enabled villagers to adapt easily to commercial literacy practices required by their growing involvement in the world economy as fruit exporters. Rote memorization of Islamic texts, Street suggests, instilled respect for the importance of format and exact positioning of words, learning traits that were then transferred to commercial literate practices such as accounting and record keeping.[27] In a somewhat similar way, the workpoint literacy learned in China's collectives may have facilitated a transference of skills, paving the way for the success of peasant entrepreneurialism in the postcollective era.

It is true that many of the issues that have surrounded basic rural education in China throughout the twentieth century continue to confront Chinese leaders today. Although rural illiteracy may have been largely eliminated on a national scale, the question of education for rural needs is still unresolved. Local voluntarism remains a central feature of state educational policy. The economic environment in which the choices regarding local educational development are being made, however, has changed dramatically in recent years. In the long run, that may make all the difference.

Appendix

Educational levels in Guangdong by district, city, and county, 1982 (thousands)

Locality	Total	Junior middle school	Primary school	Illiterate	Per cent illiterate	Illiterates aged 12 years and over
Total	51,760	10,024	24,086	12,672	24.4	9,747
Guangzhou City	5,088	1,177	2,137	726	14.2	565
Guangzhou						
City Proper	2,919	739	1,015	295	10.0	239
Hua County	374	87	180	66	17.6	50
Conghua County	319	69	153	61	19.3	44
Xinfeng County	162	35	73	35	22.0	27
Longmen County	215	48	98	50	23.6	36
Zengcheng County	490	92	271	98	20.0	68
Panyu County	605	104	342	118	19.5	98
Shaoguan City	600	145	251	12	18.7	88
Shaoguan						
City Proper	312	90	115	37	12.0	29
Qujiang County	288	54	135	74	25.9	58
Shenzhen City	305	74	131	66	22.0	52
Shenzhen						
City District	101	29	35	13	13.0	10
Baoan County	203	44	95	53	26.0	42
Zhuhai City	119	28	55	19	16.0	15
Hainan						
Admin. District	3,239	653	1,298	894	28.0	734
Haikou City	240	70	76	40	17.0	34
Qiongshan County	431	80	184	118	27.4	97
Wenchang County	409	91	181	86	21.0	74
Qionghai County	330	79	143	64	19.0	55
Wanning County	350	70	148	90	26.0	71

▶

◀ *Hainan Admin. District*

Locality	Total	Junior middle school	Primary school	Illiterate	Per cent illiterate	Illiterates aged 12 years and over
Dingan County	208	43	88	49	24.0	40
Tunchang County	177	35	73	48	28.0	40
Dengmai County	315	61	130	88	28.0	73
Lingao County	262	39	91	101	39.0	82
Dan County	513	81	179	206	40.0	163
Hainan Li, Miao						
Autonomous Prefecture	1,578	289	590	537	34.0	393
Ya County	247	52	95	75	30.0	53
Dongtang County	214	29	64	101	48.0	77
Ledong County	310	51	116	113	36.0	82
Qiongzhong County	160	33	64	43	27.0	31
Baoting County	170	35	67	42	25.0	30
Lingshui County	208	40	85	63	30.0	48
Baisha County	120	21	48	38	32.0	27
Changjiang County	147	25	46	60	41.0	42
Shantou District	9,193	1,345	4,555	2,694	29.0	2,148
Shantou City	658	145	290	134	20.0	111
Chaozhou City	150	40	65	20	13.5	16
Chaoan County	886	134	496	204	23.0	168
Chenghai County	562	81	285	154	27.0	130
Raoping County	646	80	288	245	38.0	196
Nanao County	51	6	22	18	36.0	16
Chaoyang County	1,442	162	785	425	30.0	326
Jieyang County	1,131	193	667	189	17.0	151
Jiexi County	524	107	271	98	19.0	78
Puning County	1,017	160	569	228	22.0	171
Huilai County	572	57	219	269	47.0	216
Lufeng County	897	89	328	440	49.0	352
Haifeng County	651	85	262	265	41.0	210
Meixian District	3,267	800	1,461	609	19.0	470
Meizhou City	100	32	27	8	9.0	6
Mei County	526	154	216	80	15.0	65
Dapu County	373	92	171	66	18.0	52
Fengshun County	429	82	225	87	20.0	65
Wuhua County	709	134	347	161	23.0	116
Xingning County	775	219	318	138	18.0	109
Pingyuan County	183	38	86	37	20.0	30
Jiaoling County	169	45	68	29	17.0	23
Huiyang District	4,566	967	2,240	1,034	23.0	779
Huizhou City	150	43	55	22	15.0	17
Huiyang County	361	82	174	81	23.0	63

▶

◀ *Huiyang District*

Locality	Total	Junior middle school	Primary school	Illiterate	Per cent illiterate	Illiterates aged 12 years and over
Zijin County	476	101	227	114	24.0	86
Heping County	315	59	160	77	25.0	53
Lianping County	245	47	114	66	27.0	50
Heyuan County	475	108	212	117	25.0	84
Boluo County	526	115	255	120	23.0	86
Dongguan County	1,011	205	562	182	18.0	149
Huidong County	448	80	206	139	31.0	107
Longchuan County	554	123	271	111	20.0	79
Shaoguan District	4,020	701	1,872	1,148	29.0	887
Shixing County	176	33	85	43	24.0	33
Nanxiong County	342	49	150	117	34.0	99
Renhua County	131	26	58	34	26.0	26
Lechang County	363	66	150	114	31.0	87
Lian County	370	72	173	91	25.0	71
Yangshan County	352	50	174	106	30.0	84
Yingde County	712	110	323	228	32.0	167
Qingyuan County	779	143	387	208	27.0	161
Foteng County	204	43	100	42	21.0	32
Wengyuan County	261	52	121	64	25.0	49
Lianshan Zhuang Yao Autonomous County	77	15	37	16	21.0	13
Liannan Yao Autonomous County	108	19	46	32	30.0	24
Ruyuan Yao Autonomous County	139	19	60	49	35.0	37
Foshan District	6,187	1,297	3,299	1,075	17.0	879
Foshan City	262	67	112	36	14.0	31
Jiangmen City	198	51	90	25	13.0	21
Sanshui County	263	58	129	50	19.0	40
Nanhai County	733	133	431	125	17.0	106
Shunde County	721	142	407	129	18.0	108
Zhongshan County	909	178	502	164	18.0	137
Doumen County	212	42	107	44	21.0	37
Xinhui County	722	136	396	134	19.0	108
Taishan County	838	174	458	125	15.0	98
Enping County	332	78	155	66	20.0	52
Kaiping County	530	125	274	85	16.0	72
Heshan County	274	63	137	50	19.0	38
Gaoming County	187	44	93	35	19.0	26
Zhaoqing District	4,252	799	2,149	959	23.0	723
Zhaoqing City	156	42	60	20	13.0	17
Gaoyao County	622	97	347	146	24.0	114

▶

◀ *Zhaoqing District*

Locality	Total	Junior middle school	Primary school	Illiterate	Per cent illiterate	Illiterates aged 12 years and over
Sihui County	297	60	150	63	21.0	52
Guangning County	383	72	202	79	21.0	60
Huaiji County	526	74	260	153	29.0	107
Fengkai County	316	55	165	71	23.0	53
Deqing County	263	52	129	57	22.0	43
Yuntu County	371	65	184	95	26.0	70
Xinxing County	315	61	163	64	20.0	48
Yunan County	334	71	159	71	21.0	56
Luoding County	664	146	324	134	20.0	99
Zhanjiang District	9,339	1,745	4,044	2,792	30.0	2,008
Zhanjiang City	749	160	288	186	25.0	148
Maoming City	358	82	150	77	21.0	62
Yangjiang County	999	168	453	315	32.0	226
Yangchun County	706	121	336	204	29.0	140
Xinyi County	726	135	340	195	27.0	145
Gaozhou County	960	189	445	246	26.0	207
Dianbai County	915	122	368	373	41.0	298
Wuchuan County	529	104	234	154	30.0	127
Huazhou County	793	183	336	200	25.0	158
Lianjiang County	850	187	361	237	28.0	19
Suixi County	522	102	233	144	28.0	114
Haikang County	817	117	312	333	41.0	262
Xuwen County	408	68	182	121	30.0	96

Source: *Disanci quanguo renkou pucha shougong huizong ziliao huibian,* vol. 5 (Beijing: Zhongguo tongji ju chubanshe 1983), 122-9.

Notes

Chapter 1: Introduction

1 Klaus Belde, *Saomang: Kommunistische Alphabetisierungsarbeit* (Bochum: Brockmeyer 1982).

2 Previous works on the subject include, in addition to Belde's study mentioned above, Ronald F. Price, *Education in Modern China* (London: Routledge and Kegan Paul 1979), especially 202-10 (originally published in 1970 as *Education in Communist China*); Jonathan Unger, *Education under Mao: Class and Competition in Canton Schools, 1960-1980* (New York: Columbia University Press 1982); the various contributions in Ruth Hayhoe, ed., *Contemporary Chinese Education* (London: Croom Helm 1984), especially 12-13, 16-17, 19, 21, 31-3, 48, 58, 60, 80, 82, 201; Charles W. Hayford, 'Literacy Movements in Modern China,' in Robert F. Arnove and Harvey J. Graff, eds., *National Literacy Campaigns: Historical and Comparative Perspectives* (New York: Plenum Press 1987), 147-71; Suzanne Pepper, *China's Education Reform in the 1980s: Policies, Issues and Historical Perspectives* (Berkeley: Institute of East Asian Studies, University of California 1990), 28-65; Vilma Seeberg, *Literacy in China: The Effects of the National Development Context and Policy on Literacy Levels, 1949-1979* (Bochum: Brockmeyer 1990); Alexander Woodside, 'Real and Imagined Continuities in the Chinese Struggle for Literacy,' in Ruth Hayhoe, ed., *Education and Modernization: The Chinese Experience* (Oxford: Pergamon Press 1992), 23-45; and Suzanne Pepper, *Radicalism and Education Reform in 20th-Century China* (Cambridge and New York: Cambridge University Press 1996), especially 194-5, 212, 215, 252, 417, 439-40, 526.

3 Hayford, 'Literacy Movements in Modern China,' 167.

4 Gilbert Rozman, ed., *The Modernization of China* (New York: Free Press 1981), 373, 401-19; H.S. Bhola, *Campaigning for Literacy: Eight National Experiences of the Twentieth Century, with a Memorandum to Decision-Makers* (Paris: UNESCO 1984), 74; Jay Taylor, *The Dragon and the Wild Goose: China and India* (New York: Greenwood Press 1987), 179; Jean C. Robinson, 'Stumbling on Two Legs: Education and Reform in China,' *Comparative Education Review* 35.1 (1991):179.

5 Seeberg, *Literacy in China*, 268, 278-9.

6 *China Daily*, 6 April 1989:3.

7 'Xia Yan de feifu zhi yan: jianguo yilai sanda cuowu,' *Yangcheng wanbao* 18 November 1988; 'Lu Dingyi tongzhi huijian benkan jizhe qiangdao zhichu: minzhu fazhi bixu jiaqiang zhongshi zhishi shifen biyao,' *Minzhu yu fazhi* 4 (1983):2-3; Fang Lizhi, *Tearing Down the Great Wall: Writings on Science, Culture, and Democracy in China* (New York: W.W. Norton 1990), 256.

8 Philip H. Coombs, *The World Crisis in Education: The View from the Eighties* (Oxford: Oxford University Press 1985), 268. *UNESCO Statistical Yearbook*, 1.15-1.22; *The Social Sectors: Population, Health, Nutrition and Education*, vol. 3 of *China: Socialist Economic Development* (Washington, DC: World Bank 1983), 147, 152-3, 211. For an interesting comparison of literacy rates in China and India that supports this interpretation, see Jean Dreze and Jackie Loh, 'Literacy in China and India,' *Economic and Political Weekly* (India), 11 November 1995:2868-78.

9   Xie Guodong, 'Wancheng saomang lishi renwu de tiaojian yu duice,' *Jiaoyu yanjiu* 12 (1991):47.

10 Evelyn Sakakida Rawski, *Education and Popular Literacy in Ch'ing China* (Ann Arbor: University of Michigan Press 1979), 1.

11 John K. Fairbank, 'The Reunification of China,' in Roderick MacFarquhar and John K. Fairbank, eds., *The People's Republic, Part 1: The Emergence of Revolutionary China 1949-1965*, vol. 14 of *The Cambridge History of China* (Cambridge, UK: Cambridge University Press 1987), 18.

12 John K. Fairbank, *The United States and China*, 4th ed. (Cambridge, MA: Harvard University Press 1983), 43.

13 Rawski, *Education and Popular Literacy*, 140.

14 Lu Hongji [Bernard Luk], *Zhongguo jinshi de jiaoyu fazhan* (Hong Kong: Huafeng shuju chubanshe 1983), 74-8, cited in Alexander Woodside and Benjamin A. Elman, 'Afterword: The Expansion of Education in Ch'ing China,' in Benjamin A. Elman and Alexander Woodside, eds., *Education and Society in Late Imperial China, 1600-1900* (Berkeley: University of California Press 1994), 531.

15 Woodside, 'Real and Imagined Continuities,' 26, 37, 38. For another attempt to show how literacy was conditioned by the 'structure of dominance' in late-imperial Chinese society, see David Johnson, 'Communication, Class and Consciousness in Late Imperial China,' in David Johnson, Andrew J. Nathan, and Evelyn S. Rawski, eds., *Popular Culture in Late Imperial China* (Berkeley: University of California Press 1985), 34-72.

16 Woodside and Elman, 'Afterword,' 549.

17 The preeminent statement of this view is in Jack Goody and Ian Watt, 'The Consequences of Literacy,' in Jack Goody, ed., *Literacy in Traditional Societies* (Cambridge, UK: Cambridge University Press 1968), 27-68. See also Daniel Lerner, *The Passing of Traditional Society: Modernizing the Middle East* (New York: Free Press 1958); and Alex Inkeles and David H. Smith, *Becoming Modern* (Cambridge, MA: Harvard University Press 1974).

18 Harvey J. Graff, *The Literacy Myth: Literacy and Social Structure in the Nineteenth Century City* (New York: Academic Press 1979). See also Graff's introduction in Harvey J. Graff, ed., *Literacy and Social Development in the West: A Reader* (Cambridge, UK: Cambridge University Press 1981), 1-13. For a comprehensive overview of the field, see David Barton, *Literacy: An Introduction to the Ecology of Written Language* (Oxford: Basil Blackwell 1994).

19 Brian V. Street, *Literacy in Theory and Practice* (Cambridge, UK: Cambridge University Press 1984), 8.

20 Kenneth Levine, *The Social Context of Literacy* (London: Routledge and Kegan Paul 1986), 43. See also Jennifer Cook-Gumperz, *The Social Construction of Literacy* (Cambridge, UK: Cambridge University Press 1986).

21 Rawski, *Education and Popular Literacy*, 2. See also Hayford, 'Literacy Movements in Modern China,' 150-1; and Glen Peterson, 'Recent Trends in Literacy Studies and Their Application to China,' *Journal of Educational Thought* 28.2 (1994):138-52.

22 Zhou Youguang, 'The Modernization of the Chinese Language,' *International Journal of the Sociology of Language* 59 (1986):13.

23 John DeFrancis, *The Chinese Language: Fact and Fantasy* (Honolulu: University of Hawaii Press 1984), 84, 129.

24 Chen Heqin, *Yuti wen yingyong zihui* (Shanghai: Commercial Press 1931).

25 Cited in Johnson, 'Communication,' 63-4.

26 Kenneth Levine, 'Functional Literacy: Fond Illusions and False Economies,' *Harvard Educational Review* 52.3 (1982):264-5.

27 Graff, ed., *Literacy and Social Development*, 3.

28 Woodside, 'Real and Imagined Continuities,' 30.

29 On the history of plague in China, see Carol Benedict, 'Bubonic Plague in Nineteenth-Century China,' *Modern China* 14.2 (1988):107-55.

30 See Xiao Xiangyong, 'Dui shehui jiaoyu de yidian yijian,' *Guangdong jiaoyu yu wenhua* 1.5 (1950):10-11.

31 'Zhongshan xian Xinping xiang dijiu nonye shengchan hezuoshe de qingnian tujidui,' in Zhonggong zhongyang bangong ting, ed., *Zhongguo nongcun de shehui zhuyi gaochao* (Beijing:

Renmin chubanshe 1956), 3:961; Zheng Xihong, 'Nongmin yeyu jiaoyu de xin fangxiang' *Renmin jiaoyu* 6 (1958):5.

32   Peng Pai, *Haifeng nongmin yundong* (n.p.: Guangdong sheng nongmin xiehui 1926), 18.

33   'Nongcun de xuexi rechao,' *Dagongbao* (Hong Kong), 21 August 1950, in *Union Research Institute* LO136 4222 3235.

34   'Nongcun zhong pochu mixin kaizhan weisheng gongzuo de jingyan,' in Renmin jiaoyushe, ed., *Nongmin shizi jiaoyu de zuzhi xingshi he jiaoxue fangfa*, vol. 1 (Beijing: Renmin jiaoyushe 1950).

35   François Furet and Jacques Ozouf, *Reading and Writing: Literacy in France from Calvin to Jules Ferry* (Cambridge, UK: Cambridge University Press 1982), 2; Woodside, 'Real and Imagined Continuities,' 39. See also Sally Borthwick, *Education and Social Change in China: The Beginnings of the Modern Era* (Stanford: Hoover Institution Press 1983), 66.

36   Paul Bailey, *Reform the People: Changing Attitudes towards Popular Education in Early 20th Century China* (Vancouver: University of British Columbia Press 1990), 2. On the late-Qing educational reforms, see also Marianne Bastid, *Educational Reform in Early Twentieth Century China* (Ann Arbor: University of Michigan Press 1988); and Borthwick, *Education and Social Change*.

37   Hayford, 'Literacy Movements in Modern China,' 153. See also his *To the People: James Yen and Village China* (New York: Columbia University Press 1990), 9.

38   Wolfgang Franke, *The Reform and Abolition of the Chinese Examination System* (Cambridge, MA: Harvard University Press 1960).

39   Bailey, *Reform the People*; Ming K. Chan and Arif Dirlik, *Schools into Fields and Factories: Anarchists, the Guomindang and the National Labour University in Shanghai, 1927-1932* (Durham, NC: Duke University Press 1991).

40   Bailey, *Reform the People*, 143-4.

41   John DeFrancis, *Nationalism and Language Reform in China* (Princeton: Princeton University Press 1950). On the Esperanto movement in China, see Gerald Chan, 'China and the Esperanto Movement,' *Australian Journal of Chinese Affairs* 15 (1986):1-18. The quotation is from S. Robert Ramsey, *The Languages of China* (Princeton: Princeton University Press 1987), 3.

42   For James Yen, see Hayford, *To the People*; for Liang Shuming, see Guy Alitto, *The Last Confucian: Liang Shu-ming and the Chinese Dilemma of Modernity* (Berkeley: University of California Press 1981). Tao Xingzhi's lifework still awaits a book-length study, but see Hubert O. Brown, 'American Progressivism in Chinese Education: The Case of T'ao Hsing-chih,' in Ruth Hayhoe and Marianne Bastid, eds., *China's Education and the Industrialized World* (Armonk, NY: M.E. Sharpe 1987), 120-38. For the CCP's literacy programs during the Jiangxi Soviet, see Wang Hsueh-wen, 'A Study of Chinese Communist Education during the Kiangsi Period,' *Issues and Studies* 9.7 (1973):59-74; 9.8 (1973):69-83; 9.9 (1973):68-81.

43   Hayford, *To the People*, especially xiii-xiv, 11-12, 32-9, 61-2, 111-14. See also Myron L. Cohen, 'The Case of the Chinese "Peasant,"' *Daedalus* 122.2 (1993):151-70; and Chang-tai Hung, *Going to the People: Chinese Intellectuals and Folk Literature, 1918-1937* (Cambridge, MA: Harvard University Press/Council on East Asian Studies 1985).

44   Cohen, 'Case of the Chinese "Peasant,"' 155-6.

45   The issue of Guangdong's representativeness is discussed in William L. Parish and Martin King Whyte, *Village and Family in Contemporary China* (Chicago: University of Chicago Press 1978), especially 28-9, 360 note 11.

46   William Lavely et al., 'The Rise of Female Education in China: National and Regional Patterns,' *China Quarterly* 121 (1990):61.

47   Edward J.M. Rhoads, *China's Republican Revolution: The Case of Kwangtung, 1895-1913* (Cambridge, MA: Harvard University Press 1975), 13.

48   Feng Bingkui, *Zhongguo wenhua yu lingnan wenhua* (Taibei: Taibei zhongxing daxue fashang xueyuan 1962). See also Chen Xujing, 'Kuang-tung yu Chung-kuo,' *Dongfang Zazhi* 36.2 (1939):41-5. For a contemporary celebration of these differences, see Huang Naizhao, He Wenguang, and Gu Zuoyi, *Guangzhou ren: Zuori yu jinri* (Guangzhou: Guangzhou wenhua chubanshe 1987); and the journal *Lingnan wenshi* (Culture and History of Lingnan), which began publication in the early 1980s.

49   See, for example, Helen Siu, 'Cultural Identity and the Politics of Difference in South China,' *Daedalus* 122.2 (1993):19-44. See also Edward Friedman, 'Reconstructing China's National

Identity: A Southern Alternative to Mao-Era Anti-Imperialist Nationalism,' *Journal of Asian Studies* 53.1 (1994):67-91; and Lynn White and Li Cheng, 'China Coast Identities: Regional, National, and Global,' in Lowell Dittmer and Samuel S. Kim, eds., *China's Quest for a National Identity* (Ithaca: Cornell University Press 1993), 154-93.

50 For Guangdong's position among China's macroregions, see the chapters by Skinner in G. William Skinner, ed., *The City in Late Imperial China* (Stanford: Stanford University Press 1977).

51 Guangdong sheng tongji ju, ed., *Guangdong sheng shi di xian gaikuang* (Guangzhou: Guangdong sheng ditu chubanshe 1985). See also Wu Yuwen, ed., *Guangdong sheng jingji dili* (Beijing: Xinhua chubanshe 1986); and Zhu Yuncheng, ed., *Zhongguo renkou: Guangdong fence* (Beijing: Zhongguo caizheng jingji chubanshe 1988).

52 Herold J. Wiens, *China's March to the Tropics* (Hamden, CT: Shoe String Press 1954); Ezra Vogel, *Canton under Communism: Programs and Politics in a Provincial Capital, 1949-1968* (Cambridge, MA: Harvard University Press 1969), 22-4. For a brief summary of Guangdong's early and modern history, see Lau Yee-cheung, 'History,' in Y.M. Yeung and David K.Y. Chu, eds., *Guangdong: Survey of a Province Undergoing Rapid Change* (Hong Kong: Chinese University Press 1994), 430-47.

53 On the linguistic variety of Guangdong, see Leo J. Moser, *The Chinese Mosaic: The Peoples and Provinces of China* (Boulder: Westview Press 1985), 203-55. Interested readers should also consult the many references listed in Moser's extensive bibliography on Cantonese and Hakka. Another vital source is Ramsey, *The Languages of China*.

54 Susan Naquin and Evelyn S. Rawski, *Chinese Society in the Eighteenth Century* (New Haven: Yale University Press 1987), 178.

55 Ibid., 178-81. For the history of lineages, see David Faure, 'The Lineage as a Cultural Invention: The Case of the Pearl River Delta,' *Modern China* 15.1 (1989):4-36; and the early chapters of Helen F. Siu, *Agents and Victims in South China: Accomplices in Rural Revolution* (New Haven: Yale University Press 1989).

56 Qin Mu, 'Guangdong wenhua jiaoyu lunkuo shu,' *Guangdong jiaoyu yu wenhua* 1.6 (1950):2-6.

Chapter 2: Minban Schools

1 On land reform in China, see John Wong, *Land Reform in the People's Republic of China: Institutional Transformation in Agriculture* (New York: Praeger 1973); and Victor Lippit, *Land Reform in China: A Study of Institutional Change and Development* (White Plains, NY: International Arts and Sciences Press 1974).

2 On land reform in Guangdong, see Ezra Vogel, *Canton under Communism: Programs and Politics in a Provincial Capital, 1949-1968* (Cambridge, MA: Harvard University Press 1969), 91-124.

3 David Faure, 'The Lineage as a Cultural Invention: The Case of the Pearl River Delta,' *Modern China* 15.1 (1989):4-36.

4 Huang Yanpei, 'Qingji gesheng xingxue shi' (xu), *Renwen yuekan* 1.8 (1930):10, as cited in Sally Borthwick, *Education and Social Change in China: The Beginnings of the Modern Era* (Stanford: Hoover Institution Press 1983), 63.

5 On late-imperial academies (*shuyuan*) in Guangdong, see Tilemann Grimm, 'Academies and Urban Systems in Kwangtung,' in G. William Skinner, ed., *The City in Late Imperial China* (Stanford: Stanford University Press 1977), 475-98. For the impact of the late-Qing educational reforms on lineage and gentry sponsorship of modern schools in Guangdong, see Edward J.M. Rhoads, *China's Republican Revolution: The Case of Kwangtung, 1895-1913* (Cambridge, MA: Harvard University Press 1975), 72-7.

6 Lineages owned 40 per cent of land in the southern and middle parts of Guangdong, 35 per cent of land in the east, 25 per cent of land in the north, and 23 per cent of land in the southwest. See Chen Han-seng, *Landlord and Peasant in China: A Study of the Agrarian Crisis in South China* (New York: International Publishers 1936), 35-6.

7 Ibid., 73-4; Robert Y. Eng, 'Institutional and Secondary Landlordism in the Pearl River Delta, 1600-1949,' *Modern China* 12 (1986):3-38.

8 Borthwick, *Education and Social Change in China*, 97-8, 103. Popular resentment of modern schools was also often linked to the expropriation of local temples for use by modern schools.

9 Prasenjit Duara, *Culture, Power and the State: Rural North China, 1900-1942* (Stanford: Stanford University Press 1988), 111-12.
10 Merchant-sponsored schools were found mainly in southwestern Guangdong, especially in the area surrounding Maoming, where private merchant associations (*huiguan*) had been active since the seventeenth century in sponsoring local schools. By contrast, in the delta region, where nearly all corporate land was held by lineages, such schools were rare.
11 For the development of modern schooling in Guangdong up to 1949, see Wu Qingsheng, 'Weichi nongcun xiaoxue de daolu,' *Guangdong jiaoyu yu wenhua* 3.1 (1951):3. See also Zhang Mingsheng, 'Guangdong chudeng jiaoyu de qingkuang yu wenti,' *Guangdong jiaoyu yu wenhua* 3.2 (1951):10-13; and Shen Hengsong, 'Guangdong sili zhongdeng xuexiao de guoqu he weilai,' *Guangdong jiaoyu yu wenhua* 2.4 (1951):14-15. For an interesting comparison of educational development in different provinces during the republican period, see Ruth Hayhoe, 'Cultural Tradition and Educational Modernization: Lessons from the Republican Era,' in Ruth Hayhoe, ed., *Education and Modernization: The Chinese Experience* (Oxford: Pergamon Press 1992), 60-7.
12 Reliable estimates of sishu attendance are extremely difficult to find, due to the nature of the institution – attendance was non-compulsory and flexible depending on the needs of individual students – and because the sishu was officially proscribed, which meant a furtive existence for most. One official report estimated the total number of sishu pupils in Guangdong in 1940 at around 139,000, which is almost certainly an underestimate. See Guangdong sheng zhengfu mishu chu bianyi shi, ed., *Guangdong jiaoyu* (Guangzhou: Guangdong sheng zhengfu mishu chu dier ke 1943), Table 4.
13 'Jiefang qian Maoming de shuyuan he sishu,' *Maoming jiaoyu* 2 (1992):35-6.
14 On the sishu's place in society, see Liao T'ai-ch'u, 'Rural Education in Transition: A Study of the Old-Fashioned Chinese Schools (Szu-Shu) in Shantung and Szechuan,' *Yenching Journal of Social Studies* 4.1 (1948):1240-2. See also Sally Borthwick, *Education and Social Change in China: The Beginnings of the Modern Era* (Stanford: Hoover Institution Press 1983), 63, 17-37.
15 Cited in Borthwick, *Education and Social Change*, 81.
16 The official proscription of sishu started with Zhang Zhidong's 1904 school regulations, which banned all sishu except those with thirty or more pupils from participating in the new educational system. See Ibid.
17 The expression 'Teacher Eight Legs' referred to the abstruse and highly stylized 'eight-legged essay' format required of candidates in the imperial civil service examinations. Peng's use of the term was intended to denigrate classically educated village teachers, whose pedagogical traditions Peng regarded as unfit for the modern classroom.
18 Peng Pai, *Haifeng nongmin yundong* (n.p.: Guangdong sheng nongmin xiehui 1926), 17-18.
19 Guangdong nongmin yundong jiangxi suo jiuzhi jinian guan, ed., *Guangzhou nongmin yundong jiangxi suo ziliao xuanbian* (Beijing: Renmin Chubanshe 1987), 205-6.
20 Peng, *Haifeng nongmin yundong*, 1; Qian Chunrui, 'Xuexi he guanche Mao zhuxi de jiaoyu sixiang: Wei jinian zhongguo gongchang dang de sanshi zhounian erzuo,' *Guangdong jiaoyu yu wenhua* 3.4 (1951):5.
21 *Zijin xian jiaoyu zhi* (n.p.: n.p. 1987), 15; *Xinxing xian jiaoyu zhi*, rev. ed. (n.p.: n.p. 1978), 8; *Huazhou xian jiaoyu zhi (jianben)* (n.p.: n.p. 1987), 3.
22 Zheng Huihao, ed., *Zijin xian jiaoyu zhi*, 47; Panyu xian renmin zhengfu jiaoyu ke, ed., *Panyu xian jiaoyu zhi (chugao)* (n.p.: n.p. 1988), 6, 11-13; Taishan xian jiaoyu zhi bianxie zu, eds., *Taishan xian jiaoyu zhi (neibu faxing)* (n.p.: n.p. 1987), 87.
23 Liu Lequn, 'Xuexi Mao Zedong tongzhi guanyu nongmin jiaoyu sixiang de jidian tihui,' *Shenyang shiyuan xuebao* 4 (1983), in *Fuyin baokan ziliao* series G5 6 (1983):49.
24 'Pengbo fazhan de Haifeng yexiao,' *Guangdong jiaoyu yu wenhua* 1.5 (1950):29.
25 *Taishan xian jiaoyu zhi*, 18. For the collapse of school enrolment in Guangdong in the early 1950s, see Zhong Zhong, 'Zhujiang qu yiban jiaoyu qingkuang suxie,' *Guangdong jiaoyu yu wenhua* 11.15 (1950):15. See also Nanlu zhuanshu wenjiao ke, 'Nanlu qu wenhua jiaoyu de zhuangtai,' *Guangdong jiaoyu yu wenhua* 1.5 (1950):21.
26 For the resurgence of sishu after 1949, see Nanhai xian wenjiao ke, 'Sishu shi de zhuanbian,' *Guangdong jiaoyu yu wenhua* 1.4 (1950):54-5. See also Zhang, 'Guangdong chudeng jiaoyu,' 11; Shen Hengsong, 'Duiyu jinhou chuli sishu de yijian,' *Guangdong jiaoyu yu wenhua* 1.2

(1950):14; and Su Hongtong, 'Yue zhongnan lu yiban jiaoyu qingkuang de jieshao,' *Guangdong jiaoyu yu wenhua* 1.5 (1950):16-20.

27 Shen, 'Duiyu jinhou chuli sishu de yijian.' See also Su, 'Yue zhongnan lu yiban jiaoyu,' 18.

28 'Guangzhou de sishu shi xuexi dahui,' *Guangdong jiaoyu yu wenhua* 1.6 (1950):36-7.

29 Shen, 'Duiyu jinhou chuli sishu de yijian.'

30 'Jiaoyubu guangyu jieban sili zhong, xiaoxue de zhishi,' in Zhongguo jiaoyu nianjian bianji bu, ed., *Zhongguo jiaoyu nianjian 1949-1984* (Beijing: Zhongguo dabaike quanshu chubanshe 1984), 731-2.

31 Shen, 'Guangdong sili zhongdeng xuexiao.' See also Guangdong jiaoyu nianjian bianji bu, ed., *Guangdong jiaoyu nianjian* (Guangzhou: Guangdong jiaoyu ting 1986), 19, 51, 76.

32 For the Yanan educational reforms, see Peter J. Seybolt, 'The Yenan Revolution in Mass Education,' *China Quarterly* 48 (1971):641-69; see also Suzanne Pepper, 'Education for the New Order' in Roderick MacFarquhar and John K. Fairbank, eds., *The People's Republic, Part 1: The Emergence of Revolutionary China, 1949-1965*, vol. 14 of *The Cambridge History of China* (Cambridge, UK: Cambridge University Press 1987), 195.

33 Mark Selden, *The Yenan Way in Revolutionary China* (Cambridge, MA: Harvard University Press 1971), cited in Pauline Keating, 'The Ecological Origins of the Yan'an Way,' *Australian Journal of Chinese Affairs* 32 (1994):140; see also 143.

34 *Zhongguo jiaoyu nianjian*, 123.

35 For the problems faced by the early minban schools, see 'Sanshui xian gongnong yeyu jiaoyu de jidian jingyan jiaoxun,' *Guangdong jiaoyu yu wenhua* 2.5 (1951):2. See also 'Minxiao gongzuo zhong de jige wenti,' *Renmin jiaoyu* 2.1 (1950):3.

36 In the mid-1950s, school management committees were relocated under township (*xiang*) governments.

37 Xin Ming, 'Banxue de liangtiao luxian,' *Renmin jiaoyu* 6 (1957):14-18. On the efforts to implement the plan in Guangdong, see *Xinfeng xian jiaoyu zhi* (Zhaoqing: Xinfeng xian jiaoyu ju 1978), 132; *Zijin xian jiaoyu zhi*, 63-7. Use of the land tax to finance local education represented a historic departure. Under the republic, township officials preferred to fund schools and other public works by means of commercial taxes and other ad hoc levies rather than surcharges on the land tax, because the latter generated revenues that had to be shared with counties and provinces. See Helen R. Chauncey, *Schoolhouse Politicians: Locality and State during the Chinese Republic* (Honolulu: University of Hawaii Press 1992), 112.

38 *Zhongguo jiaoyu nianjian*, 89; 'Zhengwuyuan guanyu zhengdun he gaijin xiaoxue jiaoyu de zhishi,' in *Zhongguo jiaoyu nianjian*, 732-3.

39 *Zhongguo jiaoyu nianjian*, 732.

40 'Zhengwuyuan guanyu zhengdun he gaijin xiaoxue jiaoyu de zhishi,' 732-3. See also the speech by Education Minister Zhang Xiruo, reprinted in *Xinhua yuebao* 70.8 (1955):62. Minority districts and former communist base areas were exempt from the decision not to establish additional state-funded schools in rural areas.

41 Xin, 'Banxue de liangtiao luxian,' 16; Li Pingjie, 'Strive to Bring Universalization of Obligatory Primary School Education into Realization at an Early Date,' *Guangming ribao*, 22 February 1956, in *Survey China Mainland Press* 1246 (13 March 1956):18-22.

42 *Zhongguo jiaoyu nianjian*, 123; 'Shitan zenyang guanche qunzhong banxue de fangzhen,' *Renmin jiaoyu* 6 (1957):18.

43 *Zijin xian jiaoyu zhi*, 67. See also 'Xijiang minxiao fadong qunzhong ruxue ji jiejue jingfei wenti jingyan zongjie,' in *Guangdong sheng diyijie gongnong jiaoyu huiyi (yi)*, 96-7; and 'Guanyu kaizhan yiwu wuyi nian dongxue gongzuo de zhishi,' *Changjiang ribao*, 18 November 1951, in *Union Research Institute* LOl35 4222 3135.

44 'Yi suo wanquan you nongmin ziban de xuexiao,' *Guangming ribao*, 17 July 1953, in *Union Research Institute* LO136 4222 3235.

45 Barry Naughton, 'The Pattern and Legacy of Economic Growth in the Mao Era,' in Kenneth Lieberthal et al., eds., *Perspectives on Modern China: Four Anniversaries* (Armonk, NY: M.E. Sharpe 1991), 235-6.

46 *Zhongguo jiaoyu nianjian*, 123.

47 Naughton, 'Pattern and Legacy,' 235-7.

48 Ernest Gellner, *Nations and Nationalism* (Oxford: Basil Blackwell 1983). See also Francisco O. Ramirez and John Boli-Bennett, 'Global Patterns of Educational Institutionalization,' in Robert F. Arnove and Gail Kelly, eds., *Comparative Education* (New York: Macmillan 1988), 15-36.

49 Vivienne Shue, *The Reach of the State: Sketches of the Chinese Body Politic* (Stanford: Stanford University Press 1988), 130-48.

50 *Xinxing xian jiaoyu zhi*, 78-86. For additional examples of this pattern, see *Zijin xian jiaoyu zhi*, 20-2; and *Taishan xian jiaoyu zhi*, 127-34.

51 Vilma Seeberg, *Literacy in China: The Effects of the National Development Context and Policy on Literacy Levels, 1949-1979* (Bochum: Brockmeyer 1990), 152, 161-2.

52 Jean Robinson, 'Minban Schools in Deng's Era,' in Irving Epstein, ed., *Chinese Education: Problems, Policies, and Prospects* (New York: Garland 1991), 166.

53 Alexander Woodside, 'Real and Imagined Continuities in the Chinese Struggle for Literacy,' in Ruth Hayhoe, ed., *Education and Modernization: The Chinese Experience* (Oxford: Pergamon Press 1992), 36. See also Rawski, *Education and Popular Literacy*, 128-39.

Chapter 3: Contested Priorities

1 Edgar Snow, *Red Star over China*, rev. and enl. ed. (New York: Bantam 1978), 59.

2 See Kenneth Lieberthal and Michel Oksenberg, *Policy Making in China: Leaders, Structures, and Processes* (Princeton: Princeton University Press 1988), especially 20-1, 137-51.

3 Elizabeth J. Perry, 'State and Society in Contemporary China,' *World Politics* 41, 4 (1989):587. For an overview of recent conceptualizations of the state, see Stephen D. Krasner, 'Approaches to the State: Alternative Conceptions and Historical Dynamics,' *Comparative Politics* 16.2 (1984):223-46.

4 Paul Bailey, *Reform the People: Changing Attitudes towards Popular Education in Early 20th Century China* (Vancouver: University of British Columbia Press 1990), 227-62. See also Ming K. Chan and Arif Dirlik, *Schools into Fields and Factories: Anarchists, the Guomindang and the National Labour University in Shanghai, 1927-1932* (Durham, NC: Duke University Press 1991), 322 n. 4.

5 For a discussion of the institutional conflicts in Soviet education, see Sheila Fitzpatrick, *Education and Social Mobility in the Soviet Union, 1921-1934* (Cambridge, UK: Cambridge University Press 1979), 10-17.

6 On the concept of policy arenas in Chinese politics, see David Lampton, 'Policy Arena and the Study of Chinese Politics,' *Studies in Comparative Communism* 7 (1974):409-13.

7 Vilma Seeberg, *Literacy in China: The Effects of the National Development Context and Policy on Literacy Levels, 1949-1979* (Bochum: Brockmeyer 1990), 55-64.

8 Zhongguo jiaoyu nianjian bianji bu, ed., *Zhongguo jiaoyu nianjian 1949-1984* (Beijing: Zhongguo dabaike quanshu chubanshe 1984), 576.

9 'Jiaoyubu dangzu guanyu diyici quanguo nongmin yeyu wenhua jiaoyu huiyi de baogao' and 'Zhonggong zhongyang dui jiaoyubu dangzu guanyu diyi quanguo nongmin yeyu wenhua jiaoyu huiyi de baogao,' in Zhonghua renmin gongheguo jiaoyubu gongnong jiaoyu si, ed., *Gongnong jiaoyu wenxian huibian (nongmin jiaoyu)* (Beijing: n.p. 1979), 47-54; 46-47.

10 For a more complete discussion of the association and its activities, see Chapter 6.

11 For a full discussion of the various pre-1949 influences that shaped Chinese education after 1949, see Suzanne Pepper, *Radicalism and Education Reform in 20th Century China* (Cambridge and New York: Cambridge University Press 1996), 37-154.

12 Ma served as minister of higher education after the ministry was divided in 1952 and was vice-chair of the Culture and Education Committee of the Government Administration Council, forerunner of the State Council. For a detailed biography of Ma's life and contributions, see Jinyang xuekan bianji bu, comp., *Zhongguo xiandai shehui kexuejia zhuanlue*, vol. 2 (Taiyuan: Shanxi renmin chubanshe 1983), 10-31. See also Donald W. Klein and Ann B. Clark, eds., *Biographical Dictionary of Chinese Communism, 1921-1965*, vol. 1 (Cambridge, MA: Harvard University Press 1971), 465-8.

13 The Russian, Cuban, and Nicaraguan literacy campaigns are discussed in Robert F. Arnove and Harvey J. Graff, eds., *National Literacy Campaigns: Historical and Comparative Perspectives* (New York: Plenum Press 1987). For the Vietminh literacy campaign, see Alexander

Woodside, 'The Triumphs and Failures of Mass Education in Vietnam,' *Pacific Affairs* 56.3 (1988):401-27.

14 Ma Xulun, 'Guanyu diyici quanguo gongnong jiaoyu huiyi de baogao,' in *Gongnong jiaoyu wenxian huibian (nongmin jiaoyu)*, 13. See also 'Ma Xulun buzhang zai diyici quanguo gongnong jiaoyu huiyi shang de kaimu ci,' in the same source, 6.

15 See Ma, 'Guanyu diyici quanguo gongnong jiaoyu huiyi de baogao.' See also Qian Chun, 'Wei tigao gongnong de wenhua shuping manzu gongnong ganbu de wenhua yaoqiu er fendou,' *Renmin jiaoyu* 3.1 (1951):12-16; and Guo Moruo, *Guanyu wenhua jiaoyu gongzuo de baogao: Zai zhongguo renmin zhengzhi xieshang huiyi diyijie quanguo weiyuanhui disanci huiyi shang de baogao* (Beijing: Renmin chubanshe 1951), especially 9-11.

16 The two stimuli echoed in a general way the former imperial state's view that education (*jiaoyu*) performed two separate functions: the cultivation of bureaucratic talent (*yucai*), and the moral transformation or improvement of the masses (*jiaohua*). See Sally Borthwick, *Education and Social Change in China: The Beginnings of the Modern Era* (Stanford: Hoover Institution Press 1983), 4.

17 David Holm, *Art and Ideology in Revolutionary China* (Oxford: Clarendon Press 1991), 21.

18 Benedict Anderson, *Imagined Communities: Reflections on the Origin and Spread of Nationalism*, rev. ed. (New York: Verso 1991), 54 n. 28.

19 Holm, *Art and Ideology*, 18-26. See also Chang-tai Hung, *War and Popular Culture: Resistance in Modern China, 1937-45* (Berkeley: University of California Press 1994), 221-69; and Peter J. Seybolt, 'The Yenan Revolution in Mass Education,' *China Quarterly* 48 (1971):641-69.

20 Barbara Ward, 'Regional Operas and Their Audiences: Evidence from Hong Kong,' in David Johnson, Andrew J. Nathan, and Evelyn S. Rawski, eds., *Popular Culture in Late Imperial China* (Berkeley: University of California Press 1985), 187. Since the Song local magistrates had attempted to propagate agricultural techniques using cartoons posted on *yamen* walls, in the late nineteenth century public poster campaigns were the favoured means of local gentry seeking to defame Christian missionaries in the eyes of peasants. See Evelyn Sakakida Rawski, *Education and Popular Literacy in Ch'ing China* (Ann Arbor: University of Michigan Press 1979), 15; and Paul Cohen, *China and Christianity: The Missionary Movement and the Growth of Chinese Antiforeignism, 1860-1870* (Cambridge, MA: Harvard University Press 1963). On party efforts to co-opt traditional storytelling arts, see Chang-Tai Hung, 'Re-Educating a Blind Storyteller: Han Qixiang and the Chinese Communist Storytelling Campaign,' *Modern China* 19.4 (1993):395-426. On the importance of the performing arts in general in CCP strategies for peasant mobilization, see Ellen R. Judd, 'Cultural Articulation in the Chinese Countryside, 1937-1947,' *Modern China* 16.3 (1990):269-308. See also David Johnson, 'Actions Speak Louder Than Words,' in David Johnson, ed., *Ritual Opera, Operatic Ritual* (Berkeley: Institute of East Asian Studies, Chinese Popular Culture Project 1989), 1-45; and Colin Mackerras, *The Chinese Theatre in Modern Times: From 1840 to the Present Day* (London: Thames and Hudson 1975).

21 This quotation is from Mao's 1927 'Report on the Investigation into the Peasant Movement in Hunan,' as cited in 'Xuexi he guanche Mao zhuxi de jiaoyu sixiang: Wei jinian zhongguo gongchang dang de sanshi zhounian er zuo,' *Guangdong jiaoyu yu wenhua* 3.4 (1951):1-7.

22 Helen R. Chauncey, *Schoolhouse Politicians: Locality and State during the Chinese Republic* (Honolulu: University of Hawaii Press 1992), 191.

23 Richard Madsen, *Morality and Power in a Chinese Village* (Berkeley: University of California Press 1984).

24 On the Shan-Gan-Ning Border Region, see Mark Selden, *The Yenan Way in Revolutionary China* (Cambridge, MA: Harvard University Press 1971), 159, 214, 221. The 1949 illiteracy figure is from *China Review* (Hong Kong: Sing Tao Group 1989), 29. See also Hung Yung Lee, *From Revolutionary Cadres to Party Technocrats in Socialist China* (Berkeley: University of California Press 1991).

25 Qian Chunrui, 'Wei tigao gongnong de wenhua shuiping manzu gongnong ganbu de wenhua yaoqiu er fendou,' *Renmin jiaoyu* 3.1 (1951):12-16. For Ma Xulun's views, see 'Guanyu diyici quanguo gongnong jiaoyu huiyi de baogao,' 13; and, in the same collection, 'Ma Xulun buzhang zai diyici quanguo gongnong jiaoyu huiyi shang de kaimu ci,' 6. For the Ministry

of Education statement on worker-peasant education, see Zhongguo jiaoyu nianjian bianji bu, ed., *Zhongguo jiaoyu nianjian, 1949-1981* (Beijing: Zhongguo dabaike quanshu chubanshe 1984), 895.

26 'Jianshe xin Zhongguo bixu zhansheng er da luohou,' in *Guangdong sheng diyijie gongnong jiaoyu huiyi ji jiaoyu gonghui daibiao dahui cailiao*, vol. 1 (n.p.: n.p. 1951), 28.

27 Local cadres were instructed to compile and submit written reports of grain collection in their areas every ten days, but illiterate cadres were allowed to send in their reports by telephone or telegraph. See Vivienne Shue, *Peasant China in Transition: The Dynamics of Development toward Socialism, 1949-56* (Berkeley: University of California Press 1980), 130, 137 n. 54, 138.

28 On entrepreneurial state brokers, see Prasenjit Duara, *Culture, Power and the State: Rural North China, 1900-1942* (Stanford: Stanford University Press 1988).

29 'Shiqi jiguan yeyu wenhua xuexiao qingkuang jieshao,' in *Guangdong sheng diyijie gongnong jiaoyu huiyi ji jiaoyu gonghui daibiao dahui cailiao*, vol. 1, 1. Mao was aware of the danger as early as 1948, when he denounced as impractical the view that 'the poor peasants, having conquered the rivers and mountains, should now rule the rivers and mountains' (*pinnong da jiangshan, zuo jiangshan*), or that 'a democratic government is simply a peasants' government' (*minzhu zhengfu zhishi nongmin dezhengfu*). See Stuart R. Schram, 'Party Leader or True Ruler? Foundations and Significance of Mao Zedong's Personal Power,' in Stuart R. Schram, ed., *Foundations and Limits of State Power in China* (Hong Kong: Chinese University Press 1987), 229.

30 See the question box in *Renmin jiaoyu* 2.4 (1951):50-1.

31 *Zhongguo jiaoyu nianjian*, 580-2.

32 'Sulian saochu wenmang de jingguo,' in *Guangdong sheng diyijie gongnong jiaoyu huiyi ji jiaoyu gonghui daibiao dahui cailiao (yi)*, 24, 26.

33 Chao Yimin, 'Dongxue jiaoyu de fangzhen ji youguan de jige wenti,' *Changjiang ribao*, 20 August 1951, in *Union Research Institute* LO135 4222 3135.

34 See the question box in *Renmin jiaoyu* 2.4 (1951):50-1.

35 *Zhongguo jiaoyu nianjian*, 578.

36 In fact, the National Anti-Illiteracy Work Committee in 1953 decreed that a score of 60 per cent (600 characters) was sufficient to pass the character-recognition component in literacy tests. See 'Saochu wenmang gongzuo weiyuanhui guanyu saomang biaozhun biye kaoshi deng zanxing banfa de tongzhi,' in *Gongnong jiaoyu wenxian huibian (nongmin jiaoyu)*, 33-4.

37 'Gongnong ganbu wenhua buxi xuexiao zanxing shishi banfa,' in Zhonghua renmin gongheguo jiaoyu bu gongnong jiaoyu si, ed., *Gongnong jiaoyu wenxian huibian (zhigong ganbu jiaoyu)* (Beijing: n.p. 1979), 18-22. In the same collection, see 'Zhonggong zhongyang guanyu jiaqiang ganbu wenhua jiaoyu gongzuo de zhishi,' 30-4.

38 Figures on the increase in the number of party and state personnel are from Gordon White, 'The Postrevolutionary Chinese State,' in Victor Nee and David Mozingo, eds., *State and Society in Contemporary China* (Ithaca: Cornell University Press 1983), 30-1. Slightly different figures are given in Victor C. Funnell, 'Bureaucracy and the Chinese Communist Party,' *Current Scene* 9.5 (1976):6.

39 Du Guoxiang, 'Guangdong sheng diyijie gongnong jiaoyu huiyi ji jiaoyu gonghui daibiao dahui kaimu ci,' *Guangdong jiaoyu yu wenhua* 2.6 (1951):2-3. See also Li Zhaohan, 'Guangdong diyi suo gongnong sucheng zhongxue jieshao,' *Guangdong jiaoyu yu wenhua* 3.1 (1951):6-7; and *Guangdong jiaoyu nianjian*, 103.

40 'Gongnong jiaoyu de gezhong zuzhi xingshi he neirong,' in *Guangdong sheng diyijie gongnong jiaoyu huiyi ji jiaoyu gonghui daibiao dahui cailiao*, vol. 1.

41 'Jiaoyubu guanyu jiaqiang jinnian dongxue zhengzhi shishi jiaoyu de zhishi,' in *Gongnong jiaoyu wenxian huibian (nongmin jiaoyu)*, 23-4.

42 Ibid. See also 'Jiaoyubu guanyu jiaqiang nongmin yeyu jiaoyu zhong kangmei yuanchao shishi jiaoyu de zhishi,' in *Gongnong jiaoyu wenxian huibian (nongmin jiaoyu)*, 19-20.

43 'Fengshun xian wenhua guan gongzuo bao,' in *Guangdong jiaoyu yu wenhua* (1952):10-11. See also Cai Fei, 'Shehui jiaoyu de fangxiang,' *Guangdong jiaoyu yu wenhua* 1.1 (1950):37-8; and 'Jiji tigao dongxue jiaoshi de zhengzhi he wenhua shuiping,' *Changjiang ribao*, 30 December 1951, in *Union Research Institute* LO135 4222 3135.

44 Zhonggong zhongyang Huanan fenju, ed., *Guanyu jiaqiang zai tudi gaige zhong dui nongmin de sixiang fadong gongzuo de fangan* (Guangzhou: Huanan renmin chubanshe 1952), 4-7.
45 'Guanyu yijiu wuer nian dongxue yundong de tongzhi'; 'Jiaoyubu, saochu wenmang gongzuo weiyuanwei guanyu yijiu wusan nian dongxue gongzuo de zhishi'; and 'Jiaoyubu, qingniantuan zhongyang guanyu yijiu wusi nian dongxue gongzuo de zhishi,' all in *Gongnong jiaoyu wenxian huibian (nongmin jiaoyu)*, 27-9, 35-8, 42-5.
46 *Guangdong nianjian, 1987* (Guangzhou: Guangdong renmin chubanshe 1987), 102.
47 Zhongguo renmin zhengzhi xieshang huiyi Guangdong sheng guangzhou shi weiyuanhui, wenshi ziliao yanjiu weiyuanhui, ed., *Guangzhou jin bainian jiaoyu shiliao* (Guangzhou: Guangdong renmin chubanshe 1983).
48 Helen F. Siu, *Agents and Victims in South China: Accomplices in Rural Revolution* (New Haven: Yale University Press 1989), 108-10, 122.
49 On the purge of Cantonese cadres during land reform, see Ezra Vogel, *Canton under Communism: Programs and Politics in a Provincial Capital, 1949-1968* (Cambridge, MA: Harvard University Press 1969), 101-24.
50 *Guanyu guangdong sheng saochu wenmang gongzuo quanmian guihua de baogao (jimi wenjian)* (Guangzhou: Guangdong jiaoyu ting 1956), 3. See also *Guangdong jiaoyu nianjian*, 23.
51 *Zhongguo jiaoyu nianjian*, 580. See also Zhongyang jiaoyu kexue yanjiu suo, ed., *Zhonghua renmin gongheguo jiaoyu dashi ji* (Beijing: Jiaoyu kexue chubanshe 1983), 52; and Vincent Tsing Ching Lin, 'Adult Education in the People's Republic of China, 1950-58' (Ph.D. diss., University of California, Berkeley, 1963), 256-7.
52 'Jiaoyubu guanyu gedi zhankai "sucheng shizi fa" de jiaoxue shijian gongzuo de tongzhi,' in *Gongnong jiaoyu wenxian huibian (nongmin jiaoyu)*, 26-7; *Zhongguo jiaoyu nianjian*, 577.
53 'Zhenge cun minxiao xiaozhang ying dong xueyuan shang minxiao, buyao dengdai jin sucheng shizi ban,' *Fujian ribao*, 2 March 1953, in *Union Research Institute* LO136, 4222 3237.
54 *Guangdong jiaoyu nianjian*, 102. See also Yang Guang, *Sucheng shizi de gushi* (Guangzhou: Nanfang tongsu duben lianhe chubanshe 1952). The latter was comprised of letters by newly literate peasants praising the advantages of the accelerated literacy method.
55 For criticisms of the accelerated literacy method, see 'Jiaoyubu guanyu zhengdun gongnong yeyu xuexiao gaoji ban yu zhongxue wenti de tongzhi,' in *Gongnong jiaoyu wenxian huibian (nongmin jiaoyu)*, 30-2. See also Qu Naisheng, 'Fuwu shengchang, yikao qunzhong, kaizhan dongxue yundong guanche guojia guodu shiqi zongluxian de jiaoyu,' *Jiaoyu banyue kan* 23 (1953):4; and *Zhongguo jiaoyu nianjian*, 577.
56 On the collapse of the literacy movement after 1953, see *Gongnong jiaoyu wenxian huibian (nongmin jiaoyu)*, 46-9, 52, 54, 60. See also 'Geji jiaoyu bumen bixu jiaqiang gongnong jiaoyu de lingdao,' *Renmin jiaoyu* 12 (1955):4-5.

Chapter 4: The Problem of the Teachers

1 Cited in Ross Terrill, *Mao: A Biography* (New York: Harper and Row 1980), 45.
2 On minban teachers, see Li Jiangang, *Xiaoxue jiaoyu daquan* (Jinan: Shandong jiaoyu chubanshe 1987), 94; Vilma Seeberg, *Literacy in China: The Effects of the National Development Context and Policy on Literacy Levels, 1949-1979* (Bochum: Brockmeyer 1990), 136-7, 146-9; and Joan Robinson, 'People-Run Schools in China,' *Comparative Education Review* 30.1 (1986):73-88.
3 Gordon White, *Party and Professionals: The Political Role of Teachers in Contemporary China* (New York: M.E. Sharpe 1981). See also his 'Distributive Politics and Educational Development: Teachers as a Political Interest Group,' in David S. Goodman, ed., *Groups and Politics in the People's Republic of China* (Cardiff: University of Cardiff Press 1984), 102-25; and Joel Glassman, 'The Political Experience of Primary School Teachers in the PRC,' *Comparative Education* 15.2 (1979):159-73.
4 Mao Zedong, 'Speeches at the Second Session of the Eighth Party Congress,' *Miscellany of Mao Zedong Thought Part 1*, cited in White, 'Distributive Politics,' 117.
5 Between 1951 and the early 1980s, the proportion of female primary school teachers in China increased from 18.4 per cent to 36 per cent. See Zhongguo jiaoyu nianjian bianji bu, ed., *Zhongguo jiaoyu nianjian, 1949-1981* (Beijing: Zhongguo dabaike quanshu chubanshe 1984), 1024.

6 Arthur Smith, *Village Life in China: A Study in Sociology* (New York: Revell 1899), 70-135; Daniel H. Kulp, *Country Life in South China* (New York: Teachers College, Columbia University 1925), 221-2; Liao T'ai-ch'u, 'Rural Education in Transition: A Study of the Old-Fashioned Chinese Schools (Szu-Shu) in Shantung and Szechuan,' *Yenching Journal of Social Studies* 4.1 (1948):1240-2; James Hayes, 'Specialists and Written Materials in the Village World,' in David Johnson, Andrew J. Nathan, and Evelyn S. Rawski, eds., *Popular Culture in Late Imperial China* (Berkeley: University of California Press 1985), 102.

7 See the various images of the schoolmaster depicted in Allan Barr, 'Four Schoolmasters: Educational Issues in Li Hai-kuan's *Lamp at the Crossroads*,' in Benjamin A. Elman and Alexander Woodside, eds., *Education and Society in Late Imperial China, 1600-1900* (Berkeley: University of California Press 1994), 50-75.

8 Jerry Dennerline, *Qian Mu and the World of Seven Mansions* (New Haven: Yale University Press 1988), 155.

9 Cited in Patricia Buckley Ebrey, ed., *Chinese Civilization and Society: A Sourcebook* (New York: Free Press 1981), 213.

10 Li, *Xiaoxue jiaoyu daquan*, 82. On village teachers in late-imperial China, see also Evelyn Sakakida Rawski, *Education and Popular Literacy in Ch'ing China* (Ann Arbor: University of Michigan Press 1979), 42-3, 54-61, 95-7, 101-4.

11 Cited in Fernando Galbiati, *P'eng P'ai and the Hai-Lu-feng Soviet* (Stanford: Stanford University Press 1985), 77.

12 Zheng Huihao, ed., *Zijin xian jiaoyu zhi* (n.p.: n.p. 1987), 63.

13 Zhang Ruxin, 'Zuo yige renmin jiaoshi shifou guangrong?' in *Zenyang zuo yige renmin de xiaoxue jiaoshi* (Chongqing: Xinan qingnian chubanshe 1952), 33-7.

14 'Shitan zenyang guanche qunzhong banxue de fangzhen,' *Renmin jiaoyu* 6 (1957):17-21. See also Zhang Mingshen, 'Guangdong chudeng jiaoyu de qingkuang yu wenti,' *Guangdong jiaoyu yu wenhua* 3.2 (1951):10-13; *Zijin xian jiaoyu zhi*, 63; Wu Yen-yin, 'We Should Pay Enough Attention to the Middle and Primary School Education and Teachers,' *Guangming ribao*, 16 August 1956, in *Survey China Mainland Press* 1380 (10 October 1956):13; *Zhongguo jiaoyu nianjian*, 124.

15 Wu Xun was a nineteenth-century orphaned beggar who founded free schools for the poor. Honoured by the emperor after his death in 1896, Wu's educational philanthropy was celebrated in a 1950 film biography supported by Zhou Yang, Xia Yan, Guo Moruo (the latter's calligraphy graced the film title), and other leading cultural figures. The party reacted strongly, launching a campaign to decry what it called the 'spirit of Wu Xun': the notion that education alone can dissolve class-based social and economic inequalities. On the Wu Xun affair, see *Wu Xun Lishi diaocha zhi* (Guangzhou: n.p. 1951); and Roxanne Witke, *Comrade Ch'iang Ch'ing* (Boston: Little, Brown 1977), 238-44.

16 Sheila Fitzpatrick emphasizes the same point in explaining the political vulnerability of rural school teachers in the Soviet Union. See her *Education and Social Mobility in the Soviet Union, 1921-1934* (Cambridge, UK: Cambridge University Press 1979), 30.

17 'Discrimination against Primary Teachers Cannot Be Allowed,' *Renmin ribao*, 5 October 1956, in *Survey China Mainland Press* 1398 (26 October 1956):3-4. On the complaints expressed by teachers during the Hundred Flowers Movement, see 'Jiaqiang xuexiaozhong dangyuan he qunzhong de lianxi,' *Renmin jiaoyu* 2 (1957):21; and 'Jiaoshi tan jiaoyu gongzuo neibu maodun,' *Renmin jiaoyu* 6 (1957):6-13.

18 Mao Zedong, 'Talks at the Chengtu Conference,' March 1958, in Stuart R. Schram, ed., *Mao Tse-tung Unrehearsed: Talks and Letters, 1956-71* (Harmondsworth, UK: Penguin 1974), 116.

19 'Discrimination against Primary School Teachers Cannot Be Allowed.'

20 Chao Yimin, 'Dongxue jiaoyu de fangzhen ji youguan de jige wenti,' *Changjiang ribao*, 20 August 1951, in *Union Research Institute* LO135 4222 3135.

21 'Jianchi lixue shiwu nian de longlou cun yexiao,' *Guangdong jiaoyu* 2 (1966):49-51. See also Wu Qingsheng, 'Weichi nongcun xiaoxue de daolu,' *Guangdong jiaoyu yu wenhua* 3.1 (1951):3; Xin Ming, 'Ban xiaoxue de liangtiao luxian,' *Renmin jiaoyu* 6 (1957):16; Zhang Mingsheng, 'Guangdong sheng diyijie gongnong jiaoyu huiyi ji jiaoyu gonghui daibiao dahui zongjie baogao,' in *Guangdong sheng diyijie gongnong jiaoyu huiyi ji jiaoyu gonghui daibiao dahui cailiao (yi)*, reprinted in *Guangdong jiaoyu yu wenhua* 2.6 (1951):5-10; Chao Yimin, 'Dongxue jiaoyu de fangzhen.'

22 Lyon Sharman, *Sun Yatsen, His Life and Its Meaning: A Critical Biography* (New York: John Day 1934), 16-19.

23 Alexander Woodside, 'Problems of Education in the Chinese and Vietnamese Revolutions,' *Pacific Affairs* 49 (1976-7):648-9.

24 Ka-che Yip, 'Warlordism and Educational Finances, 1916-1927,' in Joshua A. Fogel and William T. Rowe, eds., *Perspectives on a Changing China: Essays in Honor of Professor C. Martin Wilbur on the Occasion of His Retirement* (Boulder: Westview Press 1979), 183-96.

25 On teacher opposition to party involvement in schools and education in Guangdong during the early 1950s, see Zhou Ping, 'Jinhou de renwu he gongzuo: Quansheng wenjiao gongzuo huiyi zongjie baogao,' *Guangdong jiaoyu yu wenhua* 1.5 (1950):2. See also Zhang, 'Guangdong sheng diyijie gongnong jiaoyu huiyi'; and Xiao Xiangyong, 'Dui shehui jiaoyu de yidian yijian,' *Guangdong jiaoyu yu wenhua* 1.5 (1950):10-11.

26 Taishan xian jiaoyu zhi bianxie zu, eds., *Taishan xian jiaoyu zhi (neibu faxing)* (n.p.: n.p. 1987), 99. See also Xiao Xiangyong, 'Dui shehui jiaoyu de yidian yijian.' For the late-1953 primary education directive, see 'Zhengwuyuan guanyu zhengdun he gaijin xiaoxue jiaoyu de zhishi,' 26 November 1953, in *Zhongguo jiaoyu nianjian*, 732-3.

27 Lu Lan, 'Xiangcun jiaoshi ye er yao qingsuan zichan jieji jiaoyu sixiang ma?' *Guangdong jiaoyu yu wenhua* (1952):6-7.

28 'Zhigong jiaoyu bixu jinxing jiaoxue gaige,' *Guangdong saomang* 2 (25 November 1958):23-5. See also Nanhai xian wenjiao ke, 'Sishu shi de zhuanbian,' *Guangdong jiaoyu yu wenhua* 1.4 (1950):54-5.

29 *Educational Theory in the People's Republic of China: The Report of Ch'ien Chun-jui*, com. and trans. John N. Hawkins (Honolulu: University of Hawaii Press 1971), 64-5.

30 Ibid., 65.

31 Zhou Ping, 'Jinhou de renwu he gongzuo,' 2; 'Guanyu jiaoshi xuexi wenti de baogao,' in *Guangdong sheng diyijie gongnong jiaoyu huiyi ji jiaoyu gonghui daibiao dahui cailiao (yi)*, 75-87. See also *Guangdong jiaoyu nianjian*, 17-18.

32 Zhou Ping, 'Xin jiu jiaoyu you shenmo butong? Zai Lingnan daxue he Guangzhou ge daxue de yanjiang,' *Guangdong jiaoyu yu wenhua* 1.2 (1950):8-13.

33 'Tuanjie quansheng aiguo jiaoyu gongzuozhe wei banhao renmin de jiaoyu shiye er douzheng,' in *Guangdongsheng diyijie gongnong jiaoyu huiyi ji jiaoyu gonghui daibiao dahui cailiao (yi)*, 63-74; Zhang, 'Guangdong sheng diyijie gongnong jiaoyu huiyi.' On the Soviet Teachers' Union, see Fitzpatrick, *Education and Social Mobility*, 60-1.

34 David E. Apter, *The Politics of Modernisation* (Chicago: University of Chicago Press 1965); White, 'Distributive Politics.' Intellectuals' 'social bargaining power' has become a valid subject of debate in China since 1978. For an introduction to recent views on the subject, see Shi Ping, *Zhishi fenzi de lishi yundong he zuoyong* (Shanghai: Shanghai shehui kexue yuan chubanshe 1988).

35 White, 'Distributive Politics,' 119. This point builds on Hungarian sociologist Andras Hegedus's theory of the role of the technical division of labour in determining social interest groups.

36 *Guangdong jiaoyu nianjian*, 57. Nationally, CCP membership levelled off at about 6 million just after 1949. It began to grow rapidly in 1954. Within a year and a half, it had grown to 10.75 million. By mid-1957, there were 12.5 million party members, more than double the 1954 figure. See Craig Dietrich, *People's China: A Brief History* (New York: Oxford University Press 1986), 93.

37 *Xinxing xian jiaoyu zhi*, 149; *Huazhou xian jiaoyu zhi*, 26-7; Lin Liming, 'Guanyu dangqian jiaoyu gongzuo zhong de jige wenti,' *Guangdong jiaoyu*, 10 April 1956:4.

Chapter 5: Collectivization

1 Vivienne Shue, *Peasant China in Transition: The Dynamics of Development toward Socialism, 1949-56* (Berkeley: University of California Press 1980).

2 On the Soviet theory of a planned economy, see Alec Nove, 'Toward a Theory of Planning,' in Alec Nove and Jane Degras, eds., *Soviet Planning: Essays in Honour of Naum Jasny* (Oxford: Basil Blackwell 1964). See also his *The Soviet Economic System* (London: George Allen and Unwin 1977). Chinese journals in the mid-1950s carried numerous articles on creating a Soviet-style planned economy in China. See Luo Gengmo, 'Xuexi sulian de jingyan: Guanyu

jingji jianshe de jihua wenti,' *Xuexi* 3 (1953):9-10; Yang Jianbai, 'A Comparative Analysis of China's First Five Year Plan and the Soviet Union's First Five Year Plan,' *Tongji gongzuo tongxin* 8 (1955), in *Extracts China Mainland Magazines* 10 (1955):15-27.

3 Stanislav Strumilin, 'The Economics of Education in the U.S.S.R.,' in *Economic and Social Aspects of Educational Planning* (Paris: UNESCO 1964); and, by the same author, *The Economic Significance of National Education* (Paris: UNESCO 1968). On Strumilin's contribution to the development of Soviet education, see Joseph L. Wieczynski, ed., *The Modern Encyclopedia of Russian and Soviet History*, vol. 37 (Gulf Breeze, FL: Academic International Press 1984), 228-9. See also Vilma Seeberg, *Literacy in China: The Effects of the National Development Context and Policy on Literacy Levels, 1949-1979* (Bochum: Brockmeyer 1990), 57. Strumilin's ideas entered the discourse of Western development economics in the 1960s via international bodies such as UNESCO, which heavily promoted the human capital concept. For one of the earliest and most influential statements of human capital theory in the West, see Theodore W. Schultz, *The Economic Value of Education* (New York: Columbia University Press 1963); see also George S. Becker, *Human Capital: A Theoretical and Empirical Analysis, with Special Reference to Education* (New York: Columbia University Press 1963).

4 On the educational aspirations of the First Five-Year Plan, see 'Jiaoyubu dangzu guanyu diyici quanguo nongmin yeyu wenhua jiaoyu huiyi de baogao' and 'Zhonggong zhongyang dui jiaoyubu dangzu guanyu diyici quanguo nongmin yeyu wenhua jiaoyu huiyi de baogao,' both in *Gongnong jiaoyu wenxian huibian (nongmin jiaoyu)*, 47-54, 46-7. See also Li Fuchun, *Report on the First Five Year Plan for Development of the National Economy of the People's Republic of China* (Beijing: Foreign Language Press 1955). The plan's requirements for various kinds of specialized talent (*zhuanmen rencai*) can be found in Yang Xiufeng, 'Peiyang nongcun zhuanmen rencai yaozou ziji de lu,' in *Yang Xiufeng jiaoyu wenji* (Beijing: Beijing shifan daxue chubanshe 1987), 43-53.

5 *Guangdong jiaoyu nianjian*, 23.

6 'Jianshe xin zhongguo bixu zhansheng erda luohou,' 27-8. On the urban growth rate in the 1950s, see Witold Rodzinski, *The People's Republic of China: Reflections on Chinese Political History since 1949* (London: Fontana Press 1988), 56. For urban growth in Guangdong during the 1950s, see Wu, *Guangdong jingji dili*, 67, 88. Urban growth in Guangdong during this period was a result of two developments: official efforts to expand modern economic activity from its traditional centre in the Pearl River Delta to southwestern and northern parts of the province (the northern city of Shaoguan, for example, was developed into a centre for heavy industry), and the huge influx of peasants into urban areas during the Great Leap Forward.

7 Peter Nolan, 'Collectivization in China: Some Comparisons with the USSR,' *Journal of Peasant Studies* 3 (1976):192-220; Thomas Bernstein, 'Mass Mobilization in the Soviet and Chinese Collectivization Campaigns of 1929-30 and 1955-56: A Comparison,' *China Quarterly* 31 (1969):1-47.

8 See Kenneth Levine, 'Functional Literacy: Fond Illusions and False Economies,' *Harvard Educational Review* 52.3 (1982):249-66.

9 'Nongye hezuohua xuyao wenhua,' *Guangming ribao* (Beijing), 2 September 1949, in *Union Research Institute* LO135 42222. The official view of the relationship of literacy to collectivization was also spelled out by the Guangdong bureau of education in 'Dali kaizhan nongcun saochu wenmang yundong,' in *Dali kaizhan saochu wenmang yundong*, ed. Guangdong jiaoyu ting (Guangzhou: Guangdong renmin chubanshe 1956), 47-8, originally published as an editorial in *Nanfang ribao*, 5 January 1956.

10 Mao's July 1955 speech was addressed to a group of provincial and regional bosses meeting in Beijing. The speech stunned the Central Committee, which had just reaffirmed a policy of gradual collectivization. The level of surprise and the opposition to Mao's unilateral action are suggested by the fact that the leading theoretical journal for cadre consumption, *Xuexi* (Study) subsequently published two full issues without so much as even mentioning Mao's speech. The text of the speech was finally reprinted in full, with accompanying editorials in full support of the new policy, three months later. See *Xuexi* 11 (1955), which is devoted almost entirely to the subject.

11 Benedict Stavis, *The Politics of Agricultural Mechanization in China* (Ithaca: Cornell University Press 1978).

12 For the first, unpublished preface, see Michael Y.M. Kau and John K. Leung, eds., *The Writings of Mao Zedong, 1949-1976* (Armonk, NY: M.E. Sharpe 1986) vol. 1, 622-5. For Mao's comment on literacy work in the published edition, see 691. The original text is in *Zhongguo nongcun de shehui zhuyi gaochao*, vol. 1.

13 'Geji jiaoyu bumen bixu jiaqiang gongnong yeyu jiaoyu de lingdao,' *Renmin jiaoyu* 12 (1955):4-5.

14 For the comparison of Soviet and Chinese literacy rates, see the comments by Chen Yi, chair of the National Anti-Illiteracy Association, in *New China News Agency* (Beijing), 15 March 1956, in *Survey China Mainland Press* 1251 (20 March 1956):4-5. See also *New China News Agency* (Beijing) (English), 20 June 1956, in *Current Background* 400. The comparison was based on information provided in a widely read speech by the famous Soviet educator I.A. Kairov, given to the first national conference on worker-peasant education, in 1951, on the Soviet Union's experience in literacy education. See 'Sulian saochu wenmang de jingguo,' in *Guangdong sheng diyijie gongnong jiaoyu huiyi ji jiaoyu gonghui daibiao dahui cailiao (yi)*, 21-6. The most optimistic Soviet data from the 1920s claimed a literacy rate of 51-55 per cent, which most Western specialists and contemporary Soviet sources now reject as too high, while even Krupskaia herself complained in 1929 that ten years after the anti-illiteracy decree not a single article had been implemented. See Ben Eklof, 'Russian Literacy Campaigns, 1861-1939,' in Robert F. Arnove and Harvey J. Graff, eds., *National Literacy Campaigns: Historical and Comparative Perspectives* (New York: Plenum Press 1987), 123-45; and Sheila Fitzpatrick, *Education and Social Mobility in the Soviet Union, 1921-1934* (Cambridge, UK: Cambridge University Press 1979), 169-70, 175-6.

15 Chinese writers on the subject appear to have relied on official Soviet figures claiming that primary schooling was all but universal by the late 1920s, a claim rejected by many Western scholars. Fitzpatrick estimates only 50-60 per cent of school-age children attended Soviet primary schools on the eve of collectivization – about the same proportion as in China. Given the relatively small size of the Soviet school-age population compared with that in China, the latter's progress was probably more impressive, not less. See Fitzpatrick, *Education and Social Mobility*, 159, 169-71, 174-5. On the growth of primary education in China, see *New China News Agency* (Beijing), 20 June 1956, in *Current Background* 400; and 'Universalization of Obligatory Education,' *Renmin ribao*, 27 February 1956, in *Survey China Mainland Press* 1246 (13 March 1956):16-18.

16 Hu argued that China could only realistically aspire to rapid elimination of illiteracy among youth, because the 'memory capacity' (*jiyi li*) required to master Chinese characters declined significantly after age thirty. See Hu Yaobang, 'Guanyu nongcun saochu wenmang gongzuo,' in *Dali kaizhan saochu wenmang yundong*, 25. Others, however, disagreed, arguing that this view had 'no scientific basis' and that, if there was a decline in learning performance among adults, it was because they had more responsibilities than youth and less time for study. See Xiang Loruo, '"Chengnian ren lijie liqiang jiyi li ruo" de shuofa shi meiyou kexue gengjude,' *Renmin jiaoyu* 2 (1957):52-4.

17 *Zhongguo jiaoyu nianjian*, 578, 1034.

18 *Guanyu Guangdong sheng saochu wenmang gongzuo quanmian guihua de baogao (jimi wenjian)* (Guangzhou: Guangdong jiaoyuting 1956), 3; *Guangdong jiaoyu nianjian*, 23, 109.

19 Xiang Nan, 'Let the Whole Youth League Take a Hand in Wiping Out Illiteracy,' *Zhongguo qingnian bao* 21 (1956), in *Extracts China Mainland Magazines* 20 (1956):33-4.

20 Tian Xin, 'Jiji zhudong, xianqi yige xuexi wenhua de gaochao,' in Guangdong sheng jiaoyu ting, ed., *Dali kaizhan saochu wenmang yundong* (Guangzhou: Guangdong renmin chubanshe 1956), 42-6; Ezra Vogel, *Canton under Communism: Programs and Politics in a Provincial Capital, 1949-1968* (Cambridge, MA: Harvard University Press 1969), 150-1.

21 Liang Weilin, 'Liji dongshou, zuzhi liliang, dali kaizhan quansheng fanwei de nongcun saochu wenmang yundong,' in *Dali kaizhan saochu wenmang yundong*, 36.

22 Dong Chuncai, 'Diyici quanguo nongmin yeyu jiaoyu huiyi de zongjie baogao,' *Renmin jiaoyu* 9 (1955):29-34. See also 'Dali kaizhan nongcun saochu wenmang yundong,' 47-51.

23 Tian Xin, 'Jiji zhudong, xianqi yige xuexi wenhua de gaochao,' 42; *Zhongguo nongcun de shehui zhuyi gaochao: Xuanben* (Beijing: Renmin chubanshe 1956), 364-5.

24 'Jixu qianjin, juexin zuoge you wenhua zhishi, you shehui zhuyi juewu de xinshi nongmin,' in *Guangdong sheng saochu wenmang jiji fenzi daibiao dahui huikan* (Guangzhou: Guangdong sheng saochu wenmang jiji fenzi daibiao dahui mishuchu), 98-9.

25 'Saochu shengchan shuangfang shou,' in *Guangdong sheng saochu wenmang jiji fenzi daibiao dahui huikan*, 95.

26 On the lack of numeracy skills in Guangdong collectives, see the examples in *Zhongguo nongcun de shehui zhuyi gaochao*, vol. 3, especially 956. On the management problems in cooperatives caused by lack of skilled personnel, see Lo Zicheng, 'Guanyu nongye hezuoshe gonggu de gongzuo,' *Xuexi* 6 (1955):5-8. Jan Myrdal, *Report from a Chinese Village*, trans. Maurice Michael (New York: Pantheon Books 1965), 96-101, 183-95, describes similar problems in northern Chinese villages. The figure on collectives and mutual-aid teams disbanded in 1955 is from Stavis, *Politics of Agricultural Mechanization*, 58.

27 Xiang Nan, 'Let the Whole Youth League Take a Hand.'

28 Jinyang xuekan bianji bu, comp., *Zhongguo xiandai shehui kexuejia zhuanlue*, vol. 4 (Taiyuan: Shanxi renmin chubanshe 1983), 159-68.

29 Lin Handa, 'Wei shehui zhuyi jianshe kaizhan saomang gongzuo,' *Wenhuibao* (Shanghai), 2 November 1955 and 3 November 1955, in *Union Research Institute* LO364 42222.

30 (Editor's note to) 'The Experience of the Youth League Branch of Gaojialiugou Village of Junan County in Setting Up a Class in Workpoint Recording.' The translation given here is based, with minor modifications, on Kau and Leung, eds., *The Writings of Mao Zedong*, vol. 1, 713. The original version is in *Zhongguo nongcun de shehui zhuyi gaochao: Xuanben*, 362-4.

31 Vivienne Shue, *The Reach of the State: Sketches of the Chinese Body Politic* (Stanford: Stanford University Press 1988), 132-3.

32 Hu Yaobang, 'Guanyu nongcun saochu wenmang gongzuo,' 27-8.

Chapter 6: National Literacy Campaigns

1 'Zhonggong zhongyang, guowuyuan guanyu saochu wenmang de jueding.' The full text of the decision is reprinted in *Zhongguo jiaoyu nianjian*, 895-7, and in *Renmin jiaoyu* 4 (1956):4-6. English translations can be found in *New China News Agency* (Beijing), 30 March 1956, in *Survey China Mainland Press* 1266 (12 April 1956):3-7; and in Hu Shiming and Eli Saifman, eds., *Towards a New World Outlook: A Documentary History of Education in the PRC, 1949-1976* (New York: AMS Press 1976), 74-7.

2 *Zhongguo jiaoyu nianjian*, 598-9.

3 This left an additional 86 million illiterates officially remaining in the twelve- to forty-year-old age cohort. See *Zhongguo jiaoyu nianjian*, 577-8, 1037.

4 *Guangdong jiaoyu nianjian*, 15, 103-4; Wu Yuwen, ed., *Guangdong sheng jingji dili* (Beijing: Xinhua chubanshe 1986), 69; Zhu Yuncheng, ed. *Zhongguo renkou: Guangdong fence* (Beijing: Zhongguo caizheng jingji chubanshe 1988), 389-90.

5 See, for example, Suzanne Pepper, 'Education for the New Order,' in Roderick MacFarquhar and John K. Fairbank, eds., *The People's Republic, Part 1: The Emergence of Revolutionary China, 1949-1965*, vol. 14 of *The Cambridge History of China* (Cambridge, UK: Cambridge University Press 1987), 198.

6 *Educational Theory in the People's Republic of China: The Report of Ch'ien Chun-jui*, com. and trans. John N. Hawkins (Honolulu: University of Hawaii Press 1971), 87-94.

7 See 'Jiaoyubu guanyu yijiu wuwu niandong dao yijiu wuliu nianchun zuzhi nongmin xuexi de tongzhi'; 'Jiaoyubu guanyu chouban geji saochu wenmang xiehui de tongzhi'; 'Jiaoyubu, saomang xiehui han zhuan guowuyuan zhuanfa de guanyu geji saomang xiehui renyuan bianzhi de fangan,' all in *Gongnong jiaoyu wenxian huibian (nongmin jiaoyu)*, 60-3, 64-7, 137-8. On the commission membership, see *New China News Agency* (Beijing), 15 March 1956, in *Survey China Mainland Press* 1251 (20 March 1956):4-5.

8 'Guanyu yong jida de nuli jiaqiang dui saomang gongzuo lingdao de zhishi,' cited in *Guangdong jiaoyu nianjian*, 103. On Xinxing county, see *Xinxing xian jiaoyu zhi*. On the membership of the Guangdong anti-illiteracy commission, see *Dagongbao* (Hong Kong), 17 May 1956, in *Survey China Mainland Press* 1293 (22 May 1956):21.

9   Hu Yaobang, 'Guanyu nongcun saochu wenmang gongzuo,' 22-31. On the role of the Youth League, see 'Qingniantuan zhongyang tongzhi pubian jianli qingnian saomangdui,' *Renmin ribao*, 2 January 1956, in *Union Research Institute* LO364 42222; and *Zhongguo qingnianbao*, 27 December 1955, in *Survey China Mainland Press* 1202 (6 January 1956):5.

10   Sheila Fitzpatrick, *Education and Social Mobility in the Soviet Union, 1921-1934* (Cambridge, UK: Cambridge University Press 1979), 162.

11   Soviet influence on Chinese literacy education was controversial in the eyes of many Chinese educators. During the Hundred Flowers Movement of 1957, for example, critics accused Chinese communist educators of harbouring a 'colonial learning attitude' (*zhimin de xuefeng*) toward the Soviet Union. See Wang Tongqi, 'Jiaoyu fangzhen de taolun he yixie xuyao yanjiu jiejue de wenti,' *Renmin jiaoyu* 2 (1957):22-3. Others cited worship of the Soviet Union as a main reason for the relative lack of emphasis on adult literacy education compared to regular school education. One critic compared officials engaged in spare-time education to 'blind men trying to make their way down a road,' because leading education journals were full of articles such as 'Leadership Work of Principals in Soviet Regular Schools' and 'Teaching History ... in Soviet Regular Schools,' but rarely mentioned rural literacy education. See 'Duo wei yeyu jiaoyu xiangxiang,' *Renmin jiaoyu* 6 (1957):64-5.

12   Gong Kuoru, 'Yuenan de pingmin jiaoyu gongzuo,' *Renmin jiaoyu* 2 (1957):57-9. Gong belonged to a delegation of Chinese educational, cultural, and health care officials who visited the Democratic Republic of Vietnam in the mid-1950s. On Chinese efforts to learn from Vietnam's experience with literacy education, see *Renmin ribao*, 30 October 1956, in *Survey China Mainland Press* 1431 (14 December 1956):24-5.

13   Lin Handa, 'Wei shehui zhuyi jianshe kaizhan saomang gongzuo,' *Wenhuibao* (Shanghai), 2 November 1955 and 3 November 1955, in *Union Research Institute* LO364 42222. See also 'Qingnian tuan zhongyang tongzhi pubian jianli qingnian saomang dui,' *Renmin ribao*, 2 January 1956, in *Union Research Institute* LO364 42222.

14   *Guanyu Guangdong sheng saochu wenmang gongzuo quanmian guihua de baogao (jimi wenjian)* (Guangzhou: Guangdong jiaoyu ting 1956). On teacher training estimates, see 'Yijiu waliu nian Guangdong sheng putong jiaoyu he shifan jiaoyu de gongzuo renwu,' *Guangdong jiaoyu* 11-12 (10 June 1956):8, 14; and 'Fachu guanyu pubian jianli qingnian saomang dui de tongzhi,' *Nanfang ribao*, 6 January 1956, in *Union Research Institute* LO364 42222.

15   Hu Yaobang, 'Guanyu nongcun saochu wenmang gongzuo,' 26; 'Yijiu wuliu nian guangdong sheng putong jiaoyu he shifan jiaoyu de gongzuo renwu.'

16   *Guanyu guangdong sheng saochu wenmang gongzuo quanmian guihua de baogao (jimi wenjian)*. In prosperous regions such as the Pearl River Delta, illiteracy was to be eliminated even sooner, within three years.

17   Rudolf Lowenthal, 'Printing Paper: Its Supply and Demand in China,' *Yenching Journal of Social Studies* 1.1 (1938):107-21. On the organization of publishing after 1949, see Gayle Feldman, 'The Organization of Publishing in China,' *China Quarterly* 107 (1986):519-29.

18   'Strive to Meet the Demand of Peasants for Popular Reading Material,' *Renmin ribao*, 8 January 1956, in *Survey China Mainland Press* 1213 (23 January 1956):16-18.

19   'Jiaoyubu, wenhuabu guanyu yijiu wuliu nian liqian gongnong saomang ji yeyu xiaoxue jiaoxue yongshu wenti de jueding' and 'Jiaoyubu, wenhuabu guanyu gongnong yeyu wenhua xuexiao keben gongying wenti de lianhe tongzhi,' both in *Gongnong jiaoyu wenxian huibian (nongmin jiaoyu)*, 127-9, 130-1.

20   'Jiaoyubu, wenhuabu guanyu yijiu wuliu nian liqian gongnong saomang ji yeyu xiaoxue jiaoxue yongshu wenti de jueding.'

21   I have drawn the notion of literate 'survival skills' from Ben Eklof's important study of the growth of Russian rural education, *Russian Peasant Schools: Officialdom, Village Culture, and Popular Pedagogy, 1861-1914* (Berkeley: University of California Press 1986).

22   Michael Schoenhals, *Doing Things with Words in Chinese Politics: Five Studies* (Berkeley: Institute of East Asian Studies, University of California 1992).

23   Gu Hua, *A Small Town Called Hibiscus*, trans. Gladys Yang (Beijing: Panda Books 1983), 109. On the social uses of China's state language, see Perry Link, *Evening Chats in Beijing: Probing China's Predicament* (New York: W.W. Norton 1992), 173-91. On revolutionary language, see Lynn Hunt, *Politics, Culture and Class in the French Revolution* (Berkeley: University of California Press 1984), 19-26.

24 Clifford Geertz, *Negara: The Theater State of Nineteenth Century Bali* (Princeton: Princeton University Press 1987). On mass campaigns in the PRC, see Gordon Bennett, *Yundong: Mass Campaigns in Chinese Communist Leadership* (Berkeley: University of California Press 1976); and Charles Cell, *Revolution at Work: Mobilization Campaigns in China* (New York: Academic Press 1977). On Soviet rituals, see Christel Lane, *The Rites of Rulers: Ritual in Industrial Society – the Soviet Case* (Cambridge, UK: Cambridge University Press 1981).

25 On the social construction of deviance and the use of labels, see Howard S. Becker, *The Outsiders: Studies in the Sociology of Deviance* (New York: Free Press 1973).

26 As quoted in Fitzpatrick, *Education and Social Mobility*, 162.

27 'Jiji xuexi he dali guanche guanyu saochu wenmang de jueding,' *Renmin jiaoyu* 4 (1956):6; 'Lead Positively the Movement for Eliminating Illiteracy,' *Renmin ribao*, 1 April 1956, in *Survey China Mainland Press* 1269 (17 April 1956):3; 'Zuodao shengchan, saomang liang buwu,' *Guangming ribao*, 4 December 1955, in *Union Research Institute* LO364 4222.

28 'Zenyang jiasu saochu nongcun wenmang gongzuo,' *Guangming ribao*, 28 November 1955, in *Union Research Institute* LO364 4222; *Zhongguo nongcun de shehui zhuyi gaochao: Xuanben*, 365.

29 Lin Liming, 'Guanyu dangqian jiaoyu gongzuo zhong de jige wenti,' *Guangdong jiaoyu*, 10 April 1956:6.

30 'Jiaoyubu guanyu saochu wenmang gongzuo de tongzhi,' in *Gongnong jiaoyu wenxian huibian (nongmin jiaoyu)*, 93-5, describes the 'falling off' of the literacy campaign across the country in late 1956-7; on the situation in one Guangdong locality, see 'Wo shi zheiyang dang yige saomang ganbu,' in *Guangdong sheng saochu wenmang jiji fenzi daibiao dahui huikan* (Guangzhou: Guangdong sheng saochu wenmang jiji fenzi daibiao dahui mishuchu 1958), 91-2.

31 *Zhongguo jiaoyu nianjian*, 577.

32 *Xiaoxue jiaoyu*, 16 April 1958:2, 11.

33 *Zhongguo xinwen*, 3 April 1958; *Nanfang ribao*, 11 May and 9 June 1958; Guo Jianfang, 'Qingzhu yijiu wuba nian de weida chengjiu, yingjie yijiu wujiu nian de weida renwu,' *Guangdong gongnong jiaoyu* 1 (1959):5.

34 The literacy campaign in Puning is described in Guangdong jiaoyu ting, comp., *Wenhua geming de shangyou Puning: Jieshao Puning xian saochu wenmang de jingyan* (Guangzhou: Guangdong renmin chubanshe 1958). See also Puning gongnong jiaoyu diaocha zu, 'Liangzhong taidu, liangzhong xiaoguo,' *Guangdong gongnong jiaoyu* 2 (1959):7-8; and 'Wei shenme zhei wushiwu ge xiang, she neng tiqian saochu qingzhuannian wenmang?' in Guangdong sheng saochu wenmang xiehui, ed., *Xianqi daguimo zhuangkuo de saomang dayuejin* (Guangzhou: Guangdong renmin chubanshe, n.d.).

35 'Gonggu saomang chengguo, daban yeyu jiaoyu,' *Guangdong saomang* 1 (1958):11-14; *Dagongbao* (Hong Kong), 29 September 1958. On Heilongjiang, see Liang Zhichao, 'Heilongjiang sheng wancheng jiben saochu wenmang renwu de chubu tihui' and Heilongjiang sheng daili xian wenjiao ju, 'Du baiben shu, xie wange zi,' both in *Renmin jiaoyu* 8 (1958).

36 'Jixu kaizhan saomang yundong daban yeyu chudeng jiaoyu: Sheng jiaoyu gongzuo huiyi tichu fazhan gongnong jiaoyu de renwu,' *Guangdong gongnong jiaoyu* 5 (1959):6-8; Puning gongnong jiaoyu diaocha zu, 'Liangzhong taidu, liangzhong xiaoke,' 7-8; *Guangdong jiaoyu nianjian*, 104. In 1959, central authorities estimated around 30 per cent of peasants nationwide had 'relapsed' into illiteracy since the start of the Great Leap Forward literacy campaign. See 'Nuli gonggu kuoda saomang chengguo,' *Guangdong gongnong jiaoyu* 1 (1959):18-20.

37 Puning gongnong jiaoyu diaocha zu, 'Liangzhong taidu liangzhong xiaoke' and 'Zou qunzhong luxian wancheng saomang renwu de guanjian,' in *Guangdong sheng saochu wenmang jiji fenzi daibiao dahui huikan*, 21.

38 On the social and economic breakdown that accompanied the failure of the Great Leap Forward, see the essays by Nicholas Lardy and Kenneth Lieberthal in Roderick MacFarquhar and John K. Fairbank, eds., *The People's Republic, Part 1: The Emergence of Revolutionary China, 1949-1965*, vol. 14 of *The Cambridge History of China* (Cambridge, UK: Cambridge University Press 1987). On the famine, see Basil Ashton et al., 'Famine in China: 1958-61,' *Population and Development Review* 10 (1984):613-45.

39 'Zhonggong zhongyang guanyu jiaqiang nongcun saomang he yeyu jiaoyu gongzuo de lingdao he guanli de tongzhi' and 'Zhonghua renmin gongheguo jiaoyu bu guanyu chedi zhixing zhonggong zhongyang "guanyu jiaqiang nongcun saomang he yeyu jiaoyu gongzuo de lingdao he guanli de tongzhi,"' in *Gongnong jiaoyu wenxian huibian (nongmin jiaoyu)*, 107-8, 139-40.

40 On the breakdown of the statistical system during the Great Leap Forward, see Li Chohming, *The Statistical System of Communist China* (Berkeley: University of California Press 1962), 83-108.

41 Chen Ziyun, 'Dali zhiyuan nongye, jiji kaizhan yi zhuyin shizi wei zhongxin de qunzhong xuexi yundong, wei tiqian wancheng saomang he puji yeyu jiaoyu de guangrong renwu er fendou,' *Guangdong jiaoyu (yeyu jiaoyu ban)* 5.6 (1960):3.

42 Only since the 1980s has literacy 'inspection' come to be associated with learner performance rather than bureaucratic discipline. On inspection procedures, see Vilma Seeberg, *Literacy in China: The Effects of the National Development Context and Policy on Literacy Levels, 1949-1979* (Bochum: Brockmeyer 1990), 168-9. See also *Literacy Situation in Asia and the Pacific Country Studies: China* (Bangkok: UNESCO Regional Office for Education in Asia and the Pacific 1984), 37-8.

43 'Zuohao wenmang qingdi gongzuo,' *Guangdong jiaoyu (yeyu jiaoyu ban)* 3 (1960):20.

44 *Shanghai saomang*, 14 February 1957, in *Union Research Institute* 42207.

45 'Bixu shifen zhongshi quanrizhi xuexiao jiaoxue zhiliang de tigao,' *Guangdong jiaoyu* 1 (1960):3-4. See also 'Zhengque renshi jiaoyu gongzuo de jige jiben wenti,' *Guangdong jiaoyu* 12 (1962):3-5; and Xia Jing, 'Wei shenme yao tiaozheng jiaoyu shiye?' *Guangdong jiaoyu* 6 (1962):4-5.

46 Evelyn S. Rawski, 'The Social Agenda of May Fourth,' in Kenneth Lieberthal et al., eds., *Perspectives on Modern China: Four Anniversaries* (Armonk, NY: M.E. Sharpe 1991), 144.

47 *Guangdong jiaoyu nianjian*, 104.

48 Chen Bixiang, ed., *Zhongguo xiandai yuwen jiaoyu zhan shi* (Kunming: Yunnan jiaoyu chubanshe 1987), 248-9.

Chapter 7: Beijing's Language Reform

1 See 'Guowuyuan guanyu tuiguang putonghua de zhishi,' *Renmin jiaoyu* 2 (1956):21-2, 30-4. See also Wei Ke, 'Dali tuixing hanyu pinyin fangan, wei puji jiaoyu chuangzao tiaojian,' *Renmin jiaoyu* 4 (1958):20-2.

2 The academies are discussed in Alexander Woodside, 'The Political Inevitability of School Reform in Late Imperial China,' in Benjamin A. Elman and Alexander Woodside, eds., *Rapporteur's Report: Conference on Education and Society in Late Imperial China* (US Joint Committee on Chinese Studies, Studies on China, no. 19), 8.

3 Quoted in Chiu-sam Tsang, *Nationalism in School Education in China* (Hong Kong: South China Morning Post 1933), 66.

4 While the use of the term *guoyu* in reference to a Chinese vernacular appears in Buddhist records as early as the sixth century, its modern usage dates to the turn of this century when the scholar and educator Wu Rulun returned from studying the educational system in Japan and urged the Qing government to copy Japan's success in promoting the Tokyo dialect as *kokugo* (*guoyu*). However, the dynasty, which responded positively to Wu's suggestion, fell before it could be realized. See S. Robert Ramsey, 'The Polysemy of the Term *Kokugo*,' in Victor H. Mair, ed., *Schriftfestschrift: Essays on Writing and Language in Honor of John DeFrancis on His Eightieth Birthday*, issue of *Sino-Platonic Papers* 27 (August 1991), 37-47.

5 On the use of Mandarin in Cantonese opera, see Barbara E. Ward, 'Regional Operas and Their Audiences: Evidence from Hong Kong,' in David Johnson, Andrew J. Nathan, and Evelyn S. Rawski, eds., *Popular Culture in Late Imperial China* (Berkeley: University of California Press 1985), 167 n. 7. On the Cantonese vernacular literature movement, see Qin Mu, 'Guangdong wenhua jiaoyu lunkuo shu,' *Guangdong jiaoyu yu wenhua* 1.6 (1950):6. The movement had roots in famous works such as the mid-nineteenth-century collection of Cantonese popular ballads known as *Yue ou*. The movement was revived in Hong Kong in the late 1940s and spread rapidly to Guangdong, where it collided after 1949 with the communist effort to suppress dialect literature.

6   John DeFrancis, *Nationalism and Language Reform in China* (Princeton: Princeton University Press 1950) 53.

7   The earliest romanization scheme devised by a Chinese was published in 1892 by Lu Zhuangzhang, an impoverished lower degree holder from Fujian whose scheme was based on the romanization method used by Catholic missionaries in his native Xiamen and on Lu's knowledge of English acquired during three years in Singapore. See Ni Haishu zhuzuo bianji xiaozu, ed., *Ni Haishu yuwen lunji* (Shanghai: Shanghai jiaoyu chubanshe 1991), 83. On Wang Bingyue, see DeFrancis, *Nationalism and Langauge Reform*, 38.

8   Ni Haishu zhuzuo bianji, *Ni Haishu lunji*, 100-2. On Qu Qiubai's role in the formation of early CCP language policy, see also Paul L.M. Serruys, *Survey of the Chinese Language Reform and the Anti-Illiteracy Movement in China* (Berkeley: Center for Chinese Studies, Institute of International Studies, University of California 1962), 46-7; and S. Robert Ramsey, *The Languages of China* (Princeton: Princeton University Press 1987), 46-7. On Wu Yuzhang's role, see Jinyang xuekan bianji bu, comp., *Zhongguo xiandai shehui kexue xuejia zhuanlue*, vol. 3 (Taiyuan: Shanxi renmin chubanshe 1983), 230-46. A founding member of Sun Yatsen's Tongmenhui, Wu was educated in Japan, France, and the Soviet Union and was one of the leading founders of the work-study movement in Paris in 1915.

9   David Holm, *Art and Ideology in Revolutionary China* (Oxford: Clarendon Press 1991), 33-4. See also Paul Pickowicz, 'Ch'u Ch'iu-pai and the Chinese Marxist Conception of Revolutionary Literature and Art,' *China Quarterly* 70 (1971):298.

10 Edgar Snow, *Red Star over China*, rev. and enl. ed. (New York: Bantam 1978), 446.

11 See, for example, *Hu Qiaomu Wenji*, vol. 1 (Beijing: Renmin chubanshe 1992), 39-40; Wang Yunfeng, *Xu Teli zai Yanan* (Xi'an: Shanxi renmin chubanshe 1991), 9.

12 As late as 1948, Ni Haishu, one of the CCP's leading language reformers, published a list of romanization schemes for the major regional dialects. See Ni Haishu, *Zhongguo pinyin wenzi gailun* (Shanghai: Shidai shubao chubanshe 1948), 42-61.

13 Simplified characters had been promoted by the Communist Party since the early 1930s. See Wang Hsueh-wen, 'A Study of Chinese Communist Education during the Kiangsi Period,' Part 2, *Issues and Studies* 9.8 (1973):79.

14 *Guangming ribao, xueshu lun wenji: Wenzi gaige*, 2 vols. (Washington, DC: Center for Chinese Research Materials 1972).

15 Mae Chu-Chang, 'Issues for a Bilingual Population: The Case of China,' in June Y. Mei, ed., *Reading in China: Report of the U.S. Reading Study Team to the People's Republic of China* (New York: National Committee on U.S.-China Relations n.d.), 84.

16 Fan Liu, Tong Lequan, and Song Jun, 'The Characteristics of Chinese Language and Children's Learning to Read and Write,' in Daniel A. Wagner, ed., *The Future of Literacy in a Changing World* (Oxford: Pergamon Press 1987), 89.

17 On the political foundations of language reform, see DeFrancis, *Nationalism and Language Reform*.

18 Quoted in John DeFrancis, 'Mao Tse-tung and Writing Reform,' in Joshua A. Fogel and William T. Rowe, eds., *Perspectives on a Changing China: Essays in Honor of Professor C. Martin Wilbur on the Occasion of His Retirement* (Boulder: Westview Press 1979), 139-42.

19 Charles W. Hayford, 'Literacy Movements in Modern China,' in Robert F. Arnove and Harvey J. Graff, eds., *National Literacy Campaigns: Historical and Comparative Perspectives* (New York: Plenum Press 1987), 169.

20 Critics, however, continued to charge that *hanyu pinyin* was a foreign import that slighted China's cultural and linguistic heritage; hence, the search for a more perfect alphabet continued. According to a recent source, a further 1,667 proposals for alphabets were put forward by PRC linguists between 1958 and 1980. Zhou Youguang, 'The Modernization of the Chinese Language,' *International Journal of the Sociology of Language* 59 (1986):17.

21 On early post-1949 efforts to promote Mandarin in Guangdong, see 'Guangdong renmin zhengfu wenjiao ting yijiu wuling nian wenjiao gongzuo jihua caoan,' *Guangdong jiaoyu yu wenhua* 1.2 (1950):5-6; and 'Wei shenmo xuexi guoyu?' *Guangdong jiaoyu yu wenhua* 2.4 (1951):27-8.

22 Zhang Xiruo, 'Resolutely Promote the Standard Vernacular Based on Peking Pronunciation,' in Peter J. Seybolt and Gregory Kuei-ke Chiang, eds., *Language Reform in China: Documents and Commentary* (White Plains, NY: M.E. Sharpe 1979), 65-6, 68. These aims were

formally promulgated in the State Council decree of 1956, 'Guowuyuan guanyu tuiguang putonghua de zhishi,' *Renmin jiaoyu* 2 (1956):21-2, also in *Zhongguo jiaoyu nianjian*, 687-8.

23 See *Renmin jiaoyu* 2 (1956):21-2, 30-4. See also Wei Ke, 'Dali tuixing hanyu pinyin fangan, wei puji jiaoyu chuangzao tiaojian,' *Renmin jiaoyu* 4 (1958):20-2.

24 'Yijiu wuliu nian guangdong sheng putong jiaoyu he shifan jiaoyu de gongzuo renwu,' *Guangdong jiaoyu* 10-11 (10 June 1956):12-13.

25 'Jianchi tuiguang putonghua he putonghua jiaoxue: Chaoan di er zhongxue,' *Guangdong jiaoyu*, 16 February 1960:15.

26 Huang Muliang, 'Yinian lai wo shi zenyang jinxing putonghua jiaoxue de,' *Guangdong jiaoyu*, September 1956:26-7. See also Huang Heyang, 'Wo shi zheiyang yong putonghua jinxing jiaoxue de,' *Guangdong jiaoyu*, July 1956:29-30.

27 Lin Handa, 'Wei shehui zhuyi jianshe kaizhan saomang gongzuo,' Part 2, *Wenhuibao* (Shanghai), 3 November 1955, in *Union Research Institute* LO364 42222. See also his 'Relie zhankai hanyu pinyin fangan (caoan) de taolun, jiji tigong xiugai de yijian,' *Renmin jiaoyu* 3 (1956):25-8. The various State Council and Central Committee directives are described in *Zhongguo jiaoyu nianjian*, 145.

28 Hu Yaobang, 'Guanyu nongcun saochu wenmang gongzuo,' *Renmin ribao*, 16 November 1955, in *Union Research Institute* LO364 4222. See also Zhang Xiruo, 'Resolutely Promote the Standard Vernacular,' 71.

29 'Fu: Shanxi shengwei guanyu zai quansheng tuiguang wanrong xian zhuyin shizi jingyan zhengqu tiqian shi shanxi chengwei wumang sheng xiang zhongyang de baogao,' *Guangdong jiaoyu*, 10 June 1960:4. See also 'Dali tuiguang zhuyin shizi zhengqu tiqian saochu wenmang,' *Guangdong jiaoyu*, 10 June 1960:5.

30 'Zhuyin shizi shi saochu wenmang de jiejing,' *Guangdong jiaoyu (yeyu jiaoyuban)*, 15 August 1960:10-11.

31 'Dali tuiguang zhuyin shizi zhengqu tiqian saochu wenmang.'

32 'Zhuyin shizi shi saochu wenmang de jiejing.' See also He Liu, 'Tuixing zhuyin shizi, jiakuai saomang sudu: Ji Tanshui gongshe Dongming dadui kaizhan zhuyin shizi yundong,' *Guangdong jiaoyu (yeyu jiaoyuban)*, 15 July 1960:3-4. The pinyin scheme published in the Guangdong education bureau's official journal contained many letters that were printed upside down or wrongly used, indicating that peasants were not the only ones who found it difficult to master pinyin. See 'Zhuyin shizi pinyin jiaoxue dagang (chugao)' *Guangdong jiaoyu (yeyu jiaoyuban)*, 15 January 1960:14-17.

33 H.S. Bhola, *Campaigning for Literacy: Eight National Experiences of the Twentieth Century, with a Memorandum to Decision-Makers* (Paris: UNESCO 1984), 85.

34 John DeFrancis, *The Chinese Language: Fact and Fantasy* (Honolulu: University of Hawaii Press 1984), 269.

35 Ibid., 295 n. 4.

36 'Dali kaizhan saomang gongzuo, daban gezhong yeyu jiaoyu, jixu tigao jiaoxue zhiliang, jiji jinxing jiaoxue gaige,' *Guangdong jiaoyu*, 10 June 1960:7-8; Che Mu, 'Wei shenmo yong fangyan zhuyin shizi?' *Guangdong jiaoyu (yeyu jiaoyuban)*, 15 August 1960:16.

37 'Guangzhou hua pinyin fangan,' *Guangdong jiaoyu (yeyu jiaoyuban)*, 10 October 1960:12-13; 'Kejia hua pinyin fangan,' 'Chaozhou hua pinyin fangan,' and 'Hainan hua pinyin fangan,' in *Guangdong jiaoyu (yeyu jiaoyuban)*, 20 November 1960:16-17, 24-5, 32-3.

38 On the Great Leap Forward famine of 1958-61, see Basil Ashton et al., 'Famine in China: 1958-61,' *Population and Development Review* 10 (1984):613-45.

39 Chen Ziyun, 'Dali zhiyuan nongye, jiji kaizhan yi zhuyin shizi wei zhongxin de qunzhong xuexi yundong, wei tiqian wancheng saomang he puji yeyu jiaoyu de guangrong renwu er fendou,' *Guangdong jiaoyu (yeyu jiaoyuban)*, 20 November 1960:2-5. See also 'Renzhen zongjie zhuyin shizi de shidian jingyan,' *Guangdong jiaoyu (yeyu jiaoyuban)*, 10 October 1960:10.

40 'Renzhen zongjie zhuyin shizi de shidian jingyan.'

41 Eugen Weber, *Peasants into Frenchmen: The Modernization of Rural France, 1870-1914* (Stanford: Stanford University Press 1976).

Chapter 8: Literacy Expansion and Social Contraction

1 Jonathan Unger, 'Bending the School Ladder: The Failure of Chinese Educational Reform in the 1960s,' *Comparative Education Review* 24.2, Part 1 (1980):221-37. See also Joel Glassman,

'Educational Reform and Manpower Needs Policy in China 1955-58,' *Modern China* 3.3 (1977):259-90; and Robert D. Barendson, 'The Agricultural Middle Schools in Communist China,' *China Quarterly* 8 (1961):106-34.

2 Kenneth Levine, 'Functional Literacy: Fond Illusions and False Economies,' *Harvard Educational Review* 52.3 (1982):261-2.

3 David F.K. Ip, 'The Design of Development: Experiences from South China, 1949-1976' (Ph.D. diss., University of British Columbia 1979).

4 On supravillage networks, see Helen F. Siu, *Agents and Victims in South China: Accomplices in Rural Revolution* (New Haven: Yale University Press 1989), 3-7, 15-87, which traces these networks over the course of five centuries in the Pearl River Delta of Guangdong. On state efforts to broker its authority through such networks, see Prasenjit Duara, *Culture, Power and the State: Rural North China, 1900-1942* (Stanford: Stanford University Press 1988).

5 Cited in Tiejun Cheng, 'The Dialectics of Control: The Household Registration (*Hukou*) System in Contemporary China' (Ph.D. diss., State University of New York at Binghampton 1991), 81.

6 Jean Oi, *State and Peasant in Contemporary China* (Berkeley: University of California Press 1989), 42. Grain rationing was implemented in the Soviet Union during the period of 'war communism' to combat severe economic shortages and was subsequently disbanded. By contrast, the PRC rationing system was introduced in 1953, after the period of economic recovery, and was subsequently extended to cover not only food grain but most other staple commodities as well. The PRC rationing system, which operated in close conjunction with residence controls, was implemented and maintained until the 1980s for reasons of political economy more than economic exigency.

7 Until recently, the broad social and political significance of the *hukou* was overlooked in most Western scholarship on the PRC. For the first important attempt to understand its significance, see Sulamith Heins Potter, 'The Position of Peasants in Modern China's Social Order,' *Modern China* 9.4 (1983):465-99. See also Sulamith H. Potter and Jack M. Potter, *China's Peasants: The Anthropology of a Revolution* (Cambridge, UK: Cambridge University Press 1990), 300-2; and Tiejun Cheng and Mark Selden, 'The Origins and Social Consequences of China's *Hukou* System,' *China Quarterly* 139 (1994):644-68. The latter provides an extensive analysis of the system's evolution from the early 1950s onward. The most comprehensive available description of the system in an official Chinese source, which also traces the evolution of Chinese population registration methods from antiquity, is Liu Guangren, ed., *Hukou guanli xue* (Beijing: Zhongguo jiancha chubanshe [gongan jiguan neibu faxing] 1992), published for internal circulation among public security organs.

8 Cheng, 'Dialectics of Control,' i; Kam Wing Chan, 'Economic Growth Strategy and Urbanization Policies in China, 1949-1982,' *International Journal of Urban and Regional Research* 16 (1992):275-306; and, by the same author, *Cities with Invisible Walls* (Hong Kong: Oxford University Press 1994).

9 Especially significant was the fact that residency status was inherited matrilineally, since, as the authors of the study point out, China remained in every other respect a patrilineal society after 1949. Residential status was assigned matrilineally presumably in order to minimize changes in status, since males were more likely to achieve upward mobility than females. See Potter and Potter, *China's Peasants*, 97.

10 Ibid.; Siu, *Agents and Victims*, 6, 168.

11 Y.C. Wang, 'Western Impact and Social Mobility in China,' *American Sociological Review* 25 (1960):843-55.

12 James Hayes, 'Specialists and Written Materials in the Village World,' in David Johnson, Andrew J. Nathan, and Evelyn S. Rawski, eds., *Popular Culture in Late Imperial China* (Berkeley: University of California Press 1985), 75-111. Hayes identifies two main groups of literate specialists in pre-1949 Cantonese villages: those versed in protective rituals and the manipulation of natural forces, and those expert in performing social rites and prescribed forms of social intercourse.

13 In the Guangdong commune studied by Potter and Potter, villagers recounted only a single instance of a member actually leaving the commune to become an urban resident by means of education in a state school – so rare that the story had formed part of local folklore. See Potter and Potter, *China's Peasants*, 306-11. See also Huang Shu-min, *The Spiral Road: Change*

in a Chinese Village through the Eyes of a Communist Party Leader (Boulder: Westview Press 1989), 54.

14 Hung Yung Lee, *From Revolutionary Cadres to Party Technocrats in Socialist China* (Berkeley: University of California Press 1991). The attributes of local team and brigade leaders have been analyzed for a number of Guangdong localities; see Siu, *Agents and Victims*, 122-3, 135, 166-7, 305 n. 15; Potter and Potter, *China's Peasants*, 277; and Richard Madsen, *Morality and Power in a Chinese Village* (Berkeley: University of California Press 1984), 47.

15 An excellent 'thick' description of the role of literate team functionaries is provided in Potter and Potter, *China's Peasants*, 99-101.

16 Mervyn Matthews, 'Soviet Students: Some Sociological Perspectives,' *Soviet Studies* 27.1 (1975):97.

17 'Shiyong nongye hezuoshehua xuyao, dali kaizhan nongcun saomang gongzuo,' *Renmin Jiaoyu* 1 (1956):33.

18 'Quanri zhi xuexiao bixu yi jiaoxue weizhu,' *Guangdong jiaoyu*, 16 January 1960:3-4.

19 On the origins of the work-study movement, see Paul Bailey, *Reform the People: Changing Attitudes towards Popular Education in Early 20th Century China* (Vancouver: University of British Columbia Press 1990).

20 Lian Ruiqing, '"Liangzhong jiaoyu zhidu, liangzhong laodong zhidu" de tichu jiqi xianshi yiyi,' in Lu Xingdou, ed., *Liu Shaoqi he tade shiye* (Beijing: Zhonggong dangshi chubanshe 1991), 455-7. See also *Zhongguo dabaike quanshu: Jiaoyu* (Beijing: Zhongguo dabaike quanshu chubanshe 1985), 224-5.

21 Cited in 'Daliang fazhan nongye zhongxue,' *Guangdong jiaoyu*, January 1960:26.

22 Guojia tongji ju, ed., *Zhongguo tongji nianjian, 1987* (Beijing: Zhongguo tongji chubanshe 1987), 764. Altogether, more than two million primary and middle school graduates were sent back to their villages to work between 1955 and 1957. 'Youxiu de yiwu minxiao jiaoshi,' *Renmin jiaoyu* 11 (1955):38-9; *Zhongguo jiaoyu nianjian*, 416.

23 *Guangdong jiaoyu nianjian*, 76.

24 For a succinct refutation of the notion, long popular in Western academic writing, that the Maoist strategy for economic development was characterized by an 'antiurban bias,' see Chan, 'Economic Growth Strategy.'

25 See Lu Dingyi, 'Nongye zhongxue chuangban er zhounian,' *Guangdong jiaoyu*, 16 March 1960:3. For Lu's major statement on the subject, see his *Education Must Be Combined with Productive Labour* (Beijing: Foreign Language Press 1958), 8.

26 On the curriculum of agricultural middle schools in Guangdong, see 'Cong shiji chufa wei dangdi shengchan fuwu: Xingning longtian nongzhong de yixie banxue jingyan,' in *Guangdong sheng nongcun bannong bandu jiaoyu huiyi ziliao*, 1-6; and 'Guzu ganjin daban nongye zhongxue, jiji zhiyuan nongye jishu gaizao,' *Guangdong jiaoyu*, April 1960:4-8.

27 'Jianchi jieji douzheng, jianchi bannong bandu de banxue fangxiang: Guanyu xinhui hetang nongye zhongxue de diaocha baogao,' in *Guangdong sheng nongcun bannong bandu jiaoyu huiyi ziliao*, 1-14.

28 Kong Xiangxing, 'Wei nongye shengchan jianshe peiyang laodong houbei liliang,' *Guangdong jiaoyu*, 1 March 1964:9-13.

29 Yang Xiufeng, 'Peiyang nonglin zhuanmen rencai yaozou ziji de lu,' in *Yang Xiufeng jiaoyu wenji* (Beijing: Beijing shifan daxue chubanshe 1987), 44-5. See also Unger, 'Bending the School Ladder,' 233-4. Yang's career was far more cosmopolitan than the one he advocated for Chinese youth. After graduating from Beijing Teachers' College in 1921, Yang taught at several colleges and universities before he left China for Paris in 1929. There he joined the French Communist Party and spent the next three years living in France, Germany, England, the Soviet Union, and Japan before finally returning to China in the early 1930s.

30 Lin Liming, 'Guanyu dangqian jiaoyu gongzuo zhong de jige wenti,' *Guangdong jiaoyu*, 10 April 1956:3-6.

31 'Guzu ganqin daban nongye zhongxue, jiji zhiyuan nongye jishu gaizao,' 6.

32 'Jianchi jieji douzheng, jianchi bannong bandu de banxue fangxiang: Guanyu xinhui hetang nongye zhongxue de diaocha baogao,' 5-7.

33 Qu Mengjue et al., *Hong you zhuan* (Guangzhou: Guangdong renmin chubanshe 1958), 6. On another occasion, Qu described graduates of the agricultural middle schools as

possessed of both literary (*wen*) and martial (*wu*) qualities (in traditional Chinese political philosophy, the two were always juxtaposed), capable of any kind of labour.

34   Victoria J. Baker, 'Education for Its Own Sake: The Relevance Dimension in Rural Areas,' *Comparative Education Review* 33 (1989):507-18.

35   Alexander Woodside, 'Some Mid-Qing Theorists of Popular Schools: Their Innovations, Inhibitions, and Attitudes toward the Poor,' *Modern China* 9.1 (1983):26-7. The traditional symbolic dissociation of schools and vocational education is suggested by the efforts of the eighteenth-century popular educational reformer Chen Hongmou to spread techniques of sericulture among Shaanxi peasants. As Woodside points out, Chen arranged for peasants to be taught these techniques not in schools but in special 'silkworm bureaus' (*canju*), and not by teachers but by special 'silkworm chiefs' (*canzhang*).

36   Unger, 'Bending the School Ladder,' 224.

37   'Shi xuexiao you shi nongye jishu tuiguang zhan: Jieyang xian baita nongye zhongxue jieshao,' *Guangdong jiaoyu*, 10 June 1960:28-9; 'Jishu yexiao yu xinren,' *Guangdong jiaoyu*, January 1965:23-4.

38   'Cong shiji chufa wei dangdi shengchan fuwu: Xingning longtian nongzhong de yixie banxue jingyan.'

39   'Xingning xian nongye zhongxue banxue qinian,' in *Guangdong sheng nongcun bannong bandu jiaoyu huiyi ziliao*, 1-10.

40   *Zhongguo jiaoyu nianjian*, 180-1. Regular middle school enrolment in 1965 was over 9 million.

41   *Guangdong jiaoyu nianjian*, 24-5, 79, 134-5.

Chapter 9: The Cultural Revolution

1   The editors' first 'error' was to refer to a party policy of 'exterminating landlords and bureaucrats' – a possible reference to Mao's dismissal of Defence Minister Peng Dehuai for daring to criticize Mao's policies during the Great Leap Forward – which should have read 'exterminating landlords and bureaucratic capitalists.' The second 'error' was to describe the massive water conservancy works built during the Great Leap Forward as a transformation of the 'rivers and mountains' (*jiangshan*), which critics pointed out was a classical reference to the political realm; the lyrics should have referred to 'mountains and rivers' (*shanjiang*). The third thinly disguised 'error' was to use the word *yao* ('to shake') rather than *yang* ('to raise') to describe the fluttering of the 'red flag,' since the former – the critics charged – implied a 'faltering' flag. 'Women de jiantao,' *Guangdong jiaoyu*, May 1966:27.

2   Li Dachao and Deng Qin, '"Guangdong jiaoyu" wei shei fuwu?' *Guangdong jiaoyu*, June 1966:26.

3   *Zhongguo jiaoyu nianjian*, 603, 1021, 1037; *Guangdong jiaoyu nianjian*, 105. See also Vilma Seeberg, *Literacy in China: The Effects of the National Development Context and Policy on Literacy Levels, 1949-1979* (Bochum: Brockmeyer 1990), 171.

4   Suzanne Pepper, 'New Directions in Education,' in Roderick MacFarquhar and John K. Fairbank, eds., *The People's Republic, Part 1: The Emergence of Revolutionary China, 1949-1965*, vol. 14 of *The Cambridge History of China* (Cambridge, UK: Cambridge University Press 1987), 402-3.

5   *Zhongguo jiaoyu nianjian*, 123-4.

6   'Daban gengdu xiaoxue, duokuai duosheng de shixian puji nongcun jiaoyu,' in *Guangdong sheng nongcun bannong bandu jiaoyu huiyi ziliao* (Guangzhou: n.p. 1965), 1-12. See also *Zhongguo jiaoyu nianjian*, 123-4; and *Guangdong jiaoyu nianjian*, 24, 52, 54, 56, 133.

7   Zhonggong gaozhou xian dongan gongshe weiyuanhui, 'Mianxiang pinxia zhongnong jiji banhao gengdu xiaoxue,' *Guangdong jiaoyu*, 2 February 1966:34-42.

8   Liu Shaoqi's educational views are examined in Lu Xingdou, ed., *Liu Shaoqi he tade shiye* (Beijing: Zhonggong dangshi chubanshe 1991), 454-66.

9   Zhenjiang zhuanshu jiaoyu ji, 'Daban gengdu xiaoxue dukuai haosheng de puji nongcun jiaoyu,' *Guangdong jiaoyu*, July 1965:8-10.

10   Tao Zhan, 'Mianxiang nongcun, wei nongye fuwu de Changpo xiaoxue,' *Guangdong jiaoyu*, 11 June 1964: 14-16.

11 'Daban gengdu xiaoxue, duokuai duosheng de shixian puji nongcun jiaoyu,' 3; Luo Guang, 'Jieshao Niaoshi nongchang gengdu xiaoxue,' *Guangdong jiaoyu*, November 1964:15.
12 Qiu Tian, 'Dui xiaoxue shougong laodong ke de yijian,' *Guangdong jiaoyu*, June 1965:24-5.
13 Richard Baum, *Prelude to Revolution: Mao, the Party and the Peasant Question 1962-1966* (New York: Columbia University Press 1975). For the Socialist Education Movement in Guangdong, see Anita Chan, Richard Madsen, and Jonathan Unger, *Chen Village: The Recent History of a Peasant Community in Mao's China* (Berkeley: University of California Press 1984); and Richard Madsen, *Morality and Power in a Chinese Village* (Berkeley: University of California Press 1984), 67-101, 130-50.
14 On the army's role in the Socialist Education Movement in Guangdong, see Ezra Vogel, *Canton under Communism: Programs and Politics in a Provincial Capital, 1949-1968* (Cambridge, MA: Harvard University Press 1969), 302, 308, 310-13.
15 'Jiji zhiyuan nongye,' *Guangdong jiaoyu* 2 (1962):3-4.
16 Thomas Bernstein, *Up to the Mountains and Down to the Villages: The Transfer of Youth from Urban to Rural China* (New Haven: Yale University Press 1977). On the rustication movement in Guangdong, see Jonathan Unger, *Education under Mao: Class and Competition in Canton Schools, 1960-1980* (New York: Columbia University Press 1982); and Stanley Rosen, *Red Guard Factionalism and the Cultural Revolution in Guangzhou* (Boulder: Westview Press 1982).
17 'Jiji kaizhan nongcun saomang he yeyu jiaoyu: Guangdong sheng jiaoyu ting Rao Huangxiang fu tingzhan zai quansheng nongcun saomang he yeyu jiaoyu huiyi de baogao disan bufen,' *Guangdong jiaoyu*, 1 January 1964:3-5. For local descriptions of the movement, see *Panyu xian jiaoyu zhi*, 15-16; and *Xinxing xian jiaoyu zhi*, 142.
18 Lianjiang xian jiaoyu ju, 'Jinmi jiehe nongcun shehui zhuyi jiaoyu yundong kaizhan yeyu jiaoyu gongzuo,' *Guangdong jiaoyu*, 1 April 1964:25-6; and 'Yunyong duozhong duoyang de xingshi dui xuesheng jinxing jieji jiaoyu,' *Guangdong jiaoyu* 10 (1963):5-6.
19 'Fayang jianku fendou, qinjian ban xue de geming jingshen,' *Guangdong jiaoyu*, August 1964:12-13.
20 Madsen, *Morality and Power*, 73, 75-6.
21 Gu Hua, *A Small Town Called Hibiscus*, trans. Gladys Yang (Beijing: Panda Books 1983), 149-50. Gu termed these beliefs and ceremonies, which were clearly meant to appeal to peasants' religious sensibility, the 'modern superstitions' of New China, a 'new variety of the benighted feudal ideas which had prevailed in China for thousands of years.' See 151.
22 See David E. Apter, 'Yan'an and the Narrative Reconstruction of Reality,' *Daedalus* 122.2 (1993):223. I have borrowed the author's characterization of the CCP's Yanan narrative and applied it to the use of written texts in the Socialist Education Movement, for which the characterization appears to be equally if not more apt.
23 Madsen, *Morality and Power*, 16, 34-5, 131-2.
24 'Women shi zheyang jianchi xuexi Mao zhuxi zhuzuo de,' *Guangdong jiaoyu*, December 1964:10-11. On the miraculous powers attributed to Mao's thought, see George Urban, ed., *The Miracles of Chairman Mao* (London: Tom Stacey 1971).
25 Unger, *Education under Mao*; Rosen, *Red Guard Factionalism*; Susan L. Shirk, *Competitive Comrades: Career Incentives and Student Strategies in China* (Berkeley: University of California Press 1982).
26 Byung-joon Ahn, *Chinese Politics and the Cultural Revolution: Dynamics of Policy Processes* (Seattle: University of Washington Press 1976). See also Lee Hong-yung, *The Politics of the Chinese Cultural Revolution: A Case Study* (Berkeley: University of California Press 1978). On the unfolding of the Cultural Revolution in Guangdong, see Vogel, *Canton under Communism*, 321-49.
27 This paragraph is based on the analysis presented by Marianne Bastid, 'Economic Necessity and Political Ideals in Educational Reform during the Cultural Revolution,' *China Quarterly* 42 (1970):16-45. See also John Gardner and Wilt Idema, 'China's Educational Revolution,' in Stuart R. Schram, ed., *Authority, Participation and Cultural Change in China* (Cambridge, UK: Cambridge University Press 1973), 257-89.
28 'Chronology of the Two Road Struggle on the Educational Front for the Past Seventeen Years,' *Jiaoyu geming*, 6 May 1967; trans. in Peter J. Seybolt, ed., *Revolutionary Education in*

China: Documents and Commentary (New York: International Arts and Sciences Press 1971), 5-59.

29   Suzanne Pepper, 'Education,' in Roderick MacFarquhar and John K. Fairbank, eds., *The People's Republic, Part 2: Revolutions within the Chinese Revolution, 1966-1982*, vol. 15 of *The Cambridge History of China* (Cambridge, UK: Cambridge University Press 1978), 560. See also Pepper, *Radicalism*, 350-1; and Lowell Dittmer, *Liu Shaoqi and the Chinese Cultural Revolution: The Politics of Mass Criticism* (Berkeley: University of California Press 1974), 270-7.

30   *Zhongguo jiaoyu nianjian*, 578, 604. See also *Literacy Situation in Asia and the Pacific Country Studies: China* (Bangkok: UNESCO Regional Office for Education in Asia and the Pacific 1984), 5.

31   *Xinfeng xian jiaoyu zhi*, 103.

32   Guo Lin, 'Qiantan yuwen jiaoxue gaige,' *Jiaoyu yanjiu* 1 (1980):47-54.

33   *Xinxing xian jiaoyu zhi*, 142. See also Zhou Yixian, *Woguo nongcun jiaoyu de huigu yu sikao* (Beijing: Beijing shifan daxue nongcun jiaoyu yanjiu shi 1988). My thanks to Professor Zhou for providing me with a copy of this document.

34   *Guangdong jiaoyu nianjian*, 105.

35   Yunfu xian weiyuanhui zhenggong zu jiaoyu geming bangongshi, *Yunfu xian hongyexiao wenhua keben* (n.p.: n.p. 1972); Shandong sheng geming weiyuanhui zhengzhi bu jiaoyu zu, ed., *Sheyuan shizi*, vols. 1 and 2 (n.p.: Shandong renmin chubanshe 1973).

36   *Guangdong jiaoyu nianjian*, 16, 105; *Xinxing xian jiaoyu zhi*, 142; *Panyu xian jiaoyu zhi*, 16-17. For the increase in Guangdong's illiteracy rate during the Cultural Revolution decade, see Lin Hong, 'Wosheng chengren chu, gaodeng jiaoyu shinian fazhan huigu,' *Guangdong jiaoyu* 5 (1989):11.

37   *Pinxia zhongnong ban xuexiao* (Guangzhou: Guangdong renmin chubanshe 1973).

38   'Draft Program for Primary and Middle Schools in the Chinese Countryside,' trans. in Hu Shiming and Eli Saifman, eds., *Toward a New World Outlook: A Documentary History of Education in the People's Republic of China*, (New York: AMS Press 1976), 230-6. The model was said to have originated in the form of a letter published by *Renmin ribao* in November 1968 by two cadres from Shandong's Maji commune. The letter called for the transferring of the management and finance of all rural state-run primary schools to production brigades. *Zhongguo jiaoyu nianjian*, 126.

39   *Zhongguo jiaoyu nianjian*, 468.

40   *Xinxing xian jiaoyu zhi*, 66; *Huazhou xian jiaoyu zhi*, 13. On curricular reforms, see also Gardner and Idema, 'China's Educational Revolution,' 268-71.

41   Suzanne Pepper, 'Education and Revolution: The "Chinese Model" Revisited,' *Asian Survey* 18 (1978):853.

42   *Huazhou xian jiaoyu zhi*, 13; *Xinfeng xian jiaoyu zhi*, 76. On the quota system for higher education, see William L. Parish and Martin King Whyte, *Village and Family in Contemporary China* (Chicago: University of Chicago Press 1978), 370 n. 13.

43   *Guangdong jiaoyu nianjian*, 52.

44   Ibid., 18; *Xinfeng xian jiaoyu zhi*, 77, 126. In 1979, the county officially exonerated the teachers who had been killed during the Cultural Revolution, and future employment was arranged for their children.

45   *Guangdong jiaoyu nianjian*, 52; *Zhongguo jiaoyu nianjian*, 1024; Parish and Whyte, *Village and Family*, 78-85, 371 n. 17.

46   See Glen D. Peterson, 'Socialist China and the Huaqiao: The Transition to Socialism in the Overseas Chinese Areas of Rural Guangdong,' *Modern China* 14.3 (1988):309-35.

47   *Guangdong jiaoyu nianjian*, 124-5.

Chapter 10: Literacy and Economic Development

1   For a comprehensive examination of the post-Mao reforms, see Harry Harding, *China's Second Revolution: Reform after Mao* (Washington, DC: Brookings Institution 1987). For a fine collection of analytical essays on the politics of reform, including agriculture, see Elizabeth J. Perry and Christine Wong, eds., *The Political Economy of Reform in Post-Mao China* (Cambridge, MA: Council on East Asian Studies, Harvard University 1985). On Deng's rise to power, see Richard Baum, *Burying Mao: Chinese Politics in the Age of Deng Xiaoping*

(Princeton: Princeton University Press 1994). For a comprehensive account of reform in Guangdong, see Ezra F. Vogel, *One Step Ahead in China: Guangdong under Reform* (Cambridge, MA: Harvard University Press 1989).

2 'Guowuyuan guanyu saochu wenmang de zhishi (zhailu),' *Zhongguo jiaoyu nianjian*, 6 November 1978:900.

3 Jack Gray and Maisie Gray, 'China's New Agricultural Revolution,' in Stephen Feuchtwang and Arthur Hussain, eds., *The Chinese Economic Reforms* (New York: St. Martin's Press 1983), 151-84.

4 See David Zweig, *Agrarian Radicalism in China, 1960-1981* (Cambridge, MA: Harvard University Press 1989); and Daniel Kelliher, *Peasant Power in China: The Era of Rural Reform, 1979-1989* (New Haven: Yale University Press 1992).

5 On the implementation of the household responsibility system, see David Zweig, 'Household Contracts and Decollectivization, 1977-1983,' in David M. Lampton, ed., *Policy Implementation in Post-Mao China* (Berkeley: University of California Press 1987); and Kathleen Hartford, 'Socialist Agriculture Is Dead: Long Live Socialist Agriculture! Organizational Transformation in Chinese Agriculture,' in Perry and Wong, eds., *Political Economy of Reform*, 31-62. On the process as it unfolded in Guangdong after 1979, see Graham E. Johnson, 'The Production Responsibility System in Chinese Agriculture: Some Examples from Guangdong,' *Pacific Affairs* 55 (1982):430-51.

6 Vogel, *One Step Ahead*, 92-7. The administrative structure adopted in 1984 lasted only briefly. Administrative restructuring occurred continuously throughout the 1980s and into the 1990s.

7 Du Runsheng, *Many People, Little Land: China's Rural Economic Reform* (Beijing: Foreign Languages Press 1989), 15, 27-9. For a trenchant analysis of changing state policy toward commerce during the Maoist and early post-Mao eras, see Dorothy J. Solinger, *Chinese Business under Socialism: The Politics of Domestic Commerce, 1949-1980* (Berkeley: University of California Press 1984).

8 'Yanjiu xin qingkuang, xin tedian, renzhen gaohao gongnong jiaoyu,' *Guangming ribao*, 5 January 1982.

9 *Deng Xiaoping Wenxuan* (Beijing: Renmin chubanshe 1983), 83-8; *Zhongguo jiaoyu nianjian*, 60-1. See also Marianne Bastid, 'Chinese Educational Policies in the 1980s and Economic Development,' *China Quarterly* 98 (1984):189-219.

10 On 'Saint-Simonianism' in post-Mao China, see Alexander Woodside, 'The Asia-Pacific Idea as a Mobilization Myth,' in Arif Dirlik, ed., *What Is in a Rim? Critical Perspectives on the Pacific Region Idea* (Boulder: Westview Press 1993), 15-16.

11 Cited in ibid., 17.

12 He Dongchang, 'Nongcun jiaoyu zhuyao wei dangdi jianshe fuwu,' *Renmin jiaoyu* 3 (1988):2-4.

13 'Gaige chengren jiaoyu, fazhan chengren jiaoyu: Li Peng tongzhi zai quanguo chengren jiaoyu gongzuo huiyi shang de jianghua,' *Zhongguo jiaoyu bao*, 20 December 1986:1; Lin Li, 'Shitan chengren jiaoyu de diwei he zuoyong,' *Chengren jiaoyu* 1 (1982):22-6.

14 On the introduction and influence of Western educational terms and concepts into China after 1978, see Jurgen Henze, 'Educational Modernization as a Search for Higher Efficiency,' in Marianne Bastid and Ruth Hayhoe, eds., *China's Education and the Industrial World* (Armonk, NY: M.E. Sharpe 1987), 252-70. On the role of the UN in Chinese education in the reform period, see 'Lianheguo jiaokewen zuzhi yatai diqu saomang, chengren jiaoyu shidi kaocha zuotanhui zai Guangzhou zhaokai,' *Guangdong jiaoyu* 12 (1982):2. See also Yu Bo, 'Zhongguo chengren jiaoyu de qiyuan wenti,' *Chengren jiaoyu* 1 (1982):18-21 for an interesting exploration into the origins of adult education in China.

15 'Nongcun saomang ruxue renshu zaidu huisheng,' *Renmin ribao*, 16 October 1985:1; Huang Shiqi, 'Nonformal Education,' in *Education and Modernization*, 148-9; Jacques Lamontagne, 'Chinese Educational Development before and during the 1980s,' unpublished ms., 16. I thank Professor Lamontagne for providing me with a copy of this manuscript.

16 'Jinggao!' *Yangcheng wanbao*, 14 December 1988:1; 'Renkou: Shuliang yu zhiliang,' *Guangming ribao*, 13 April 1989:1. See also Stanley Rosen, 'Women, Education and Modernization,' in Ruth Hayhoe, ed., *Education and Modernization: The Chinese Experience* (Oxford: Pergamon Press 1992), 257.

17 Suzanne Pepper, *China's Education Reform in the 1980s: Policies, Issues, and Historical Perspectives* (Berkeley: Center for Chinese Studies, Institute of East Asian Studies, University of California 1990), 79-84.
18 'Guojia jiaowei biaozhang yibai ge saomang xianjin xian,' *Zhongguo jiaoyu bao*, 3 November 1988:1. See also Li Yunhong, 'Nutong ruxue wenti zhide zhongshi,' *Renmin jiaoyu* 7-8 (1988):12-13; and Li Xiaojiang, 'Zenyang kan dangqian funu wenti he funu yanjiu,' *Qiushi* 11 (1988):32-6.
19 The figures on rural-urban educational differences do not take into account the fact that official definitions of 'urban' and 'rural' changed considerably after 1978. Many formerly rural locations were redesignated as towns and cities, while residents of these areas normally retained their rural residency (*hukou*) status. Nonetheless, conferring official urban status had considerable fiscal impact, since urban areas were normally included in county and provincial budgets, which meant more state funds to support schools and other public expenditures. See Laurence J.C. Ma and Chusheng Lin, 'Development of Towns in China: A Case Study of Guangdong Province,' *Population and Development Review* 19 (1993):583-606. On the policy of truncated primary schools in rural areas, see Jurgen Henze, 'The Formal Education System and Modernization: An Analysis of Developments since 1978,' in Hayhoe, ed., *Education and Modernization*, 115.
20 Barry Naughton, 'The Pattern and Legacy of Economic Growth in the Mao Era,' in Kenneth Lieberthal et al., eds., *Perspectives on Modern China: Four Anniversaries* (Armonk, NY: M.E. Sharpe 1991), 251.
21 'Xin "dushu wuyong" lun yige jingji genyuan de peiyuan,' *Jiaoyu yanjiu* 9 (1988):19-23.
22 'Gengxin guannian luoshi cuoshi zhuzhong shixiao zhuahao saomang,' *Nongcun chengren jiaoyu* (Zhengzhou) 6 (1988):8-10.
23 'Jiji gaige he fazhan nongcun jiaoyu,' *Guangdong jiaoyu* 3 (1983):4-5.
24 *The Social Sectors: Population, Health, Nutrition and Education*, vol. 3 of *China: Socialist Economic Development* (Washington, DC: World Bank 1983), 180, 183-4.
25 Vivienne Shue, 'The Fate of the Commune,' *Modern China* 10.3 (1984):264.
26 Zhao Yimin, 'Wei "liangzhong jiaoyu zhidu" huifu mingyu,' *Jiaoyu yanjiu* 2 (1980):12-14.
27 *Zhongguo jiaoyu nianjian*, 709; Guan Shixiong, *Chengren jiaoyu de lilun yu shijian* (Beijing: Beijing chubanshe 1986), 176-7.
28 Cheng Youxin, 'Xiandai jiaoyu he shangpin jingji de tizhi lianxi yiji dui wo guo jiaoyu gaige de jidian sikao,' *Jiaoyu yanjiu* 9 (1992):28. See also Yu Zhenming, 'Weiji yu chulu: Jiaoyu fazhan de sikao,' *Guangdong yanjiu* 9 (1988):32-6; and He Bochuan, *Shanao shang de Zhongguo: Wenti, kunjing, tongku de xuanze* (Guiyang: Guizhou renmin chubanshe 1988), 364-419.
29 Jean Robinson, 'Minban Schools in Deng's Era,' in Irving Epstein, ed., *Chinese Education: Problems, Policies and Prospects* (New York: Garland 1991), 163-9. See also Suzanne Pepper, 'Chinese Education after Mao: Two Steps Forward, Two Steps Backward and Begin Again?' *China Quarterly* 81 (1980):1-65.
30 *Guangdong jiaoyu nianjian*, 106.
31 Wu Yuwen, ed., *Guangdong sheng jingji dili* (Beijing: Xinhua chubanshe 1986), 85.
32 Vogel, *One Step Ahead*, 80-8. See also Peter T.Y. Cheung, 'Relations between the Central Government and Guangdong,' in Y.M. Yeung and David K.Y. Chu, eds., *Guangdong: Survey of a Province Undergoing Rapid Change* (Hong Kong: Chinese University Press 1994), 22-30.
33 Graham E. Johnson, 'Rural Transformation in South China? Views from the Locality,' *Revue Européenne des sciences sociales* 37 (1989): especially 208-24.
34 Specialized households and keypoint households were often difficult to distinguish in practice, and definitions of the two varied from locality to locality. See ibid., 212; and 'Jiji gaige he fazhan nongcun jiaoyu.'
35 Graham E. Johnson, 'The Political Economy of Chinese Urbanization: Guangdong and the Pearl River Delta Region,' in Gregory Eliyu Guldin, ed., *Urbanizing China* (New York: Greenwood Press 1992), 202.
36 On the growth of small towns in Guangdong since 1978, see Ma and Chusheng, 'Development of Towns in China.' On the erosion of the *hukou* system and increased rural-urban migration, see Kam Wing Chan, 'Urbanization and Rural-Urban Migration in China since 1982: A New Baseline,' *Modern China* 20.3 (1994):243-81.

37 'Nuli fazhan saomang chengren jiaoyu.'

38 Guangdong sheng tongji ju, ed., *Guangdong tongji nianjian 1993* (Beijing: Zhongguo tongji chubanshe 1993), 445.

39 'Zhujiang sanjiaozhou zai jingji kaifang xingshi xia de jiaoyu xianzhuang ji duice,' *Guangdong jiaoyu* 12 (1987):3-6.

40 A further 13.5 million of twelve to forty year olds possessed only primary education, however, which meant that 55 per cent of the population aged twelve to forty had a primary school education or less in 1982. See 'Nuli kaichuang wosheng gongnong yeyu jiaoyu de xin jumian,' *Guangdong jiaoyu* 2 (1984):13-14; and *Guangdong jiaoyu nianjian*, 108.

41 Author's interviews with Liu Huan, chair of the Panyu county adult education committee general office, Panyu, December 1988. In contrast, the 1982 (and later the 1990) census figures were based entirely on self-evaluation by respondents. Enumerators simply asked respondents who had not attended school to rate their ability to read and write (school attendance itself was taken as a proxy for literacy). The instructions to 1982 census enumerators were that, 'For those age 6 and over who are illiterate or know fewer than 1,500 characters, who cannot read ordinary books and newspapers and who cannot write simple messages, enumerate as "know no characters or know few characters."' As cited in William Lavely et al., 'The Rise of Female Education in China: National and Regional Patterns,' *China Quarterly* 121 (1990):63.

42 *Guangdong jiaoyu nianjian*, 107; 'Nuli fazhan saomang chengren jiaoyu,' *Guangdong jiaoyu* 7-8 (1985):93.

43 Lin Hong, 'Saochu wenmang baituo yumei,' *Guangdong jiaoyu* 1 (1990):7; Guojia tongji ju renkou tongji si, ed., *Zhongguo renkou tongji nianjian 1990* (Beijing: Kexue jishu wenjian chubanshe 1991), 72-3.

44 'Chen Jinduo futingzhan jiu jiejue wosheng zhongxiaoxue weifang wenti da benjizhe wen,' *Guangdong jiaoyu* 5 (1990):2-3.

45 The main overseas Chinese areas in Guangdong are in the Pearl River Delta and the adjacent region encompassing Kaiping, Taishan, Xinhui, and Enping; the northeastern coastal region, especially Shantou, Denghai, Chaoan, and Puning; and the Meixian district. Significant numbers of overseas Chinese also trace their origins to Hainan Island.

46 Huang Jiaju, Yan Zexian, and Feng Zengjun, eds., *Gaige dachaozhong de Zhujiang sanjiaozhou jiaoyu* (Guangzhou: Guangdong gaodeng jiaoyu chubanshe 1993), 6. See also *Taishan xian jiaoyu zhi*, 206-10; and *China Official Yearbook 1983/84* (Hong Kong: Dragon Pearl Publishers n.d.), 459.

47 Yuen-Fong Woon, 'International Links and the Socioeconomic Development of Rural China: An Emigrant Community in Guangdong,' *Modern China* 16.2 (1990):139-72.

48 Li Peiliang, ed., *Renmin gongshe yu nongcun fazhan: Taishan xian doushan gongshe de jingyan* (Hong Kong: Chinese University Press 1981), 121. See also *Guangdong jiaoyu nianjian*, 27, 52-3.

49 Qian Daoyuan et al., 'Guangdong yiwu jiaoyu jieduam xuesheng liushi, liuji wenti de yanjiu baogao,' *Jiaoyu luncong* 1 (1990):15; Liang Ziling, 'Maoming shi renkou wenhua goucheng fenxi,' *Nanfang renkou* 2 (1991):55-7.

50 He Bochuan, *Shanao shang de Zhongguo*, 397. See also Li Ji, 'Liushisheng yu diling fanzui, *Guangdong jiaoyu* 7-8 (1991):9-10.

51 By the late 1980s, much of this factory labour was taken up by Guangdong's large 'floating population' (*liudong renkou*) of migrant labourers from other provinces, especially Sichuan, Hunan, and Guangxi. These factory labourers were usually unmarried young women between the ages of sixteen and twenty-five, many of whom were middle school graduates. Li Si-ming and Siu Yat-ming, 'Population Mobility,' in Yeung and Chu, eds., *Guangdong*, 387-95. See also Ke Qiaowen, 'Ba chengren jiaoyu naru qiye jingji fazhan de guidao,' *Xueshu yanjiu* (Guangzhou) 1.9 (1986):90-4. Educational planners acknowledged that eliminating illiteracy and raising the educational level among China's 'floating population' – estimates of which range as high as 80-120 million in the 1990s – would be extremely difficult. See Xie Guodong, 'Wancheng saomang lishi renwu de tiaojian yu duice,' *Jiaoyu yanjiu* 12 (1991):46, 48.

52 Yu Zhenming, 'Weiji yu chulu'; Yu Mingdi et al., 'Zhujiang sanjiaozhou jiaoyu fazhan zhanlue yanjiu baogao,' *Jiaoyu yanjiu* 12 (1991):30-4.

53   Carlo Cipolla, *Literacy and Development in the West* (Harmondsworth, UK: Penguin 1969), 32-4, 68; François Furet and Jacques Ozouf, *Reading and Writing: Literacy in France from Calvin to Jules Ferry* (Cambridge, UK: Cambridge University Press 1982), 217-18.

Chapter 11: The Struggle for Literacy in Guangdong

1   Dai Xingyi, 'Qianxi woguo de wenmang renkou wenti,' *Renkou yu jingji* 6 (1990):23, 25.
2   François Furet and Jacques Ozouf, *Reading and Writing: Literacy in France from Calvin to Jules Ferry* (Cambridge, UK: Cambridge University Press 1982).
3   'Jiji fazhan nongmin jiaoyu,' *Guangdong jiaoyu* 10 (1986):15-16; *Disanci quanguo renkou pucha shougong huizong ziliao huibian*, vol. 5, *Renkou wenhua chengdu* (Beijing: Guowuyuan renkou pucha bangongshi 1983), 122-9.
4   He Guohua, 'Kejia ren de jiaoyu guan chutan,' *Lingnan wenshi* 22.2 (1992):9-15.
5   *Disanci quanguo renkou pucha*, vol. 5, 122-9.
6   David Faure, 'The Lineage as a Cultural Invention: The Case of the Pearl River Delta,' *Modern China* 15.1 (1989):4-36.
7   Furet and Ozouf, *Reading and Writing*, 149.
8   Ibid., 304.
9   Vilma Seeberg, *Literacy in China: The Effects of the National Development Context and Policy on Literacy Levels, 1949-1979* (Bochum: Brockmeyer 1990), 10.
10 *Disanci quanguo renkou pucha*, vol. 5, 124.
11 G. William Skinner, 'Marketing and Social Structure in Rural China,' *Journal of Asian Studies* 24.1 (1964):3-43; 24.2 (1965):195-228; 24.3 (1965):363-9.
12 G. William Skinner, 'Differential Development in Lingnan,' in Thomas Lyons and Victor Nee, eds., *The Economic Transformation of South China: Reform and Development in the Post-Mao Era* (Ithaca: Cornell University Press 1994), 17-54.
13 Yu Mingdi et al., 'Zhujiang sanjiaozhou jiaoyu fazhan zhanlue yanjiu baogao,' *Jiaoyu yanjiu* 12 (1991):31.
14 Zhu Yuanxing, 'Dui Guangdong jiaoyu fazhan de yixie sikao,' *Guangdong jiaoyu* 12 (1992):6; Pan Guangyi, 'Chuangzao tiaojian: Tuijin wosheng shanqu yiwu jiaoyu,' *Guangdong jiaoyu* 5 (1990):5; Wen Yinggan and Liao Liqiong, 'Zhenxing shanqu jingji de zhongyao huanjie: Lun Guangdong shanqu de zhili kaifa,' *Xuebao* (Zhongshan University) 2 (1987):17-24.
15 *Disanci quanguo renkou pucha*, vol. 5, 122-9; *Guangdong jiaoyu nianjian*, 51-2.
16 Peng Xizhe, 'Major Determinants of China's Fertility Transition,' *China Quarterly* 117 (1989):1-37.
17 Jacques Lamontagne, 'Education and Employment in China: Variations according to Gender, Region, Ethnicity, and Age,' (paper presented at the Canadian Learned Societies Conference, Hamilton, 1987).
18 Guangdong sheng tongji ju renkou pucha bangongshi, eds., *Zhongguo 1987 nian 1% renkou chouyang diaocha ziliao* (Guangzhou: Zhongguo tongji ju chubanshe 1988), 288-93. On the steady improvement of female literacy in the Lingnan macroregion after 1949, see William Lavely et al., 'The Rise of Female Education in China: National and Regional Patterns,' *China Quarterly* 121 (1990):79 fig. 7.
19 *UNESCO Statistical Yearbook* (Paris: UNESCO 1987), 1.15-1.22.
20 Donald J. Munro, 'Egalitarian Ideal and Educational Fact in Communist China,' in John M.H. Lindbeck, ed., *China: Management of a Revolutionary Society* (Seattle: University of Washington Press 1971), 263.
21 Barry Naughton, 'The Pattern and Legacy of Economic Growth in the Mao Era,' in Kenneth Lieberthal et al., eds., *Perspectives on Modern China: Four Anniversaries* (Armonk, NY: M.E. Sharpe 1991), 235-7.
22 Victoria J. Baker, 'Education for Its Own Sake: The Relevance Dimension in Rural Areas,' *Comparative Education Review* 33 (1989):507-18.
23 R.H. Tawney, *Land and Labour in China* (London: George Allen and Unwin 1932), 91. The report is described in Suzanne Pepper, 'New Directions in Education,' in Roderick MacFarquhar and John K. Fairbank, eds., *The People's Republic, Part 1: The Emergence of Revolutionary China, 1949-1965*, vol. 14 of *The Cambridge History of China* (Cambridge, UK: Cambridge University Press 1987), 190-2.

24 Charles W. Hayford, 'Literacy Movements in Modern China,' in Robert F. Arnove and Harvey
    J. Graff, eds., *National Literacy Campaigns: Historical and Comparative Perspectives* (New York:
    Plenum Press 1987), 159-67; Evelyn Sakakida Rawski, *Education and Popular Literacy in Ch'ing
    China* (Ann Arbor: University of Michigan Press 1979), 167-73.
25 Paul Bailey, *Reform the People: Changing Attitudes towards Popular Education in Early 20th
    Century China* (Vancouver: University of British Columbia Press 1990), 266-8. See also Pep-
    per, *Radicalism*.
26 Naughton, 'Pattern and Legacy,' 236, 251-2. See also Dreze and Loh, 'Literacy in China and
    India,' 2876. They argue that China's advances in basic education during the Mao era
    constitute 'one of the pre-reform social achievements that have permitted and sustained
    participatory growth in China after the reforms.'
27 Brian V. Street, *Literacy in Theory and Practice* (Cambridge, UK: Cambridge University Press
    1984), especially 158-80.

Bibliography

Works from Guangdong

'Baiyu xueyuan chufa gongzuo' (Initial work of Baiyu college). *Nanfang ribao*, 8 June 1952. In *Union Research Institute* 4242

'Bixu shifen zhongshi quanrizhi xuexiao jiaoxue zhiliang de tigao' (We must pay full attention to raising teaching quality in full-time schools). *Guangdong jiaoyu* 1 (1 January 1960):3-4

Cai Fei. 'Shehui jiaoyu de fangxiang' (The direction of social education). *Guangdong jiaoyu yu wenhua* 1.1 (May 1950):37-8

Chang Gong et al. *Guangdong de jiefang* (The liberation of Guangdong). Guangzhou: n.p. 1950

'Chaoshan qu yeyu jiaoyu kefu jingfei kunnan de shili' (The strength of Chaoshan district in overcoming funding difficulties in spare-time education). *Guangdong jiaoyu yu wenhua* 2.6 (April 1951):20-1

'Chaozhou hua pinyin fangan' (Phonetic scheme for Chaozhou speech). *Guangdong jiaoyu (yeyu jiaoyuban)* 5-6 (20 November 1960):24-5

Che Mu. 'Wei shenmo yong fangyan zhuyin shizi?' (Why use dialect phonetic symbols for reading?) *Guangdong jiaoyu (yeyu jiaoyuban)* 2 (15 August 1960):16

Chen Zhou. 'Laoqu nongmin jiaoyu gezhong fangshi de jieshao' (Introduction to various patterns of peasant education in old base areas). *Guangdong jiaoyu yu wenhua* 2.5 (March 1951):27-9

Chen Ziyun. 'Dali zhiyuan nongye, jiji kaizhan yi zhuyin shizi wei zhongxin de qunzhong xuexi yundong, wei tiqian wancheng saomang he puji yeyu jiaoyu de guangrong renwu er fendou' (Vigorously support agriculture, strive to actively develop the mass study movement with phonetic reading at the centre in order to achieve early completion of the glorious task of eliminating illiteracy and popularizing spare-time education). *Guangdong jiaoyu (yeyu jiaoyuban)* 5-6 (20 November 1960):2-5

'Chen Jinduo futingzhan jiu jiejue wosheng zhongxiaoxue weifang wenti da benjizhe wen' (This reporter asks Vice-Bureau Chief Chen Jinduo about solving the problem of our province's dangerous primary and middle school buildings). *Guangdong jiaoyu* 5 (1990):2-3

'Chuangban liunian zhuo chengji' (Grasping six years of success). *Wenhuibao* (Hong Kong), 26 March 1954. In *Union Research Institute* LO136, 4222 3235

'Cong shiji chufa wei dangdi shengchan fuwu: Xingning longtian nongzhong de yixie banxue jingyan' (Proceed from practice in serving local production: Some experiences of Xingning's Longtian agricultural middle school in setting up a school). In *Guangdong sheng nongcun bannong bandu jiaoyu huiyi ziliao* (Materials recollecting village half-farming, half-study education in Guangdong province), 1-6. Guangzhou: n.p. 1965

Conghua xian geming weiyuanhui. 'Woxian kaizhan saomang gongzuo de yixie zuofa' (Some methods of developing anti-illiteracy work in our county). *Guangdong jiaoyu* 3 (1979):6

'Daban gengdu xiaoxue, duokuai haosheng de shixian puji nongcun jiaoyu' (Go in for ploughing-reading primary schools, popularize village education faster and more economically). In *Guangdong sheng nongcun bannong bandu jiaoyu huiyi ziliao* (Materials recollecting village half-farming, half-study education in Guangdong province), 1-12. Guangzhou: n.p. 1965

Dai Tieshan. *Sanyuanli nongmin xue wenhua* (Sanyuanli peasants study culture). N.p.: Huanan renmin chubanshe 1953

'Dali kaizhan nongcun saochu wenmang yundong' (Go in for developing the village anti-illiteracy movement). In *Dali kaizhan saochu wenmang yundong* (Go in for developing the village anti-illiteracy movement), ed. Guangdong jiaoyu ting, 47-8. Guangzhou: Guangdong renmin chubanshe 1956

'Dali kaizhan saomang gongzuo, daban gezhong yeyu jiaoyu, jixu tigao jiaoxue zhiliang, jiji jinxing jiaoxue gaige' (Vigorously develop anti-illiteracy work, go in for various kinds of spare-time education, continue to raise teaching quality, actively implement teaching reform). *Guangdong jiaoyu* 11-12 (10 June 1960):7-8

'Dali tuiguang zhuyin shizi zhengqu tiqian saochu wenmang' (Vigorously promote phonetic symbols for reading, strive to eliminate illiteracy ahead of time). *Guangdong jiaoyu* 11-12 (10 June 1960):5

'Daliang fazhan nongye zhongxue' (Develop agricultural middle schools on a large scale). *Guangdong jiaoyu* 1 (January 1960):26

Dingan xian geming weiyuanhui. 'Fadong qunzhong nuli saochu wenmang' (Launch a great mass effort to eliminate illiteracy). *Guangdong jiaoyu* 3 (1979):5

Disanci renkou pucha ziliao huibian (Compiled materials of the third population census). Vol. 2. Guangzhou: Guangdong sheng renkou pucha bangongshi 1984

'Dongjiang qu qunzhong banxue de juti shili' (Specific strengths of mass efforts to establish schools in the East River district). *Guangdong jiaoyu yu wenhua* 3.2 (June 1951):25

Du Guoxiang. 'Guangdong sheng diyijie gongnong jiaoyu huiyi ji jiaoyu gonghui daibiao dahui kaimu ci' (Opening speech to the first Guangdong worker-peasant education conference and educational workers union delegates plenary session). *Guangdong jiaoyu yu wenhua* 2.6 (April 1951):3-4

'Fachu guanyu pubian jianli qingnian saomang dui de tongzhi' (Circular issued concerning universal establishment of youth anti-illiteracy troops). *Nanfang ribao*, 6 January 1956. In *Union Research Institute* LO364 4 2222

'Fayang jianku fendou, qinjian banxue de geming jingshen' (The revolutionary spirit of carrying forward arduous struggle, running schools industriously and thriftily). *Guangdong jiaoyu* 8 (August 1954):12-13

Feng Bingkui. *Zhongguo wenhua yu lingnan wenhua* (Chinese culture and Lingnan culture). Taibei: Taibei zhongxing daxue fashang xueyuan 1962

'Fengshun xian wenhua guan gongzuo bao' (Work bulletin of Fengshun county cultural hall). *Guangdong jiaoyu yu wenhua* (March 1952):10-11

'Fu: Shanxi shengwei guanyu zai quansheng tuiguang wanrong xian zhuyin shizi jingyan zhengqu tiqian shi Shanxi chengwei wumang sheng xiang zhongyang de baogao' (Attached: Report of the Shanxi party committee to the Central Committee concerning striving to make Shanxi illiteracy free ahead of schedule by the provincewide promotion of Wanrong county's experience in phonetic reading). *Guangdong jiaoyu* 11-12 (10 June 1960):4

'Gonggu saomang chengguo, daban yeyu jiaoyu' (Consolidate anti-illiteracy achievements, make great efforts in spare-time education). *Guangdong saomang* 1 (25 October 1958):11-14

'Gongnong jiaoyu de gezhong zuzhi xingshi he neirong' (Contents and various organizational forms of worker-peasant education). In *Guangdong sheng diyijie gongnong jiaoyu huiyi ji jiaoyu gonghui daibiao dahui cailiao* (Materials from the first Guangdong worker-peasant education conference and educational workers union delegates plenary session). Vol. 1. N.p.: n.p. 1951

Guangdong jiaoyu nianjian, 1949-1985 (Guangdong educational yearbook). Guangzhou: Guangdong jiaoyu ting 1986

Guangdong jiaoyu ting, comp. *Wenhua geming de shangyou Puning: Jieshao Puning xian saochu wenmang de jingyan* (Puning's advanced cultural revolution: Introduction to Puning county's anti-illiteracy experience.) Guangzhou: Guangdong renmin chubanshe 1958

Guangdong nianjian 1987 (Guangdong yearbook, 1987). Guangzhou: Guangdong renmin chubanshe 1987

Guangdong nianjian 1988 (Guangdong yearbook, 1988). Guangzhou: Guangdong renmin chubanshe 1988

Guangdong sheng diyijie gongnong jiaoyu huiyi ji jiaoyu gonghui daibiao dahui cailiao (Materials from the first Guangdong worker-peasant education conference and educational workers union delegates plenary session). 3 vols. N.p.: n.p. 1951

Guangdong ershisan niandu jiaoyu gaifang (Educational report on Guangdong in the twenty-third year of the republic). Guangzhou: Guangdong jiaoyu ting 1934

'Guangdong renmin zhengfu wenjiao ting yijiu wuling nian wenjiao gongzuo jihua caoan' (Guangdong people's government culture and education bureau draft plan for cultural and educational work in 1950). *Guangdong jiaoyu yu wenhua* 1.2 (June 1950):5-6

Guangdong sheng tongji ju, ed. *Guangdong sheng shi di xian gaikuang* (Survey of Guangdong cities, districts, and counties). Guangzhou: Guangdong sheng ditu chubanshe 1985

Guangdong sheng tongji ju, ed. *Guangdong tongji nianjian 1993* (Guangdong statistical yearbook 1993). Beijing: Zhongguo tongji chubanshe 1993

Guangdong sheng tongji ju renkou pucha bangongshi, ed. *Zhongguo 1987 nian 1% renkou chouyang diaocha ziliao* (China 1987 1 per cent population sample survey data). Guangzhou: Zhongguo tongji ju chubanshe 1988

Guangdong sheng zhengfu mishu chu bianyi shi, ed. *Guangdong jiaoyu* (Guangdong education). Guangzhou: Guangdong sheng zhengfu mishu chu dier ke 1943

'Guangzhou hua pinyin fangan' (Phonetic scheme for Guangzhou speech). *Guangdong jiaoyu (yeyu jiaoyuban)* 3 (10 October 1960):12-13

Guangzhou jiaoyu ju shejiao ke. 'Fazhan zhong de guangzhou gongnong yeyu jiaoyu' (Ongoing development of worker-peasant spare-time education in Guangzhou). *Guangdong jiaoyu yu wenhua* 1.2 (June 1950):50-1

Guangzhou nongmin yundong jiangxi suo jiuzhi jinian guan, ed. *Guangzhou nongmin yundong jiangxi suo ziliao xuanbian* (Selected materials from the Guangzhou Peasant Movement Training Institute). Beijing: Renmin chubanshe 1987

'Guangzhou qingzhen xiaoxue benqi xuesheng zengduo' (Students in Guangzhou Qingzhen primary school increasing this term). *Dagongbao* (Hong Kong), 14 January 1953. In *Union Research Institute* LO139 424125

Guanyu guangdong sheng saochu wenmang gongzuo quanmian guihua de baogao (jimi wenjian) (Report concerning the Guangdong comprehensive provincial plan for anti-illiteracy work [classified document]). Guangzhou: Guangdong jiaoyu ting 1956

'Guanyu jiaoshi he xuesheng canjia saomang gongzuo de tongzhi' (Circular concerning participation of teachers and students in anti-illiteracy work). *Xiaoxue jiaoyu* (Guangdong), 16 April 1958:2, 11

'Guanyu jiaoshi xuexi wenti de baogao' (Report concerning the problem of teachers' studies). In *Guangdong sheng diyijie gongnong jiaoyu huiyi ji jiaoyu gonghui daibiao dahui cailiao* (Materials from the first Guangdong worker-peasant education conference and educational workers union delegates plenary session), 75-87. Vol. 1. N.p.: n.p. 1951

'Guli jiaoshimen genghao de ban Yaozu jiaoyu shiye fuwu' (Urge teachers to better serve the cause of Yao people's education). *Nanfang ribao*, 21 September 1954. In *Union Research Institute* LO139 424125

Guo Jianfang. 'Qingzhu yijiu wuba nian de weida chengjiu, yingjie yijiu wujiu nian de weida renwu' (Celebrate the great achievements of 1958, greet the great tasks of 1959). *Guangdong gongnong jiaoyu* 1 (25 January 1959):4-7

Guo Moruo. 'Guanyu wenhua jiaoyu gongzuo, yijiu wuling nian liuyue shiqi ri zai renmin zhengxie quanguo weiyuanhui dierci huiyi de baogao' (Report to second conference of the national people's consultative committee concerning cultural and educational work). *Guangdong jiaoyu yu wenhua* 1.4 (August 1950):2-6

'Guzu ganjin daban nongye zhongxue, jiji zhiyuan nongye jishu gaizao' (Go all out for agricultural middle schools, actively support technical reforms in agriculture). *Guangdong jiaoyu* 7 (April 1960):4-8

'Hainan hua pinyin fangan' (Phonetic scheme for Hainan speech). *Guangdong jiaoyu (yeyu jiaoyuban)* 5-6 (20 November 1960):32-3

He Guohua. 'Kejia ren de jiaoyu guan chutan' (A preliminary exploration of the Hakka view of education). *Lingnan wenshi* 22.2 (1992):9-15

He Hanmin. 'Zai wenhua da geming zhong gongxian chu wo bisheng de liliang' (The strength of our graduates' contributions in the Cultural Revolution shows through). *Guangdong jiaoyu* 9 (May 1960):15-16

He Liu. 'Tuixing zhuyin shizi, jiakuai saomang sudu: Ji Tanshui gongshe dongming dadui kaizhan zhuyin shizi yundong' (Practise phonetic reading, speed up elimination of illiteracy: Notes on development of the phonetic reading movement in Tanshui commune, Dongming brigade). *Guangdong jiaoyu (yeyu jiaoyuban)* 1 (15 July 1960):3-4

He Weijun. 'Bannong banjiao neng cushi jiaoshi youhong youzhuan' (Half-farming, half-study education can spur teachers to become red and expert). *Guangdong jiaoyu* 12 (December 1964):3

Hu Yaobang. 'Guanyu nongcun saochu wenmang gongzuo' (Concerning village anti-illiteracy work). In *Dali kaizhan saochu wenmang yundong* (Vigorously develop the anti-illiteracy movement), ed. Guangdong sheng jiaoyu ting (Guangdong education bureau), 22-31. Guangzhou: Guangdong renmin chubanshe 1956

Huang Heyang. 'Wo shi zheiyang yong putonghua jinxing jiaoxue de' (This is how I conducted teaching in the common language). *Guangdong jiaoyu* (July 1956):29-30

Huang Jiaju, Yan Zexian, and Feng Zengjun, eds. *Gaige dachaozhong de Zhujiang sanjiaozhou jiaoyu.* Guangzhou: Guangdong gaodeng jiaoyu chubanshe 1993

Huang Muliang. 'Yinian lai wo shi zenyang jinxing putonghua jiaoxue de' (This is how I conducted teaching in the common language over the past year). *Guangdong jiaoyu* (September 1956):26-7

Huang Naizhao, He Wenguang, and Gu Zuoyi. *Guangzhou ren: Zuori yu jinri* (Guangzhou people: Yesterday and today). Guangzhou: Guangdong wenhua chubanshe 1987

Huang Ningying. 'Yueju gaijin de juti wenti' (Concrete problems in improving Cantonese opera). *Guangdong jiaoyu yu wenhua* 2.5 (March 1951):53-5

Huang Shan. 'Guangzhou de sishu shi xuexi dahui' (Mass-study meeting for Guangzhou sishu teachers). *Guangdong jiaoyu yu wenhua* 1.6 (October 1950):36-7

Huazhou xian jiaoyu zhi (jianben) (Huazhou county educational history [abbreviated]). N.p.: n.p. 1987

'Huigao yichi, daogao yizhang' (The correct way will always triumph). *Guangdong jiaoyu* 2 (1 February 1964):4

'Jiakuai bufa zhuajin saomang' (Quicken the pace, firmly grasp the elimination of illiteracy). *Guangdong jiaoyu* 3 (1979):4

'Jianchi jieji douzheng, jianchi bannong bandu de banxue fangxiang: Guanyu xinhui hetang nongye zhongxue de diaocha baogao' (Uphold class struggle, uphold the half-farming, half-study direction in schooling: Investigative report concerning Xinhui Hetang agricultural middle school). In *Guangdong sheng nongcun bannong bandu jiaoyu huiyi ziliao* (Materials recollecting village half-farming, half-study education in Guangdong province), 1-14. Guangzhou: n.p. 1965

'Jianchi lixue shiwu nian de longlou cun yexiao' (Uphold the fifteen-year experience of Longlou village evening school). *Guangdong jiaoyu* 2 (February 1966):49-51

'Jianchi tuiguang putonghua he putonghua jiaoxue: Chaoan dier zhongxue' (Uphold promotion of the common language and teaching in the common language: Chaoan Number Two Middle School). *Guangdong jiaoyu* (16 February 1960):15

'Jianshe xin zhongguo bixu zhansheng er da luohou' (Building New China requires overcoming two great backwardnesses). In *Guangdong sheng diyijie gongnong jiaoyu huiyi ji jiaoyu gonghui daibiao dahui cailiao* (Materials from the first Guangdong worker-peasant education conference and educational workers union delegates plenary session). Vol. 1. N.p.: n.p. 1951

'Jiaqiang liangdao, banhao nongmin xiaoxue' (Strengthen leadership, firmly establish agricultural middle schools). *Guangdong jiaoyu* 6 (1962):25

'Jiefang qian Maoming de shuyuan he sishu' (Academies and private schools in preliberation Maoming). *Maoming jiaoyu* 2 (1992):35-6

'Jieshao "nongmin shizi jiaoyu de zuzhi xingshi he jiaoxue fangfa"' (Introducing 'Organizational forms and teaching methods in peasant literacy education'). *Guangdong jiaoyu yu wenhua* 2.5 (March 1951):62

'Jiji fazhan nongmin jiaoyu' (Actively develop peasant education) *Guangdong jiaoyu* 10 (1986):15-16

'Jiji gaige he fazhan nongcun jiaoyu' (Actively reform and develop village education). *Guangdong jiaoyu* 3 (1983):4-5

'Jiji kaizhan nongcun saomang he yeyu jiaoyu: Guangdong sheng jiaoyu ting Rao Huangxiang fu tingzhan zai quansheng nongcun saomang he yeyu jiaoyu huiyi de baogao disan bufen' (Actively develop village anti-illiteracy work and spare-time education: Part 3 of Guangdong education bureau vice-head Rao Huangxiang's speech to the provincial conference on village anti-illiteracy work and spare-time education). *Guangdong jiaoyu* 1 (1 January 1964):3-5

'Jiji zhiyuan nongye' (Actively support agriculture). *Guangdong jiaoyu* 2 (1962):3-4

'Jinggao!' (Warning!). *Yangcheng wanbao*, 14 December 1988:1

'Jishu yexiao yu xinren' (Evening technical schools and new people). *Guangdong jiaoyu* 1 (January 1965):23-4

'Jixu kaizhan saomang yundong daban yeyu chudeng jiaoyu: Sheng jiaoyu gongzuo huiyi tichu fazhan gongnong jiaoyu de renwu' (Continue to develop the anti-illiteracy movement: Go all out for primary education). *Guangdong gongnong jiaoyu* 5 (19 May 1959):6-8

'Jixu qianjin, juexin zuoge you wenhua zhishi, you shehui zhuyi juewu de xinshi nongmin' (Continue advancing, be determined to become a new kind of peasant with cultural knowledge and socialist consciousness). In *Guangdong sheng saochu wenmang jiji fenzi daibiao dahui huikan* (Proceedings from the Guangdong anti-illiteracy activists delegates' mass meeting), 98-9. Guangzhou: Guangdong sheng saochu wenmang jiji fenzi daibiao dahui mishuchu 1958

Ke Qiaowen. 'Ba chengren jiaoyu naru qiye jingji fazhan de guidao' (Put adult education on the track of developing the enterprise economy). *Xueshu yanjiu* (Guangzhou) 1.9 (1986):90-4.

'Kejia hua pinyin fangan' (Phonetic scheme for Kejia speech). *Guangdong jiaoyu (yeyu jiaoyuban)* 5-6 (20 November 1960):16-17

Kong Xiangxing. 'Wei nongye shengchan jianshe peiyang laodong houbei liliang' (In order to build agricultural production, raise a reserve labour force). *Guangdong jiaoyu* 3 (1 March 1964):9-13

Li Dachao and Deng Qin, '"Guangdong jiaoyu" wei shei fuwu?' (Who does 'Guangdong jiaoyu' serve?). *Guangdong jiaoyu*, June 1966:26

Li Ji. 'Liushisheng yu diling fanzui' (School dropouts and crime). *Guangdong jiaoyu* 7-8 (1991):9-10

Li Peiliang, ed. *Renmin gongshe yu nongcun fazhan: Taishan xian doushan gongshe de jingyan* (People's communes and village development: The experiences of Taishan county's Doushan commune). Hong Kong: Chinese University Press 1981

Li Shouzhi. 'Zenyang zhangwo Guangzhou yin he Beijing yin de duiying guilu' (Laws for mastering the correspondence of Guangzhou speech sounds with Beijing speech sounds). *Guangdong jiaoyu* (July 1956):27-9

'Li Tieying tongzhi guancha zhuhai tequ shi tichu yao dali tuiguang putonghua' (Comrade Li Tieying advances the necessity of vigorously promoting the common speech while surveying Zhuhai special district). *Pujiao jianbao* (Nanhai county), 3 July 1988:2-3

Li Zhaohan. 'Guangdong diyi suo gongnong sucheng zhongxue jieshao' (Introduction to the first Guangdong worker-peasant accelerated middle school). *Guangdong jiaoyu yu wenhua* 3.1 (May 1951):6-7

Liang Weilin. 'Liji dongshou, zuzhi liliang, dali kaizhan quansheng fanwei de nongcun saochu wenmang yundong' (Promptly mobilize, organize strength, vigorously develop a provincewide village anti-illiteracy movement). In *Dali kaizhan saochu wenmang yundong*

(Vigorously develop the anti-illiteracy movement), ed. Guangdong sheng jiaoyu ting, 36-41. Guangzhou: Guangdong renmin chubanshe 1956

Liang Ziling. 'Maoming shi renkou wenhua goucheng fenxi' (An analysis of the cultural composition of the population of Maoming city). *Nanfang renkou* 2 (1991):55-7

'Lianheguo jiaokewen zuzhi yatai diqu saomang, chengren jiaoyu shidi kaocha zuotanhui zai Guangzhou zhaokai' (UN Asia-Pacific regional teaching and curriculum organization anti-illiteracy, adult education on-site inspection symposium convened in Guangzhou). *Guangdong jiaoyu* 12 (1982):2

Lianjiang xian jiaoyu ju. 'Jinmi jiehe nongcun shehui zhuyi jiaoyu yundong kaizhan yeyu jiaoyu gongzuo' (Closely integrate the village Socialist Education Movement with the development of spare-time education work). *Guangdong jiaoyu* 4 (1 April 1964): 25-6

Lin Hong. 'Wosheng chengren chu, gaodeng jiaoyu shinian fazhan huigu' (A ten-year review of our province's elementary- and middle-level adult educational development). *Guangdong jiaoyu* 5 (1989):11

–. 'Saochu wenmang baituo yumei' (Sweep away illiteracy, cast off ignorance). *Guangdong jiaoyu* 1 (1990):7

Lin Liming. 'Guanyu dangqian jiaoyu gongzuo zhong de jige wenti' (Some problems concerning present educational work). *Guangdong jiaoyu* 7-8 (10 April 1956):3-6

Lu Dingyi. 'Nongye zhongxue chuangban er zhounian' (The second anniversary of agricultural middle schools). *Guangdong jiaoyu* 6 (16 March 1960):3

Lu Lan. 'Xiangcun jiaoshi ye er yao qingsuan zichan jieji jiaoyu sixiang ma?' (Must village teachers also expose and criticize capitalist education thought?). *Guangdong jiaoyu yu wenhua* (April 1952):6-7

Luo Guang. 'Jieshao Niaoshi nongchang gengdu xiaoxue' (Introducing Niaoshi state farm half-ploughing, half-study primary school). *Guangdong jiaoyu* 11 (November 1964):15

'Mei sanren you yiren shangxue de Heyuan laoqu' (In Heyuan old base area one out of every three persons is attending school). *Guangdong jiaoyu yu wenhua* 1.5 (September 1950):28

'Meixian saomang gongzuo' (Anti-illiteracy in Meixian). *Lian jiada xinbao*, 29 January 1954. In *Union Research Institute* LO136 4222 3235

Nanhai xian wenjiao ke. 'Sishu shi de zhuanbian' (The transformation of *sishu* teachers). *Guangdong jiaoyu yu wenhua* 1.4 (August 1950):54-5

'Nanhai xian xuexiao tuipu gongzuo qingkuang' (The situation with respect to the task of promoting the common language in Nanhai county schools). *Pujiao jianbao* (Nanhai county), 20 January 1987:1-5

Nanlu zhuanshu wenjiao ke. 'Nanlu qu wenhua jiaoyu de zhuangtai' (The condition of cultural education in Nanlu district). *Guangdong jiaoyu yu wenhua* 1.5 (September 1950):21

'1956 nian guangdong sheng putong jiaoyu he shifan jiaoyu de gongzuo renwu' (Work assignment for general education and teacher-training education in Guangdong province, 1956). *Guangdong jiaoyu* 11-12 (10 June 1956):8-15

'Nongcun de xuexi rechao' (Upsurge of learning in the villages). *Dagongbao* (Hong Kong), 21 August 1950. In *Union Research Institute* LO136 4222 3235

Nongmin fanshen sanzijing (Three-character classic of peasant liberation). Guangzhou: Nanfang tongsu duwu lianhe chubanshe 1952

'Nongmin wanren ru xuexiao' (Ten thousand peasants enter schools). *Wenhuibao* (Hong Kong), 8 December 1951. In *Union Research Institute* LO136 4222 3235

'Nuli fazhan saomang chengren jiaoyu' (Struggle to develop anti-illiteracy adult education). *Guangdong jiaoyu* 7-8 (1985):93

'Nuli gonggu kuoda saomang chengguo' (Struggle to consolidate and enlarge anti-illiteracy achievements). *Guangdong gongnong jiaoyu* 1 (25 June 1959):18-20

'Nuli kaichuang nongmin jiaoyu de xin jumian' (Struggle to initiate the new phase of peasant education). *Guangdong jiaoyu* 5 (1983):9

'Nuli kaichuang wosheng gongnong yeyu jiaoyu de xin jumian' (Struggle to initiate the new phase of our province's worker-peasant spare-time education). *Guangdong jiaoyu* 2 (1984):14

Ouyang Shuiwang and Lai Wanjin. 'Banhao nongye zhongxue de yixie jingyan' (Some experiences in firmly establishing agricultural middle schools). *Guangdong jiaoyu* 7 (1 April 1960):9-10

Pan Guangyi. 'Chuangzao tiaojian: Tuijin wosheng shanqu yiwu jiaoyu' (Create the conditions: Push forward compulsory education in our province's mountain areas). *Guangdong jiaoyu* 5 (1990):5

Panyu xian renmin zhengfu jiaoyu ke, ed. *Panyu xian jiaoyu zhi (chugao)* (Panyu county educational history [draft]). N.p.: n.p. 1988

Peng Pai. *Haifeng nongmin yundong* (The Haifeng peasant movement). N.p.: Guangdong sheng nongmin xiehui 1926

'Pengbo fazhan de Haifeng yexiao' (The vigorous development of Haifeng evening schools). *Guangdong jiaoyu yu wenhua* 1.5 (September 1950):29

Pinxia zhongnong ban xuexiao (Poor and lower middle peasants run schools). Guangzhou: Guangdong renmin chubanshe 1973

Puning gongnong jiaoyu diaocha zu. 'Liangzhong taidu, liangzhong xiaoguo' (Two kinds of attitudes, two kinds of effects). *Guangdong gongnong jiaoyu* 2 (25 February 1959):7-8

Puning xian wenjiao ju. 'Jixu zuohao gonggu tigao gongzuo' (Continue to complete the work of consolidation and improvement). *Guangdong gongnong jiaoyu* 1 (25 January 1959):21-2

Qian Chunrui. 'Xuexi he guanche Mao zhuxi de jiaoyu sixiang: Wei jinian zhongguo gongchang dang de sanshi zhounian erzuo' (Study and implement Chairman Mao's educational thought: Serve this year's thirtieth anniversary of the Chinese Communist Party). *Guangdong jiaoyu yu wenhua* 3.4 (August 1951):5

Qian Daoyuan et al. 'Guangdong yiwu jiaoyu jieduam xuesheng liushi, liuji wenti de yanjiu baogao' (Research report on compulsory education, cutting off the problem of student dropouts and failures in Guangdong). *Jiaoyu luncong* 1 (1990):15

Qian Fei et al. *Xue wenhua de gushi* (Stories about learning culture). Guangzhou: Guangdong renmin chubanshe 1956

Qin Mu. 'Guangdong wenhua jiaoyu lunkuo shu' (A sketch of Guangdong culture and education). *Guangdong jiaoyu yu wenhua* 1.6 (October 1950):2-6

Qiu Tian. 'Dui xiaoxue shougong laodong ke de yijian' (Some opinions regarding manual labour classes in primary schools). *Guangdong jiaoyu* 6 (June 1965):24-5

Qu Mengjue. 'Cong Xinhui xian de banxue shijian kan bangong (nong) bandu de jiaoyu zhidu' (View the half-work [farming], half-study education system from the perspective of Xinhui county's practice in running schools). *Guangdong jiaoyu* 11 (November 1964):3-7

Qu Mengjue et al. *Hong you zhuan* (Red and expert). Guangzhou: Guangdong renmin chubanshe 1958

'Quanri zhi xuexiao bixu yi jiaoxue weizhu' (Full-time schools must give first place to teaching). *Guangdong jiaoyu* 2 (16 January 1960):3-4

'Raoping xian jianku banxue de jingyan' (Raoping county's arduous experience running schools). *Guangdong jiaoyu yu wenhua* 3.2 (June 1951):23-4

'Renzhen zongjie zhuyin shizi de shidian jingyan' (Conscientiously summarize experimental experience in phonetic reading). *Guangdong jiaoyu yeyu jiaoyuban* 3 (10 October 1960):10

'Sanshui xian gongnong yeyu jiaoyu de jidian jingyan jiaoxun' (Some lessons from Sanshui county's experience in spare-time education). *Guangdong jiaoyu yu wenhua* 2.6 (March 1951):21-2

'Saomang shengchan shuangfang shou' (Eliminate illiteracy and raise production at the same time). In *Guangdong sheng saochu wenmang jiji fenzi daibiao dahui huikan* (Proceedings from the Guangdong anti-illiteracy activists delegates' mass meeting), 95. Guangzhou: Guangdong sheng saochu wenmang jiji fenzi daibiao dahui mishuchu 1958

Shen Hengsong. 'Duiyu jinhou chuli sishu de yijian' (Opinions regarding the present and future handling of *sishu*). *Guangdong jiaoyu yu wenhua* 1.2 (June 1950):14-15

–. 'Guangdong sili zhongdeng xuexiao de guoqu he weilai' (The past and future of Guangdong private secondary schools). *Guangdong jiaoyu yu wenhua* 2.4 (February 1951):14-15

Shi jiaoyu ju Wan Maji fuzhang zai shi nongcun yeyu jiaoyu he jiji fenzi daibiao dahui shang de jianghua (neibu) (Speech by city education bureau vice-head Wan Maji to the city rural spare-time education and activist delegates meeting [classified]). N.p.: n.p. 1964

'Shi xuexiao you shi nongye jishu tuiguang zhan: Jieyang xian Baita nongye zhongxue jieshao' (A school is also an agrotechnical extension station: Introduction to Jieyang county Baita agricultural middle school). *Guangdong jiaoyu* 11-12 (10 June 1960):28-9

'Shiqi jiguan yeyu wenhua xuexiao qingkuang jieshao' (Introduction to the situation of spare-time cultural schools in seventeen organizations). In *Guangdong sheng diyijie gongnong jiaoyu huiyi ji jiaoyu gonghui daibiao dahui cailiao* (Materials from the first Guangdong worker-peasant education conference and educational workers union delegates plenary session). Vol. 3. N.p.: n.p. 1951

Su Hongtong. 'Yue zhongnan lu yiban jiaoyu qingkuang de jieshao' (Introduction to the general education situation in the south-central region of Guangdong). *Guangdong jiaoyu yu wenhua* 1.5 (September 1950):16-20

'Sui qingzhen guoguang liang xiaoxue ji xueqi lai da you gaijin' (Great improvements in Sui primary school and Guoguang Islamic primary school in the past few school terms). Hong Kong *Wenhuibao*, 22 April 1954. In *Union Research Institute* LO139 424125

'Sulian saochu wenmang de jingguo' (The Soviet Union's experience in eliminating illiteracy). In *Guangdong sheng diyijie gongnong jiaoyu huiyi ji jiaoyu gonghui daibiao dahui cailiao* (Materials from the first Guangdong worker-peasant education conference and educational workers union delegates plenary session). Vol. 1. N.p.: n.p. 1951

Taishan xian jiaoyu zhi bianxie zu, ed. *Taishan xian jiaoyu zhi (neibu faxing)* (Taishan county educational history [internal circulation]). N.p.: n.p. 1987

Tan Ruihong. *Dali tanbian xiaoxue zhi* (Dali Tanbian primary school history). N.p.: n.p. 1978

Tao Zhan. 'Mianxiang nongcun, wei nongye fuwu de Changpo xiaoxue' (Changpo primary school faces the village and serves agriculture). *Guangdong jiaoyu* 6 (11 June 1964):14-16

Tian Xin. 'Jiji zhudong, xianqi yige xuexi wenhua de gaochao' (Actively initiate, set in motion a high tide in learning culture). In *Dali kaizhan saochu wenmang yundong* (Vigorously develop the anti-illiteracy movement), ed. Guangdong sheng jiaoyu ting, 42-6. Guangzhou: Guangdong renmin chubanshe 1956

'Tuanjie quansheng aiguo jiaoyu gongzuozhe wei banhao renmin de jiaoyu shiye er douzheng' (Unite the whole province's patriotic educational workers in the struggle to firmly establish the cause of people's education). In *Guangdong sheng diyijie gongnong jiaoyu huiyi ji jiaoyu gonghui daibiao dahui cailiao* (Materials from the first Guangdong worker-peasant education conference and educational workers union delegates' plenary session). Vol. 1. N.p.: n.p. 1951

'Wei shenme zhei wushiwu ge xiang, she neng tiqian saochu qingzhuangnian wenmang?' (Why have these fifty-five townships and collectives eliminated illiteracy among youth and adults ahead of schedule?). In *Xianqi daguimo zhuangkuo de saomang dayuejin*, ed. Guangdong sheng saochu wenmang xiehui. Guangzhou: Guangdong renmin chubanshe n.d.

'Wei shenmo xuexi guoyu?' (Why study the common language?). *Guangdong jiaoyu yu wenhua* 2.4 (February 1951):27-8

Wen Yinggan and Liao Liqiong. 'Zhenxing shanqu jingji de zhongyao huanjie: Lun Guangdong shanqu de zhili kaifa' (Vigorously develop the key link in the mountain region economies: On opening up the power of knowledge in Guangdong's mountain regions). *Xuebao* (Zhongshan University) 2 (1987):17-24

'Wo shi zheiyang dang yige saomang ganbu' (This is how I became an anti-illiteracy cadre). In *Guangdong sheng saochu wenmang jiji fenzi daibiao dahui huikan* (Proceedings from the Guangdong anti-illiteracy activists delegates' mass meeting), 91-2. Guangzhou: Guangdong sheng saochu wenmang jiji fenzu daibiao dahui mishuchu 1958

'Women de jiantao' (Our self-criticism). *Guangdong jiaoyu* (May 1966):27

'Women shi zheiyang jianchi xuexi Mao zhuxi zhuzuo de' (This is how we supported the study of Mao's works). *Guangdong jiaoyu* 12 (December 1964):10-11

Wu Ming. 'Huiyang xian gongnong yeyu jiaoyu de qingxing' (The situation of worker-peasant spare-time education in Huiyang county). *Guangdong jiaoyu yu wenhua* 3.3 (July 1951):22

Wu Qingsheng. 'Weichi nongcun xiaoxue de daolu' (Maintain the path of village primary education). *Guangdong jiaoyu yu wenhua* 3.1 (May 1951):8-9

Wu Yuwen, ed. *Guangdong sheng jingji dili* (Economic geography of Guangdong province). Beijing: Xinhua chubanshe 1986

Xia Jing. 'Wei shenmo yao tiaozheng jiaoyu shiye?' (Why the education system must be revised). *Guangdong jiaoyu* 6 (1962):4-5

'Xia Yan de feifu zhi yan: Jianguo yilai sanda cuowu' (Straight talk from Xia Yan: Three great mistakes since the setting up of the country). *Yangcheng wanbao*, 18 November 1988:1

Xiao Xiangyong. 'Dui shehui jiaoyu de yidian yijian' (Some opinions on social education). *Guangdong jiaoyu yu wenhua* 1.5 (September 1950):10-11

'Xijiang minxiao fadong qunzhong ruxue ji jiejue jingfei wenti jingyan zongjie' (Summary of Xijiang people school's experiences initiating mass education and solving funding problems). In *Guangdong sheng diyijie gongnong jiaoyu huiyi ji jiaoyu gonghui daibiao dahui cailiao* (Materials from the first Guangdong worker-peasant education conference and educational workers union delegates' plenary session). Vol. 1. N.p.: n.p. 1951

Xinfeng xian jiaoyu zhi (Xinfeng county educational history). Zhaoqing: Xinfeng xian jiaoyu ju 1978

'Xingning xian nongye zhongxue banxue qinian' (Xingning county agricultural middle school established for seven years). In *Guangdong sheng nongcun bannong bandu jiaoyu huiyi ziliao* (Materials recollecting village half-farming, half-study education in Guangdong province), 1-10. Guangzhou: n.p. 1965

'Xinhui nongye jishu xuexiao de chengji he jiben jingyan' (Basic experiences and results of Xinhui agrotechnical school). In *Guangdong sheng nongcun bannong bandu jiaoyu huiyi ziliao* (Materials recollecting village half-farming, half-study education in Guangdong province), 48-54. Guangzhou: n.p. 1965

Xinxing xian jiaoyu zhi (Xinxing county educational history). Rev. ed. N.p.: n.p. 1978

'Xuexi he guanche Mao zhuxi de jiaoyu sixiang: Wei jinian zhongguo gongchang dang de sanshi zhounian er zuo' (Study and implement Chairman Mao's educational thought: Serve the thirtieth anniversary of the Chinese Communist Party). *Guangdong jiaoyu yu wenhua* 3.4 (August 1951):1-7

Yang Guang. *Sucheng shizi de gushi* (Accelerated literacy stories). Guangzhou: Nanfang tongsu duben lianhe chubanshe 1952

'Yige shizi buduo nongmin xianzai yineng shuxie zichuan' (A barely literate peasant can already write). *Dagongbao* (Hong Kong), 4 March 1953. In *Union Research Institute* LO136 4222 3235

'Yige zhansheng zhongzhong kunnan banhao gengdu xuexiao de nu jiaoshi' (A woman teacher who triumphed over numerous difficulties to set up a half-ploughing, half-study school). In *Guangdong sheng nongcun bannong bandu jiaoyu huiyi ziliao* (Materials recollecting village half-farming, half-study education in Guangdong province), 1-4. Guangzhou: n.p. 1965

'Yijiu wuliu nian guangdong sheng putong jiaoyu he shifan jiaoyu de gongzuo renwu' (1956 Guangdong general education and teacher-training work assignment). *Guangdong jiaoyu* 11-12 (10 June 1956):8, 14

'Yijiu wuyi nian kaizhan gongnong jiaoyu gongzuo chubu fangan' (A 1950 preliminary draft plan for opening up worker-peasant educational work). In *Guangdong sheng diyijie gongnong jiaoyu huiyi ji jiaoyu gonghui daibiao dahui cailiao* (Materials from the first Guangdong worker-peasant education conference and educational workers union delegates' plenary session). Vol. 3. N.p.: n.p. 1951

'Yinian lai Guangdong sheng nongcun wenyi yundong gaikuang' (Survey of the village literature and art movement in Guangdong over the past year). *Guangdong jiaoyu yu wenhua* 2.4 (February 1951):13-14

Yu Zhenming. 'Weiji yu chulu: Jiaoyu fazhan de sikao' (The Crisis and the way out: Reflections on educational development). *Guangdong yanjiu* 9 (1988):32-6

Yunfu xian weiyuanhui zhenggong zu jiaoyu geming bangongshi. *Yunfu xian hongyexiao wenhua keben* (Yunfu county red evening school cultural primer). N.p.: n.p. 1972

'Yunyong duozhong duoyang de xingshi dui xuesheng jinxing jieji jiaoyu' (Utilize multiple ways of carrying out class education among students). *Guangdong jiaoyu* 10 (1963):5-6

'Zai saomang gongzuo shang duanlian tigao ziji' (Strive to improve oneself in anti-illiteracy work). In *Guangdong sheng saochu wenmang jiji fenzi daibiao dahui huikan* (Proceedings from the Guangdong anti-illiteracy activists delegates' mass meeting), 81-2. Guangzhou: Guangdong sheng saochu wenmang jiji fenzu daibiao dahui mishuchu 1958

Zhang Bailin. 'Guanyu banli nongmin yeyu jiaoyu de jidian tiyan' (Some experiences concerning management of peasant spare-time education). *Guangdong jiaoyu yu wenhua* 4.1 (November 1951):24-5

Zhang Mingshen. 'Guangdong chudeng jiaoyu de qingkuang yu wenti' (Situation and problems with respect to Guangdong primary education). *Guangdong jiaoyu yu wenhua* 3.2 (June 1951):10-13

–. 'Guangdong sheng diyijie gongnong jiaoyu huiyi ji jiaoyu gonghui daibiao dahui zongjie baogao' (Summary report to the first Guangdong worker-peasant education conference and educational workers delegates' plenary session). In *Guangdong sheng diyijie gongnong jiaoyu huiyi ji jiaoyu gonghui daibiao dahui cailiao* (Materials from the first Guangdong worker-peasant education conference and educational workers union delegates' plenary session). Vol. 1. N.p.: n.p. 1951

Zheng Huihao, ed. *Zijin xian jiaoyu zhi* (Zijin county educational history). N.p.: n.p. 1987

'Zhengque renshi jiaoyu gongzuo de jige jiben wenti' (Some fundamental problems in correctly understanding educational work). *Guangdong jiaoyu* 12 (1962):3-5

Zhenjiang zhuanshu jiaoyu ju. 'Daban gengdu xiaoxue duokuai haosheng de puji nongcun jiaoyu' (Go all out for half-ploughing, half-study primary schools, popularize village education faster and more economically). *Guangdong jiaoyu* 7 (July 1965):8-10

'Zhigong jiaoyu bixu jinxing jiaoxue gaige' (Teaching must be reformed in staff and worker education). *Guangdong saomang* 2 (25 November 1958):23-5

Zhong Zhong. 'Zhujiang qu yiban jiaoyu qingkuang suxie' (A brief sketch of the general education situation in Zhujiang district). *Guangdong jiaoyu yu wenhua* 1.5 (September 1950):15

Zhonggong gaozhou xian dongan gongshe weiyuanhui. 'Mianxiang pingxia zhongnong jiji banhao gengdu xiaoxue' (Face the villages, actively establish half-ploughing, half-study primary schools). *Guangdong jiaoyu* (2 February 1966):38-42

Zhonggong zhongyang Huanan fenju, ed. *Guanyu jiaqiang zai tudi gaige zhong dui nongmin de sixiang fadong gongzuo de fangan* (Program concerning the strengthening of ideological mobilization work among peasants during land reform). Guangzhou: Huanan renmin chubanshe 1952

Zhongguo renmin zhengzhi xieshang huiyi Guangdong sheng guangzhou shi weiyuanhui, wenshi ziliao yanjiu weiyuanhui, ed. *Guangzhou jin bainian jiaoyu shiliao* (Historical materials on education in Guangzhou over the past 100 years). Guangzhou: Guangdong renmin chubanshe 1983

'Zhongshan xian Xinping xiang dijiu nongye shengchan hezuoshe de qingnian tujidui' (New year assault troops of Zhongshan county, Xinping township, number nine agricultural producers cooperative). In *Zhongguo nongcun de shehui zhuyi gaochao* (Socialist upsurge in the Chinese countryside), ed. Zhonggong zhongyang bangong ting, 961. Vol. 3. Beijing: Renmin chubanshe 1956

Zhou Ping. 'Guangzhou shi diyici gongnong jiaoyu huiyi zongjie baogao' (Summary report to the Guangzhou first worker-peasant education conference). *Guangdong jiaoyu yu wenhua* 2.3 (January 1951):28-33

–. 'Guanyu quanguo gongnong jiaoyu huiyi de chuanda baogao' (Relayed report concerning the national worker-peasant education conference). *Guangdong jiaoyu yu wenhua* 2.2 (December 1950):4-6

–. 'Jinhou de renwu he gongzuo: Quansheng wenjiao gongzuo huiyi zongjie baogao' (Present and future tasks and work: Summary report to the provincial culture and education work conference). *Guangdong jiaoyu yu wenhua* 1.5 (September 1950):2

–. 'Xin jiu jiaoyu you shenmo butong? Zai Lingnan daxue he Guangzhou ge daxue de yanjiang' (What are the differences between the old and the new education? Speech to Lingnan university and other Guangzhou universities). *Guangdong jiaoyu yu wenhua* 1.2 (June 1950):8-13

Zhu Yuanxing. 'Dui Guangdong jiaoyu fazhan de yixie sikao' (Some reflections on Guangdong's educational development). *Guangdong jiaoyu* 12 (1992):6

Zhu Yuncheng, ed. *Zhongguo renkou: Guangdong fence* (China's population: Guangdong volume). Beijing: Zhongguo caizheng jingji chubanshe 1988

'Zhujiang sanjiaozhou zai jingji kaifang xingshi xia de jiaoyu xianzhuang ji duice' (The contemporary educational situation and countermeasures under the situation of economic openness in the Pearl River Delta). *Guangdong jiaoyu* 12 (1987):3-6

'Zhuyin shizi pinyin jiaoxue dagang (chugao)' (Teaching outline for phonetic reading [draft]). *Guangdong jiaoyu (yeyu jiaoyuban)* 1 (15 January 1960):14-17

'Zhuyin shizi shi saochu wenmang de jiejing' (Phonetic spelling is a shortcut to eliminating illiteracy). *Guangdong jiaoyu (yeyu jiaoyuban)* 2 (15 August 1960):10-11

'Zhuyin shizi zhong de xinren xinshi: Ji Chaoan jiangdong gongse yangguang dadui zhuyin shizi shidian' (New people and new things produced by phonetic reading: Report on Chaoan county Jiangdong commune Yangguang brigade's experiments in phonetic reading). *Guangdong jiaoyu (yeyu jiaoyu ban)* 4 (16 October 1960):12

'Zou qunzhong luxian wancheng saomang renwu de guanjian' (The key to walking the mass line and completing the anti-illiteracy task). In *Guangdong sheng saochu wenmang jiji fenzi daibiao dahui huikan* (Proceedings from the Guangdong anti-illiteracy activists delegates' mass meeting), 21. Guangzhou: Guangdong sheng saochu wenmang jiji fenzu daibiao dahui mishuchu 1958

'Zuohao wenmang qingdi gongzuo' (Complete the work of cleaning up illiteracy). *Guangdong jiaoyu (yeyu jiaoyu ban)* 3 (10 October 1960):20

Chinese-Language Works

Cai Zhentang. 'Zhengshe heyi bibing duo' (There are too many evils in the fusion of government and collective). *Lilun yu shijian* 1 (1981):27. In *Fuyin baokan ziliao: Nongye jingji* 3 (1981):34

Chao Yimin. 'Dongxue jiaoyu de fangzhen ji youguan de jige wenti' (The policy of winter school education and certain related problems). *Changjiang ribao*, 20 August 1951. In *Union Research Institute* LO135 4222 3135

Chen Bixiang, ed. *Zhongguo xiandai yuwen jiaoyu zhanshi* (An extended history of contemporary Chinese language education). Kunming: Yunnan jiaoyu chubanshe 1987

Chen Heqin. *Yuti wen yingyong zihui* (Glossary of common Chinese characters). Shanghai: Commercial Press 1931

Cheng Youxin. 'Xiandai jiaoyu he shangpin jingji de benzhi lianxi yiji dui wo guo jiaoyu gaige de jidian sikao' (Some reflections on the nature of the relationship between education and the commodity economy and its impact on our country's educational reform). *Jiaoyu yanjiu* 9 (1992):24-9

'Chuantou nongmin xiaozhang Yu Hongduan bu lianxi qunzhong, minxiao wei banhao' (Principal Yu Hongduan of Chuantou peasant school failed to link up with the masses, and the school is not yet well established). *Fujian ribao*, 23 January 1953. In *Union Research Institute* LO136 4222 3237

Dai Xingyi. 'Qianxi woguo de wenmang renkou wenti' (A brief analysis of our country's illiterate population problem). *Renkou yu jingji* 6 (1990):23-6

Deng Xiaoping Wenxuan (Selected works of Deng Xiaoping). Beijing: Renmin chubanshe 1983

Disanci quanguo renkou pucha shougong huizong ziliao huibian: Vol. 5: Renkou wenhua chengdu (Compendium of manually compiled materials of the third national population census: Vol. 5: Population cultural levels). Beijing: Guowuyuan renkou pucha bangongshi 1983

Dong Chuncai. 'Diyici quanguo nongmin yeyu jiaoyu huiyi de zongjie baogao' (Summary report to the first national peasant spare-time education conference). *Renmin jiaoyu* 9 (1955):31

'Dui shaoshu minzu jiaoxue shang de jidian yijian' (Some opinions regarding teaching minority peoples). *Guangming ribao*, 30 January 1954. In *Union Research Institute* LO139 42411

'Duo wei yeyu jiaoyu xiangxiang' (More reflections on spare-time education). *Renmin jiaoyu* 6 (1957):64-5

Feng Decai. 'Nongcun renmin gongshe yinggai chengwei danchun de jingji zuzhi' (The rural people's communes should be only an economic unit). *Jingji yanjiu* 2 (1980):80-1

'Gaige chengren jiaoyu, fazhan chengren jiaoyu: Li Peng tongzhi zai quanguo chengren jiaoyu gongzuo huiyi shang de jianghua' (Reform adult education, develop adult education: Comrade Li Peng's speech to the national adult-education work conference). *Zhongguo jiaoyu bao*, 20 December 1986

'Geji jiaoyu bumen bixu jiaqiang gongnong jiaoyu de lingdao' (Education departments must strengthen leadership in worker-peasant education). *Renmin jiaoyu* 12 (1955):4-5

'Gengxin guannian luoshi cuoshi zhuzhong shixiao zhuahao saomang' (Renew the emphasis on practical effects, pay attention to results, and take charge of anti-illiteracy work). *Nongcun chengren jiaoyu* (Zhengzhou) 6 (1988):8-10

Gong Kuoru. 'Yuenan de pingmin jiaoyu gongzuo' (Vietnam's work in mass education). *Renmin jiaoyu* 2 (1957):57-9

Guan Shixiong. *Chengren jiaoyu de lilun yu shijian* (The theory and practice of adult education). Beijing: Beijing chubanshe 1986

Guangming ribao xueshu lun wenji: Wenzi gaige (Guangming daily academic collection: Language reform). 2 vols. Repr. Washington, DC: Center for Chinese Research Materials 1972

'Guanyu dongyuan xuesheng zai hanjiaqi zhong canjia saomang gongzuo de tongzhi' (Circular concerning the mobilization of students to participate in anti-illiteracy work during winter vacation). *Xinhua ribao* (Nanjing), 6 January 1956. In *Union Research Institute* LO364 42222

'Guanyu jiaqiang xiaoxuesheng xiezi xunlian de tongzhi' (Circular concerning strengthening writing drills for primary school students). In *Xiaoxue jiaoyu daquan*, ed. Li Jiangang, 1123-4. Jinan: Shandong jiaoyu chubanshe 1987

'Guanyu kaizhan yijiu wuyi nian dongxue gongzuo de zhishi' (Directive concerning the development of winter school education for 1950). *Changjiang ribao*, 18 November 1951. In *Union Research Institute* LO135 4222 3135

'Guanyu zai zhong, xiaoxue he geji shifan xuexiao dali tuiguang putonghua de zhishi' (Directive concerning the vigorous promotion of the common language in middle, primary, and teacher-training schools). *Renmin jiaoyu* 12 (1955):9-11

Guo Lin. 'Qiantan yuwen jiaoxue gaige' (A preliminary discussion of language-teaching reform). *Jiaoyu yanjiu* 1 (1980):47-54

Guo Moruo. *Guanyu wenhua jiaoyu gongzuo de baogao: Zai zhongguo renmin zhengzhi xieshang huiyi diyijie quanguo weiyuanhui disanci huiyi shang de baogao* (Report concerning cultural and educational work: Report to the third conference of the first national committee of the Chinese political consultative conference). Beijing: Renmin chubanshe 1951

–. *Guanyu wenhua jiaoyu gongzuo, yijiu wuling nian liuyue shiqi ri zai renmin zhengxie quanguo weiyuanhui dierci huiyi de baogao* (Report concerning cultural and educational work to the second conference of the national people's consultative committee, June 1950). Beijing: Renmin chubanshe 1951

'Guojia jiaowei biaozhang yibai ge saomang xianjin xian' (The State Education Commission cites 100 advanced anti-illiteracy counties). *Zhongguo jiaoyu bao*, 3 November 1988:1

Guojia tongji ju, ed. *Zhongguo tongji nianjian, 1987* (Chinese statistical yearbook, 1987). Beijing: Zhongguo tongji chubanshe 1987

Guojia tongji ju renkou tongji si, ed. *Zhongguo renkou tongji nianjian 1990* (Chinese population statistics yearbook 1990). Beijing: Kexue jishu wenjian chubanshe 1991

'Guowuyuan guanyu saochu wenmang de zhishi (zhailu)' (State Council directive concerning the elimination of illiteracy [excerpts]). In *Zhongguo jiaoyu nianjian, 1949-1981* (China educational yearbook), ed. Zhongguo jiaoyu nianjian bianji bu, 900. Beijing: Zhongguo dabaike quanshu chubanshe 1984

'Guowuyuan guanyu tuiguang putonghua de zhishi' (Directive concerning the promotion of the common language). *Renmin jiaoyu* 2 (1956):21-2

He Bochuan. *Shanao shang de zhongguo: Wenti, kunjing, tongku de xuanze* (China in a depression: A selection of problems, predicaments, and suffering). Guiyang: Guizhou renmin chubanshe 1988

He Dongchang. 'Nongcun jiaoyu zhuyao wei dangdi jianshe fuwu' (Village education should primarily serve local construction). *Renmin jiaoyu* 3 (1988):2-4

Heilongjiang sheng Tailai xian wenjiao ju. 'Du baiben shu, xie wange zi' (Read 100 books, write 10,000 characters). *Renmin jiaoyu* 8 (1958)

Hu Yaobang. 'Guanyu nongcun saochu wenmang gongzuo' (Concerning village anti-illiteracy work). *Renmin ribao*, 16 November 1955. In *Union Research Institute* LO364 42222

Hu Qiaomu Wenji (Collected Writings of Hu Qiaomu). Vol. 1. Beijing: Renmin chubanshe 1992

Jian Yueren. 'Ping "xiao xiansheng zhi"' (A critique of the 'Little teacher system'). *Renmin jiaoyu* 3.4 (1 August 1951):34-7

Jiang Liu, ed. *Zhongguo shehui zhuyi jingsheng wenming yanjiu* (Research into Chinese socialist spiritual civilization). Beijing: Zhonggong zhongyang dangxiao chubanshe 1987

'Jiaoshi tan jiaoyu gongzuo neibu maodun' (The internal contradictions of teachers' discussions of educational work). *Renmin jiaoyu* 6 (1957):6-13

'Jiaoyu bu guanyu kaizhan nongmin yeyu jiaoyu de zhishi' (Ministry of Education directive concerning the development of peasant spare-time education). In *Zhongguo jiaoyu nianjian, 1949-1981* (China educational yearbook), ed. Zhongguo jiaoyu nianjian bianji bu, 895. Beijing: Zhongguo dabaike quanshu chubanshe 1984

'Jiaoyubu guanyu jieban sili zhong, xiaoxue de zhishi' (Ministry of Education directive concerning takeover of private middle and primary schools). In *Zhongguo jiaoyu nianjian, 1949-1981* (China educational yearbook), ed. Zhongguo jiaoyu nianjian bianji bu, 731-2. Beijing: Zhongguo dabaike quanshu chubanshe 1984

'Jiaoyubu guanyu kaizhan nongmin yeyu jiaoyu de zhishi' (Ministry of Education directive concerning the development of peasant spare-time education). In *Union Research Institute* LO13 4222 322

'Jiaqiang xuexiaozhong dangyuan he qunzhong de lianxi' (Strengthen the unity between party members and the masses in the schools). *Renmin jiaoyu* 2 (1957):21

'Jiji tigao dongxue jiaoshi de zhengzhi he wenhua shuiping' (Actively raise the political and cultural level of winter school teachers). *Changjiang ribao*, 30 December 1951. In *Union Research Institute* LO135 4222 3135

'Jiji xuexi he dali guanche guanyu saochu wenmang de jueding' (Actively study and implement the decision concerning elimination of illiteracy). *Renmin jiaoyu* 4 (1956):6

'Jin yibu zuohao minzu jiaoyu gongzuo' (Progress in carrying out minority peoples' educational work). *Guangming ribao*, 25 October 1954. In *Union Research Institute* LO139 42411

Jinyang xuekan bianji bu, comp. *Zhongguo xiandai shehui kexuejia zhuanlue* (Biographical sketches of contemporary Chinese social scientists). 10 vols. Taiyuan: Shanxi renmin chubanshe 1983

Lao Han. 'Jieshao "nongmin shizi jiaoyu de zuzhi xingshi he jiaoxue fangfa"' (Introduction to 'organizational forms and teaching methods in peasant literacy education'). *Renmin jiaoyu* 2.1 (November 1950):46

Li Botang. *Xiaoxue yuwen jiaocai jianshi* (A brief history of Chinese language teaching materials). Jinan: Shandong jiaoyu chubanshe 1985

Li Jiangang, ed. *Xiaoxue jiaoyu daquan* (Encyclopedia of primary education). Jinan: Shandong jiaoyu chubanshe 1987

Li Jun. 'Lun sixue yu zhongguo chuantong wenhua' (On private schools and China's traditional culture). *Jiaoyu yanjiu* 12 (1991):70-3

Li Xiaojiang. 'Zenyang kan dangqian funu wenti he funu yanjiu' (How to look at current women's problems and women's research). *Qiushi* 11 (1988):32-6

Li Yunhong. 'Nutong ruxue wenti zhide zhongshi' (The problem of girls' school participation is worth paying attention to). *Renmin jiaoyu* 7-8 (1988):12-13

Liang Zhichao. 'Heilongjiang sheng wancheng jiben saochu wenmang renwu de chubu tihui' (Preliminary experience from the basic elimination of illiteracy in Heilongjiang). *Renmin jiaoyu* 8 (1958):10-12

Lin Handa. 'Relie zhankai hanyu pinyin fangan (caoan) de taolun, jiji tigong xiugai de yijian' (Enthusiastically open up discussion on the Han language phonetic scheme, actively offer opinions for improvement). *Renmin jiaoyu* 3 (1956):25-8

–. 'Wei shehui zhuyi jianshe kaizhan saomang gongzuo' (Develop anti-illiteracy work in order to build socialism). *Wenhuibao* (Shanghai), 2 and 3 November 1955. In *Union Research Institute* LO364 42222

Lin Li. 'Shitan chengren jiaoyu de diwei he zuoyong' (An exploration of the position and significance of adult education). *Chengren jiaoyu* 1 (1982):22-6

Liu Guangren, ed. *Hukou guanli xue* (A study of household registration management). Beijing: Zhongguo jiancha chubanshe (gongan jiguan neibu faxing) 1992

Liu Lequn. 'Xuexi Mao Zedong tongzhi guanyu nongmin jiaoyu sixiang de jidian tihui' (Some experiences studying comrade Mao Zedong's thought on peasant education). *Shenyang shiyuan xuebao* 4 (1983). In *Fuyin baokan ziliao* ser. G5 6 (1983):49

Lo Zicheng. 'Guanyu nongye hezuoshe gonggu de gongzuo' (Concerning the work of consolidating agricultural producers cooperatives). *Xuexi* 6 (June 1955):5-8

Lu Can. 'Shanxi pingxun xian shixing nongye shengchan hezuoshe ban minban xiao de jingyan' (Experiences of Shanxi province Pingxun county in implementing the policy of agricultural producers cooperatives establishing people-run schools). *Renmin jiaoyu* 8 (1985):52-4

'Lu Dingyi tongzhi huijian benkan jizhe qiangdao zhichu: Minzhu fazhi bixu jiaqiang zhongshi zhishi shifen biyao' (Comrade Lu Dingyi met with our journal's reporters to emphasize: Democracy and law must be strengthened, respecting knowledge is extremely necessary). *Minzhu yu fazhi* 4 (1983):2-3

Lu Hongji [Bernard Luk]. *Zhongguo jinshi de jiaoyu fazhan* (Modern educational development of China). Hong Kong: Huafeng shuju chubanshe 1983

Lu Xingdou, ed. *Liu Shaoqi he tade shiye*. Beijing: Zhonggong dangshi chubanshe 1991

Luo Gengmo. 'Xuexi sulian de jingyan: Guanyu jingji jianshe de jihua wenti' (Study the experience of the Soviet Union: Concerning problems of economic construction and planning). *Xuexi* 3 (1953):9-10

Mao Zedong. 'Hunan nongmin yundong kaocha baogao' (Report on an investigation into the peasant movement in Hunan). In *Mao zhuxi lun jiaoyu geming* (Chairman Mao on educational revolution). Beijing: Renmin chubanshe 1967

Ni Haishu. *Zhongguo pinyin wenzi gailun* (Introduction to China's phonetic alphabet). Shanghai: Shidai shubao chubanshe 1948

Ni Haishu zhuzuo bianji xiaozu, ed. *Ni Haishu yuwen lunji* (Collected opinions of Nu Haishu on Chinese). Shanghai: Shanghai jiaoyu chubanshe 1991

Ning Hongbin. *Zenyang tigao yuedu nengli* (How to improve reading). Beijing: Beijing ligong daxue chubanshe 1988

'Nongcun saomang ruxue renshu zaidu huisheng' (Village anti-illiteracy and school attendance is once again returning to a state of defeat). *Renmin ribao*, 16 October 1985

'Nongcun zhong pochu mixin kaizhan weisheng gongzuo de jingyan' (Village experiences in abolishing superstition and developing health work). In *Nongmin shizi jiaoyu de zuzhi xingshi he jiaoxue fangfa* (Organizational forms and teaching methods in peasant reading education), ed. Renmin jiaoyushe, vol. 1. 4 vols. Beijing: Renmin jiaoyushe 1950

'Nongcun zhong pochu mixin kaizhan weisheng gongzuo de jingyan' (Village experiences abolishing superstition and developing health work). *Renmin jiaoyu* 1.2 (1950):122-8

'Nongye hezuo hua xuyao wenhua' (Agricultural collectivization requires culture). *Guangming ribao*, 2 September 1949. In *Union Research Institute* LO135 42222

Nongye shengchan hezuoshe shifan zhangcheng caoan tujie (Illustrated explanation of draft model regulations for agricultural producers cooperatives). Shenyang: Liaonong Renmin chubanshe 1956

Population Census Office under the State Council and Department of Population Statistics, State Statistical Bureau, ed. *1982 Population Census of China (Results of Computer Tabulation)* (in Chinese). Beijing: Zhongguo tongji chubanshe n.d.

Qian Chunrui. 'Wei tigao gongnong de wenhua shuiping manzu gongnong ganbu de wenhua yaoqiu er fendou' (Struggle to raise worker-peasant cultural levels and satisfy worker-peasant cadre cultural demands). *Renmin jiaoyu* 3.1 (1 May 1951):12-16

'Qingnian tuan zhongyang tongzhi pubian jianli qingnian saomang dui' (Youth League central committee circular calls for universal establishment of anti-illiteracy youth troops). *Renmin ribao*, 2 January 1956. In *Union Research Institute* LO364 42222

'Qionghai renmin xuexi wenhua' (The people of Qionghai study culture). *Renmin ribao*, 31 March 1950. In *Union Research Institute* LO139 4242

Qu Naisheng. 'Fuwu shengchang, yikao qunzhong, kaizhan dongxue yundong guanche guojia guodu shiqi zongluxian de jiaoyu' (Serve production, rely on the masses, develop the winter school movement, and implement education according to the general line for the transition period). *Jiaoyu banyue kan* 23 (1953):4

'Renkou: Shuliang yu zhiliang' (Population: Quantity and quality). *Guangming ribao*, 13 April 1989:1

Renmin jiaoyu 2.4 (1 February 1951):50-1 (Question box)

Renmin jiaoyushe, ed. *Nongmin shizi jiaoyu de zuzhi xingshi he jiaoxue fangfa* (Organizational forms and teaching methods in peasant reading education). 4 vols. Beijing: Renmin jiaoyushe 1950

Shandong sheng geming weiyuanhui zhengzhi bu jiaoyu zu, ed. *Sheyuan shizi* (Commune members' reader). 2 vols. N.p.: Shandong renmin chubanshe 1973

Shanghai saomang, 14 February 1957. In *Union Research Institute* 42207

Shi Ping. *Zhishi fenzi de lishi yundong he zuoyong* (The historical movement and functions of intellectuals). Shanghai: Shanghai shehui kexue yuan chubanshe 1988

'Shitan zenyang guanche qunzhong banxue de fangzhen' (Explorations into how to implement the policy of the masses running schools). *Renmin jiaoyu* 6 (1957):17-21

'Shiying nongye hezuoshe xuyao, dali kaizhan nongcun saomang gongzuo' (Adapt to the requirements of collectives, vigorously develop anti-illiteracy work). *Renmin jiaoyu* 1 (1956):32-3

Wang Tongqi. 'Jiaoyu fangzhen de taolun he yixie xuyao yanjiu jiejue de wenti' (A discussion on educational policy and some problems that need research and solutions). *Renmin jiaoyu* 2 (1957):22-3

Wang Yunfeng. *Xu Teli zai Yanan* (Xu Teli in Yanan). Xian: Shanxi renmin chubanshe 1991

'Wei cujin hanzi gaige, tuiguang putonghua, shixian hanyu guifanhua er nuli' (Strive to promote character reform, promote the common language, bring about the standardization of Han speech). *Renmin jiaoyu* 11 (1955):15-17

Wei Ke. 'Dali tuixing hanyu pinyin fangan, wei puji jiaoyu chuangzao tiaojian' (Vigorously practise the Han speech phonetic scheme, in order to create the conditions for popularizing education). *Renmin jiaoyu* 4 (1958):20-2

'Wenhua jianxun' (Culture brief). *Renmin ribao*, 18 July 1953. In *Union Research Institute* LO139 424125

Xiang Laoruo. '"Chengnian ren lijie liqiang jiyi liruo" de shuofa shi meiyou kexue genjude' (There is no scientific basis to the theory that 'adults have strong reasoning faculties and weak memory capacity'). *Renmin jiaoyu* 2 (1957):52-4

Xie Guodong. 'Wancheng saomang lishi renwu de tiaojian yu duice' (Conditions and strategies for completing the historical task of sweeping away illiteracy). *Jiaoyu yanjiu* 12 (1991):46-50

'Xin "dushu wuyong" lun yige jingji genyuan' (An opinion on the economic roots of the new 'study is useless' attitude). *Jiaoyu yanjiu* 9 (September 1988):19-23

Xin Ming. 'Ban xiaoxue de liangtiao luxian' (The two lines in running schools). *Renmin jiaoyu* 6 (1957):14-18

'Xu Teli tongzhi jieda guanyu jiaoyu fangzhen de jige wenti' (Comrade Xu Teli responds to problems concerning educational policy). *Renmin jiaoyu* 4 (1958):8-10

'Yanjiu xin qingkuang, xin tedian, renzhen gaohao gongnong jiaoyu' (Research the new situation, new characteristics, earnestly engage in worker-peasant education). *Guangming ribao*, 5 January 1982:1

Yang Xiufeng. 'Peiyang nonglin zhuanmen rencai yaozou ziji de lu' (Specialized talent trained in agriculture and forestry must follow its own road). In *Yang Xiufeng jiaoyu wenji* (Collected works of Yang Xiufeng), 43-53. Beijing: Beijing shifan daxue chubanshe 1987

'Yaomin jiaoyu you henda fazhan' (Big developments in Yao education). *Changjiang ribao*, 3 December 1951. In *Union Research Institute* LO139 424125

'Yi suo wanquan you nongmin ziban de xuexiao' (A school that was completely set up by peasants). *Guangming ribao*, 17 July 1953. In *Union Research Institute* LO136 4222 3235

'Youxiu de yiwu minxiao jiaoshi' (An exemplary volunteer people's school teacher). *Renmin jiaoyu* 11 (1955):38-9

Yu Bo. 'Zhongguo chengren jiaoyu de qiyuan wenti' (The fundamental problems of adult education). *Chengren jiaoyu* 1 (1982):18-21

Yu Mingdi et al. 'Zhujiang sanjiaozhou jiaoyu fazhan zhanlue yanjiu baogao' (Research report on an educational development strategy for the Pearl River Delta). *Jiaoyu yanjiu* 12 (1991):30-4

'Zenyang jiasu saochu nongcun wenmang gongzuo' (How to speed up village anti-illiteracy work). *Guangming ribao*, 28 November 1955. In *Union Research Institute* LO364 42222

Zhang Jian. 'Xuexi sulian jingyan de chengji bushi zhuyao de ma?' (Is it not important to study the achievements of Soviet experience?). *Renmin jiaoyu* 8 (March 1957):16-18

Zhang Ruxin. 'Zuo yige renmin jiaoshi shifou guangrong?' (Is it glorious to be a people's teacher or not?). In *Zenyang zuo yige renmin de xiaoxue jiaoshi* (How to be a people's primary school teacher), 33-7.Chongqing: Xinan qingnian chubanshe 1952

Zhang Xiruo. 'Dali tuiguang yi beijing yuyin wei biaozhun yin de putonghua' (Vigorously promote the common speech with Beijing pronunciation as the standard). *Renmin jiaoyu* 12 (1955):12-15

–. 'Guanyu zhong xiaoxue biye shang sheng, jiuye he xuesui ertong ruxue wenti' (Concerning the problems of higher education for middle and primary school graduates and school-age children attending school). *Renmin jiaoyu* 4 (1957):4-7

'Zhankai sixiang' (Open up your thinking). *Renmin jiaoyu* 2.1 (November 1950):88-9

Zhao Yimin. 'Wei "liangzhong jiaoyu zhidu" huifu mingyu' (On restoring the reputation of the 'two kinds of education system'). *Jiaoyu yanjiu* 2 (1980):12-14

Zheng Xihong. 'Nongmin yeyu jiaoyu de xin fangxiang' (The new direction in peasant spare-time education). *Renmin jiaoyu* 6 (1958):5

'Zhenge cun minxiao xiaozhang ying dong xueyuan shang minxiao, buyao dengdai jin sucheng shizi ban' (All village people's school principals should mobilize students to attend school, do not wait for them to enter accelerated literacy classes). *Fujian ribao*, 2 March 1953. In *Union Research Institute* LO136 4222 3237

'Zhengwuyuan guanyu zhengdun he gaijin xiaoxue jiaoyu de zhishi' (Political affairs council directive concerning the rectification and improvement of primary school education). In *Zhongguo jiaoyu nianjian, 1949-1981* (China educational yearbook), ed. Zhongguo jiaoyu nianjian bianji bu, 732-3. Beijing: Zhongguo dabaike quanshu chubanshe 1984

Zhonggong zhongyang bangong ting, ed. *Zhongguo nongcun de shehui zhuyi gaochao* (Socialist upsurge in the Chinese countryside). 3 vols. Beijing: Renmin chubanshe 1956

'Zhonggong zhongyang, guowuyuan guanyu saochu wenmang de jueding' (Decision of the Central Committee and State Council concerning the elimination of illiteracy). In *Zhongguo jiaoyu nianjian, 1949-1981* (China educational yearbook), ed. Zhongguo jiaoyu nianjian bianji bu, 895-7. Beijing: Zhongguo dabaike quanshu chubanshe 1984

Zhongguo dabaike quanshu: Jiaoyu. Beijing: Zhongguo dabaike quanshu chubanshe 1985

Zhongguo jiaoyu nianjian bianji bu, ed. *Zhongguo jiaoyu nianjian, 1949-1981* (China educational yearbook, 1949-1981). Beijing: Zhongguo dabaike quanshu chubanshe 1984

Zhongguo renkou qingbao ziliao zhongxin. *Zhongguo renkou ziliao shouce* (Chinese population materials handbook) (for internal circulation only). Beijing: Zhongguo renkou qingbao ziliao zhongxin 1983

Zhonghua renmin gongheguo jiaoyubu gongnong jiaoyu si, ed. *Gongnong jiaoyu wenxian huibian (nongmin jiaoyu)* (Compendium of documents on worker-peasant education [peasant education]). Beijing: n.p. 1979

Zhongyang jiaoyu kexue yanjiu suo, ed. *Zhonghua renmin gongheguo jiaoyu dashiji, 1949-1982* (People's Republic of China educational chronicle). Beijing: Jiaoyu kexue chubanshe 1983

Zhou Enlai. 'Zhonghua renmin gongheguo guowuyuan guanyu jiaqiang nongmin yeyu wenhua jiaoyu de zhishi' (People's Republic of China State Council directive concerning the strengthening of peasant spare-time education). *Renmin jiaoyu* 8 (1955):50-1

Zhou Yixian. *Woguo nongcun jiaoyu de huigu yu sikao* (Retrospective and reflection on our country's peasant education). Beijing: Beijing shifan daxue nongcun jiaoyu yanjiu shi 1988

'Zunzhong shaoshu minzu tongxue de shenghuo xiguan' (Respect the living habits of your minority classmates). *Zhongguo qingnianbao*, 6 November 1953. In *Union Research Institute* LO139 42411

'Zuodao shengchan, saomang liang buwu' (Accomplish production and eliminate illiteracy, miss neither). *Guangming ribao*, 4 December 1955. In *Union Research Institute* LO364 4222

Western-Language Works

'Actively and Steadily Eliminate Illiteracy.' *Renmin ribao*, 25 November 1956. In *Survey China Mainland Press* 1431 (14 December 1956):20-2

Ahn, Byung-joon. *Chinese Politics and the Cultural Revolution: Dynamics of Policy Processes*. Seattle: University of Washington Press 1976

Alitto, Guy. *The Last Confucian: Liang Shu-ming and the Chinese Dilemma of Modernity*. Berkeley: University of California Press 1981

Anderson, Benedict. *Imagined Communities: Reflections on the Origin and Spread of Nationalism*. Rev. ed. New York: Verso 1991

Apter, David E. *The Politics of Modernisation*. Chicago: University of Chicago Press 1965

–. 'Yan'an and the Narrative Reconstruction of Reality.' *Daedalus* 122 (Spring 1993):207-32

Arnove, Robert F., and Gail P. Kelly, eds. *Comparative Education*. New York: Macmillan 1988

Arnove, Robert F., and Harvey J. Graff, eds. *National Literacy Campaigns: Historical and Comparative Perspectives*. New York: Plenum Press 1987

Bailey, Paul J. *Reform the People: Changing Attitudes towards Popular Education in Early Twentieth Century China*. Edinburgh: Edinburgh University Press 1990

Barendson, Robert D. 'The Agricultural Middle Schools in Communist China.' *China Quarterly* 8 (October-December 1961):106-34

Barr, Allan. 'Four Schoolmasters: Educational Issues in Li Hai-kuan's *Lamp at the Crossroads*.' In *Education and Society in Late Imperial China, 1600-1900*, ed. Alexander Woodside and Benjamin A. Elman, 50-75. Berkeley: University of California Press 1994

Barton, David. *Literacy: An Introduction to the Ecology of Written Language*. Oxford: Basil Blackwell 1994

Bastid, Marianne. 'Economic Necessity and Political Ideals in Educational Reform during the Cultural Revolution.' *China Quarterly* 42 (April-June 1970):16-45

–. 'Levels of Economic Decision-Making.' In *Authority, Participation, and Cultural Change in China*, ed. Stuart R. Schram, 159-97. Cambridge: Cambridge University Press 1973

–. 'Chinese Educational Policies in the 1980s and Economic Development.' *China Quarterly* 98 (June 1984):189-219

–. *Educational Reform in Early Twentieth Century China*. Ann Arbor: n.p. 1988

Bastid, Marianne, and Ruth Hayhoe, eds. *China's Education and the Industrial World*. Armonk, NY: M.E. Sharpe 1987

Baum, Richard. *Prelude to Revolution: Mao, the Party and the Peasant Question 1962-1966*. New York: Columbia University Press 1975

–. *Burying Mao: Chinese Politics in the Age of Deng Xiaoping*. Princeton: Princeton University Press 1994

Becker, George S. *Human Capital: A Theoretical and Empirical Analysis, with Special Reference to Education*. New York: Columbia University Press 1963

Becker, Howard S. *The Outsiders: Studies in the Sociology of Deviance*. New York: Free Press 1973

Belde, Klaus. *Saomang: Kommunistische Alphabetisierungsarbeit*. Bochum: Brockmeyer 1982

Benedict, Carol. 'Bubonic Plague in Nineteenth-Century China.' *Modern China* 14.2 (April 1988):107-55

Bennett, Gordon. *Yundong: Mass Campaigns in Chinese Communist Leadership*. Berkeley: University of California Press 1976

Bernstein, Thomas P. 'Mass Mobilization in the Soviet and Chinese Collectivization Campaigns of 1929-30 and 1955-56: A Comparison.' *China Quarterly* 31 (1969):1-47

–. *Up to the Mountains and Down to the Villages: The Transfer of Youth from Urban to Rural China*. New Haven: Yale University Press 1977

Bhola, H.S. *Campaigning for Literacy: Eight National Experiences of the Twentieth Century, with a Memorandum to Decision-Makers*. Paris: UNESCO 1984

Borthwick, Sally. *Education and Social Change in China: The Beginnings of the Modern Era*. Stanford: Hoover Institution Press 1983

Brown, Hubert O. 'American Progressivism in Chinese Education: The Case of T'ao Hsing-chih.' In *China's Education and the Industrialized World*, ed. Ruth Hayhoe and Marianne Bastid, 120-38. Armonk, NY: M.E. Sharpe 1987

Buck, John Lossing. *Land Utilization in China*. Nanking: University of Nanking Press 1937

Cell, Charles P. *Revolution at Work: Mobilization Campaigns in China*. New York: Academic Press 1977

Chan, Anita, Richard Madsen, and Jonathan Unger. *Chen Village: The Recent History of a Peasant Community in Mao's China*. Berkeley: University of California Press 1984

Chan, Gerald. 'China and the Esperanto Movement.' *Australian Journal of Chinese Affairs* 15 (January 1986):1-18

Chan, Kam Wing. *Cities with Invisible Walls*. Hong Kong: Oxford University Press 1994

–. 'Economic Growth Strategy and Urbanization Policies in China, 1949-1982.' *International Journal of Urban and Regional Research* 16 (1992):275-306

–. 'Urbanization and Rural-Urban Migration in China since 1982: A New Baseline.' *Modern China* 20 (July 1994):243-81

Chan, Ming K., and Arif Dirlik. *Schools into Fields and Factories: Archivists, the Guomindang and the National Labor University in Shanghai, 1927-1932*. Durham, NC: Duke University Press 1991

Chauncey, Helen R. *Schoolhouse Politicians: Locality and State during the Chinese Republic*. Honolulu: University of Hawaii Press 1992

Chen, Han-seng. *Landlord and Peasant in China: A Study of the Agrarian Crisis in South China*. New York: International Publishers 1936

Cheng, Tiejun. 'The Dialectics of Control: The Household Registration (*Hukou*) System in Contemporary China.' Ph.D. diss., State University of New York at Binghampton, 1991

Cheng, Tiejun, with Mark Selden. 'The Origins and Social Consequences of China's *Hukou* System.' *China Quarterly* 139 (September 1994):644-68

Cheung, Peter T.Y. 'Relations between the Central Government and Guangdong.' In *Guangdong: Survey of a Province Undergoing Rapid Change*, ed. Y.M. Yeung and David K.Y. Chu, 19-51. Hong Kong: Chinese University Press 1994

China: Issues and Prospects for Education (Annex 1 to *China: Long-Term Development Issues and Options*). Washington, DC: World Bank 1985

'Chronology of the Two Road Struggle on the Educational Front for the Past Seventeen Years.' *Jiaoyu geming*, 6 May 1967. In *Revolutionary Education in China: Documents and Commentary*, ed. Peter J. Seybolt, 5-59. New York: International Arts and Sciences Press 1971

Cipolla, Carlo. *Literacy and Development in the West*. Harmondsworth, UK: Penguin 1969

Cohen, Myron L. 'The Case of the Chinese "Peasant."' *Daedalus* 122.2 (Spring 1993): 151-70

Cook-Gumperz, Jennifer. *The Social Construction of Literacy*. Cambridge, UK: Cambridge University Press 1986

Coombs, Philip H. *The World Crisis in Education: The View from the Eighties*. Oxford: Oxford University Press 1985

Dagongbao (Hong Kong), 17 May 1956. In *Survey China Mainland Press* 1293 (22 May 1956):21

'Decision of the Central Committee and the State Council concerning the Elimination of Illiteracy.' *New China News Agency* (Beijing), 30 March 1956. In *Survey China Mainland Press* 1266 (12 April 1956):3-7. Reprint, *Towards a New World Outlook: A Documentary History of Education in the PRC, 1949-1976*, ed. Hu Shiming and Eli Saifman, 74-7. New York: AMS Press 1976

DeFrancis, John. 'Mao Tse-tung and Writing Reform.' In *Perspectives on a Changing China: Essays in Honor of Professor C. Martin Wilbur on the Occasion of His Retirement*, ed. Joshua A. Fogel and William T. Rowe, 137-54. Boulder: Westview Press 1979

–. *Nationalism and Language Reform in China*. Princeton: Princeton University Press 1950

–. *The Chinese Language: Fact and Fantasy*. Honolulu: University of Hawaii Press 1984

Dietrich, Craig. *People's China: A Brief History*. New York: Oxford University Press 1986

Dennerline, Jerry. *Qian Mu and the World of the Seven Mansions*. New Haven: Yale University Press 1988

'Discrimination against Primary School Teachers Cannot Be Allowed.' *Renmin ribao*, 5 October 1956. In *Survey China Mainland Press* 1398 (26 October 1956):3-4

Dittmer, Lowell. *Liu Shaoqi and the Chinese Cultural Revolution: The Politics of Mass Criticism*. Berkeley: University of California Press 1974

Dittmer, Lowell, and Samuel S. Kim, eds. *China's Quest for National Identity*. Ithaca: Cornell University Press 1993

'Draft Program for Primary and Middle Schools in the Chinese Countryside.' *Renmin ribao*, 12 May 1969. In *Toward a New World Outlook: A Documentary History of Education in the People's Republic of China*, ed. Hu Shiming and Eli Saifman, 230-6. New York: AMS Press 1976

Dreze, Jean, and Jackie Loh. 'Literacy in China and India.' *Economic and Political Weekly* (India), 11 November 1995:2868-78

Du Runsheng. *Many People, Little Land: China's Rural Economic Reform*. Beijing: Foreign Languages Press 1989

Duara, Prasenjit. *Culture, Power and the State: Rural North China, 1900-1942*. Stanford: Stanford University Press 1988

Ebrey, Patricia Buckley, ed. *Chinese Civilization and Society: A Sourcebook*. New York: Free Press 1981

Eklof, Ben. 'Russian Literacy Campaigns, 1861-1939.' In *National Literacy Campaigns: Historical and Comparative Perspectives*, ed. Robert F. Arnove and Harvey J. Graff, 123-45. New York: Plenum Press 1987

–. *Russian Peasant Schools: Officialdom, Village Culture, and Popular Pedagogy, 1861-1914*. Berkeley: University of California Press 1986

Elman, Benjamin A., and Alexander Woodside, eds. *Education and Society in Late Imperial China, 1600-1900*. Berkeley: University of California Press 1994

Eng, Robert Y. 'Institutional and Secondary Landlordism in the Pearl River Delta, 1600-1949.' *Modern China* 12 (1986):3-38

Fairbank, John K. 'The Reunification of China.' In *The People's Republic, Part 1: The Emergence of Revolutionary China 1949-1965*, ed. Roderick MacFarquhar and John K. Fairbank, 1-47. Vol. 14 of *The Cambridge History of China*. Cambridge, UK: Cambridge University Press 1987

–. 'The State That Mao Built.' *World Politics* 19 (July 1967):664-77

–. *The United States and China*. 4th ed. Cambridge, MA: Harvard University Press 1983

Fairbank, John K., Alexander Eckstein, and L.S. Yang. 'Economic Change in Early Modern China: An Analytic Framework.' *Economic Development and Cultural Change* 9.1 (October 1960):1-26

Fang Lizhi. *Tearing Down the Great Wall: Writings on Science, Culture, and Democracy in China*. New York: W.W. Norton 1990

Faure, David. 'The Lineage as a Cultural Invention: The Case of the Pearl River Delta.' *Modern China* 15 (January 1989):4-36

Feldman, Gayle. 'The Organization of Publishing in China.' *China Quarterly* 107 (September 1986):519-29

Feuchtwang, Stephen, and Arthur Hussain, eds. *The Chinese Economic Reforms*. New York: St. Martin's Press 1983

Fitzpatrick, Sheila. *Education and Social Mobility in the Soviet Union 1921-1934*. Cambridge, UK: Cambridge University Press 1979

Fogel, Joshua A., and William T. Rowe, eds. *Perspectives on a Changing China*. New York: Columbia University Press 1981

Franke, Wolfgang. *The Reform and Abolition of the Chinese Examination System*. Cambridge, MA: Harvard University Press 1960

Friedman, Edward. 'Reconstructing China's National Identity: A Southern Alternative to Mao-Era Anti-Imperialist Nationalism.' *Journal of Asian Studies* 53.1 (February 1994): 67-91

Furet, François, and Jacques Ozouf. *Reading and Writing: Literacy in France from Calvin to Jules Ferry*. Cambridge, UK: Cambridge University Press 1982

Galbiati, Fernando. *P'eng P'ai and the Hai-Lu-Feng Soviet*. Stanford: Stanford University Press 1985

Gardner, John, and Wilt Idema. 'China's Educational Revolution.' In *Authority, Participation and Cultural Change in China*, ed. Stuart R. Schram, 257-89. Cambridge, UK: Cambridge University Press 1973

Geertz, Clifford. *Negara: The Theater State of Nineteenth Century Bali*. Princeton: Princeton University Press 1987

Gellner, Ernest. *Nations and Nationalism*. Oxford: Basil Blackwell 1983

Glassman, Joel. 'Educational Reform and Manpower Needs Policy in China, 1955-58.' *Modern China* 3 (1977):259-90

–. 'The Political Experience of Primary School Teachers in the PRC.' *Comparative Education* 15.2 (June 1979):159-73

Goodman, David S., ed. *Groups and Politics in the People's Republic of China*. Cardiff: University of Cardiff Press 1984

Goody, Jack, and Ian Watt. 'The Consequences of Literacy.' In *Literacy in Traditional Societies*, ed. Jack Goody, 27-68. Cambridge, UK: Cambridge University Press 1968

Graff, Harvey J., ed. *Literacy and Social Development in the West: A Reader*. Cambridge, UK: Cambridge University Press 1981

–. *The Literacy Myth: Literacy and Social Structure in the Nineteenth Century City*. New York: Academic Press 1979

Gray, Jack, and Maisie Gray. 'China's New Agricultural Revolution.' In *The Chinese Economic Reforms*, ed. Stephen Feuchtwang and Arthur Hussain, 151-84. New York: St. Martin's Press 1983.

Grimm, Tilemann. 'Academies and Urban Systems in Kwangtung.' In *The City in Late Imperial China*, ed. G. William Skinner, 475-98. Stanford: Stanford University Press 1977

Gu Hua. *A Small Town Called Hibiscus*. Trans. Gladys Yang. Beijing: Panda Books 1983

Guo Moruo. 'Correctly Understand the Meaning of Overall Development.' *Zhongguo qingnianbao* 14 (16 July 1956). In *Extracts China Mainland Magazines* 49 (27 August 1956): 18-20

Harding, Harry. *China's Second Revolution: Reform after Mao*. Washington, DC: Brookings Institution 1987

–. 'The Study of Chinese Politics: Toward a Third Generation of Scholarship.' *World Politics* 36 (January 1984):284-307

Hartford, Kathleen. 'Socialist Agriculture Is Dead: Long Live Socialist Agriculture! Organizational Transformation in Chinese Agriculture.' In *The Political Economy of Reform in Post-Mao China*, ed. Elizabeth J. Perry and Christine P. Wong, 31-62. Cambridge, MA: Harvard University Press 1985

Hayes, James. 'Specialists and Written Materials in the Village World.' In *Popular Culture in Late Imperial China*, ed. David Johnson, Andrew J. Nathan, and Evelyn S. Rawski, 75-111. Berkeley: University of California Press 1985

Hayford, Charles W. 'Literacy Movements in Modern China.' In *National Literacy Campaigns: Historical and Comparative Perspectives*, ed. Robert F. Arnove and Harvey J. Graff, 147-71. New York: Plenum Press 1987

–. 'Rural Reconstruction in China: Y.C. James Yen and the Mass Education Movement.' Ph.D. diss., Harvard University, 1973

–. *To the People: James Yen and Village China*. New York: Columbia University Press 1990

Hayhoe, Ruth. 'Cultural Tradition and Educational Modernization: Lessons from the Republican Era.' In *Education and Modernization: The Chinese Experience*, ed. Ruth Hayhoe, 47-72. Oxford: Pergamon Press 1992

–, ed. *Education and Modernization: The Chinese Experience*. Oxford: Pergamon Press 1992

Hayhoe, Ruth, and Marianne Bastid, eds. *China's Education and the Industrial World*. Armonk, NY: M.E. Sharpe 1987

Henze, Jurgen. 'Educational Modernization as a Search for Higher Efficiency.' In *China's Education and the Industrial World*, ed. Ruth Hayhoe and Marianne Bastid, 252-70. Armonk, NY: M.E. Sharpe 1987

–. 'The Formal Education System and Modernization: An Analysis of Developments since 1978.' In *Education and Modernization: The Chinese Experience*, ed. Ruth Hayhoe, 103-39. Oxford: Pergamon Press 1992.

Holm, David. *Art and Ideology in Revolutionary China*. Oxford: Clarendon Press 1991

Hu Shiming and Eli Saifman, eds. *Towards a New World Outlook: A Documentary History of Education in the PRC, 1949-1976*. New York: AMS Press 1976

Huang Shiqi. 'Nonformal Education and Modernization.' In *Education and Modernization: The Chinese Experience*, ed. Ruth Hayhoe, 141-80. Oxford: Pergamon Press 1992

Huang Shu-min. *The Spiral Road: Change in a Chinese Village through the Eyes of a Communist Party Leader*. Boulder: Westview Press 1989

Hung, Chang-Tai. *Going to the People: Chinese Intellectuals and Folk Literature, 1918-1937*. Cambridge, MA: Harvard University Press, Council on East Asian Studies, 1985

–. 'Re-Educating a Blind Storyteller: Han Qixiang and the Chinese Communist Storytelling Campaign.' *Modern China* 19 (October 1993):395-426

–. *War and Popular Culture: Resistance in Modern China, 1937-45*. Berkeley: University of California Press 1994

Hunt, Lynn. *Politics, Culture and Class in the French Revolution*. Berkeley: University of California Press 1984

Inkeles, Alex, and David H. Smith. *Becoming Modern*. Cambridge, MA: Harvard University Press 1974

Ip, David F.K. 'The Design of Development: Experiences from South China, 1949-1976.' Ph.D. diss., University of Britsh Columbia, 1979

Johnson, David. 'Communication, Class and Consciousness.' In *Popular Culture in Late Imperial China*, ed. David Johnson, Andrew J. Nathan, and Evelyn S. Rawski, 34-72. Berkeley: University of California Press 1985

Johnson, David, Andrew J. Nathan, and Evelyn S. Rawski, eds. *Popular Culture in Late Imperial China*. Berkeley: University of California Press 1985

Johnson, Graham E. 'The Political Economy of Chinese Urbanization: Guangdong and the Pearl River Delta Region.' In *Urbanizing China*, ed. Gregory Eliyu Guldin, 185-220. New York: Greenwood Press 1992

–. 'The Production Responsibility System in Chinese Agriculture: Some Examples from Guangdong.' *Pacific Affairs* 55 (Fall 1982):430-51

–. 'Rural Transformation in South China? Views from the Locality.' *Revue Européenne des sciences sociales* 37 (1989):208-24

Judd, Ellen R. 'Cultural Articulation in the Chinese Countryside, 1937-1947.' *Modern China* 16 (July 1990):269-308

Kau, Michael Y.M., and John K. Leung, eds. *The Writings of Mao Zedong, 1949-1976*. 2 vols. Armonk, NY: M.E. Sharpe 1986

Keating, Pauline. 'The Ecological Origins of the Yan'an Way.' *Australian Journal of Chinese Affairs* 32 (July 1994):123-53

Kelliher, Daniel. *Peasant Power in China: The Era of Rural Reform, 1979-1989*. New Haven: Yale University Press 1992

Klein, Donald W., and Ann B. Clark, eds. *Biographical Dictionary of Chinese Communism, 1921-1965*. 2 vols. Cambridge, MA: Harvard University Press 1971

Krasner, Stephen D. 'Approaches to the State: Alternative Conceptions and Historical Dynamics.' *Comparative Politics* 16.2 (January 1984):223-46

Kulp, Daniel H. *Country Life in South China*. New York: Teachers College, Columbia University 1925

Lamontagne, Jacques. 'Chinese Educational Development before and during the 1980s.' Unpublished ms.

–. 'Education and Employment in China: Variations according to Gender, Region, Ethnicity and Age.' Paper presented at the Canadian Learned Societies Conference, Hamilton, 1987

Lampton, David. 'Policy Arenas and the Study of Chinese Politics.' *Studies in Comparative Communism* 7 (Winter 1974):409-13

–, ed. *Policy Implementation in Post-Mao China*. Berkeley: University of California Press 1987

Lane, Christel. *The Rites of Rulers: Ritual in Industrial Society – the Soviet Case*. Cambridge, UK: Cambridge University Press 1981

Lavely, William et al. 'The Rise of Female Education in China: National and Regional Patterns.' *China Quarterly* 121 (March 1990):61-93

'Lead Positively the Movement for Eliminating Illiteracy.' *Renmin ribao*, 1 April 1956. In *Survey China Mainland Press* (17 April 1956):3-5

Lee, Hung Yung. *From Revolutionary Cadres to Party Technocrats in Socialist China*. Berkeley: University of California Press 1991

–. *The Politics of the Chinese Cultural Revolution: A Case Study*. Berkeley: University of California Press 1978

Lerner, Daniel. *The Passing of Traditional Society: Modernizing the Middle East*. New York: Free Press 1958

Levine, Kenneth. 'Functional Literacy: Fond Illusions and False Economies.' *Harvard Educational Review* 52.3 (August 1982):249-66

Li Choh-ming. *The Statistical System of Communist China*. Berkeley: University of California Press 1962

Li Fuchun. *Report on the First Five Year Plan for Development of the National Economy of the People's Republic of China*. Beijing: Foreign Languages Press 1955

Li Pingjie. 'Strive to Bring Universalization of Obligatory Primary School Education into Realization at an Early Date.' *Guangming ribao*, 22 February 1956. In *Survey China Mainland Press* 1246 (13 March 1956):18-22

Li Si-ming and Siu Yat-ming. 'Population Mobility.' In *Guangdong: Survey of a Province Undergoing Rapid Change*, ed. Y.M. Yeung and David K.Y. Chu, 373-400. Hong Kong: Chinese University Press 1994

Liao T'ai-ch'u. 'Rural Education in Transition: A Study of the Old-Fashioned Chinese Schools (Szu-Shu) in Shantung and Szechuan.' *Yenching Journal of Social Studies* 4.1 (August 1948):1240-42

Lieberthal, Kenneth, and Michel Oksenberg. *Policy Making in China: Leaders, Structures, and Processes*. Princeton: Princeton University Press 1988

Lieberthal, Kenneth et al. *Perspectives on Modern China: Four Anniversaries*. Armonk, NY: M.E. Sharpe 1991

Lin, Vincent Tsing Ching. 'Adult Education in the People's Republic of China, 1950-58.' Ph.D. diss., University of California, Berkeley, 1963

Lindbeck, John M.H., ed. *China: Management of a Revolutionary Society*. Seattle: University of Washington Press 1971

Link, Perry. *Evenings Chats in Beijing: Probing China's Predicament*. New York: W.W. Norton 1992

Lippit, Victor. *Land Reform in China: A Study of Institutional Change and Development*. White Plains, NY: International Arts and Sciences Press 1974

Literacy Situation in Asia and the Pacific Country Studies: China. Bangkok: UNESCO 1984

Literacy Situation in Asia and the Pacific Country Studies: Socialist Republic of Vietnam. Bangkok: UNESCO 1984

Lo, Leslie Nai-Kwai. 'The Changing Educational System: Dilemma of Disparity.' In *China Review 1993*, ed. Joseph Cheng Yu-shek and Maurice Brosseau, 22.1-41. Hong Kong: Chinese University Press 1993.

Lofstedt, Jan-Ingvar. *Chinese Educational Policy: Changes and Contradictions, 1949-1979*. Atlantic Highlands, NJ: Humanities Press 1980

Lowenthal, Rudolf. 'Printing Paper: Its Supply and Demand in China.' *Yenching Journal of Social Studies* 1.1 (June 1938):107-21

Lu Dingyi. *Education Must Be Combined with Productive Labour*. Beijing: Foreign Languages Press 1958

Lyons, Thomas P., and Victor Nee, eds. *The Economic Transformation of South China: Reform and Development in the Post-Mao Era*. Ithaca: Cornell University Press 1994

Ma, Laurence J.C., and Chusheng Lin. 'Development of Towns in China: A Case Study of Guangdong Province.' *Population and Development Review* 19 (September 1993): 583-606

MacFarquhar, Roderick, and John K. Fairbank, eds. *The People's Republic, Part 1: The Emergence of Revolutionary China, 1949-1965*. Vol. 14 of *The Cambridge History of China*. Cambridge, UK: Cambridge University Press 1987

Madsen, Richard. *Morality and Power in a Chinese Village*. Berkeley: University of California Press 1984

Mae Chu-Chang. 'Issues for a Bilingual Population: The Case of China.' In *Reading in China: Report of the U.S. Reading Study Team to the People's Republic of China*, ed. June Y. Mei, 75-85. New York: National Committee on US-China Relations n.d.

Mao Zedong. 'Talks at the Chengtu Conference' (March 1958). In *Mao Tse-tung Unrehearsed: Talks and Letters, 1956-71*, ed. Stuart R. Schram, 96-124. Harmondsworth, UK: Penguin 1974

Mei, June Y., ed. *Reading in China: Report of the U.S. Reading Study Team to the People's Republic of China*. New York: National Committee on US-China Relations n.d.

Moser, Leo J. *The Chinese Mosaic: The Peoples and Provinces of China*. Boulder: Westview Press 1985

Munro, Donald J. 'Egalitarian Ideal and Educational Fact in Communist China.' In *China: Management of a Revolutionary Society*, ed. John M.H. Lindbeck, 256-301. Seattle: University of Washington Press 1971

Myrdal, Jan. *Report from a Chinese Village*. Trans. Maurice Michael. New York: Pantheon Books 1965

Naquin, Susan, and Evelyn S. Rawski. *Chinese Society in the Eighteenth Century*. New Haven: Yale University Press 1987

Naughton, Barry. 'The Pattern and Legacy of Economic Growth in the Mao Era.' In *Perspectives on Modern China: Four Anniversaries*, ed. Kenneth Lieberthal et al., 226-54. Armonk, NY: M.E. Sharpe 1991

Nove, Alec. *The Soviet Economic System*. London: George Allen and Unwin 1977

–. 'Toward a Theory of Planning.' In *Soviet Planning: Essays in Honour of Naum Jasny*, ed. Alec Nove and Jane Degras. Oxford: Basil Blackwell 1964

Oi, Jean. *State and Peasant in Contemporary China*. Berkeley: University of California Press 1989

Parish, William L., and Martin King Whyte. *Village and Family in Contemporary China*. Chicago: University of Chicago Press 1978

Peng Xizhe. 'Major Determinants of China's Fertility Transition.' *China Quarterly* 117 (March 1989):1-37

Pepper, Suzanne. *China's Education Reform in the 1980s: Policies, Issues, and Historical Perspectives*. Berkeley: Center for Chinese Studies, Institute of East Asian Studies, University of California 1990

–. 'Chinese Education after Mao: Two Steps Forward, Two Steps Backward and Begin Again?' *China Quarterly* 81 (March 1980):1-65

–. 'Education.' In *The People's Republic, Part 2: Revolutions within the Chinese Revolution, 1966-1982*, ed. Roderick MacFarquhar and John K. Fairbank, 540-93. Vol. 15 of *The Cambridge History of China*. Cambridge, UK: Cambridge University Press 1991

–. 'Education for the New Order.' In *The People's Republic, Part 1: The Emergence of Revolutionary China, 1949-1965*, ed. Roderick MacFarquhar and John K. Fairbank, 185-217. Vol. 14 of *The Cambridge History of China*. Cambridge, UK: Cambridge University Press 1987

–. 'New Directions in Education.' In *The People's Republic, Part 1: The Emergence of Revolutionary China, 1949-1965*, ed. Roderick MacFarquhar and John K. Fairbank, 398-431. Vol. 14 of *The Cambridge History of China*. Cambridge, UK: Cambridge University Press 1987

–. *Radicalism and Education Reform in 20th Century China*. Cambridge and New York: Cambridge University Press 1996

Perry, Elizabeth J. 'State and Society in Contemporary China.' *World Politics* 41.4 (1989):579-91

–. 'Trends in the Study of Chinese Politics: State-Society Relations.' *China Quarterly* 139 (September 1994):704-13

Perry, Elizabeth J., and Christine P. Wong, eds. *The Political Economy of Reform in Post-Mao China*. Cambridge, MA: Harvard University Press 1985

Peterson, Glen D. 'Recent Trends in Literacy Studies and Their Application to China.' *Journal of Educational Thought* 28.2 (August 1994):138-52

–. 'Socialist China and the Huaqiao: The Transition to Socialism in the Overseas Chinese Areas of Rural Guangdong.' *Modern China* 14 (July 1988):309-35

–. 'State Literacy Ideologies and the Transformation of Rural China.' *Australian Journal of Chinese Affairs* 32 (July 1994):95-120

–. 'The Struggle for Literacy in Postrevolutionary Guangdong.' *China Quarterly* 140 (December 1994):926-43

Pickowicz, Paul. 'Ch'u Ch'iu-pai and the Chinese Marxist Conception of Revolutionary Literature and Art.' *China Quarterly* 70 (June 1977):296-314

Potter, Sulamith Heins. 'The Position of Peasants in Modern China's Social Order.' *Modern China* 9 (1983):465-99

Potter, Sulamith Heins, and Jack M. Potter. *China's Peasants: The Anthropology of a Revolution*. Cambridge, UK: Cambridge University Press 1990

Price, Ronald F. *Education in Modern China*. London: Routledge and Kegan Paul 1979

Ramirez, Francisco O., and John Boli-Bennett. 'Global Patterns of Educational Institutionalization.' In *Comparative Education*, ed. Robert F. Arnove and Gail P. Kelly, 15-36. New York: Macmillan 1988

Ramsey, S. Robert. *The Languages of China*. Princeton: Princeton University Press 1987

–. 'The Polysemy of the Term *Kokugo*.' In *Schriftfestschrift: Essays on Writing and Language in Honor of John DeFrancis on His Eightieth Birthday*, ed. Victor H. Mair. Spec. issue of *Sino-Platonic Papers* 27 (August 1991):37-47

Rawski, Evelyn Sakakida. *Education and Popular Literacy in Ch'ing China*. Ann Arbor: University of Michigan Press 1979

–. 'The Social Agenda of May Fourth.' In *Perspectives on Modern China: Four Anniversaries*, ed. Kenneth Lieberthal et al., 139-57. Armonk, NY: M.E. Sharpe 1991

Rhoads, Edward J.M. *China's Republican Revolution: The Case of Kwantung, 1895-1913*. Cambridge, MA: Harvard University Press 1975

Robinson, Jean C. 'Minban Schools in Deng's Era.' In *Chinese Education: Problems, Policies and Prospects*, ed. Irving Epstein, 163-9. New York: Garland 1991

–. 'Stumbling on Two Legs: Education and Reform in China.' *Comparative Education Review* 35.1 (February 1991):177-89

Rodzinski, Witold. *The People's Republic of China: Reflections on Chinese Political History since 1949*. London: Fontana Press 1988

Rosen, Stanley. *Red Guard Factionalism and the Cultural Revolution in Guangzhou*. Boulder: Westview Press 1982

–. 'Women, Education and Modernization.' In *Education and Modernization: The Chinese Experience*, ed. Ruth Hayhoe, 255-84. Oxford: Pergamon Press 1992

Rozman, Gilbert, ed. *The Modernization of China*. New York: Free Press 1981

Schoenhals, Michael. *Doing Things with Words in Chinese Politics: Five Studies*. Berkeley: Institute of East Asian Studies, University of California 1992

Schram, Stuart, ed. *Authority, Participation, and Cultural Change in China*. Cambridge, UK: Cambridge University Press 1973

–. 'The Cultural Revolution in Historical Perspective.' In *Authority, Participation, and Cultural Change in China*, ed. Stuart Schram, 1-108. Cambridge, UK: Cambridge University Press 1973

–, ed. *Mao Tse-tung Unrehearsed: Talks and Letters, 1956-71*. Harmondsworth, UK: Penguin 1974

–. 'Party Leader or True Ruler? Foundations and Significance of Mao Zedong's Personal Power.' In *Foundations and Limits of State Power in China*, ed. Stuart R. Schram, 203-56. Hong Kong: Chinese University Press 1987

–, ed. *Foundations and Limits of State Power in China*. Hong Kong: Chinese University Press 1987

Schultz, Theodore W. *The Economic Value of Education*. New York: Columbia University Press 1963

Seeberg, Vilma. *Literacy in China: The Effect of the National Development Context and Policy on Literacy Levels, 1949-1979*. Bochum: Brockmeyer 1990

Selden, Mark. *The Yenan Way in Revolutionary China*. Cambridge, MA: Harvard University Press 1971

Serruys, Paul L.M. *Survey of the Chinese Language Reform and the Anti-Illiteracy Movement in China*. Berkeley: Center for Chinese Studies, Institute of International Studies, University of California 1962

Seybolt, Peter J., ed. *Revolutionary Education in China: Documents and Commentary*. New York: International Arts and Sciences Press 1971

–. 'The Yenan Revolution in Mass Education.' *China Quarterly* 48 (1971):641-69

Sharman, Lyon. *Sun Yatsen, His Life and Its Meaning: A Critical Biography*. New York: John Day 1934

Shirk, Susan L. *Competitive Comrades: Career Incentives and Student Strategies in China*. Berkeley: University of California Press 1982

Shue, Vivienne. 'The Fate of the Commune.' *Modern China* 10 (July 1984):259-83

–. *Peasant China in Transition: The Dynamics of Development toward Socialism, 1949-56*. Berkeley: University of California Press 1980

–. *The Reach of the State: Sketches of the Chinese Body Politic*. Stanford: Stanford University Press 1988

Siu, Helen F. *Agents and Victims in South China: Accomplices in Rural Revolution*. New Haven: Yale University Press 1989

–. 'Cultural Identity and the Politics of Difference in South China.' *Daedalus* 122.2 (Spring 1993):19-44

Skinner, G. William, ed. *The City in Late Imperial China*. Stanford: Stanford University Press 1977

–. 'Differential Development in Lingnan.' In *The Economic Transformation of South China: Reform and Development in the Post-Mao Era*,' ed. Thomas P. Lyons and Victor Nee, 17-54. Ithaca: Cornell University Press 1994

–. 'Marketing and Social Structure in Rural China.' *Journal of Asian Studies* 24.1 (1964):3-43; 24.2 (1965):195-228; 24.3 (1965):363-9

Smith, Arthur. *Village Life in China: A Study in Sociology*. New York: Revell 1899

Snow, Edgar. *Red Star over China*. Rev. and enl. ed. New York: Bantam 1978

Stavis, Benedict. *The Politics of Agricultural Mechanization in China*. Ithaca: Cornell University Press 1978

Street, Brian V. *Literacy in Theory and Practice*. Cambridge, UK: Cambridge University Press 1984

'Strengthen the Concrete Leadership of the Work of Eliminating Illiteracy.' *Renmin ribao*, 21 January 1956. In *Survey China Mainland Press* 1221 (2 February 1956):8-10

'Strive to Meet the Demand of Peasants for Popular Reading Material.' *Renmin ribao*, 8 January 1956. In *Survey China Mainland Press* 1213 (23 January 1956):16-18

Strumilin, Stanislav. 'The Economics of Education in the U.S.S.R.' In *Economic and Social Aspects of Educational Planning*. Paris: UNESCO 1964

–. *The Economic Significance of National Education*. Paris: UNESCO 1968

Taylor, Jay. *The Dragon and the Wild Goose: China and India*. New York: Greenwood Press 1987

Tsang, Chiu-sam. *Nationalism in School Education in China*. Hong Kong: South China Morning Post 1933

UNESCO Statistical Yearbook. Paris: UNESCO 1987

Unger, Jonathan. 'Bending the School Ladder: The Failure of Chinese Educational Reform in the 1960s.' *Comparative Education Review* 24.2, Part 1 (June 1980):221-37

–. *Education under Mao: Class and Competition in Canton Schools, 1960-1980*. New York: Columbia University Press 1982

'Universalization of Obligatory Education.' *Renmin ribao*, 27 February 1956. In *Survey China Mainland Press* 1246 (13 March 1956):16-18

Urban, George, ed. *The Miracles of Chairman Mao*. London: Tom Stacey 1971

Venezky, Richard L. 'Language, Script, and Reading in China.' In *Reading in China: Report of the U.S. Reading Study Team to the People's Republic of China*, ed. June Y. Mei, 48-66. New York: National Committee on US-China Relations n.d.

Vogel, Ezra. *Canton under Communism: Programs and Politics in a Provincial Capital, 1949-1968*. Cambridge, MA: Harvard University Press 1969

–. *One Step Ahead in China: Guangdong under Reform*. Cambridge, MA: Harvard University Press 1989

Wang Hsueh-wen. 'A Study of Chinese Communist Education during the Kiangxi Period.' *Issues and Studies* 9.7 (April 1973):59-73; 9.8 (May 1973):69-83; 9.9 (June 1973):68-81

Wang, Y.C. 'Western Impact and Social Mobility in China.' *American Sociological Review* 25 (1960):843-55

Ward, Barbara E. 'Regional Operas and Their Audiences: Evidence from Hong Kong.' In *Popular Culture in Late Imperial China*, ed. David Johnson, Andrew J. Nathan, and Evelyn S. Rawski. Berkeley: University of California Press 1985

Weber, Eugen. *Peasants into Frenchmen: The Modernization of Rural France, 1870-1914*. Stanford: Stanford University Press 1976

White, Gordon. 'Distributive Politics and Educational Development: Teachers as a Political Interest Group.' In *Groups and Politics in the People's Republic of China*, ed. David S. Goodman. Cardiff: University of Cardiff Press 1984

–. *Party and Professionals: The Political Role of Teachers in Contemporary China*. New York: M.E. Sharpe 1981

White, Lynn, and Li Cheng. 'China Coast Identities: Regional, National, and Global.' In *China's Quest for National Identity*, ed. Lowell Dittmer and Samuel S. Kim, 154-93. Ithaca: Cornell University Press 1993

Wieczynski, Joseph L., ed. *The Modern Encyclopedia of Russian and Soviet History*. Vol. 37. Gulf Breeze, FL: Academic International Press 1984

Wiens, Herold J. *China's March to the Tropics*. Hamden, CT: Shoe String Press 1954

Wong, Christine P., and Elizabeth J. Perry, eds. *The Political Economy of Reform in Post-Mao China*. Cambridge, MA: Harvard University Press 1985

Wong, John. *Land Reform in the People's Republic of China: Institutional Transformation in Agriculture*. New York: Praegar 1973

Woodside, Alexander. 'The Asia-Pacific Idea as a Mobilization Myth.' In *What Is in a Rim? Critical Perspectives on the Pacific Region Idea*, ed. Arif Dirlik, 13-28. Boulder: Westview Press 1993

–. *Community and Revolution in Modern Vietnam*. Boston: Houghton Mifflin 1976

–. 'The Political Inevitability of School Reform in Late Imperial China.' In *Rapporteur's Report, Conference on Education and Society in Late Imperial China*, ed. Benjamin A. Elman and Alexander Woodside. US Joint Committee on Chinese Studies, Studies on China, no. 19. Montecito, June 1989

–. 'Problems of Education in the Chinese and Vietnamese Revolutions.' *Pacific Affairs* 49 (Winter 1976-7):648-9

–. 'Real and Imagined Continuities in the Chinese Struggle for Literacy.' In *Education and Modernization: The Chinese Experience*, ed. Ruth Hayhoe, 23-45. Oxford: Pergamon Press 1992

–. 'Some Mid-Qing Theorists of Popular Schools: Their Innovations, Inhibitions, and Attitudes toward the Poor.' *Modern China* 9 (January 1983):3-35

–. 'The Triumphs and Failures of Mass Education in Vietnam.' *Pacific Affairs* 56 (Fall 1988):401-27

Woodside, Alexander, and Benjamin A. Elman. 'Afterword: The Expansion of Education in Ch'ing China.' In *Education and Society in Late Imperial China, 1600-1900*, ed. Alexander Woodside and Benjamin A. Elman, 525-60. Berkeley: University of California Press 1994

Woon, Yuen-Fong. 'International Links and the Socioeconomic Development of Rural China: An Emigrant Community in Guangdong.' *Modern China* 16 (April 1990):139-72

Wu Yen-yin. 'We Should Pay Enough Attention to the Middle and Primary School Education and Teachers.' *Guangming ribao*, 16 August 1956. In *Survey China Mainland Press* 1380 (10 October 1956):12-13

Xiang Nan. 'Let the Whole Youth League Take a Hand in Wiping Out Illiteracy.' *Zhongguo qingnian bao* 21 (1 November 1956). In *Extracts China Mainland Magazines* 20 (3 January 1956):33-4

Yang Jianbai. 'A Comparative Analysis of China's First Five Year Plan and the Soviet Union's First Five Year Plan.' *Tongji gongzuo tongxin* 8 (August 1955). In *Extracts China Mainland Magazines* 10 (16 October 1955):15-27

Yeung, Y.M., and David K.Y. Chu, eds. *Guangdong: Survey of a Province Undergoing Rapid Change*. Hong Kong: Chinese University Press 1994

Yip, Ka-che. 'Warlordism and Educational Finances, 1916-1927.' In *Perspectives on a Changing China*, ed. Joshua A. Fogel and William T. Rowe, 183-96. New York: Columbia University Press 1981

Zhang Xiruo. 'Resolutely Promote the Standard Vernacular Based on Peking Pronunciation.' In *Language Reform in China: Documents and Commentary*, ed. Peter J. Seybolt and Gregory Kuei-ke Chiang, 65-77. White Plains, NY: M.E. Sharpe 1979

Zhou Youguang. 'The Modernization of the Chinese Language.' *International Journal of the Sociology of Language* 59 (1986):7-23

Zweig, David. *Agrarian Radicalism in China, 1960-1981*. Cambridge, MA: Harvard University Press 1989

–. 'Household Contracts and Decollectivization, 1977-1983.' In *Policy Implementation in Post-Mao China*, ed. David M. Lampton, 255-83. Berkeley: University of California Press 1987

Index

Instructional methods, in literacy campaign, 90-1
Intellectuals: critiques of mass literacy campaigns, 100-1; use of, by CCP, 49-50, 54-5. *See also* Teachers
International Monetary Fund, 155
Iran, literacy education in, 180-1

J

Japan: military prowess of, and popular literacy, 13; occupation of 1937-45, and school curriculum, 25, 28; social education in, 14; universal primary schooling in, 5-6
Jiaoxue dian (minischools), 157-8
Jiashu (family schools), 25. *See also* Sishu
Jishu jiaoyu (continuing education), 156
Joint Decision concerning Some Problems in Popularizing Primary Schooling (1980), 161

K

Kaimen banxue ('open-door schooling'), 146
Kang Youwei, 18
Keypoint schools (*zhongdian xuexiao*), 37, 136, 174
Korean War: and concern over teachers' loyalty, 69; effect on literacy campaign, 53

L

Labour. *See* Peasants; Teachers; Technicians; Workers
Land reform: and breakdown of class structure, 66; and education, in Guangdong villages, 22; and lineage schools, undermining of, 29; and literacy education, 52-3; and political education, 53-4
Language: dialects, and romanization, 114, 115; dialects, in Guangdong, 17-18, 111; Mandarin, promotion of, 42-3, 103, 107-9, 111-16; national standard, attempts at, 15, 103, 106-11; romanization attempts, 42-3, 107-9. *See also* Writing system
Language Reform Committee, 109
League of Nations, report on Chinese education system, 179
Lei Feng, 64
Lenin, Vladimir Ilyich, 40, 45
Li Chang, 44
Li Peng, 155
Li people, of Guandong, 17
Li Wenhui, 141
Liang Qichao, 18, 26
Liang Shuming, 15, 179
Liang Weilin, 78
Liao Hanzhao, 28

Liao Luyan, 88
Lin Biao, 138, 145
Lin Feng: critique of, during Cultural Revolution, 143; and literacy campaign, 88
Lin Handa: on anti-illiteracy army, 90; and Anti-Illiteracy Work Committee, 44; critique of literacy education methods of, 144; and National Anti-Illiteracy Association, 88; and official ideology of peasant literacy, 80-4; and use of Mandarin-based pinyin in literacy training, 112
Lin Liming, 128-9
Lineages: of Guangdong, 18, 19; and literacy education, 174-5; and private schools, 18, 23-5; and sishu, 25
Linguists, and formation of literacy policy, 42
Literacy: acquisition rates 1949-81, 87; certificates, 50; and collectivization, 73-84; compared with other developing countries, 5-6, 178; complexity of, 6, 7, 9-10; definitions, 50-1; gender differential in, 177-8; geographic distribution of, 172-4, 176-7; incentives, 77-80, 122-5; and peasants, official ideology of, 80-4; policy, 41-6; and political mobilization, 46-52; research on, 3-5, 7-11; statistics, national census of 1982, 4-5; Western models, 13-14. *See also* Illiteracy; Literacy campaigns; Literacy education; Writing system; types of schools
Literacy campaigns: of 1956, 90-6; of 1958 (Great Leap Forward), 96-102, 114, 116-17; of 1978, 150-1
Literacy education: demand for, in Guangdong, 166-7; demise of, under Cultural Revolution, 143-5; effect of Korean War on, 53; enrolment decline, after decollectivization, 156-7; in half-farming, half-study schools, 137-8; instructional formats, 90-1; and lineage, 174-5; model zones, in terms of success, 171; and political education, 46-53, 144-5; in post-collective economy, 153-4; problems, 55-7, 135, 145; and 'production contracts' for teachers, 159-60; prohibition of, in early 1950s, 52-5; as responsibility of local agricultural bureaus, 116; strategies, 55-7, 80-4, 114-15, 150-1; traditional, revival of, 144
Liu Shaoqi: critique of, during Cultural Revolution, 142-3, 146, 149, 150; on education system priorities, 180; on expansion of school system, 126; liberal economic policies of, 138; and restoration of academic standards, 135

Set in Stone by Artegraphica Design Co. Ltd.

Printed and bound in Canada by Friesens

Copy-editor: Dallas Harrison

Proofreader: Edward Wagstaff

Indexer: Annette Lorek